The Sun of Jesús del Monte

Writing the Early Americas
Anna Brickhouse and Kirsten Silva Gruesz, Editors

The Sun of Jesús del Monte
A Cuban Antislavery Novel

ANDRÉS AVELINO DE ORIHUELA

A critical edition translated and edited by
David Luis-Brown

University of Virginia Press
Charlottesville and London

University of Virginia Press
© 2022 by the Rector and Visitors of the University of Virginia
All rights reserved

First published 2022

Library of Congress Cataloging-in-Publication Data

Names: Orihuela, Andrés Avelino de, 1818–1873, author. | Luis-Brown, David, translator, editor.
Title: The sun of Jesús del Monte : a Cuban antislavery novel / Andrés Avelino de Orihuela ; translated and edited by David Luis-Brown.
Other titles: Sol de Jesús del Monte. English.
Description: Charlottesville : University of Virginia Press, 2021. | Series: Writing the early Americas | Includes bibliographical references.
Identifiers: LCCN 2020051343 (print) | LCCN 2020051344 (ebook) | ISBN 9780813946207 (hardcover) | ISBN 9780813946214 (paperback) | ISBN 9780813946221 (ebook)
Classification: LCC PQ6552.O76 S6413 2021 (print) | LCC PQ6552.O76 (ebook) | DDC 863/.5—dc23
LC record available at https://lccn.loc.gov/2020051343
LC ebook record available at https://lccn.loc.gov/2020051344

Publication of this volume has been supported by *New Literary History*.

Cover art: "Aduana de la Habana" (Customs House, Havana), by Frédéric Mialhe. From *Isla de Cuba Pintoresca, histórica, política, literaria, mercantile é industrial,* edited by J. M. de Andueza (Madrid: Boix, 1839). (University of Miami Libraries, Cuban Heritage Collection)

Contents

Acknowledgments   vii

Introduction   xi

Textual Essay   xxxix

Note on the Translation   xlv

The Sun of Jesús del Monte   1

Afterword   209

Notes   229

Bibliography   243

Acknowledgments

I was fortunate to stumble upon the edition of Orihuela's novel then recently published in the Canary Islands while on sabbatical leave from the University of Miami and during my stay as a Sheila Biddle Ford Foundation Fellow at the W. E. B. Du Bois Institute for African and African American Research at Harvard University in the spring of 2009. My thanks go to both institutions and to my colleagues there. Sabbatical leaves from Claremont Graduate University in the spring of 2012, the fall of 2015, and the spring of 2019 helped me to bring this project closer to completion, as did a National Endowment for the Humanities Summer Stipend in 2015. I am grateful to the staffs of the Biblioteca Nacional of Havana, Cuba, the Houghton Library at Harvard, the Library of Congress, and the New York Public Library, where I conducted research on this book.

I am grateful to Miguel David Hernández Paz for bringing Orihuela's novel back into print in 2007. Many thanks to my parents, Brenda and Donal Brown, and to my wife, Tina Luis-Brown, as well as to the two anonymous readers for the University of Virginia Press for their suggestions on drafts of this translation. Many thanks to my research assistant, Gene Luzala, a PhD student at Claremont Graduate University, who read through the penultimate draft of the translation and offered invaluable suggestions. My thanks also go to Agnes Lugo Ortiz for her comments on a chapter of the translation and on an article on Orihuela's novel and to Marlene Daut for her insightful comments on a draft of my introduction. I am also very grateful to Raúl Fernández for reading the entire manuscript and for his suggestions pertaining to language, culture, and history in nineteenth-century Cuba. Thanks as well to Enrico Mario Santí for clarifying the meaning of a few particularly thorny *cubanismos*. I also thank Eric Brandt, assistant director and editor in chief of the University of Virginia Press; Helen Chandler, acquisitions assistant; Ellen Satrom, managing editor; Joanne Allen, copyeditor; and Anna Brickhouse and Kirsten Silva Gruesz, coeditors of the Writing the Early Americas series at the University of Virginia Press, for their support of this project and for their patience as my work progressed. Many thanks to my colleagues in the Departments of Cultural Studies and English at Claremont Graduate University, who have made working there such a pleasure: Eric Bulson, Nadine Chan, Marlene

Daut (now at the University of Virginia), Lori Anne Ferrell, Joshua Goode, Wendy Martin, Darrell Moore, Eve Oishi, Linda Perkins, and Enrico Mario Santí. I am also grateful to my colleagues at the Claremont Colleges, including Isabel Balseiro and Alfred Flores (Harvey Mudd College), Grace Dávila-López, Jonathan Lethem, April Mayes, Nivia Montenegro, Kyla Tompkins, and Valorie Thomas (Pomona College), Gabriela Bacsán, Myriam Chancy, Martha González, Thomas Koenigs, and Warren Liu (Scripps College), the Intercollegiate Department of Africana Studies, particularly Maryan Soliman and Sidney Lemelle, and the Intercollegiate Department of Chicana/o and Latina/o Studies. Finally, I thank Alberto Abreu Arcia, Magalí Armillas-Tiseyra, Isabel Caldeira, Nahum Chandler, Ada Ferrer, Claire Fox, Susan Gillman, Sara Johnson, George Lipsitz, Laura Lomas, William Luis, Anne Garland Mahler, Stephen Silverstein, Monica Mohseni Sisiruca, José Saldívar, and Ramón Saldívar for their support of my work. And I owe much to the inspiring teaching of Norma Klahn, Lourdes Martínez Echazabal, and Julio Ramos many years ago.

Capoeira has kept me kicking through the long process of writing this book. My thanks go to Mestre Jelon Vieira and Contra Mestre Esquilo Preto of Capoeira Luanda and to Mestre Boneco, Formanda Pavao, Formando Chegado, and Instructor Quebrado of Capoeira Brasil, Los Angeles, and to all of their students and fellow teachers who have pushed me forward in the art of capoeira. I'm grateful to Casca Grossa and Glamorosa for being my carpool buddies and my best friends in Claremont.

I want to thank my cousins in Orihuela's "dos hemisferios" for keeping me connected and grounded: Kristin and Neil in Mexico; Susan, Frank, Sophia, and Lars in Berlin; Dario, Jenan, and Raffaele in London; Alessia, Jonas (whom I have dubbed DJ Heavy J), Luciana, and Renzo in Milano; Fabio, Maria Giovanna, and Rebecca in Bologna; and in Tuscany Chiara and Michele; Cecilia, Giulio, and Martino; Michelangelo and Luana; Franca and Francesco; Mauro and Anamaria: Samantha, Andrea, Emmanuele, and Martina; Roberto and Maura; Filippo, Samuela, and Emma; Biagio, Gianna, and Camilla. And thanks to my extended family in California as well: Tia Carmen, Little Luis, Alexis, Gilbert, Mark, Stuey, Little Alex, Nicole, Fili, Cody, Marisa, Karla, Hondi, Tio George, and all of their family members.

I published an earlier set of reflections on *El Sol de Jesús del Monte* in "Slave Rebellion and the Conundrum of Cosmopolitanism: Plácido and *La*

Escalera in a Neglected Antislavery Novel by Orihuela," *Atlantic Studies* 9, no. 2 (2012): 209–30, followed by a brief excerpt from my translation on pages 231–43.

This book is for Tina. It is also dedicated to my parents, Donal and Brenda Brown, and to the future of my children, Dante and Sofia; my sister, Paula, and her children, Erin and Evan; mis cuates, Claudia, Silvia, Emilio, and Kamilo; Jenny, Josh, and Noah; my cousins in England, Germany, Italy, Mexico, and the United States; Capoeira; and Cuba. Finally, it is dedicated with great respect to Black Lives Matter.

Introduction

An *Uncle Tom's Cabin* for Cuba?

In 1852, the year that Harriet Beecher Stowe published her bestselling novel *Uncle Tom's Cabin,* a migrant from the Canary Islands to Cuba then in exile in Paris, Andrés Avelino de Orihuela, set out to build on her success. He published what he claimed was the first Spanish-language translation of Stowe's novel, *La cabaña del tío Tom,* and his own antislavery novel set in Cuba, *El Sol de Jesús del Monte: Novela de costumbres cubanas* (The Sun of Jesús del Monte: A novel of Cuban customs).[1] He also wrote *Dos palabras sobre el folleto "La situación política de Cuba y su remedio," publicado en París por D. José Antonio Saco en Octubre de 1851* (A brief note on the pamphlet "Cuba's Political Situation and its Remedy," published in Paris by Don José Antonio Saco in October of 1851), which impugned the racial politics of Cuban exiles in New York City. Since all three of these texts adapt Stowe's antislavery concerns to the political exigencies of Cuba, they could be considered differing translations of her novel. One would even be tempted to call *El Sol* an *Uncle Tom's Cabin* for Cuba, if not for Orihuela's emphasis on the plight of free people of color and his rejection of theories of racial difference, including Stowe's romantic racialist theory that held that Black people were more artistic, emotionally responsive, and nonviolent than white people and thus more Christian in their temperament.[2]

As if to register his literary ambitions, in a single year Orihuela wrote texts that attached his reputation to the premier US antislavery writer, Stowe; to the most famous Cuban writer, the mulatto poet Gabriel de la Concepción Valdés, or Plácido (1809–1844), the martyr of the Conspiracy of La Escalera (The Ladder Rebellion, 1843–44), the major anticolonial and slave rebellion in nineteenth-century Cuba; and to one of the most respected white Cuban exile intellectuals, José Antonio Saco (1797–1879), who advocated an end to the slave trade but not to slavery and opposed the annexation of Cuba. By connecting and correcting Saco and Stowe, by foregrounding Plácido's martyrdom in his own novel, which explicitly opposed slavery and implicitly countered colonialism, and by emphasizing the plight and promise of free people of color, Orihuela makes the unprecedented move in Cuban letters of linking antislavery reform to the causes of antiracism and independence in an effort to shape debates over what he calls the "cause of Cuba."³

In the letter to Stowe that Orihuela published as a prologue to his translation of *Uncle Tom's Cabin,* he pays tribute to the power of Stowe's writing: "When your newly minted book fell into my hands, I devoured its pages, and the tears provoked by that reading are the most telling testimony of the shared sentiments that unite us, the excellence of your writing, and the recognized merit of your novel. You, my lady, know how to speak to the heart, wounding it in its most delicate fibers. [. . .] A privilege has been reserved for your golden pen—that of propagating with your novel the pure and

"Eduardo y Matilde," cover page of *El Sol de Jesús del Monte: Novela de costumbres cubanas,* by Andrés Avelino de Orihuela (Paris: Boix, 1852). (Bibliothèque nationale de France)

holy seed that will soon germinate, consoling the African race and honoring modern civilization."⁴

Writing in the sentimental idiom that made Stowe's novel a transatlantic best seller, Orihuela implies that Stowe's novel will result in the abolition of slavery.⁵ The politically potent, sentimental melodrama of *Uncle Tom's Cabin* serves as one of the literary models for *El Sol*. Orihuela's invocation of Stowe's "ability to translate words into heartbeats and sobs," transforming hearts and minds to effect antislavery reform, sheds light on the fact that the aim of sentimentalism is to align feeling, reason, and morality, thereby casting benevolence and sympathy as "defining moral virtue[s]" in both the reader and the citizen.⁶ Orihuela's narrator explicitly characterizes sentimentality as central to an antislavery political consciousness: "Isn't it time for this barbarous commerce in human blood to end? The scoundrels! . . . The crime that they commit against the oppressed race of Africans—whom the vile merchants of the Spanish Antilles steal from their countries of origin and weigh down with chains—is unpardonable before the eyes of reason and before the intimate sentiment of one's conscience."⁷

Both novels deploy tears as the chief emblem of interracial sympathy. What was new in Stowe's novel was "the use of tears to cross racial barriers, to create new pictures of interracial amity and emotional intimacy," as Linda Williams has argued.⁸ When George Shelby cries after Uncle Tom's death, "for the first time in popular American [US] culture a white man weeps over the racial suffering of a slave."⁹ Orihuela's novel makes the same move in Cuban culture: the white Cuban creole Federico cries along with the free women of color Matilde and Belencita after reading an eyewitness account of Plácido's last hours prior to his execution for his alleged participation in La Escalera.¹⁰ Their tears signify their shared mourning over Plácido's death and expose the novel's daring alignment with the insurgents who shook the world's wealthiest colony. Their tears also mark Plácido—and by extension the other victims of La Escalera in the novel, the mulatto family of Matilde, Belencita, and Julio—as heroes of the melodrama, epitomizing forces of good that could redeem Cuba.¹¹

Melodrama is a narrative mode that evokes sympathy for virtuous victims caught in a clash between characters embodying primal ethical forces of good and evil.¹² As Linda Williams writes, "If emotional and moral registers are sounded, if a work invites us to feel sympathy for the virtues of beset victims, if the narrative trajectory is ultimately concerned with a retrieval and staging of virtue through adversity and suffering, then the operative mode is melodrama."¹³ Williams carefully distinguishes between the mode of *melodrama* and the uncritical term *melodramatic,* which has meant "a seemingly archaic excess of sensation and sentiment, a manipulation of the heartstrings that exceeds the bounds of good taste."[14] In my approach to Orihuela, the question of literary merit or value—the "But is it any good?" question that skeptics ask of sentimental melodrama—is far less important than questions about the racial politics of Orihuela's text.[15] Jane Tompkins resuscitated scholarly interest in *Uncle Tom's Cabin* in 1978 by refusing conventional notions of literary merit and instead asking why sentimental melodrama was so popular, taking on the mostly male literary

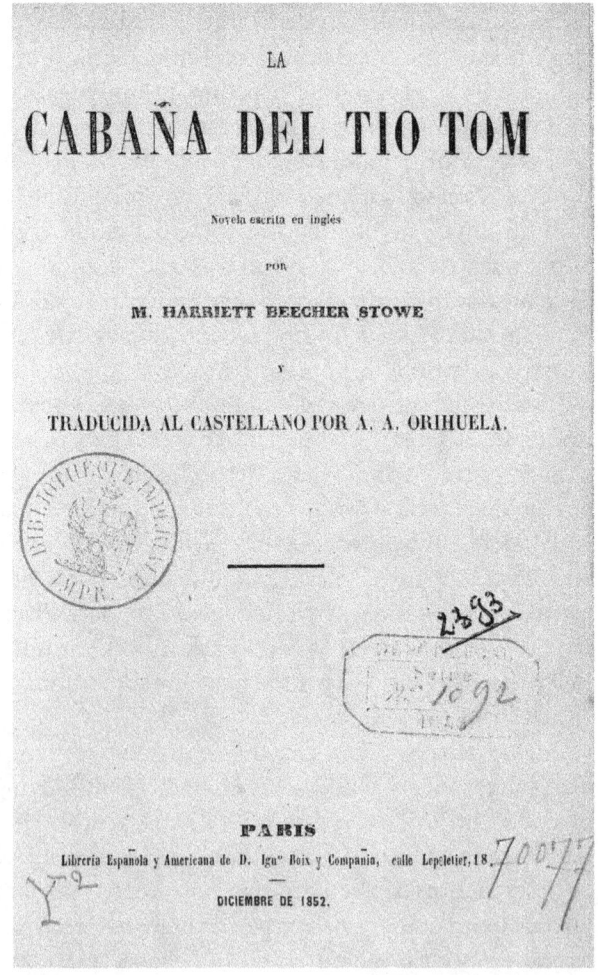

Title page of *La cabaña del tío Tom,* by Harriet Beecher Stowe, translated by Andrés Avelino de Orihuela (Paris: Librería Española y Americana de D. Ignacio Boix, 1852). (Bibliothèque nationale de France)

critics who had dismissed such writing as inferior to novels by Hawthorne and Melville.[16] For my purposes, the crucial question to pose about melodrama is not to what extent it adheres to ideas of what constitutes good writing but rather what sorts of conceptual advantages and limitations result from adopting "the point of view of the victim."[17] Orihuela's use of sentimental melodrama was new in that he sought to cast the interracial abolitionist activism of the Ladder Conspiracy as an alternative to the racist annexationism of Cuban exiles, in a bold act of remembrance that broke with the dominant discourses that criminalized Plácido and other martyrs of the rebellion.[18] As Giorgio Agamben has observed, "Remembrance restores possibility to the past."[19] Orihuela may not have accomplished the racial reforms that he envisioned, but his writings are nonetheless important for their messages of dissent and for reimagining the potential of Cuba.

Given Orihuela's work in translating *Uncle Tom's Cabin* into Spanish and his deployment of Stowe's sentimental melodrama, to what extent was *El Sol* an *Uncle Tom's Cabin* for Cuba? Orihuela implicitly placed Stowe within a much broader "hemispheric text-network," to use Susan Gillman and Kirsten Silva Gruesz's term, of cultural texts.[20] Gillman and Gruesz have argued that instead of searching for literary sources, influences, or origins, the literary critic should instead attempt to explain how "a network of crosshatched multidirectional influences" shapes the conditions for the emergence of a given text.[21] Bruno Latour's notion of the "actor-network" similarly links the local and the global by showing how "a large star-shaped web" of attachments shape subjects—and by extension, texts.[22]

For Orihuela this web of multidirectional influences includes a number of interlocutors besides Stowe, including Gustave de Beaumont (1802–1866), the travel companion of Alexis de Tocqueville and author of *Marie* (1835), an antislavery novel set in the United States; Víctor Balaguer (1824–1901), the Catalan journalist, novelist, politician, and historian who virtually invented the idiom of Catalan nationalism and to whom Orihuela dedicates his novel; Plácido, who appears in a text within the text in *El Sol;* the Cuban exile community in New York and Europe, who engaged in a series of debates on nationalism, race, and colonialism in Spanish-language newspapers, particularly *La Verdad* (1848–60) of New York; and the Del Monte circle of writers, conspicuously absent from Orihuela's writings but his immediate predecessors as Cuban writers of novels on race and slavery as well fellow alumni of the Seminario de San Carlos and co-contributors to newspapers like *Noticioso y Lucero de la Habana* (1832–44).[23] Orihuela implicitly and explicitly invoked this broad hemispheric and transatlantic text network in order to address the racial blind spots of both Stowe and Cuban exile nationalism by yoking an antislavery and antiracist vision to anticolonialism.[24]

Orihuela further distances his novel from Stowe's in that its sentimentalism does not celebrate the success of white empathy as does Stowe's but rather exposes its *failure* in effecting an enduring antiracist ethos. *El Sol* focuses on the fate of two women of modest means, one white, the other a mulatta. Tulita, a white creole, is known as the beautiful "sun" of Jesús del Monte Road.[25] The title's use of a visual metaphor is no mistake; it simultaneously signifies Tulita's arresting beauty and the widespread tendency to associate beauty with whiteness in colonial Cuba. Yet Matilde, Tulita's mulatta rival, could just as easily stake claim to that title with her beauty.

As an attractive mulatta, Matilde embodies an "erotics of politics" that defines the national romances of Latin America for Doris Sommer.[26] Sommer understands the national romance as "a cross between our contemporary use of the word [*romance*] as a love story and a nineteenth-century use that distinguished the genre as more boldly allegorical than the novel" in which "star-crossed lovers [...] represent particular regions, races, parties, economic interests, and the like."[27] In this case, the would-be union between Eduardo and Matilde signifies the possibility of a white-mulatto alliance. The novel's sympathetic portrayal of Matilde suggests that rethinking white privilege through a critique of characters like Eduardo, Federico, and Tulita is among its primary aims. Moreover, the failed union between Eduardo and Matilde points toward the novel's critique of Cuban creole nationalism's tendency to imagine the nation as exclusively white. Orihuela's sentimentalism encourages his readers to sympathize with his mulatto characters like Matilde and to distrust Eduardo; his melodrama contextualizes moments of cross-ethnic sympathy in terms of a wide array of morally polarized characters.

Orihuela emphasizes the hypocrisy of self-styled egalitarian white reformers, as embodied by the antihero of the novel, Eduardo, who betrays his high-minded ideals by ignoring his mulatta lover, Matilde, in favor of the title character, Tulita. Eduardo engages in the "exchange" or sacrifice of cosmopolitan egalitarianism in favor of "the pursuit of self-realization," to quote Max Horkheimer and Theodor Adorno's critique of Enlightenment thought.[28] Horkheimer and Adorno argue that Enlightenment ideals of freedom and egalitarianism are irrevocably "harnessed" to the capitalist mode of production, racism, and anti-Semitism, which ultimately undermine those ideals.[29] Indeed, it is as if Eduardo anticipates Horkheimer and Adorno's sardonic observation that one of the Enlightenment freedoms is the "freedom from the bite of conscience."[30] Orihuela's story of the failure of white reform—both in *Dos palabras* and in *El Sol*—served to rebuke the stubbornly persistent racism of white Cubans, who refused to include Blacks and mulattoes in their imagined community of the nation and thus failed to broaden the base of their would-be revolution against Spanish colonialism.

The subtitle of *El Sol de Jesús del Monte, Novela de costumbres cubanas,* signals that Orihuela's novel deploys *costumbrismo,* the popular Spanish-language genre that represented a country's customs and social types in literature and the visual arts. Its French analogue, the *tableau de moeurs* (portrait of customs), shapes the other novel that Orihuela names as a model for his own antislavery writing, Gustave de Beaumont's antislavery novel *Marie, ou L'esclavage aux États-Unis: Tableau de moeurs américaines* (1835). The aim of Orihuela's *costumbrismo* is to assess the perspectives and lived experiences of a wide array of social groups in Cuba in relation to race and slavery. Orihuela joins Beaumont in working within the framework of *costumbrismo,* often with the aims of celebrating national culture and engaging in moral and political critique to promote social reform. *Costumbrismo* initially crystallized in periodicals in the form of "a brief text in prose that through the telling of a simple anecdote portrays [. . .] a custom characteristic of a society [. . .] in a human type that represents" that society.[31] An anonymous critic writing in the *Eco del Comercio* (Madrid) in 1835 argues that *costumbrismo* focuses on "la copia de las prácticas y hábitos de la época" (the copy of the practices and habits of an epoch); that discourse of realism roughly corresponds to the Cuban literary critic José Manuel Mestre's perception in 1854 that Orihuela's characters bear a close resemblance to what he terms the "originals."[32]

Although for many years *costumbrismo* suffered from a lack of scholarly attention—there is no mention of it in Jean Franco's *Introduction to Spanish-American Literature* (1969)—José Fernández Montesinos argued that it was a precursor of realism in 1960, and several scholars have more recently engaged in analytically rigorous studies of the genre.[33] Scholars like José Escobar have praised *costumbrista* writers for focusing on the everyday culture of "the trivial, worthless, insignificant."[34] More recently, other scholars have pointed out that a variety of artistic, racial, social, and political discourses constitute the fabric of *costumbrismo*.³⁵ I join these scholars in arguing that *costumbrismo* spearheads a shift in representation away from the general, abstract, and universal and toward the ethnographically and historically specific and local, thereby lending itself to political imaginings.³⁶ A new critical consensus on *costumbrismo* has emerged: that it served as a relay and focal point for discourses of predisciplinary social science, race, and science, allowing for an examination of social conflicts and hierarchies in light of the latest social thought.³⁷ In Cuba and elsewhere *costumbrismo* served the additional purpose of serving as a site for the development of national consciousness.

In Cuba, the periodicals *El Faro Industrial, El Álbum, El Aguinaldo Habanero, Noticioso y Lucero,* and *El Siglo* published *costumbrista* articles. Ramón de Palma published the brief *costumbrista* stories "El cólera en La Habana" and "Una pascua en San Marcos" in *El Álbum* in 1838. The novel *Francisco* (written in 1838–39) and the *Colección de artículos* (1859), by Anselmo Súarez y Romero, were also landmark texts in Cuban *costumbrismo*. Other *costumbrista* writers in Cuba included Gaspar Betancourt Cisneros (1803–1866) and José María Cárdenas y Rodríguez (1812–1882), known by the pseudonym Jeremías de Docaransa. José Victoriano Betancourt, one of the leading Cuban *costumbristas,* began publishing his articles in 1838 in *La Cartera Cubana*. Finally, the novels and short stories of Cirilo Villaverde (1812–1894), including "La tejedora de sombreros de yarey" (1844) and *Excursión a Vuelta Abajo* (1838, 1842), abound with *costumbrista* features.³⁸ Villaverde's *Cecilia Valdés* was the single most influential novel in nineteenth-century Cuba.³⁹

The word *Sun* in Orihuera's title explicitly invokes the beauty of Eduardo's future wife, the white creole Tulita, but it implicitly also invokes the beauty of Matilde, Tulita's mulatta creole rival for Eduardo's affections. The sun in the title also implicitly signifies truth, reason, and progress—in the Spanish-speaking world the Enlightenment is known as the Siglo de las Luces (literally, the Century of Light). Moreover, the term *sun* calls to mind the anticolonial revolution Soles y Rayos de Bolívar (The Suns and Rays of Bolivar), of 1822–24. Indeed, in Orihuela's novel the father of Tulita's friend Lolita was imprisoned for his suspected participation in the Soles y Rayos de Bolívar.⁴⁰ After Félix Varela, Juan José Hernández, and Leonardo Santos Suárez traveled to the Cortes de Cádiz as Cuba's delegation from 1821 to 1823 and presented an unsuccessful proposal for abolishing slavery in Cuba and granting greater political representation to Cuban elites in the Spanish Cortes, a number of disaffected Cubans joined forces with Colombians to create a movement for the independence of Cuba.[41] The main organization for this movement was La Logia de Sol, a Masonic lodge that counted among its leadership the Colombian José Fernández Madrid (1789–1830), the Colombian Diego Tanco (1789–1849), the Argentinian José Antonio Miralla (1789–1825), and the Ecuadorian Vicente Rocafuerte (1783–1847).[42] One of its members, José Francisco Lemus, of Matanzas, exemplifies the transnational organizing that precipitated the revolution.[43] In 1817 Lemus traveled to Philadelphia, where he met with a number of Colombians, and he then traveled to Florida and finally to Spain, where he met with another group of Republicans from Colombia, including government functionaries. In 1822, Lemus returned to Cuba, where he joined a creole militia.[44] The conspiracy eventually counted more than six hundred members in Pinar del Río, Havana, and Matanzas.[45] Many participants in the incipient revolution of December 1822, including Lemus and the Cuban poet José María Heredia (1803–1839), were members of the white creole lettered elite, but this was also a cross-class movement that brought into its folds domestic slaves, "tobacco workers, itinerant salesmen, barbers, tailors, mulattoes and free blacks of various professions, and possibly slaves from sugar plantations."[46] As a cross-class and interethnic revolution, the Soles y Rayos de Bolívar was a precursor of the Ladder Rebellion, which Orihuela foregrounds in his novel.

Orihuela shifts sentimentalism's moral center of gravity and its onus of social change away from white reformers toward mulatto characters. The novel stages a moment of *cross-ethnic sympathy* à la Stowe that links Federico, a white creole man who reads the account of Placido's death, to the mulatta creoles Matilde and her mother, Belencita, because all of them cry at the story's conclusion. But it is also a moment of *intra-ethnic sympathy* that spotlights the anger, fear, and sorrow of two mulattas over the violent and unjust death of a man of color. Here I recall Sara Johnson's suggestion that scholars emphasize the "fears felt by blacks themselves" in order to create counternarratives of history.[47] These two kinds of sympathy are different. Cross-ethnic sympathy is uncertain in its outcomes because the "self-realization" of whites may conflict with antiracist egalitarianism: Tulita says that it is an "affront" that her rival for Eduardo's love is a woman of color, and Eduardo says that his love for Matilde was a "pure pastime."[48] By contrast, Orihuela's intra-ethnic sympathy explores the possibility of social change by people of color themselves. The tears in sentimental melodrama are not always signs of excess or powerlessness; they can also be "a source of future power; indeed, they are almost an investment in that power," as Williams has claimed.⁴⁹

One of the "investments" that Matilde and Belencita make with their shared tears is to implicitly construct an alliance between dark-skinned and light-skinned through their sympathy as mulattas for Plácido, a *pardo,* or light-skinned mulatto. Moreover, Orihuela's Plácido constructs an implicit alliance between free people of color and slaves. At a time when people of color in Cuba linked whiteness to the possibility of social mobility, an explicit Afro-Cuban identity did not yet exist.⁵⁰ Orihuela uses intra-ethnic sympathy to link the historical figure of Plácido—who implicitly enunciates an antislavery and anticolonial stance in this novel and at times in his published poetry—to the fictional characters Belencita, her daughter Matilde, whom the white Eduardo rejects because of her race, and Matilde's uncle Julio, whom a white soldier unjustly accuses of having participated in La Escalera.⁵¹ Orihuela thereby forms a composite figure

José Vallejo y Galeazo, "Andrés Avelino de Orihuela," in *Poetas españoles y americanos del siglo XIX,* edited by Andrés Avelino de Orihuela (Paris: M. S. Albert, 1851), 6. (Bibliothèque nationale de France)

of Cuban creole mulatto/a identity that melds a literary celebrity to those whose stories would otherwise have gone untold, a Cuban martyr to ordinary people of color who survive by emigrating to the Yucatán. These mulattos/as embody an alternative future to the exclusively white nationalism of Cuban exiles because they join the narrator in denouncing discourses of white superiority, thereby constituting the novel's ethical compass. Orihuela refigures mulatto identity as an essential component of both Cuban and Latin American futures.

El Sol de Jesús del Monte is a sentimental melodrama in the tragic mode in that the possible union between white and mulatto creoles fails to materialize in a marital union between Eduardo and Matilde.[52] The failure is twofold: the tragedy afflicting mulatto Cubans harms Cuba as a whole. Orihuela places mulatto/a and Black life in all of its variety—ranging from rural plantation slaves to urban slaves, poets, entrepreneurs and young women—at the very center of Cuban culture, further emphasizing Cuba's tragedy. He foregrounds the anticolonial and slave insurrection of La Escalera at his own moment in history, well before Black, mulatto, and white creoles fought alongside one another in the Ten Years' War for Cuban independence (1868–78).

Orihuela's Life and the Reception of *El Sol de Jesús del Monte*

The extant scholarship gives only a bare-bones outline of Orihuela's life. However, by consulting actual archives in Havana, Madrid, New York City, and Washington, DC, and by searching digital archives of newspapers in the Americas and Spain, I have been able to further flesh out his life story. Born in Las Palmas in the Canary Islands in 1818, Orihuela migrated as a toddler with his parents to Cuba. After obtaining a law degree in 1838 from the Seminario de San Carlos of Havana—the preferred college of Cuba's creole elite—Orihuela worked as a lawyer beginning in the early 1840s. In 1841 Orihuela and Pedro Martín cofounded a free Sunday school for the indigent, which they called the Institute for Free Education.[53] By holding these classes on Sunday mornings, Orihuela and Martín were able to make them informally available to Blacks and mulattoes even though the government had ordered such classes restricted to whites.[54] A prolific writer from the late 1830s on, Orihuela wrote plays, poetry, essays, novels, stories, and translations and edited or contributed to at least twenty periodicals—in Havana, Madrid, Matanzas, New York, San Francisco, Veracruz, and Paris—but *El Sol* is by far Orihuela's most important statement on Cuba. In the 1840s and 1850s Orihuela lived alternately in Havana, Veracruz, Barcelona, Madrid, London, Paris, and New York, where he became a US citizen, only to shortly thereafter resume his travels.[55] Cuban colonial authorities sent Orihuela into exile in Spain for his liberal political ideas at some point in the period 1842–44.[56] However, "D. Andres Orihuela" appears in a list of those present at an "ordinary meeting of December 12, 1843" of the Division of Industry and Commerce of the Sociedad Económica de los Amigos del País of Havana, which establishes that Orihuela had either stayed in Cuba or returned to the island by December 1843 and was therefore in a position to witness the repression of La Escalera.[57] I have not been able to determine the dates of his second banishment from Cuba. At least as early as 1844, Orihuela had established a law office on Obispo Street.[58] In 1844, the government nominated him and Manuel R. Mena to inspect the Academia de Niñas, run by Doña Felicia Beuballon in Havana.[59] There were also several announcements in the *Diario de la Marina* from April through November 1845 about ships about to set off for either Latin American or Spanish ports that named one "D. A. Orihuela" as the agent at 97 Mercaderes Street in Havana.[60] In 1845 Orihuela coedited with Teodoro Guerrero the satirical newspaper *El Quita-Pesares*—satire was one of the tools Cubans used to elude colonial censorship.[61] Orihuela also briefly married a woman in 1845 but separated from her that same year and resumed his travels to New York, Veracruz, Madrid, and Barcelona.[62]

In 1848 Orihuela traveled from New Orleans to Barcelona.[63] A tantalizing glimpse of Orihuela's multiple migrations and work as a lawyer appears in an advertisement in *El Fomento* of Barcelona: "D. Andrés Avelino de Orihuela, a lawyer in the Supreme Courts of this Nation, in the United States, in the royal tribunals of the magistrate of Havana, and in the distinguished college of this city, has opened his office on Guardia Street, number 13, on the second floor in front, where he serves the public and his friends."[64] On November, 16, 1848, Orihuela wrote a letter to Alejandro José de Atocha proposing that the Spanish businessman fund a new newspaper in New York City called *El Apostol del Pueblo,* which Orihuela envisioned as a trilingual republican daily that would be a "defender of the cause of the people [*pueblo*]."[65] Atocha was a US citizen who acted as go-between in negotiations between Santa Anna and President Polk in February 1846.[66] Orihuela planned to share the editorial and administrative duties with a group of writers he praised as "verdaderos republicanos" (true republicans), in keeping with the spirit of the republican revolutions that swept across Europe in 1848: the husband-and-wife team of Manuel Galo de Cuendias, a professor of languages, and Victoria Féréal, a writer, as well as Francisco José Orellana (1820–1891), a Spanish poet, novelist, translator, and playwright who was coeditor with Balaguer of the Barcelona newspapers *El Bien Público* and *El Universal*.[67] *El Popular* reported on November 22, 1849, that Orihuela appeared before Queen Isabella II of Spain in order to present her with a copy of his anthology of poetry, *Tesoro de los poetas españoles y americanos del siglo XIX* (Treasury of Spanish and American poets of the nineteenth century).[68]

In 1852 Orihuela was extraordinarily productive as a writer, publishing both his translation of *Uncle Tom's Cabin* and his own novel. Newspapers in Spain and Cuba reported that Orihuela was preparing for publication a "Diccionario de procedimientos judiciales" (Dictionary of judicial procedures) and soliciting subscribers to the book, which he estimated to run close to one thousand pages.[69] However, Orihuela apparently shelved this project—I have found no record of its publication. That same year, in the pamphlet *Dos palabras* (1852), Orihuela called on white Cuban exiles to make common cause with mulatto and Black Cubans and embrace antislavery at a time when Cuban nationalism was notoriously negrophobic and antislaveries were anathema. As Rodrigo Lazo has shown in his study of Cuban exile newspapers, not only were a number of prominent Cuban exile journalists slaveholders but Gaspar Betancourt Cisneros, one of the editors of *La Verdad*, regarded both slave traders and abolitionists as enemies.[70] Betancourt Cisneros also rivaled the American School of Ethnology in his racism, referring to the leaders of Haiti as "a stupid, insignificant, impotent government, of orangutans who in the blink of an eye will return to the jungle to eat cedar tree fruit and red guavas."[71] Another prominent contributor to *La Verdad*, Pedro Santacilia, raised the specter of Haiti to promote proslavery positions among Cuban exiles and associated blackness with Cuba's inability to achieve self-rule.[72] Perhaps because Orihuela's novel was ahead of its time in terms of racial politics, or perhaps because of its lengthy and distracting texts within the text, its reception was mixed. One contemporary Cuban reviewer dismissed *El Sol de Jesús del Monte* as "insignificant," and the novel fell into obscurity, at least in Cuba.[73] However, Orihuela's novel did garner positive press in Europe and elsewhere in Latin America.[74]

In the 1850s Orihuela forged friendships with a broad array of writers while contributing to several newspapers in Paris and editing a few others. In the fall of 1854, Orihuela wrote his friend and benefactor the Spanish playwright and poet Juan Eugenio Hartzenbusch (1806–1880) reporting that he had been living in London for a few months and requesting that his friend look into whether any of his contacts among editors could name him as a correspondent.[75] From 1852 to 1854, Orihuela served as the literary editor of *El Eco de Ambos Mundos,* which the Spanish government banned from all its dominions in 1852.[76] From 1854 to 1855, Orihuela served as one of the editors of *El Eco Hispano-Americano.* José Segundo Florez was the editor-in-chief of these two newspapers, both published in Paris and both focusing on Latin America. Orihuela also served as editor in chief of the monthly *Panorama universal,* also published in Paris, from 1854 to 1855.[77] From 1859 to 1860, Orihuela served as the coeditor of *La sátira de ambos mundos* in Paris along with Eugenio Guillemot. Orihuela was also a frequent contributor to Guillemot's *La Caprichosa: Revista Universal del Nuevo Mundo* from March to September 1859. Among the contributors to the August 1859 edition of *La Caprichosa,* in addition to Orihuela himself, were Gertrudis Gómez de Avellaneda, the author of the Cuban antislavery novel *Sab* (1841), Balaguer, and Ramón Zambrana (1817–1866), a Cuban doctor and poet.[78]

In 1861, Orihuela served as the secretary of the Círculo Hispano-Americano of Paris, a social club, whose members included Ramón de la Sagra (1798–1871), a Spanish naturalist and social theorist who lived in Havana from 1820 to 1835, Juan Martínez Villergas (1817–1894), the Spanish satirist, journalist, and politician who also had lived in Havana, and the Colombian poet José María Torres Caicedo (1827–1889), who was the first person to use the term *América Latina,* in his poem "Las dos Américas" (1856), and who wrote up a blueprint for Latin American unity in 1861 that was later republished in *Unión Latino-Americana* (1865).[79] In keeping with the Latin Americanist thrust of Torres Caicedo, Orihuela worked in the Uruguayan consulate of Paris for several years, first as vice consul as early as 1859 and then as consul general at least from 1862 to 1864.[80]

Orihuela's long-standing engagement with anticolonial, nationalist, and antislavery causes is evident in his writings and activities that followed *El Sol de Jesús del Monte.* In the New York Cuban exile journal *El Eco de Cuba* in 1855, in which he called himself a "citizen of the United States," Orihuela published the nationalist and anticolonial poems "El grito de Hatuey! Leyenda cubana (siglo XVI)" and "El guajiro independiente: Cantos populares cubanos."[81] Orihuela also published two long excerpts of reports to the British Parliament extolling the benefits of slave emancipation in Jamaica. Orihuela emphasized the efficiency of free Black labor in comparison with slave labor. US antislavery activists similarly invoked British West Indian emancipation to bolster their case for abolition.[82] Orihuela's endorsement of British West Indian emancipation was a stinging rebuke to the New York Cuban exile leadership. These Cuban exiles combined opposition to Spanish colonialism with proslavery views and antipathy toward Blacks in the newspaper *La Verdad*. Orihuela's rebuke of the Cuban exile leadership built on the racial reform of his earlier writings and joined the more racially inclusive and antislavery politics of Francisco Agüero Estrada's New York City Cuban exile newspapers *El Mulato* (1854) and *El Pueblo* (1855).[83]

As further evidence of his long-lasting antislavery convictions, Orihuela was one of the founding members of the Sociedad Abolicionista Española (the Spanish Abolitionist Society) in Madrid in 1864.[84] In the fall of 1864, Orihuela strode into the house of the politician, journalist, and historian Fernando Corradi (1808–1885) in Madrid, accompanied by the secretary of the British and Foreign Anti-Slavery Society, the novelist Louis Alexis Chamerovzow (1816–1875).[85] Orihuela had organized a meeting for the purpose of founding the Sociedad Abolicionista.[86] The commission that grew out of this initial meeting included Andrés de Arango (1773–1865), of Cuba, as president, Orihuela as secretary, and seven other members.[87] The commission soon disbanded as a result of conflicting political views. But the Sociedad Abolicionista of 1864 can be regarded as setting the foundations for its later, longer-lasting incarnation of 1865, since at least two members of this commission, Félix de Bona (1821?–1899) and Julio Vizcarrondo, became members of the new organization. Curiously, the leading US historian of the Spanish antislavery movement makes no mention of Orihuela.[88] From 1864 to 1866 Orihuela was also a contributor to *El Mencey* of Cuba, a Canary Islander newspaper.[89]

While José Martí was a student at the Universidad Central de Madrid from 1871 to 1873, Orihuela befriended him and helped him establish contacts with journals that published his writings, including the newspaper that Orihuela edited in 1871, *La Discusión*.[90] Although several sources give 1873 as the year of Orihuela's death, *La Correspondencia de España*, of Madrid, reported on January 29, 1874, that the Spanish government had offered Orihuela a post in the Ministry of Finance. Beyond this brief biographical sketch, scholars know very little about Orihuela's life.[91] Miguel Hernández Paz has shown that one source claims that Orihuela died in Madrid in 1873, while another source claims that he died in Paris in 1887.[92]

Just as many details of Orihuela's life have fallen into obscurity, there are few clues as to why his novel never became popular. The only contemporary Cuban critic of the novel that I have been able to find, José Manuel Mestre (1832–1886), a professor at the University of Havana, panned the novel in a review that attempted to be evenhanded but was actually dismissive and inaccurate.[93] Writing in the *Revista de la Habana* in 1854, Mestre praised the novel for its realistic characters and Orihuela for his knowledge of Cuba: "Orihuela knows our country and [. . .] his portraits are quite similar to the originals."[94] Mestre then goes on to quote approvingly from a passage in which the title character's mother hits her slave Dolores and her daughter Tulita consoles Dolores. However, Mestre's criticisms outweigh his praise. He writes that the novel's defects include Orihuela's "having poorly prepared the events and not having sufficiently developed them," and he objects to the numerous inserted narratives.[95] His most serious charge is that Orihuela's novel lacks a moral purpose and therefore "is of very little worth."[96]

Ironically, Mestre's long summary of the novel's "acción principal" (main plot) fails to mention its alignment with struggles against racial hierarchies, slavery, and colonialism—which is precisely the novel's ethical purpose.[97] Mestre misses Orihuela's suggestion that the romance of white Cubanness comes at the expense of the Black and mulatto population and the country as a whole. And although Mestre never once mentions La Escalera in his review, the conspiracy takes center stage in the novel. The importance of La Escalera directs the reader to the *other* main plot that Mestre neglects: the plot that links Plácido to Matilde, Belencita, and Julio by their shared victimization during the repression of La Escalera. Mestre therefore colludes with the novel's main antihero, Eduardo, in failing to give proper weight to the plight of Blacks and mulattoes, as if to confirm the pressing need for Orihuela's critique of whiteness.

In Europe, writers praised Orihuela's novel. On January 24, 1853, the *Diario de Palma* quoted from a review in a "well-known newspaper in Paris" that claimed that the novel had achieved "extraordinary success" and that "in very little time it had sold out two editions illustrated by the best Parisian artists. [. . .] *El Sol de Jesús del Monte* [. . .] portrays the customs of the Island of Cuba with admirable precision.[. . .] Mr. Orihuela [. . .] has just strengthened his reputation with this new work, garnering a good deal of admiration."[98] Latin American exiles in Paris were likely to have met Orihuela and to have read his writings. The Colombian poet Rafael Pombo (1833–1912) was so impressed with *El Sol* that he dedicated a poem to Orihuela in 1855 in which he wrote, "Generoso poeta que llevado / De tu destino en el torrente vas / Lanzando donde quiera que hay esclavos / Un himno de esperanza y libertad" (Generous poet, your destiny / Has swept you into a torrent / Launching a hymn of hope and liberty / Wherever there are slaves), and he predicted that Orihuela would be a "mensajer[o] profétic[o] de paz" (a prophetic messenger of peace) if Orihuela were to travel to Mexico.[99] Pombo's poem praises Orihuela's poetry yet implicitly refers to *El Sol*. And in a poem written in 1856, the Colombian poet Mariano G. Manriquer (1829–1870) praises Orihuela's "bold genius" and his unique literary voice.[100]

The only twentieth-century Cuban scholar to recognize the importance of *El Sol* was the historian Pedro Deschamps Chapeaux, who wrote an article on Orihuela's novel in 1972. Deschamps praises Orihuela's "impressive realism" and points out his important contributions to Cuban literary history: "In *El Sol de Jesús del Monte*, Orihuela recognizes the existence within slaveholding society of a sector made up of free blacks and whites who had attained some socioeconomic importance before the whirlwind of 1844 swept them away. It is significant that the work [. . .] is without a doubt the first to include within its folds the bloody events of the tragic Year of the Lash [La Escalera] and surely is also the first in which an author of a Cuban novel reveals himself to be in open opposition to [colonial] society and slavery."[101]

More recently, scholars from the Canary Islands have revived interest in Orihuela as a native son. In 1997 Paloma Jiménez del Campo published the first major article on *El Sol* since Deschamps Chapeaux's.[102] She argued that Orihuela "portrays realistically [. . .] in order to render a vivid, intimate vision of the past and thereby offer a true-to-life testimony of the epoch."[103] Jiménez del Campo also included sections on Orihuela's life and *El Sol* in her *Escritores canarios en Cuba,* which she published in the Canary Islands in 2003. In 2007 Hernández Paz came out with a new, modernized edition of *El Sol,* and in 2008 he published his critical study *Andrés Orihuela Moreno y El Sol de Jesús del Monte*. Hernández Paz explains how *El Sol* is an anticolonial text, writing that Orihuela "denounces the exclusion of Cuba from the constitutional system, which permitted [Spain] to evade the question of slavery and prevent social and political liberalism from reaching the colony"; exposes "the social hierarchy inherent to a corrupt colonial system"; and condemns racism and slavery through the character Eduardo's conversation with a racist *guajiro* (or farmer from the island's interior).[104] Hernández Paz also points out that the white characters "don't belong to the creole oligarchy, the owners of large slave estates, but rather to the middle class."[105]

Orihuela as "Cultural Editor"—Texts within the Text

The sole nineteenth-century review of *El Sol* faulted the novel for its many inserted texts by other writers, and some of today's readers of the novel might find them awkward, distracting, and lengthy and be tempted to skip them. But other nineteenth-century writers that critics have favored, like William Wells Brown in the United States or José Martí of Cuba, also tended to act as what John Ernest has termed *cultural editors,* including passages, news articles, or even whole stories written by other writers, often without citing the sources.[106] I am not interested in mounting a defense of Orihuela's choice to interrupt his story with several lengthy texts within the text; instead my aim is to attempt to understand the possible meanings of that choice.

The first such text in *El Sol* is "El palco misterioso" ("The Mysterious Theater Box"), a long story that Orihuela inserts into chapter 2, as Eduardo and Federico are traveling in a carriage to Jesús del Monte Road so that Eduardo can pay a visit to Tulita. The placement of this story is somewhat jarring to the reader since it interrupts the plot of Orihuela's novel early on in his tale. Federico reads this story to Eduardo and gives a copy of it to Lolita, a white creole widow and love interest, passing it off as his own. But Lolita, who is well-read, later exposes him as a fraud. The prolific French dramatist Eugène Scribe (1791–1861) actually wrote the story, which he published as "Judith, ou la loge d'opéra" (1838). Orihuela himself commits the literary infraction of plagiarism that he exposes Federico as having committed, as if with a wink to the reader. What is the function of this text within the text? Its inclusion sets up a clash of literary and political sensibilities contrasting European culture to the cultures of the Americas. Is Orihuela suggesting that his readers shift their attention from Europe to the Americas? Is he signaling his aim to adapt this cross-class romance, making it speak to the realities of Cuba? Including this story implicitly compares the difficulty of marrying across class hierarchies in Europe with that of marrying across racial hierarchies in Cuba. Moreover, Federico's lack of literary originality serves as a metonym for the more far-reaching and damaging fraud of the claim of white superiority.

The most important inserted text is what purports to be an eyewitness account, "Últimas horas del poeta Cubano Gabriel de la Concepción Valdés (Plácido)" (The last hours of the Cuban poet . . .), which is a text within the text that features the voice of a free person of color. I have examined the manuscript copy of "Últimas horas" in the Escoto Collection of the Houghton Library at Harvard University, and the two texts are identical. Although the Escoto Collection catalog attributes this text to Orihuela, "Salinero" signed the manuscript. Orihuela evidently copied an account by José María Salinero, the owner of the newspaper *La Aurora del Yumurí,* who had hired Plácido to be the editor of the paper's poetry section. Salinero published this account in a pamphlet, *La muerte de Plácido,* in Veracruz in 1844.[107] By featuring the conversations and poetry of Plácido, this inserted text shows that *El Sol* is an exemplar of what Antonio Cornejo Polar has termed "heterogenous literatures," which are "situated at the conflictive crossing of two societies and two cultures" and reflect on "a referent whose sociocultural identity ostensibly differs from the system that produces the literary text."[108] Whereas Cornejo Polar focuses on the linguistic and cultural alterity of indigenous groups in Peru, this text within a text focuses on the political dissent of a *pardo* poet. Indeed, as the novel shows, colonial Cuba in the mid-1840s was diverse in sociocultural groups, including free *pardos* and mulattoes, slaves, immigrants, *guajiros,* and white creoles like Federico. Rather than engaging in a toothless sentimentalism that falls short of calling for the full equality of Blacks and mulattoes, Orihuela's engaged sentimentalism allows for Plácido, a man of African ancestry, to speak for himself—and against the colonial regime—in this text within a text. That is not to say that Orihuela gives the reader access to the putatively authentic "voice" of Plácido. Instead, "Últimas horas" constructs the figure of Plácido as a poet whose words deserve to be recorded and whose martyrdom must be remembered.

The novel also includes the "Relacion de la visita ecclesiastica del ilustrisimo Señor Morel,"[109] which is a short historical document from the Spanish Inquisition telling of the exorcism of a demon and illustrating Federico's disdain for religion and superstition. However, Orihuela devotes a far more extensive section of the novel to inserted stories by Balaguer. Balaguer's "Veladas de Navidad," "La Rama del Olmo," and "Un sudario con sus trenzas" were published together in book form in 1852, the year of the publication of *El Sol de Jesús del Monte.*[110] These stories collectively address the issues of slavery and empire, which were Orihuela's urgent concerns.

"Veladas" frames the other stories by Balaguer: the narrator of "La Rama del Olmo" is Adolfo, a drunkard in the sketch "Veladas." In "La Rama del Olmo," the Count of Entenza marries a woman named Isa, thereby breaking his ties to his implicit lover, the slave Zeliska. Zeliska attempts to kill her master in revenge, but the count foils their plot. This tale of slave rebellion stemming from interracial romantic betrayal is implicitly a repudiation of white Cubans' typical manner of narrating slave rebellion as treachery in Cuba. It also calls to mind Eduardo's betrayal of Matilde. "Un sudario con sus trenzas" tells the tragic tale of Berenguer de Entenza, a fourteenth-century "catalán aventurero" (Catalan adventurer) and soldier whose brother kills him in battle and whose wife covers his corpse with a shroud of her hair.[111] In his *Bellezas de la historia de Cataluña* (1853), Balaguer recounts the history of the campaign of a mercenary army called the Compañía Catalana de Oriente, whose leader, Roger de Flor, traveled with them to Greece in 1302. The Greek Empire hired his services to repel an invasion of Turks, and one of his soldiers, Berenguer de Entenza, became the military leader upon the death of Roger de Flor in 1305. Berenguer went on to attack the territories of the Byzantine Empire. A rival succeeded in assassinating him in 1307. Orihuela's inclusion of Balaguer's stories constructs a kind of transatlantic alliance among differing nationalisms opposing the Spanish Crown or constructing a space for dissent within it.

Balaguer's biography demonstrates his considerable appeal to Orihuela as someone who joined Canary Islanders and Cubans in constructing nationalisms that contested Spanish imperial unity. Balaguer's prolific writings made him a pioneering Catalan nationalist: "The role of Víctor Balaguer in the recuperation of Catalan consciousness is unquestionable," writes Pere Anguera.[112] Like Orihuela, Balaguer was a journalist: he was the editor of numerous periodicals, including *El Laurel* (1840), *El Genio* (1844–45), *El Barcino Musical* (1846), and *El Conseller* (1856) with Lluís Cutxet. The editors of *El Genio* characterized their newspaper as a "challenge to those who have said that in Catalonia literature doesn't exist."[113] Balaguer published in both Spanish and Catalan and was the inaugural director of the Liceo Theater in 1847. Scholars have regarded his novels as contributing to the creation of a Catalan nationalist imaginary. His many novels include *La guzla del cedro o los almogávares en Oriente* (1849) and *Don Juan de Serralonga, o los bandoleros de las Guillerías* (1858). A pioneering historian of Catalonia, he held the first chair in the history of Catalonia at the Philharmonic Society of Barcelona in 1852.[114] As a historian, he published *Bellezas de la historia de Cataluña* (1853) and the five-volume *Historia de Cataluña y de la Corona de Aragón* (1860–64), which he hoped would promote "el amor al país" (love for our country).[115] He was the first author writing in Catalan to achieve popularity.[116] In 1857 he wrote the poem "A la verge de Montserrat" in Catalan, and after that date he wrote all of his poetry in that language. He was a prolific writer in the genres of history, the novel, and poetry: his *Obras completas* comprise thirty-seven volumes. In his political life, Balaguer worked to realize a constitutional and liberal monarchy in Spain, an aim that many Cuban creoles shared.[117] Balaguer led the Liberal Party in Barcelona from 1843 to 1868. He then served as overseas minister in 1871 and 1874, president of the Consejo de Ultramar (1886–89), and finally president of the Consejo de Filipinas y Posesiones del Golfo de Guinea (1894–95).[118] Balaguer thus combined Catalan nationalism in his writings with dissent from within the monarchy in his life as a politician.

As a cultural editor who included several texts written by others in his novel, Orihuela sought to signal his broad cultural affinities both within and beyond Cuba in an effort to offer an additional forum for Plácido's voice and to engage in comparative reflection on nationalism, empire, and slavery in the case of the stories by Balaguer. "Últimas horas," on Plácido, and Balaguer's stories within the novel constitute an effort to map out a series of counternationalisms in the Hispanic world, ranging from the novel's mention of the interethnic anticolonial movement of the Conspiración de los Soles y Rayos de Bolívar of 1823 and its foregrounding of La Escalera to its inclusion of the Catalan nationalist writings of Balaguer.[119] The interpolated texts in *El Sol* constitute one component of a dual Bakhtinian heteroglossia in the novel, "a multiplicity of social voices" that the novel unleashes both by borrowing liberally from other texts and by including Black and mulatto populations as members of its cosmopolitan, anticolonial imagined community.[120]

There may be a more prosaic reason why Orihuela included texts like "Judith, ou la loge d'opéra," texts removed from the concerns of *El Sol*. In an undated letter to his friend Juan Eugenio Hartzenbusch, Orihuela wrote that he was "sick and without bread for tomorrow" and asked for money. This suggests that Orihuela sought to earn a living by writing, and not just as a lawyer. Indeed, in Spain "the average price paid by an editor for eight pages [. . .] was between 250 and 300 reales from 1840 to 1860, which was no negligible amount if one compares it with the median, during this same period, of monthly salaries of wage-earning workers, which was between 200 and 400 reales."[121] If this accurately reflects what Boix paid its authors, Orihuela could earn a whole year's salary by publishing a book. And if Orihuela were paid by the page, as was common practice, it would be in his economic interest to "pad" the novel with others' writings.

Orihuela on La Escalera, Plácido, and Cuban Exile Politics

Orihuela paradoxically uses the popular literary forms of sentimental melodrama, *costumbrismo,* and texts within the text to discuss a historical event that was wildly unpopular among most sectors of the white Cuban population. Although Villaverde's *Cecilia Valdés* makes brief mention of La Escalera, to my knowledge *El Sol de Jesús del Monte* was the only nineteenth-century Cuban novel to foreground the rebellion and to emphasize its political significance, making it an indispensable comparative reference point to *Blake, or the Huts of America* (1859, 1861–62), by the African American abolitionist Martin R. Delany (1812–1885), as well as a landmark in Cuban literature.[122] *El Sol* conveys the political significance of Plácido as a historical figure—and by extension La Escalera as the defining event of the age—soon after the poet hears his death sentence. The sentence condemns Plácido—the most widely read Cuban poet in the early nineteenth century but also the most reviled for his allegedly radical politics—as the leader of the conspiracy. Plácido responds to his death sentence by endorsing the conspiracies and, implicitly, the Haitian Revolution (1791–1804), the only successful slave rebellion in the Americas: Cuban creoles "know how to die like men!"[123] Indeed, the historical Plácido hoped "to ally liberal whites with *pardos* to end slavery and win Cuba's independence," in Robert Paquette's words.[124] The significance of Orihuela's bold move to make Plácido a model of Cuban identity emerges when one considers that the Cuban colonial government punished any mention of Plácido or his poetry as a crime for decades after the poet's death.[125] Orihuela was able to do so because the novel was published in Paris and Orihuela was probably living in Paris, since he worked as the literary editor of *El Eco de Ambos Mundos* in Paris from 1852 to 1854.

La Escalera was not a single coordinated rebellion but instead comprised "several conspiracies" that were both somewhat distinct and overlapped, according to Paquette.[126] First, beginning in 1841, whites, free *pardos,* and *morenos* coalesced into two anticolonial resistance committees, with the assistance of the British consul, David Turnbull.[127] The white committee espoused independence and the gradual emancipation of slaves.[128] The committee of *pardos* and *morenos* also endorsed independence, but they also sought to bring about the immediate abolition of slavery.[129] However, according to Aisha Finch, white creoles had begun to drift away from the movement by the end of 1842, whereas free people of color heightened their activities from 1842 through 1844.[130] Second, three major slave rebellions struck Cuba in March, May, and November of 1843. On March 26, 1843, approximately one thousand slaves set fire to five sugar plantations near Matanzas and destroyed a section of the railroad tracks between Matanzas and Júcaro.[131] In May, another large slave insurrection erupted near Santiago de Cuba, followed by smaller revolts across the province of Matanzas in the summer and early fall.[132] Finally, on November 6, nearly five hundred slaves revolted on six estates in Sabanilla, in the province of Matanzas, at the Triumvirato, Ácana, La Concepción, San Miguel, San Lorenzo, and San Rafael plantations.[133]

These two sets of conspiracies overlapped in main part because of the efforts of free people of color and slaves who traveled from urban to rural areas and back spreading the news of an underground struggle with them.[134] Presumably for this very purpose of linking the urban and rural conspiracies, Plácido traveled to the town of Trinidad in Cuba, where he was arrested in April 1843 and remained in prison for six months.[135] The captain general of Cuba, Leopoldo O'Donnell, planters, and other proslavery groups began interrogating and torturing suspected participants in mid-January 1844.[136] Exaggerating the extent of the conspiracy in order to use it as an excuse to crush the ascendant artisan class of free people of color, the colonial regime imprisoned, executed, and sent into exile thousands of slaves and free people of color.[137] In March 1844, authorities accused Plácido of being the ringleader of the conspiracy. On June 29, 1844, a firing squad in Havana executed ten accused ringleaders of La Escalera, including Plácido. By crushing the community of free people of color, the colonial government engineered a shift from a three-tiered racial system—white, mulatto, Black—to a two-tiered system that pitted whites against Blacks, as Aline Helg has shown.[138]

La Escalera also set in motion an exodus of white creole intellectuals from Cuba. Facing heightened political repression and censorship, Cuban creole nationalists, most of whom were white, left the island in droves in the late 1840s and early 1850s for Veracruz, New Orleans, Philadelphia, Paris, Madrid, and especially New York, where they founded the newspaper *La Verdad* (1848–60), the leading Cuban exile paper, which was successively edited by the writers Jane Cazneau (Cora Montgomery), Betancourt Cisneros, Villaverde, Miguel Teurbe Tolón, and Pedro Santacilia.[139] Exasperated by the unwillingness of Spain to grant greater political autonomy to Cuba but also worried that increased Black rights could turn Cuba into another Haiti, the colony that became a Black republic, the US-based exiles forged an alliance with slaveholders in Cuba and the United States to annex

Cuba to the United States and excluded Blacks and mulattoes from their nationalist project. The negrophobic alliance with US slaveholders began to fall apart with the appearance of dissenting Cuban exile newspapers, including Villaverde's *El Independiente* of New Orleans in 1853, *El Filibustero* (New York, 1853–54), and Francisco Agüero Estrada's *El Mulato* (1854) and *El Pueblo* (1855), all of which appeared *after* Orihuela's novel, demonstrating that Orihuela was ahead of his time in emphasizing racial reform.[140]

Although the colonial government and creole exiles disagreed on the legitimacy of Spanish rule, they both portrayed Blacks and mulattoes as being at the heart of the problem afflicting Cuba, as if to confirm Ángel Rama's argument that the lettered city in Latin America was committed to a violent "misión civilizadora" (civilizing mission).[141] Cuban exiles routinely decried the alleged savagery of Africans and Haitians and the dangers of the "Africanization" of Cuba by the Spanish government, which was apparently only too willing to allow Blacks and mulattoes to outnumber whites. Discussing a plan by the colonial government to introduce African apprentices in 1853, an unsigned editorial in the New York Cuban exile periodical *El Filibustero* paints a lurid picture of race war in which Cuba would perform "the second act in the bloody drama of Haiti."[142] Exiles vilified Haiti in constructing a Cuban nationalism exclusively by and for whites and equated Cubanness with whiteness. Indeed, an unsigned article in *La Verdad* on May 14, 1848, called for a cross-class union of "habitantes blancos de Cuba" (white inhabitants of Cuba) for the purpose of examining their options with regard to Spanish colonial rule.[143] And in an article published in 1849, *La Verdad* revealed the limits of its imagined community with the claim that "the Spanish, the French, the Russian, the North American, etc., are Caucasian and thus of one and the same race."[144]

Orihuela realized that Plácido and La Escalera challenged that equation, which had created an impasse for Cuban exile nationalism. Following his execution, Plácido earned the praise of abolitionists in newspapers across the globe but the opprobrium of Spaniards and white Cuban exiles alike. Ironically, Cuban exile newspapers routinely published Plácido's poetry but avoided discussing his politics. It was to be expected that in Madrid the newspaper *El Laberinto* (August 16, 1844) and the editor of Plácido's *Poesías* (1847) lauded Plácido's poetic abilities, while censuring his supposed participation in the conspiracy. But surprisingly, creole exiles joined the chorus of condemnation in the Veracruz edition of his *Poesías* (1847) and in the New Orleans edition (1847), which denounced Plácido's participation in the "crazy enterprise" of La Escalera.[145] Moreover, Domingo del Monte, a prominent white creole nationalist, wrote a letter to the *Globe* of Paris in August 1844 in which he distanced himself from the "black conspiracy" and vilified Plácido.[146] Orihuela's novel differs from these accounts by portraying the poet as the martyr of the cause of Cuban independence and abolitionism, joining US abolitionist papers such as the *Liberator*, which praised his "genius" and bemoaned his "tragical end," and Douglass's *North Star*, which viewed Plácido as a leader of the Black diaspora in the style of the leaders of Haiti.[147] Although the Cuban exile community had expressed ambivalence toward Plácido, a new opportunity for antiracist thought had emerged by 1851, the year of the martyrdom of Narciso López, the military leader of the proslavery and annexationist wing of Cuban exiles, whom Spanish soldiers had executed for invading the island with a group of Cuban and US soldiers. The death of López led to a reassessment of strategies that would eventually splinter the New York exile community into rival camps that divided on questions of race and slavery.

The full significance of *El Sol de Jesús del Monte* emerges in the context of the relative dearth of antiracist writings by white Cuban creoles and Orihuela's conscious effort to fill that gap with his three publications in 1852.[148] In Orihuela's pamphlet *Dos palabras*, which he published in both New York and Paris to reach Cuban exiles across the Atlantic, he argues that the antislavery movement should be an indispensable part of the Cuban independence movement. First, Orihuela calculates that the United States is leaning more toward abolitionism than slavery: "On the one hand, the abolitionist sect finds most of its proselytes in American cities; on the other hand, in founding this great Confederation, the States placed limitations and restrictions on slavery among themselves with the aim of extinguishing it; and more specifically, the spirit and letter of the laws of the States, in keeping with the fundamental ideals of the Republic, is to destroy such an abominable institution [*tan infame institucion*]."[149] Orihuela argues that U.S. slavery is destined to perish because abolitionism is growing stronger and because the federal government has attempted to limit the spread of slavery. He thereby updates Beaumont's argument in 1835 that the progress of civilization, made concrete by the tendencies of "public opinion," logically leads to "the total extinction of slavery."[150] Turning to Cuban exile politics, Orihuela predicts that Saco will soon reveal his true colors and proclaim himself an abolitionist and an advocate of Cuban independence.[151] In making these strikingly optimistic claims, Orihuela intervenes in contemporary Cuban exile politics by criticizing Saco for his efforts to reform Spanish colonialism from within, and *La Verdad* for its *proslavery* annexationism, although he appears to support annexationism itself. He argues that a "more astute" strategy on the part of the Cuban exile junta would be to tap into what he perceives to be the growing momentum of the US antislavery movement.[152]

Thus it is telling that Orihuela returns to the historical conjuncture of La Escalera in order to create a very different narrative and set of guiding principles for the exile community. By calling on *all* Cuban creoles—white, Black, and mulatto—to die like men, Plácido's comments remind Orihuela's readers of a time before the polarizing aftermath of La Escalera, when the imperatives of revolution brought white creoles and Blacks and mulattoes into a series of alliances. While Cuban exiles like Betancourt Cisneros, Porfirio Valente, the editor of *El Filibustero,* and Villaverde rejected Plácido's politics and endorsed a US-style racist republicanism in the early 1850s, Orihuela's Plácido implicitly endorses an antiracist republicanism.[153]

Dos palabras: Orihuela's Antislavery Annexationism

In *Dos palabras,* a pamphlet published by the newspaper *La Verdad* in New York, Orihuela directly confronts the refusal of both the Del Monte circle and Cuban nationalist exiles to confront racism and challenges Cuban exile annexationists to embrace antislavery.[154] A brief discussion of the pamphlet will help to clarify the political significance of Orihuela's novel. Whereas Saco argues that US imperialism and democracy intersect and therefore opposes annexationism, Orihuela identifies a tension between US democratic ideals and the practices of imperialism and slavery, only to argue—in an enthusiastic burst of painfully naïve optimism—that those ideals have ameliorated US imperialism and will eventually result in the abolition of slavery, "tan infame institución" (such a despicable institution).[155] Orihuela is blind to the depredations of US imperialism in *Dos palabras,* as Kahlil Chaar-Pérez has pointed out: he regards the US incorporation of Texas as "voluntary" and thus endorses "the U.S. intervention against Mexico as a benevolent enterprise."[156] Orihuela also argues—again, quite optimistically—that Saco will soon correct course by endorsing antislavery and Cuban independence: "No se pasará mucho tiempo, sin que le veamos hacer públicamente una protestacion de fé política solemne, que aclarando cuantas dudas haya podido emanar de sus anteriores escritos, nos duscubran en el lleno de su splendor, á nuestro hermano, el abolicionista por escelencia, el valiente y enérgico campeon de la independencia Cubana" (It won't be long before we see him make a public, solemn declaration of faith, which will clarify the ambiguities of his previous writings. We will discover in our brother, in the full of his splendor, the abolitionist *par excellence* and the brave and forceful champion of Cuban Independence).[157]

Even though Orihuela endorses the US annexation of Cuba in this pamphlet, which is a strategic thing to do since *La Verdad,* the chief organ of the annexationists, published it, he qualifies that endorsement in two ways. First, whereas *La Verdad* called for proslavery annexationism, Orihuela calls for antislavery annexationism, which was nearly a contradiction in terms to the editors of *La Verdad* in 1852. Second, the hope that Saco, long an opponent of annexationism, will become a "forceful champion of Cuban independence" could be read as expressing the wish that Saco will endorse the annexation of Cuba to the United States. On the other hand, Orihuela could be subtly endorsing the full independence of Cuba. One should not read too much into the term *abolicionista* here. Whereas in the United States *abolitionism* referred to Black and white radical abolitionists' call for an immediate and unconditional end to slavery without the indemnification of slaveholders, the term in Cuba often denoted a more generic advocacy of antislavery causes. As Chaar-Pérez has argued, Orihuela "endorses a gradualist, pragmatic approach to abolition."[158] Although it is arguably true that Orihuela's "abolitionism was no more radical than that of Del Monte or Betancourt Cisneros," his antiracism certainly was.[159] And unlike these two others, Orihuela would later serve as the secretary of an antislavery society.

Orihuela therefore emerges as an imaginative political visionary in the pages of *Dos palabras.* First, he raises the ire of the editors of *La Verdad* for suggesting that they have not gone far enough in challenging Spanish colonialism—they include long footnotes that attempt to rebut his arguments and challenge his characterization of the newspaper and its funding. Second, he endorses a paradoxical antislavery annexationism. Third, he argues that the United States is retreating from slavery and imperialism in order to reclaim the mantle of democracy.

Conclusion

In part because it joins with *Dos palabras* in breaking with the racism and proslavery consensus among white Cuban exiles of the late 1840s and early 1850s, *El Sol de Jesús del Monte* deserves priority of place alongside Villaverde's *Cecilia Valdés* (1839, 1881–82), Suárez y Romero's *Francisco* (1839), and Gómez de Avellaneda's *Sab* (1841) as one of the most important novels of nineteenth-century Cuba.[160] It is also a novel that belongs on syllabi alongside the writings of white writers on slavery like Beaumont, Herman Melville—particularly his novella *Benito Cereno* (1855)—and Stowe, as well as African American and Cuban writers on slavery like William Wells Brown, Martin R. Delany, Frederick Douglass, Harriet Jacobs, and Juan Francisco Manzano, most of whom join Orihuela by explicitly writing either about slavery in a cross-national, hemispheric context (Brown, Delany, Douglass, and Melville) or about dissenting figures common to plantation societies in the Americas, like the slave rebel and the maroon (Beaumont, Jacobs, and Stowe).[161] Equally important, as Anna Brickhouse has suggested, all of these writers "were not only thematically influenced by emergent hemispheric sensibilities, but also embedded within an international network of literary cultures and lines of influence," a hemispheric text-network (Gilman and Gruesz) that now includes Orihuela as a hinge figure that can bring into focus both the shared concerns and conflicts among these writers.[162]

I have focused here on *El Sol de Jesús del Monte* as a novel of cultural and political critique that primarily targets slavery, racism, and sexism. However, the novel will attract a wide range of readers because it engages in a surprisingly expansive reformism that also implicitly condemns a prison system in Cuba that is itself a "punishment *corporis aflictiva* [causing harm to the body]";[163] calls for education to reach the "lowest classes [*las clases mas inferiores*]," in keeping with Orihuela's own leadership in educational-reform efforts in Cuba;[164] censures both the Catholic religion and Black *brujería* (sorcery) in Cuba for using faith and superstition to exploit the uneducated;[165] and pillories the widespread practice of Spanish immigrants in Cuba to reinforce the social "hierarchy" by obtaining royal titles, crosses, and coats of arms by bribing officials in Spain.[166] *El Sol de Jesús del Monte* is a novel that will fascinate readers with its allegorical love quadrangle interweaving issues of race, gender, and nation and its incisive social critiques and detailed portrayals of the everyday lives of Cubans across a broad array of occupations, positions in the social and racial hierarchy, and political perspectives.

Textual Essay

In translating Orihuela's novel, I have relied on the first and only edition published in the nineteenth century, *El Sol de Jesús del Monte: Novela de costumbres cubanas,* published in Paris by Editores Ignacio Boix y Compañía in 1852. To my knowledge, no other nineteenth-century editions exist of the novel, nor are there any extant manuscripts of the text. I borrowed a copy of the novel through Interlibrary Loan from Cornell University Library and created a photographic pdf of the book, which I used in lieu of the original while translating the text. The pdf is fairly clear: it reveals the wrinkles in the pages and the precise lines and shading of the illustrations, but I can't make out the names of the illustrators penned into the illustrations. On the second title page, there is an inscription in pen ink in the upper right corner that names the owner of the book in writing that is illegible on the top line, followed by "Sto. Domingo" on the second line and the date "Feb 3 1871" on the third.[1] On the page just prior to the author's preface, there is information on the printing of the novel: "PARIS, IMPRENTA DE POUSSIELGUE, MASSON Y Ca., calle de Croix-des-Petits-Champs, 29."

Ignacio Boix y Blay (1807–1862) founded the Librería de Matton y Boix in 1830 and the Imprenta de Ignacio Boix in 1833. By the 1840s his business, which held one of the most modern printing establishments in Madrid, was quite prosperous.[2] Boix himself engaged in a whirlwind of activity in the 1840s: he wrote textbooks in philosophy and philosophy of law in the early to mid-1840s and served as editor of the *Diario de Avisos* (1842–47), director of the Sociedad Literaria-Tipográfica Universal de La Ilustración (1846–47), and publisher of the magazines *El Laberinto,* ed. Antonio Flores (Madrid, November 1843–October 1845), *El Eco de Ambos Mundos* (Paris), ed. José Segundo Florez (Paris, 1852–55), and the *Revista Española de Ambos Mundos,* ed. Francisco de Paula Mellado (Paris, 1853–54).[3] Orihuela was a contributor to *El Eco de Ambos Mundos,* which was a key part of the publishing infrastructure that Boix helped to establish for Hispanophone expatriates from Latin America and Spain in Paris in the 1850s (see the introduction).

Ironically, as Ana Peña Ruiz writes, Boix moved to Paris in 1851 not because his businesses were thriving but rather because "numerous problems with subscriptions and installments, along with the debts that he had incurred, impelled him to try to revive his business in Paris. He worked there as an editor and bookseller and founded the limited partnership Boix and Company, which he directed along with the editor Apollon Lefèbvre. In only three years he established a bookstore (the Librería Española y Americana, 1851), an ambitious editorial partnership (La Madrileña, 1852) and a reading room (the Gran Círculo Literario Hispanoamericano, 1853)."[4] However, Boix declared bankruptcy in December 1853 and then in 1856 moved to Valencia, where he ran another publishing house until his death in 1862.[5]

In 1852, the Paris branch of Boix published both Orihuela's novel, *El Sol de Jesús del Monte,* and *La cabaña del tío Tom: Novela,* his translation of Harriet Beecher Stowe's *Uncle Tom's Cabin.* Boix of Paris published an array of Spanish-language texts in 1852 and 1853, including an almanac, original novels, novels in translation, poetry, plays, and two educational manuals and one religious manual. Among the novels that Boix of Paris published were *Celiar: Leyenda americana* (1852) by the Uruguayan politician and lawyer Alejandro Margariños Cervantes; *La conquista del Perú: Novela histórica original* (The conquest of Peru: An original historical novel, 1852), by the Spanish writer, jurist, and politician Pablo de la Avecilla; and *Los desposados, historia milanesa del siglo XVII* (1852), a translation of Alessandro Manzoni's *I promessi sposi* (*The Betrothed,* 1825–26). Boix of Madrid had an extensive publication list from the 1830s to the mid-1880s, with the vast majority of publications appearing between 1839 and 1846. One of the most famous titles was *Los Españoles pintados por sí mismos* (The Spaniards painted by themselves, 1843–44). The publication list of the 1840s included at least two titles on Cuba: José María de Andueza's *Isla de Cuba, pintoresca, histórica política, literaria, mercantil é industrial* (1841) and Jacinto de Salas y Quiroga's *Viages: Isla de Cuba* (1840).[6]

El Sol de Jesús del Monte is 126 pages long; all pages save for the author's preface are divided into two columns with small print. The author's preface, in the form of a letter that Orihuela wrote in Paris to his friend the novelist, historian, and politician Victor Balaguer, is dated August 2, 1852. On page 49, at the bottom of the left-hand column in print that is approximately half the size of that of the body of the text, one reads, "PRIMERA ENTREGA" (first installment). And on pages, 65, 81, 97, and 113, at the same location, one finds, "SEGUNDA ENTREGA" (second installment). In the "Sección de Anuncios" (Announcement Section) of the newspaper *La España* (Madrid) of April 10, 1853, the following advertisement appeared: "Works published and currently in press by Mister BOIX and COMPANY, editors, in

Paris, Richelieu Street, number 102. [. . .] *The Betrothed*, by Manzoni, in five installments of 64 pages [each]. *El Sol de Jesús del Monte*, by Orihuela, two installments."[7] Although it is unclear precisely how Boix divided up the installments of *El Sol*, if it followed the same practice as with *The Betrothed*, the two installments would have consisted of sixty-three pages each, and chapter 10 begins on page 63.

Publishers in the nineteenth century often delivered novels in installments to make them more affordable to their clientele. In nineteenth-century England, three-volume novels were so expensive that middle-class citizens couldn't afford to buy them, but from the 1830s through the 1860s novels appeared on installment plans to spread out the cost.[8] That is, in England publishers began to issue novels in fragments: typically from twelve to dozens of weekly or monthly pamphlets of 24 to 32 pages or, alternatively, the first four chapters of a novel. The former was the case with part 1 of Charles Dickens's *Martin Chuzzlewit* in 1843; nearly all of William Thackeray's novels also came out in such installments.[9] In Spain, the novel purchased in installments by subscription grew popular beginning in the 1840s.[10] There a courier typically delivered a new installment of a given novel every week to clients' homes. The installment was usually either 8 pages or 16 pages in length; the latter cost one real, a bit less than the cost of a pound and a half of bread and about the same price as three eggs.[11] At that cost, the price of *El Sol de Jesús del Monte* would have been around eight reales, but I have not been able to verify the price of the text and whether prices were the same in both Madrid and Paris. Compared with the 8- or 16-page installments, the two 63-page installments of *El Sol* would have been unusually large. Subscriptions made the publication of novels more lucrative for editorial houses and the purchase of novels possible for the middle classes in Spain: "The novel in installments permitted its purchase in fragments, at affordable prices."[12] One of the best-selling novels of its time, Eugène Sue's *Le Juif errante* (*The Wandering Jew*), which was published in Spain in 1844, was sold in installments.[13] In France, Paul de Kock's *Nouveau tableau de Paris* came out one installment a week in 1842 and 1843, resulting in "52 deliveries of 16 pages apiece."[14] Once readers owned all of the installments, they could have them bound by the publisher.[15] In England, the serialization of fiction in magazines meant that the sale of magazines eclipsed the sale of installment novels by the 1860s.[16]

There is no date of printing at the end of the novel. The only other edition of this novel, edited by Miguel David Hernández Paz, was published under the same title and subtitle in Santa Cruz de Tenerife, in the Canary

Islands, by Ediciones Idea in 2007. Since the 2007 edition, in 376 pages, modernizes Orihuela's Spanish, I have chosen to work with the 1852 edition instead.

Orihuela could not have published his novel in Havana, because colonial censors did not permit the publication of antislavery or proindependence literature in Cuba. Indeed, on September 28, 1852, only two months after Orihuela wrote the preface to his novel, colonial officials executed Eduardo Facciolo, the owner of the press that published the journal *La voz del pueblo cubano: Organo de independencia* (The voice of the Cuban people: An organ of independence).[17] In the 1840s and 1850s, colonial officials sought to protect Cuba's slave-based sugar economy from all threats. Cuban sugar commanded the highest prices ever in the world market in 1851, the year before the publication of Orihuela's novel.[18]

There are fifteen illustrations in the body of the novel, one of which appears on the title page. The illustrations depict characters, scenes, and dreams from the novel and from the intertexts written by other authors, but they do not depict "the most important moments of the narrative," as did the illustrations in most other installment novels.[19] The illustrations are as follows (page numbers refer to the original text from 1852; all are captioned save for item number 8, which the text describes immediately above the unusually small illustration):

1. "Eduardo y Matilde" (title page; chap. 7, p. 49).
2. "La actitud pensativa que Tulita acaba de tomar" (The thoughtful pose that Tulita had just adopted; chap. 1, p. 9).
3. "Judith" (chap. 2, p. 17).
4. "La pobre joven, turbada y fuera de si no sabía como sustraerse de las miradas de Arturo" (Disturbed and beside herself, the poor girl did not know how she could evade Arthur's gaze; chap. 2, p. 21).
5. "El baile" (The dance; chap. 3, p. 33).
6. "Pobres pidiendo limosna á las puertas de un templo" (The poor asking for change in front of the entrance to the church; chap. 10, p. 65).
7. "El cafetal 'La Reunión'" (The coffee plantation "The Reunion"; chap. 12, p. 72).
8. "Su niña bailaba con much gracia y coquetería el zapateo" (Her daughter gracefully and coquettishly danced the zapateo; chap. 13, p. 79).

9. "La baronesa deseando complacer á varios de sus amigos se puso al piano y tocó la obertura de la *Semiramis*" (In order to please her friends, the baroness sat down at the piano and played the overture to the *Semiramis;* chap. 13, p. 80).
10. "Entre un bosque de esqueletos era ya presa de los perros jíbaros" (She was menaced by wild dogs in the middle of a stretch of the forest littered with skeletons; chap. 14, p. 81).
11. "La Viuda" (The Widow; chap. 15, p. 87).
12. "Sueño de Federico" (Federico's Dream; chap. 17, p. 97).
13. "Eduardo y Tulita" (chap. 18, p. 100).
14. "Los padres de la viuda" (The widow's parents; chap. 19, p. 113).
15. "Matilde" (the unnumbered "final chapter," p. 124).

There are also several texts that Orihuela includes in the novel that he did not write. These are as follows:

1. Although the character Federico tries to pass off the novella that he reads to Eduardo as his own, it was actually Eugène Scribe who wrote "El palco misterioso" (The Mysterious Theater Box), which he published as *Judith, ou la loge d'opéra, nouvelle contemporaine*, in *Tonadillas; ou, Historiettes en action*, vol. 2 (Paris: Dumont, 1838). Orihuela inserts this novella into chapter 2 (pp. 12–32).
2. "Últimas horas del poeta Cubano Gabriel de la Concepción Valdés (Plácido)" appears in chapter 8 (pp. 55–57).[20]
3. "Relacion de la visita ecclesiastica del ilustrisimo Señor Morel," a short document from the Spanish Inquisition recounting the exorcism of a demon dated September 4, 1682 (chap. 17, pp. 95–96).
4. Balaguer's "Veladas de Navidad," "La Rama del Olmo," and "Un sudario con sus trenzas" from *Junto al hogar: Miseláneas literarias*, vol. 1 (Barcelona: Imprenta A. Brusi, 1852) (chap. 19, pp. 106–15).

Orihuela's translation of *Uncle Tom's Cabin* was published as *La cabaña del tío Tom: Novela escrita en inglés por M. Harriett Beecher Stowe* (Paris: Libreria Española y Americana de D. Ign. Boix, 1852; 322 pages) by the same publishing house that brought *El Sol de Jesús del Monte* to light. Orihuela's preface to the translation is dated October 12, 1852, and the publisher lists the publication date on the title page as December 1852. This edition is available as a free e-book in Google Books. Orihuela wrote in the preface to *La cabaña* that he was the first to translate it into Spanish, and this seems likely given that a competing translation by Wenceslao Ayguals de Izco, *La choza de Tom, ó sea Vida de los negros en el sur de los Estados Unidos, novela escrita en inglés por Enriqueta Beecher Stowe* (Madrid: Imprenta de Ayguals de Izco Hermanos, 1852), included a preface by the translator dated December 7, 1852, nearly two months after Orihuela's preface to his translation.[21] An e-book of Ayguals de Izco's translation is available. Another publisher in Europe came out with a different edition of the same translation by Orihuela one year later: *La cabaña del tío Tom: Novela escrita en inglés por M. Harriet Beecher Stowe* (Barcelona: D. Juan Oliveres, Impresor de S. M., 1853; 322 pages). This 1853 edition is also available as a free e-book in Google Books. In addition to the Paris (1852) and Barcelona (1853) editions of Orihuela's translation of *Uncle Tom's Cabin,* editions of this translation appeared in 1853 in Bogotá, Colombia, and Buenos Aires, Argentina. The Bogotá edition is available at the British Library, which lists no publisher, and the Biblioteca Nacional de Chile holds a copy of the Buenos Aires edition.

Note on the Translation

Orihuela's contemporary the Cuban writer Ramón Piña (1819–1861) wrote several translations, plays, and two novels, including *Historia de un bribón dichoso* (The tale of a happy rascal, 1860). He also wrote "Literatura: Las traducciones," an article on translation theory for *La Revista de la Habana* in 1856, in which he approvingly paraphrased the view of Jean-François Marmontel (1723–1799), the French critic, novelist, playwright, and poet, that "the translator must faithfully reproduce the thinking [of the original], rendering it with clarity, correctness, accuracy, precision, and decency."[1]

In the years between Orihuela's era and our own, translation theory has repeatedly returned to the question of the possibility of a faithful translation, but often with more skepticism. In 1923, in "The Task of the Translator," Walter Benjamin rejected the ultimate goal of fidelity in translation:

> One can demonstrate that no translation would be possible if in its ultimate essence it strove for likeness to the original. For in its afterlife [. . .] the original undergoes a change. Even words with fixed meaning can undergo a maturing process [*Nachreife*]. What sounded fresh may sound hackneyed later; what was once current may someday sound archaic. [. . .] Translation is so far removed from being the sterile equation of two dead languages that of all literary forms it is the one charged with the special mission of watching over the maturing process [*Nachreife*] of the original language and the birth pangs [*Wehen*] of its own.[2]

In his commentary on Benjamin's well-known text, Paul De Man has created the conditions for clarifying the meaning of this passage, with his claim that Harry Zohn mistranslated the German terms *Wehen* and *Nachreife*. *Wehen,* De Man argues, signifies any kind of suffering, not just childbirth. And De Man argues that "maturing process" is a woefully inadequate translation of *Nachreife,* which instead connotes "melancholy, the feeling of slight exhaustion, of life to which you are not entitled [. . .]. It is by no means a maturing process, it is a looking back on a process of maturity that is finished."[3] Although De Man does not circle back to a close reading of Benjamin's passage, his differing translations of these two terms suggests that Benjamin does not argue that translation constitutes the confident end point of a maturing process but rather that it entails a painful distancing from the original even as it seeks equivalent modes of meaning making. Benjamin will later illustrate this distance with the metaphor that translation is an "echo" and subsequent "reverberation" of the original in a new tongue.[4] Translation, then, paradoxically results in a transformation of the original as much as its preservation. When Benjamin calls the translation the "afterlife" of the original, he implies that it has a life—a history—of its own.

Benjamin further explains translation's necessary distance from the original with his distinction between the German *Brot* and the French *pain,* which points to the distinction "between what is meant and the way of meaning it."[5] Although at one moment in his unfolding argument Benjamin writes that "the two words signify the very same thing," this contradicts his claim at an earlier point in the essay that it is essential for the translator to focus on the so-called "inessential content" of literary form, style, and tone. In the *Brot*-versus-*pain* example, the "way of meaning"—the paradoxically essential "inessential content"—of these two words communicates distinct cultural and historical meanings.[6] No one would confuse the specific taste, feel, look, and purpose of German pumpernickel, a French baguette, a Tuscan *pane sciocco* (saltless bread), or a Mexican *bolillo,* even though all would recognize that they share certain generic characteristics of bread. The point here is that the "way of meaning" matters because it is culturally and historically specific. More recently, Gregory Rabassa, well known for his translation of *Cien años de soledad,* by Gabriel García Márquez, has concurred with Benjamin's skeptical take on the question of fidelity; he writes that the translator "can never enter into the author's being and even if he could the differences in languages would preclude any exact reproduction."[7]

In taking on the task of translating *El Sol de Jesús del Monte,* I knew that I faced the dual challenge of translating both Cuban Spanish into English and the language of the nineteenth century into that of the present. Since Orihuela translated Stowe's *Uncle Tom's Cabin,* I could have systematically used Stowe's choices of vocabulary—and Orihuela's translations of them—to make the translation sound like a period piece. However, I realized that such a choice was equally artificial as modernizing his prose and would have reduced Orihuela to just *one* of his stated literary models, leaving by the wayside Víctor Balaguer and Gustave de Beaumont. Instead, in mixing the vocabulary of the nineteenth century with a more readable, modernized set of word choices, I have sought a sort of middle path, an analogue to the mid-Atlantic accent by which US or Canadian actors attempt to approximate British speech. Paul Ricoeur has characterized this middle path in translation as aspiring to "equivalence without identity."[8]

Equivalence without identity is the rule rather than the exception of translation, particularly this translation. Setting a hostile tone for the visit that she and her daughter pay to Eduardo in his law office after he has ignored Matilde in favor of Tulita, Belencita says, "Al que no quiere coles, darle coles."[9] A literal rendering would be, "To the person who doesn't want cabbage, offer cabbage," but this expression would puzzle English speakers. I chose to translate the phrase as "We are unwelcome guests," which is a different expression, but one with a roughly equivalent meaning in English. Similarly, when Federico asks whether Tulita's mother had approved of their relationship, Eduardo responds, "A las mil maravillas, chico," which literally means "Like a thousand wonders," or more simply, "wonderfully."[10] In my translation, I used the roughly equivalent phrase "Things couldn't be better," since there exists no identical idiom in English.

Modernizing Orihuela's prose was by no means easy. While some translations of his sentences sounded fine at first, upon rereading them I could often find an equivalent that sounded better in today's English. For instance, Julio's rival, the white ex-soldier, says, "Un blanco no debía nunca ponerse bajo las órdenes de un mulato," which I at first translated as "A white man should never place himself under the orders of a mulatto."[11] This translation survived several revisions, but I finally decided that it sounded better in Spanish than in English. What in Spanish sounded like a straightforward and clear sentence became a somewhat clunky circumlocution in English. I therefore settled on "A white man should never subordinate himself to a mulatto." There is no such thing as a perfect translation, and this was no exception. One could argue that Orihuela didn't choose the term *subordinate*, so why should the translator? But it was the best option I could find.

According to Rabassa, Jorge Luis Borges "told his translator not to write what he said but what he wanted to say," and I have endeavored to follow that advice without trying to clarify the writer's meaning when he has left it obscure.[12] When Orihuela remarks that his friend Balaguer, "que de poeta ha pasado á positivista," I was faced with the dilemma of either translating this literally as "positivist" or choosing a term that would clarify Orihuela's meaning.[13] I opted to translate *positivista* as "politician" because I assumed that some of my readers would not understand the historical reference to positivism, which I have supplied in a footnote.

In my translation I have tried to capture the spirit of Orihuela's straightforward and lucid prose style. In the preface, a letter to Balaguer, the first thing one notes about Orihuela's writing in the Spanish original is the way several potential sentences run into one another—as if to leave the narrator breathless—via the device of the colon, which Orihuela so often employs along with *y* (and) to substitute for the period both in the preface and in the body of the novel. I have decided to break these long sentences down into shorter ones for the purpose of readability. This feature of punctuation in Orihuela accentuates the enthusiasm of his impassioned cosmopolitan and antiracist appeals, as well as the breathlessness of the text's dramatic conclusion, but is not necessary to them and is too cumbersome in English.

I have opted to retain certain terms in Spanish either because they capture particular cultural practices unique to Cuba or Latin America in the 1840s—such as the *boca-abajo* method of torturing slaves—or because they give the reader a small taste of the original as terms that were common in their circulation with important cultural or historical significance, like *criollo* (creole).[14] I have included the original *chico* (literally, boy; but figuratively, buddy or guy) in the conversations between Eduardo and Federico as part of my efforts to capture their easy informality and familiarity with each other. I have also retained the tendency of slaves to address young white people as *niño* (child, son) or *niña* (child, daughter) and white adults as *su mercé* (for *su merced,* or your grace): Dolores, the slave of Tulita, tends to call Eduardo "niño Eduardo."

In "El palco misterioso," a translated story within the novel, Orihuela chooses to include some French terms, like *foyer,* but he Hispanicizes many terms: instead of *mademoiselle, madame,* and *monsieur* he uses *señorita, señora,* and *señor;* instead of referring to the operas *Robert* and *Huguenots,* he renders them as *Roberto* and *Hugonotes*. I therefore at first chose to keep the forms of address *señorita, señora,* and *señor* to emphasize to readers that the text within the text is indeed a Spanish translation of a French original that retains key Spanish terms. It is ostensibly Federico's translation, which he passes off as his own story in the action of the novel. However, I then decided, with the help of comments from one of the press's readers of the manuscript of the translation, to retain the French terms in order to avoid a cacophony of terms from differing cultural contexts.

Federico's comically frequent recourse to folksy idiomatic expressions in Spanish challenged me as a translator: I often had to choose between a more literal translation that would preserve the precise way of meaning of the original and a more idiomatic translation for which there is an equivalent expression in English. When Federico advises his friend Eduardo to stop pursuing Matilde since Eduardo is more interested in Tulita, Federico says, "Lo que no vas a comer, déjalo bien cocer."[15] The translation that I chose loses the end rhyme but preserves the literal meaning and the folksy tone: "Let what you're not going to eat cook well." At another point in the novel, one of Federico's idiomatic expressions had me absolutely stumped: "Pues ya pueden venir, que tendran que rascarse pelo arriba y tres mas nueve."[16] Here Federico combines two sayings that were unfamiliar to me: *rascarse pelo arriba* and *tres más nueve*. I knew that a literal translation of the first phrase wouldn't help: "to scratch one's hair upright" sounds ridiculous. Fortunately, I found the answer in the online *Diccionario de la lengua española* of the Real Academia Española, not under *rascarse* but rather under *pelo*: the phrase means to "take money out of one's pocket." The second phrase took a little more detective work. I found it, finally, in *La Charca* (*The Pond*, 1894) by the Puerto Rican writer Manuel Zeno Gandía (1855–1930). *Tres más nueve* refers to something that is inevitable. It comes from the longer expression *dos por tres, seis, y tres más, nueve* (two times three equals six, plus three equals nine).[17]

Another term that I couldn't figure out in the context of its use was *cuarentena*, which we now all know means "quarantine." Eduardo uses this term in the context of praising one of Federico's many paramours, a particularly spellbinding *Sevillana* (a woman from Seville): "Eso merece cuarentena" (That deserves a *cuarentena*).[18] When I found out that *cuarentena* literally means "ensemble of 40 units," according to the online dictionary of the Real Academia Española, I was still in the dark. Then I learned of the Latin American custom of a postpartum quarantine on sex for forty days. So my translation eventually read as follows, translating what Orihuela meant to say rather than what he actually said: "She is definitely wife material." But perhaps all that was just too elaborate. Perhaps Eduardo just means that any man would like to be quarantined with such a woman.

As these various snapshots of my translation process suggest, a careful reading of a text that is not in one's mother tongue requires careful translation, and both require an investigation of cultural and linguistic norms and practices as well as historical issues. As Gayatri Spivak has argued, "Translation is the most intimate act of reading."[19] Intimacy requires respect and even delicacy, but it can also result in mistakes and an overstepping of boundaries. I hope my translation achieves the former and that readers will forgive me for the latter.

Note on the Translation

The source text for this translation is the original edition of the novel, published in 1852 in Paris and held by Cornell University Library in Ithaca, New York. I have retained Orihuela's original spellings of Spanish-language phrases and terms, but at times I have added accents that were missing in the original.

The Sun of Jesús del Monte
A Novel of Cuban Customs

Señor D. Victor Balaguer[*]

Dear friend: your arrival in Paris, the capital of the civilized world, was such a lovely surprise. Here we happily embraced each other once again, remembering the good times we had in your beautiful city, Barcelona. I doubt that we will be able to see each other again under similar circumstances, especially now, since I have no intention of returning to Spain and since you have gone from poet to politician [*positivista*] and are bound to your country by the sweetest ties of a new family. To the contrary, in keeping with my firm resolution to study men and the world, and continuing the nomadic life as a traveler that I began in 1846, it is certain that every day we will move further apart: as a true cosmopolite, with the world my country, every friend my brother, and all of humanity my family, I have resolved to relish the most complete independence in all its plenitude.[†] For that reason, I don't expect to settle in another country unless I happen to die there.[‡] That's why once I discovered that you were preparing to return so soon to your country, I felt truly sorry, because I firmly believe that we won't see each other again. I will renounce the manifold pleasures of Paris, leaving it to satisfy my restless spirit with the new sensations of traveling to the Orient, losing myself in its immense ruins, with so many graves of lost cities and past generations. Since it would not be strange if you never heard from me again, in writing the novel *El Sol de Jesús del Monte*, some of whose episodes are closely related to my own life, I would like to offer you a token of my appreciation by dedicating it to you.

Goodbye, your good friend, Orihuela.
Paris, August 2, 1852[§]

---

[*] "D." stands for *Don*. As Jane Landers has observed, the honorific *Don* was typically reserved for white men. Landers, *Atlantic Creoles*, 140. For biographical information on Víctor Balaguer (1824–1901), the Catalan novelist, politician, and historian, see the introduction.

[†] This sounds strikingly similar to the masthead for William Lloyd Garrison's *Liberator*, which read beginning in its very first edition on January 1, 1831, "Our country is the world—our countrymen are mankind."

[‡] I am grateful to one of the readers of this manuscript for this translation.

[§] For the sake of comparison, Orihuela dates the preface to his translation of *La cabaña del tío Tom*, the "Carta del traductor a Ms. Harriet Beecher Stowe, después de haber leido su novela," 12 October 1852. Stowe's *Uncle Tom's Cabin*, one of Orihuela's inspirations for writing *El Sol* but in no way a blueprint for it, appeared in weekly installments in the *National Era*, of Washington, DC, from June 1851 to April 1852. It was published in book form in 1852. Cavendish, "Publication," n.p.

1

Mother and Daughter

Only a short distance from Havana, on Jesús del Monte Road near the corner of Teja, there was in 1844 a single-story house with a long portico flanked by a wooden railing, whose jerry-rigged and uneven structure suggested that if the architect had been more sensible, he would not have been satisfied with his work. Entering the gallery of the portico, one found on the right side a barred window that extended from the top of the wall to within a foot of the ground, so that through the curtain the living room received a considerable amount of light, and on the left there was a large entryway. Beyond the humbly appointed living room there was a small alcove and another bedroom that led into a large, square patio, which allowed access to rooms for the domestic servants.

Three people lived in this house: a woman of about fifty, bitter, inconsiderate, and very vulgar in her manners; her young daughter, aged thirty, who was the flip side of the coin, since her remarkable beauty, her elegance and good manners, her courteous actions, and her friendliness and sweetness all combined in such a way that it was not possible to meet her without loving her; and a black slave of about forty, dedicated to the chores of the house.* On the island of Cuba, where the events we are about to narrate took place, there exists the custom of changing most baptismal names for special nicknames that typically correspond to those given names: you will not find a Sebastián who is not also called Chano, nor a José de Jesús who is not also named Chuchu, nor a Dolores who is not also known as Lolita, nor a Soledad who is not also called Solita. This is so obligatory for proper etiquette in that society that if one commits the indiscretion of calling Dolores, Dolores and Micaela, Micaela she will of course take it as a terrible insult, and the poor purist will expose himself as rude and insolent. It is only acceptable to call black slaves by their given names because even the class of free people of color follow the custom of the whites.† For that reason, in the

---

* Although in the critical apparatus for this volume I have chosen to capitalize *Black*, this translation follows Orihuela's lowercasing of the term.
† My translation of *gente de color* as "people of color" is in keeping with scholarly norms, even if some might find it dangerously close to the antiquated and often derogatory

family that we are describing the señora, called María de Jesús, was known despite her fifty Christmases as Chuchita by her friends and niña Chuchita by the slaves and even free people of color; the young Gertrudis as Tulita; and the slave Dolores as Dolores.

"Are you going to stop sewing so early, Tulita?" the mother asked her child, observing that she had drawn back the window curtain and sat down to eagerly watch the passersby.

"Mamá, it's already past five o'clock. You are probably tired as well."

The thoughtful pose Tulita had just adopted, resting her face on her left hand and betraying uncertainty in her expression [*fisonomía*], made such an impact on the soul of her mother that acting either out of a spontaneous impulse of her heart or out of her natural hypocrisy, she hid the anger she had felt when her daughter set down her needle so early and without replying stood up and planted a kiss on her daughter's forehead.

"Which dress do you plan to wear to María Ignacia Menocal's dance?"

"Whichever one you want, mamá."

"The pink one perfectly becomes you."

"Certainly, but now in Horcón everyone has seen me wear that dress."

"What else do you expect? Are we by chance so rich that you can wear a new dress to every dance? And not even the daughters of the captain, who are so wealthy, act like you. Our only living comes from our sewing needles, whereas they live off the fines their father charges, along with his briefs, licenses, and other various sources of income in his profession."

"On that night, if you like, I will wear the white dress with pink trim."

"As you wish, just so there is no need to head to the stores in search of some new trifle."

"No, mamá: everything is set."

"I warn you that we will not stay there past midnight. I don't want a repeat of what happened last Sunday, when we returned home at two in the morning and, worse still, on the way home we got caught in a downpour."

"colored people." Prior to the Ladder Conspiracy (1843–44) Cuba had a tripartite racial scheme of Black people, mulattoes, and whites, so to translate *gente de color* as "Black" would be historically inaccurate. Aline Helg has argued that La Escalera resulted in a shift from a tripartite racial hierarchy in colonial Cuba—whites, mulattoes, and Blacks—to a binary system of whites and Blacks. "Race and Black Mobilization," 54–55. All the terms used to designate the descendants of Africans in the Americas are potential minefields because racial discourses have appropriated them for the purposes of denigration; I hope that this translation serves as a bridge and makes a modest contribution to the intellectual activist and interdisciplinary formation of Black studies.

"Agreed, mamá. Would you like to call Dolores and ask her to bring us coffee?"

"Aren't we waiting for Don Valentin?"

"What a fool," murmured Tulita under her breath so that her mother could not hear her. "I would like to drink my coffee now," she continued out loud, "and I have not yet smoked my cigarette. Since you have already finished yours, you can easily wait for him."

"You always deny the slightest courtesy to Don Valentin. You know how eager he is to drink coffee with us, and you haven't joined him even once."

"I do it without thinking about it—and what does it matter? Hasn't he besieged us with his cigarettes, beer, and liquor when he has accompanied us to dances?"

"Well and good, but appearances [*la política*] require us to be friendly to our guests. And above all, it is an obvious snub to not wait for him before drinking your coffee."

"Please, mamá, allow me to tell you this: you shouldn't give such importance to a nobody like him who doesn't deserve it. Dolores! Dolores!"

A moment later the humble and despondent figure of a black woman presented herself in the living room.

"What does su mercé wish?"*

"Serve me coffee."

"Just a moment, niña Tulita." And the black woman quickly returned to the kitchen.

"Where have you placed the novel *The Count of Monte-Cristo?* I would like to continue reading while we wait for Don Valentín," said Chuchita, searching for her reading glasses in one of the pockets of her dress.

"On top of the side table," replied Tulita without looking away from the stretch of sidewalk that she could see from her window.

"The noise from the street is intolerable," said the mother, walking to the interior bedroom in search of the novel. "I'm going to enjoy the breezes on the patio and entertain myself for a while with the brilliance of Alejandro Dumas.† Would you like to come?"

---

* *Su mercé* is short for *su merced,* literally "your grace," a formal form of address used in speaking to someone who ranks above the speaker in the social hierarchy.

† Chuchita is referring to Alexandre Dumas (1802–1870), author of *The Three Musketeers* (1844) and *The Count of Monte Cristo* (1844–45). Ironically, given Chuchita's later disparaging remarks about people of color, Dumas's grandmother had been a slave in Haiti.

"No, mamá. I have not read the literary supplement included in today's *Prensa* and would like to see what it tells us."

"It will always contain some foolishness by Riesgo.[*] In all my years I've never seen a more inane chronicler of fashion—he is a writer who merits a plow rather than a pen. Tell me when Don Valentin comes."

Already wearing her eyeglasses, Chuchita walked into the bedroom, and since she didn't notice Dolores, who just at that moment was entering the living room by the same door, she bumped into the tray of coffee that Dolores was holding. The slave took care not to spill one drop on the tray, but before she could avoid it, some of the coffee spilled onto Chuchita's dress.

"Jesus, what an idiot!" Chuchita exclaimed angrily.

"What's wrong?" asked Tulita, who had not noticed anything since she had not taken her eyes off the street.

"That clumsy bitch spilled coffee on me." And Chuchita slapped the black woman.

"I'm sorry, señora, I was taking care to not spill any . . ."[†]

"Shut up, you shameless woman, unless you want me to send you to get a *boca-abajo*.[‡] I can't stand that woman because she is so insolent. Damn you [*maldita sea tu estampa*]!"

"Mamá don't get worked up—it was an accident."

"An accident! That little bitch doesn't have eyes in her head." Saying this, Chuchita pinched Dolores on the arm and then went to her bedroom to change her dress.

---

[*] Chuchita is probably referring to Pascual Riesgo, the author of *Conchita la habanera: Novela de costumbres* (1846), among other novels and plays. Francisco Calcagno remarks of Riesgo, "Despite his less than desirable qualities as a writer, he made money with his pen." *Diccionario biográfico cubano*, 543. Riesgo, who contributed to *El Faro Industrial*, became editor of *La Prensa* in 1843. See note on page 9; and Llaverias y Martínez, *Contribución*, 285, 289.

[†] All ellipsis points in Orihuela's novel were in the original.

[‡] Ninety to one hundred lashings with a leather whip on a naked body. As a result of such punishments slaves tend to fall ill for several days because ordinarily the wounds take a while to scab as a result of the inflammation that sets in. Nevertheless, to cure the wounds they [overseers] apply a combination of tobacco, urine and sugar cane liquor.—*Author*. Alternatively, Pichardo defines the *bocabajo* as follows: "With the mouth or with the whole front of the body facing the soil. [. . .] A rigorous punishment of lashings applied to slaves in that position, and therefore one says to give a *bocabajo*; and in Cuba *dar una tabla*. Another equivalent is *dar un fondo*." Pichardo, *Diccionario provincial*, 96.

"Now you see, niña," said the poor black woman to Tulita, "the señora always mistreats me even though it's not my fault." Two large tears rolled down her cheeks.

"You know she has a bad temper; never talk back to her. And . . . come on, give me some coffee. That's enough."

Once Tulita finished drinking her coffee, Dolores returned to her kitchen chores. Perhaps the slave meditated on the sad state of her condition in life, but she felt consoled by the observations of her young mistress.

As for Tulita, she made the most of her mother's absence by going out to pace underneath the portico, which is known by its colloquial term in Cuba as a *colgadizo,* where she could better observe the length of the avenue. Because it traced a great curve, it dominated the view even at a great distance from its approach to Jesús del Monte.

Without a doubt, a single, pressing concern preoccupied Tulita's soul, because one could see her take up the newspaper *La Prensa* without even glancing at it.* Instead, she focused all of her attention on the *volantas* and *quitrines* that passed in front of her house.† Perhaps she was waiting impatiently for the arrival of someone. Just as her anxiety reached the boiling point, at nightfall, a carriage [*quitrín*] stopped at her door, and a man of about thirty years stepped out, greeting her courteously even as he noted a certain expression of annoyance on her face that she quickly tried to conceal. That young man was Don Valentin.

---

* The Cuban journalist Luis Caso y Sola and the Andalucian José García de Arboleya, both of whom were on the editorial board of the *Faro Industrial de la Habana,* founded *La Prensa,* which began publication on 1 July 1841. It first appeared on a biweekly basis, but on 23 September 1843 it became a triweekly publication. In December 1842, Caso y Sola and García de Arboleya transferred ownership to D. Isidoro Araujo de Lira, one of the founders of the important Havana newspaper *Diario de la Marina,* which first began publication on 1 April 1844. Pascual Riesgo and Francisco C. y Villar joined Araujo de Lira as editors of *La Prensa* on 3 August 1842. On 1 January 1843, Araujo de Lira transferred the directorship of *La Prensa* to Riesgo. *La Prensa* became a daily on 30 April 1843. *La Prensa* published its last issue on 29 May 1870. Llaverias y Martínez, *Contribución,* 91, 271, 276, 280–81, 284, 289–90, 320.

† *Volanta* is a variation of *volante,* which Pichardo defines as "one of the types of luxury carriages used on the island that is similar to the *quitrin,* with the difference that its upper part is hard like that of the *calesa,* which it used to be called a long time ago." *Diccionario provincial,* 613. According to Luis Martínez-Fernández, "The main difference between *volantas* and *quitrines* was that the *quitrines* had a top that could be folded whereas the *volantas'* top was fixed. *Quitrines* were more highly esteemed than *volantas.*" Martínez-Fernández, *Fighting Slavery in the Caribbean,* 167n25.

 2

Eduardo and Federico

Two hours before Don Valentin reached Tulita's house, which we have already seen him enter, a young man around twenty-four years old, of normal stature, with his jet-black hair combed and carefully curled Roman style and dressed with polished elegance, walked down O'Reilly Street toward the Gate of Monserrate. Again and again he touched the rim of his jipi-japa hat with his right hand as if to greet passersby, and he said hello more than once during his walk from the Plaza de Armas.* For that reason the reader will undoubtedly understand that this individual was a very well connected person in this country.

Indeed, although he was not a criollo, or a son of Cuba, Eduardo had studied jurisprudence in the College of San Carlos of Havana.† Even as a newly minted lawyer, he began to enjoy prestige in the courts. If one adds that he was one of the editors of the *Faro Industrial*, an important newspaper, one of the esteemed members of the Lyceum, and the author of lovely poetic compositions, which abounded in scores of the island's periodicals, it is not strange that he had so many friends.‡

---

* Here I have translated "pronunció mas de un adios en su camino desde la plaza de Armas" as "he said hello more than once during his walk from the Plaza de Armas" because a more literal translation of *adios* would have been confusing. Here the requirements of the translation as a semiautonomous text, which Walter Benjamin has termed the "afterlife" of the original, necessarily take precedent. "Task of the Translator," 254, 256. The jipijapa was an imported straw hat from Jipijapa, Ecuador. The Plaza de Armas, which dates from the 1520s, was "the oldest and most important square in Old Havana." "Plaza de Armas."

† *Criollo* is Spanish for "creole," referring to a person born in the Americas, regardless of ethnicity. Anderson, *Imagined Communities,* 47. On the Colegio-Seminario de San Carlos, see the afterword.

‡ José M. Cárdenas, who founded *El Faro Industrial de la Habana* in 1841, using the pseudonym Jeremías Docaransa, penned "excellent chronicles on colonial life in which he identified with the oppressed and the disenfranchised." However, the proslavery US citizen John S. Thrasher, who had resided in Cuba since 1839, took over the newspaper in 1849. Marrero, *Dos siglos,* 22. The Lyceum is the Liceo de la Habana, which actually was founded on 15 September 1844, after some of the historical events that transpire in this novel, at least some of them shortly after Plácido's martyrdom on

To judge by his brisk pace, Eduardo must have been in a great hurry to go somewhere; he often caught the attention of the carriage drivers he encountered on the way, making them feel disappointed that they had already rented their carriages. As he glanced two or three times at his watch, his face registered impatience, and he neither looked at the beauties who draped themselves over the windowsills of homes nor slowed down to contemplate the elegance or the attire of those walking shoulder to shoulder with him.

Eduardo's brown [*morena*] and expressive face stood out even more against the matte white suit he wore; a frock coat of very fine linen [*tela real*], English twill pants, a black tie, and shiny [*charolado*] slip-on shoes of leather calfskin. He also wore multicolored silk socks. He walked erect and with a certain aristocratic air that revealed his distinguished education. The last toll of the bell at five o'clock sounded at the Church of Santa Catalina just as our young man entered Escauriza Café.

Outside the walls of the city and near the Gate of Monserrate, where San Rafael Street begins, there are two buildings, the Tacón Theater and the Escauriza Café, both of which look out upon the beautiful Plaza Isabel Segunda.* This café is one of the most elegant and well established of its kind outside the city walls, known for its prime location, the spaciousness of its interior, its attentive waiters, its rich sorbets of pineapple, zapote, soursop [*guanábana*], and other delicious fruits of the island, which it offers to its customers in crystal parfait glasses. And thanks to the sweet breezes that refresh those sitting on its magnificent balconies, the café hosts a select and numerous clientele from four in the afternoon until ten thirty at night.

Eduardo scanned those who were seated on the sidewalk. He warmly shook hands with various acquaintances that he recognized as he entered the spacious lower salon. There he examined all the tables where patrons enjoyed refreshments, and then, still frustrated in his search, he walked up

---

27 June 1844. Among the members of the Liceo de la Habana were Domingo del Monte, Francisco Frías, José de la Luz y Caballero, Felipe Poey, and Cirilo Villaverde. "Liceo de la Habana."

* The Café Escauriza "served flavored soda water and spirits to the crème de la crème of the city's elite" and even served as a dance hall at night. Conway, *Nineteenth-Century Spanish America,* 49. The Teatro Tacón was founded in 1838 on the corner of Paseo del Prado and San Rafael and in front of the Gate of Monserrate. It had the capacity to seat two thousand spectators. "Teatro Tacón."

to the second floor [*primer piso*],* where he passed through the circle of spectators who thronged the two billiards tables over to the balcony that looks out upon the Plaza Isabel Segunda.

"Federico is not very punctual," he said to himself, visibly annoyed while waiting on the balcony.

Eduardo had been reclining in his chair for nearly a quarter of an hour, observing the lovely spectacle on the main stretch of the avenue in front of the café—two lines of open carriages [*quitrines*] in which Cuban beauties were showing off their dresses—when he felt two pats on his back.

"I thought you had forgotten me, Federico."

"A quarter of an hour is not so late. How do you like my *flux?*"†

"It suits you."

"Chico, Uribe is the best tailor in Havana.‡ Just think, this morning he measured me for the frock coat and pants that I am wearing now, and even though he was very busy today, they were ready by four o'clock. As you see, I put them on at his house. It is true that he made me pay double, but that mulatto has golden hands. Frankly, he has not always had the golden touch, and I doubted that he would keep his word because more than once he has let me down . . ."

"Where are you going with this story?" asked Eduardo, standing up. "Are we going to Jesús del Monte or not?"

"I was looking for you."

"It's already past five and Tulita will be waiting impatiently for me on her porch to make sure that I won't miss the dance of María Ignacia Menocal."§

"That's fine; we'll take the omnibus to the corner of Teja."

---

* In Latin America the *primer piso*, which translates as "first floor," is actually the second floor, the ground floor being called the *planta baja*.

† On the island of Cuba *flux* signifies a pair of pants and frock coat, or *chopa*, of the same fabric.—*Author*

‡ *Chico* literally means "boy," but it is also a Cubanism used to signify *carnal*, "bro," "dude," "buddy," or "fellow." The mulatto Francisco Uribe was "one of the preferred tailors of well-to-do whites" from 1833 to 1844. Luis, *Literary Bondage*, 112. As William Luis has written, "In 1844 Uribe was accused of participating in the Ladder Conspiracy and was sentenced to die. The prosperous Uribe had amassed considerable wealth, which included twelve slaves, two houses and a small fortune of more than 7,398 pesos" (112).

§ In the original, Eduardo refers to "Julita" rather than Tulita, which I take to be a typo.

"Let's go downstairs to wait for it, and in the meantime we'll drink a glass of horchata."*

"Agreed."

The two friends walked downstairs after straightening their ties at one of the beautiful mirrors that adorn the high-ceilinged dining hall of the Escauriza Café.

Federico, whom we have just met, was a young man about twenty-two years old, blonde, thin, and taller than Eduardo. He was employed in an office of a businessman; his salary of six onzas allowed him to comfortably enjoy the few amusements that a city so eminently commercial as Havana offers.† His figure was svelte, his manners elegant and of good taste, and he had a uniquely sympathetic manner that would enliven any gathering. Having traveled through Europe for several years, his ample experiences always allowed him to gracefully maneuver social situations, and his naturally witty character made him the life of the party in social circles.

"By the way," Federico said, "I'm carrying a novel in my pocket, and if we take a volante taxi instead of the omnibus, you will have a good time reaching Jesús del Monte."

"As you wish, but did you write it?"

"Chico, I'm the hero in it, or rather it is a historical event that took place in Paris during my stay in that city. Since it is related to my life, I wrote it as part of my TRAVEL ALBUM."

"Well, all right. Driver! Taxi!" cried Eduardo, standing with his friend at the threshold of one of the doors of the café.

"Where is the niño going?"

"To Jesús del Monte!"

"The gentleman will pay me two pesos for the trip."‡

---

* Horchata is a drink variously made of crushed almonds, tiger nuts, or rice mixed with water and sugar. In Cuba, "typically horchata includes sesame seeds as one of the ingredients," according to Raúl Fernández. Personal communication, 3 September 2017.
† An *onza*, which literally means "ounce," is a denomination of money that derives from measurements of gold.
‡ King Ferdinand and Queen Isabella introduced the peso into Spain in 1497, but it was not until the 1780s that it came into use in Spanish America and was the rough equivalent of the US silver dollar in value and use: "The silver peso and silver real were the most widely used monetary instruments for all wholesale and a fair number of retail transactions throughout Spanish America and southern Brazil." Marichal, "Money, Taxes and Finance," 429. The peso was divided into eight reales. *Encyclopaedia Britannica Online*, s.v. "Peso," https://www.britannica.com/topic/coin/Coins-of-Latin-America.

"Six reales," said Federico.

"It is very far from the café, and the gentleman must consider..."

"Away with quibbling," replied Federico. "Get in, Eduardo."

"We'll lower the top of the carriage and enjoy the fresh air."

"But that will distract us, and for the purpose of reading it's better to leave the top up."

"All right, then we will lower it once we reach the corner of Teja."

The carriage Eduardo and Federico had just hired began to move. Federico took a notebook out of his frock coat pocket and began to read the following:

The Mysterious Theater Box

I

The Opera Theater in Paris is very beautiful.* I will not recount the miraculous scenes of the aerial grace of Taglioni, of Esler's magical enchantment, of the creative talent of Nourrit, a true Talma of lyrical tragedy, nor the inimitable harmonies of Maestro Meyerbeer, the toast of Germany, nor the seductively graceful songs of Auber, today the first among French composers.† I leave aside the illusion of the decorations, the costumes, and

---

* The prolific French dramatist Eugène Scribe (1791–1861) actually wrote this story, which he published as *Judith, ou la loge d'opéra* in 1838. According to WorldCat, this book appeared in a Spanish edition as *Judiht ó el Palco de la Opera* in 1843. Note that the title in this Spanish translation is *Judiht*, with the *h* before the *t*, and not *Judith*. When either translating the French text into Spanish or using Lesen y Moreno's Spanish translation of *Judiht*, Orihuela used *señora* and *señorita* rather than *madame* and *mademoiselle* yet was inconsistent in his use of the male characters' titles, at times using the abbreviation for *Monsieur*, as in "M. Arturo" or "M. Baraton," while at other times using Spanish, as in "el señor Rosambeau." Orihuela, *Sol*, 14–15. I have used French titles and Anglicized all first names in this story for the sake of uniformity.

† Marie Taglioni (1804–1884), an Italian dancer, was the first to dance *en pointe* for the entire time she was on stage in the ballet *La Sylphide* at the Paris Opéra in 1832. *Encyclopaedia Britannica Online*, s.v. "Marie Taglioni," https://www.britannica.com/biography/Marie-Taglioni. Louis Nourrit (1780–1831) was a French opera singer; François-Joseph Talma (1763–1826) was a famous French actor and theatrical company manager; Giacomo Meyerbeer, born Jacob Liebmann Beer (1791–1864), was a German opera composer known for the opera *Robert le diable* (1831); Daniel-François-Esprit Auber (1782–1871) was a French composer known for *Fra Diavolo* (1830).

the dance. Finally, I won't take the time to describe the building. I will only talk about the Opera Theater's hall and its audience.

There one observes the most curious, lovely, and brilliant spectacle, one full of playfulness, beauty, and splendor. Take a long look at a single spectator there: if the man in question is of good character and hasn't lost any money in the stock markets nor heard a bad speech in the assembly; if his sweetheart has not betrayed him or his wife has not mortified him with her jealousy; if he has eaten well and moves in the society of well-adjusted and witty people who are true friends; as this man is seated near the orchestra, how many colorful, fascinating, and panoramic scenes will reach his retina through his binoculars or eyeglasses! How many comic and even dramatic scenes! Above all, he should direct his view toward the side of the stage, to the dress circle and to the boxes of the front section.

And let it be understood that I don't want him to leave his assigned seat and move to the mezzanine, because how many mishaps might occur if one were to take a friend by the arm and walk through the foyer of the opera house? One could not take a step without brushing up against an ambitious or ridiculous being; without stumbling upon a deputy, a man of the State today, a minister yesterday, a man of great reputation this week, a man whose pride has never been equaled; and there, in front of a great fireplace, a man with yellow gloves who is thinking of tomorrow's chores and his bets placed at the Bois de Boulogne; a journalist and orator who in his conversation brags about his serialized novel [*folletín*] that will appear the following day; a "lion" who lives and achieves success at the expense of an actress and pays her in praise; another dandy who gets ruined by the same woman yet believes in the duty of joining in the praise of the woman, as if to justify to his friends her savings account, a burial ground for his money; finally he who visits this place must test his eyes and ears with all this sound, this movement, this liveliness, and this heady mix of self-love and ambitions, luxury and mediocrity, farce and pretensions.* The personalities found here would provide sufficient material for innumerable volumes. Despite that wealth of material, what I am going to tell here is a story in miniature.

---

* Here, given that the journalist is bragging about his own writing, I take *folletín* to mean not the literary supplement as a whole, the first meaning of *folletín* in the *Diccionario de la lengua española* of the Real Academia Española, but rather a work published in the supplement, the second meaning ("Obra publicada en el folletín"), in this case most probably a serialized novel.

One night toward the end of the year 1831, if I'm not mistaken, Mademoiselle Taglioni was dancing in a theater teeming with people. The curious had arrayed themselves on the stairs and temporary seats that together formed a kind of barricade. With much difficulty we had to cross through that Thermoplyae; I made my way through the outbursts of "paix-là!" and "silence!" from the spectators disturbed by my arrival.* One must keep in mind that when Taglioni dances, not only do the spectators watch her but they are silent. They also listen, because it appears that their admiration requires more than their eyes. Waiting near some friends whom I was supposed to meet, I found myself very embarrassed because they were so packed together that they couldn't make room for me. I then noticed that someone got up and offered me his seat, but at that moment I just had to refuse the offer because it seemed unfair to deprive him of the pleasure of comfortably watching the show.

"Accept sir," he said. "You are not taking my seat; I am going anyway." And since I did see that my gallant neighbor was about to leave, I agreed, thanking him. I noticed that while walking away he scanned the theater, stopped for a moment, and, leaning against the box of General Claparède, looked as if he were searching for someone. Later, falling into the deepest meditation, he remained at that spot. He was right that I had not deprived him of seeing the show, because having turned his back to the stage, neither seeing nor hearing anything, he appeared to have definitely forgotten even where he was. I then examined him: it was impossible to see a physiognomy that was more expressive, more noble, or more distinguished.† He was dressed

---

* The Persians under Xerxes defeated the Spartan army of Leonidas at the pass of Thermopylae in Locris, near an inlet of the Aegean Sea, in 480 BC. Lohnes and Sommerville, "Battle of Thermopylae."

† Johann Casper Lavater (1741–1800), of Zurich, was the inventor of the science of physiognomy. His four-volume *Physiognomische Fragmente* (Leipzig, 1775–78) was translated into English as *Essays on Physiognomy* (London, 1789). Lavater argued that physiognomy could, according to Martin Staum, "discern from the shape of forehead and size of facial features the 'characters in a language' revealing intellect, degree of sensuality, or moral fortitude. Eighteenth-century physiognomy ordered living characteristics by readable external signs—the form, proportion, relative size and distribution of the parts, usually of the face." Staum, "Physiognomy and Phrenology," 446. Lavater defined the science of physiognomy as "the skill of recognizing from the exterior of a person his inner being." Lyon, "'Science of Sciences,'" 257. Lavater's theories of physiognomy were popular in the fields of both science and literature; Balzac in particular spoke of his indebtedness to Lavater and deployed the methods of physiognomy in his *Comédie humaine* (1842). Rivers, *Face Value,* 105–6. Del Monte held up Balzac as

without pretensions but elegantly, and one noted grace and good taste in his manners and in his slightest movements. He seemed to be from twenty-five to twenty-eight years old; his large black eyes stayed glued to one of the secondary boxes in front, contemplating it with an expression that was sad and vaguely desperate.

I turned my head in that direction, and to my disappointment I only noticed that the box was empty. Perhaps he is waiting for someone, I said to myself; she has broken her word ... or she could be ill ... or her jealous husband has prevented her from coming ... He loves her! He waits for her! Poor man! ... And like him, I waited. I felt sorry for him and would have made any sacrifice to see the closed door of that box swing open.

The performance was winding down to its finale, and during one or two scenes in which the leading dancers weren't dancing and conversation took place at a normal volume, I heard someone mention the opera *Robert the Devil*, which was then being rehearsed and would come to the stage in a few days. The author of the libretto, a good friend of mine, had given me some tickets to take some friends to the dress rehearsal, so I invited those who were sitting next to me that night. Then the curtain fell, and I noticed that the stranger was still standing immobile in the same spot. I walked over to him to repeat my gratitude and to offer my help. To my great surprise, he called me Monsieur Meyerbeer.†

"I can't claim that honor, my friend."

"Forgive me, sir, because I was going to ask you the favor of allowing me to attend the dress rehearsal of *Robert*."

"I am delighted," I said, "to be able to help you even though I am neither the composer of the music nor the author of the libretto."

He warmly shook my hand, and we agreed to see each other the following day. He was on time for the appointment. While waiting for the rehearsal to begin, we strolled past the stage. My companion was very grave and eloquent in his amiable conversation, which was increasingly pleasant. Nevertheless, I noted that he struggled to sustain the conversation and that other thoughts preoccupied him. The singers and dancers, all beautiful

---

a model to his circle of writers, and both Anselmo Suárez y Romero and Félix Tanco viewed Balzac as a major influence on their writing. Martínez Carmenate, *Domingo del Monte*, 341, 345.

* The librettists for Meyerbeer's *Robert le diable* were Eugène Scribe and Germain Dalavigne (1790–1868). The play premiered in 1831. Pendle, "Eugène Scribe," 551.

† Orihuela renders the titles of all characters of this text within the text in Spanish, such that *Monsieur* is *Señor*.

women, were arriving one after the other. I saw him grow pale many times, and at one point his reaction was so strong that he had to lean against the side of the stage. I then guessed that he might be head over heels in love with one of our theater goddesses, a supposition that was quite possible given his age and physiognomy. But no, sir, I was completely wrong: he spoke to no one, approached no one, and ultimately no one knew him.

The rehearsal began. I searched for him among those in the orchestra stalls and did not find him. Although the building was very poorly lit, I thought I could perceive him in the same front box that he had contemplated the day before with such deep emotion. Wanting to convince myself, at the end of the rehearsal, after the laudable trio of the fifth act, I walked up to the secondary boxes. Meyerbeer, who needed to talk to me, accompanied me. We reached the box, whose door was open, and we saw a stranger holding his head in his hands, as if submerged in the deepest meditation. Upon our entry, he turned brusquely and stood up; his pallid cheeks were covered in tears. Meyerbeer jumped for joy and without saying a word shook his hand and squeezed it affectionately as if to thank him. The unknown man, trying to compose himself emotionally, babbled a few words, praising the opera in a vague and general way, which of course convinced us that he had not watched the piece and that in the two hours that the rehearsal lasted he had been thinking about something very removed from the music. Full of anger, Meyerbeer said to me,

"The wretch hasn't heard even one note!"

We all descended the stairs of the theater, and walking across the beautiful and large patio that leads to Grange-Batelière Street, the stranger greeted Monsieur Sausseret.

"Do you know that young man who just greeted you?"

"Monsieur Arthur, Helder Street, number 7, is all that I know; he has reserved a secondary box near the front all winter."

"We just saw him there."

"He undoubtedly attends the morning shows, because since he reserved the box he has not opened its door, and it always remains empty."

I had promised tickets to the grand opening of *Robert* to certain ladies, a commitment that I could not break. I arrived at the box office too late to buy tickets and consequently found myself in a difficult position. It was useless to go to Meyerbeer, because even he didn't have enough tickets, and to speak with Scribe, the author of the libretto, would also be a waste of time. Where could I go? I remembered the stranger and presented myself at his house. His apartment was very simple and modest, above all for an individual who could reserve a box at the opera.

"My friend," I said, "I come to ask you to do me a great service."

"Tell me."

"Do you plan to attend the grand opening of *Robert?*"

Something in my question bothered him, and he answered hesitatingly, "I would like to, but it is impossible."

"Have you given the box away to someone?"

"No sir."

"Would you like to give it to me? Doing so would help me meet a commitment."

Regardless of the embarrassing position in which my request placed Monsieur Arthur, he did not dare refuse me that favor . . . And as if struggling with himself, he answered,

"I agree, but under the condition that you not take ladies to that box."

"Indeed, I openly admit that I have invited two ladies."

"Do you love one of those two ladies?"

"Absolutely," I replied with energy.

"Then take my box. For my part, I leave Paris today."

I made a gesture that indicated my interest and curiosity, and he must have guessed my thoughts, because taking my hand in his he said,

"Understand, sir, that my box raises certain memories that are both very dear and very painful to me . . . I can't confide in anyone . . . What would I gain by complaining? I am a wretch, without hope . . . and above all it was all my fault!"

On the opening night *Robert* proved to be a triumph for my friend Meyerbeer; its success reverberated across Europe. Time passed along with other political and literary events and more triumphs. As for me, I didn't come across Monsieur Arthur; I didn't think about him anymore and finally forgot him.

I returned to the Opera one night and sat to the right of the orchestra. This time they weren't presenting *Robert,* but rather *The Huguenots.*[*] Five years had passed.

"You have arrived quite late," said one of my friends, a professor of jurisprudence with a season's subscription to the Opera. He exhibited as much

---

[*] *Les Huguenots* was an opera by Meyerbeer that premiered in Paris in 1836. Eugène Scribe and the poet and playwright Émile Deschamps (1791–1871) wrote the libretto.

intelligence and eloquence in the evening as he did talent and erudition during the day at his law practice.

"And you, sir, are missing it," added a man of small stature, lightly touching me on the back. It was Monsieur Baraton, a distinguished notary.

"You here!" I exclaimed. "And what has become of your business?"

"I sold it three months ago. I am now rich, a widower, and nearly sixty years old. I was married for twenty years and a notary for thirty . . . Now I can have a good time."

"He has only been a subscriber to his orchestra stall for eight days," said the professor of law.

"Yes sir, yes, it is true. I like to laugh, I am passionate about comedies, and I have subscribed to an orchestra stall at the Opera."

"Why not at the French Theater?"

"It is not as entertaining as this. Here one sees and hears the most singular things in the world. These men know everything and have met everyone, and they have told me the story behind every single theater box."

Monsieur Baraton watched the professor of law, who smiled with a modest and reserved air that, although it seemed discrete, signified: "I could say other things if I wished."

Out of habit, I turned to look at the row of secondary boxes that a few years earlier had so excited my curiosity. And to my great surprise, there in front was the one that had been empty! Satisfied that I could contribute a story to the conversation, I told it succinctly. They listened to me with great interest. My neighbors lost themselves in conjecture. The professor tried to remember the old days, and the notary smiled maliciously.

"Now then, sirs," I said, "you who know everything and know everyone, who among you can give us an explanation for this enigma? Who can tell us the full history of this mysterious theater box?"

Everyone fell silent . . . Even the professor, who passing his hand over his forehead as if to remember the story, probably would have invented one, but the notary didn't let him.

"Who will tell this story?" he asked with an air of triumph. "I will since I know all the details."

"You, Monsieur Baraton?"

"Yes, I do."

"Tell us! Tell us!" And we all gathered around the narrator.

"All right then," said the notary, with an air of importance and taking a pinch of snuff. "Who among you has met him?" At that very moment, the director of the orchestra lifted the bow of his violin to begin the symphony.

And Monsieur Baraton, who didn't want to miss a note of the introduction, stopped suddenly, saying that he would continue at the next intermission.

II

"Sirs," said the notary as soon as the first act of *The Huguenots* had concluded, "they need to dress Queen Margaret and all the maids of honor and they need to put together the set of the castle and gardens of Chenonceaux. For that reason, the intermission will be so long that I think I will have time to tell you the story that you wish to hear." And after taking another pinch of snuff, as if to help him gather his ideas, Monsieur Baraton began in the following way.

"Who among you, sirs, has met the young lady Judith?"

We looked at one another, and even the longtime subscribers could not answer.

"Judith was a dancer who about seven or eight years ago was admitted as an extra."

"Wait," said the professor of law, continuing with a somewhat pedantic tone, "a blonde who played one of the pages of the viceroy in *Muette?*"*

"She was brunette," replied the notary, "and as far as her employment, I can't say anything to the contrary because I have no knowledge that would prove it, and therefore I cede before your immense erudition."

The professor of law made a conciliatory bow.

"What no one can deny," added the notary, "is that Judith was an enchanting young woman."

"Another of the authentic facts is that Madame Bonnivet, her aunt, was the doorkeeper in a house on Richelieu Street owned by an elderly celibate. This was the house in which she had earlier worked as housekeeper, and according to others as cook, even though that didn't suit Madam Bonnivet. Despite that, as Madame Bonnivet pulled the cord of the door latch, and as she served in the different rooms of the house, her niece won over many hearts because it was impossible to pass by the bedroom of the doorkeeper without admiring the beauty of Judith even though she was then only twelve years old. Her eyes were already the most beautiful in the world, her teeth like pearls, her body graceful and svelte, and with her dress made

---

* The speaker refers to *La muette de Portici* (The mute girl of Portici), an opera by Daniel-François-Esprit Auber (1782–1871) with a libretto by Germain Delavigne (1790–1868) and revised by Eugène Scribe that premiered in Paris in 1828.

of Indian or other light fabric she had the most distinguished air that one could imagine. She also had a sincere physiognomy and the most beautiful mix of innocence and flirtatiousness. She was one of those women capable of undermining the judgment of even serious people.

"Madame Bonnivet heard so many words of praise for the extreme beauty of her niece that she finally decided to make some sacrifices to give her an education: she put her in a free school for girls, where they taught her to read and write. According to the aunt, this was a stellar education whose practical benefits she soon discovered, because as the doorkeeper she could barely decipher what was written on the envelopes that arrived and she was frequently confused as to which floors the neighbors lived on and to whom she should deliver the magazines that arrived at the house.

"Judith took charge of these matters to the satisfaction of everyone. The aunt was persuaded that with a face and an education that were so distinguished, her niece would soon make a fortune; she had only to wait for the first opportunity. Indeed, that opportunity soon arrived. Monsieur Rosambeau, the dance instructor, who lived on the sixth floor, proposed to give some lessons to Judith, and a few days later Madame Bonnivet announced to all of the doorkeepers she knew that her niece would be an extra in the chorus of the Opera, news that flew from door to door with the speed of lightning the whole length of Richelieu Street.

"Judith was innocence personified, even though she was already over 14 years old. Despite the fact that she had been educated in an honorable house in which all of the renters were married, her aunt carefully watched over her niece, accompanying her to the theater in the morning and at night planting herself in the foyer knitting stockings while her niece took her dance lessons.

"Don't ask me exactly what happened during that period while they lived on Richelieu Street. That I would not be able to tell you. What is certain, according to what I have understood, is that a friend of Madame Bonnivet took charge as doorkeeper on an interim basis, while Judith sought to make her fortune or catch a big break.

"You, sirs, know as well as I do that one does not join the Opera unless one needs a position or has to catch a break, as they say colloquially. Suddenly the scene changes, the woman gets rich, becomes honorable, and she or her daughter gets married to a broker."

"Or to a notary," added the professor.

"It's true," said Monsieur Baraton, with a grimace, "that has happened. Nevertheless, you cannot deny that neither Madame Bonnivet nor her niece nurtured similar illusions of grandeur. Persistence is indispensable for everything."

"And Judith?" I asked, noticing that the intermission was about to end.

"Judith! Let us proceed. Despite Madame Bonnivet's vigilance, nothing could prevent her niece from conversing with the other dancers. In the morning in the foyer of the dance room and above all at night when everyone was on stage... A terrible boundary that the aunt could not cross and where her vigilant observation had to come to an end a fortiori. Judith heard strange things. One of the nymphs or sylphs told her softly:

"'My friend, do you see how that guy to the right of the orchestra is looking at me?'

"'Who?'

"'That handsome guy with the cashmere vest.'

"'And?'

"'He is one of my lovers.'

"'One of your lovers!' exclaimed Judith.

"'Yes, lovers. An admirer. Don't you know what a lover means?'

"'Why no, of course.'

"'What? What? Girls, that is brilliant! Judith doesn't know what a lover is, she doesn't have boyfriends.'

"'I know; her aunt doesn't want her to.'

"'Really? I like that. Well if I were to have an aunt like that...'

"'Now don't be malicious. Judith's aunt is a wise woman; she knows what she is doing and is more sophisticated than you suppose. In order to preserve her niece from the danger of passions, she is searching for a protector!'

"'A protector? She is too dumb for such a thing; she'll never find one.'

"This conversation took place during the chorus of *La vestale*.* Judith had not missed a syllable. She did not dare ask anyone for an explanation of what she had heard, and although she could not understand everything, she felt humiliated by the image that they had formed of her; she wanted to get revenge by provoking the envy of her friends and humiliating them at the same time. That is why when Madame Bonnivet walked into the house that very night with a serious and solemn demeanor and said that she had discovered a protector for her, one who was noble and distinguished, Judith's first reaction was happiness. And although she hadn't expected it,

---

* *La vestale* (The Vestal Virgin) is an 1807 opera by the Italian composer and conductor Gaspare Spontini (1774–1851).

the aunt approved of the girl's reaction. And she continued in a sincere and satisfied manner:

"'Yes, my dear niece, a respectable man by any definition: a person who could secure your future and my fate; which is only right given all the sleepless nights and attention that I have devoted to giving you an education.' Then the aunt shed some tears, and Judith, surprised by the tenderness of Madame Bonnivet, approached her to ask her who this protector was and why she had a need for such good protection.

"'You will know in good time, my girl; you will . . . What is certain is that your friends will be sick with envy.'

"That is the only thing that Judith desired: it was extraordinary that the same night rumors and gossip about the news circulated in the foyer of the dance room.

"'Is it possible?'

"'My word of honor.'

"'That is incredible!'

"'That a little snot-nosed girl like her would have such luck! . . .'

"'An actress! Actually, just a chorus girl! . . . Maybe since I am the lead singer . . .'

"'Oh, that is incomprehensible!'

"'The truth is that it is an extraordinary thing . . . But Judith is so beautiful!'

"'And so honorable!'

"'She deserves it.'

"In truth neither the engagement of a princess nor the wedding of a queen would have produced more conjecture or conversation; and nevertheless, there was no room for doubt, because that same night the aunt had appeared in the wings of the theater in a superb Terneaux shawl.*

"But who was this unknown protector? It must have been some aged landlord or some important, respectable, wealthy gentleman with grey hair. Everyone questioned Judith so that she would reveal all, but this was in

---

* The correct spelling is *ternaux*. Guillame Louis Ternaux (1763–1833), whose first name is often Anglicized to William, was a prominent wool manufacturer in Paris who established a reputation for the excellence of his products. In 1818–19 he imported Tibetan goats to France and used their cashmere to create his shawls, which were called ternauxs. Hunt, "Cashmere," 631; Wikipedia, s.v. "William-Louis Ternaux," https://en.wikipedia.org/wiki/William-Louis_Ternaux.

vain, for Judith was scrupulously discrete under every test, and the reason for that discretion was that Judith knew absolutely nothing.

"It had already been three or four days since the aunt and her niece had traded the humble dwelling of the doorkeeper for a lovely room on Provence Street. A bedroom in perfect taste, a salon to receive visitors, elegantly adorned with a handsome carpet—a salon in which the aunt didn't dare enter because, as she put it, the kitchen persuaded her to stay in it and it was what she liked best. Despite this situation, Judith had not received a visit from the protector; in those days no one resembling such a character had appeared, and that seemed somewhat strange. Although Judith was not educated, she was not stupid: her candor and her innocence were more a result of ignorance than from a lack of intelligence. Realizing what she could understand and guessing a part of what she did not comprehend, she began to grow unsettled and to lose her natural tranquility. She would have given anything to have a friend who could give her advice . . . but since she was entirely alone, what protection could she hope to find against that protector whom she did not know but whom she already disliked? The truth is that sorting through all the ideas she had formed on the whole affair, she grew attached to the notion that he was ugly and old. Her friends had repeated many times that the person in question had to be a deformed old man suffering from gout. On the fifth day her aunt rushed in, opened the door of the salon, and with an unusual expression on her face said, 'He's here!'

"Judith wanted to get up as a sign of respect, but her legs weakened, and nearly fainting, she fell back onto the sofa. Once composed, she dared to open her eyes and saw right in front of her a man of handsome physiognomy and twenty-four years, with a noble and distinguished air. He looked at her with such sweet and expressive eyes that she instantly felt saved. It seemed to her that a man who looked at her like that would stop at nothing to defend her and that by his side she would have nothing to fear.

"'Mademoiselle,' began the stranger with a grave and respectful voice, but since he noticed that the aunt was still present he made a signal for her to leave them alone. She obeyed instantly, heading to the kitchen in order to give instructions for the meal.

"'Mademoiselle, this house belongs to you; I hope that you will be comfortable and happy in it. Excuse me for taking such a long time in paying my respects to you . . . Business has pulled me away from the pleasure of your company. I do not ask for anything from you other than one title: that of friend! And far from wanting to impose on you, I am here to satisfy your least desire!'

"Judith did not answer, but her heart beat so strongly that it lifted the light percale of her bodice.

"'As far as that aunt of yours,' and he pronounced this phrase with disdain, 'she will henceforth follow your orders, because you are the head of the house and everyone must obey you . . . beginning with me.'

"He then approached Judith, took her hand, and raised it to his lips, but noticing that she was still trembling, he said,

"'Could it possibly be my presence that causes you this fear? Because you must feel certain that I will not come back to visit you unless you need me to. Call me when you like! Goodbye, Judith, goodbye, my girl.'

"And he departed, leaving the poor young woman in turmoil and with an incomprehensible feeling of surprise that she had not before experienced."

III

"For the rest of the day the expressive face and the large black eyes of the stranger loomed in Judith's mind. She had not been able to look at him, yet not one detail about his dress or manners had escaped her. She felt that she could still hear the sweet timbre of his voice, and the words that he spoke were recorded in the depths of her soul. Although she ordinarily slept captivated by the most peaceful dreams, poor Judith couldn't sleep a wink. It was the first insomnia in her life. The next morning her face was pale and her eyes were somewhat shrunken and dull. Her aunt smiled!

"All the aunt had to do was name the young stranger, and beautiful Judith immediately blushed. Satisfied, the aunt smiled once again! But he had not returned. He did not stop by, and Judith did not dare ask him to come back! Indeed, what did she have to ask of him? Her room was most elegant; the best waiters served her table; servants and a carriage awaited her orders. Nothing was missing . . . except for him! On the other hand, her theater friends, seeing that she was so beautiful, so luminous and dressed so elegantly, never stopped questioning her! And their questions taught Judith more than she would have wished to know. Moreover, she invariably remained silent when her aunt and friends asked her what had passed between *her* and *him* without being able to explain to herself why. After everything that she had heard in the theater, she determined that there was something extraordinary in the conduct of the stranger . . . something that humiliated her and that she would have to keep to herself. She would have preferred death to speaking a single word about it.

"On the eighth day, the day of a big performance, Judith spotted the stranger, who watched her with the greatest interest, in the amphitheater, in the king's box, no less. She couldn't suppress a shout of joy and surprise that made her falter in her balance and timing at the moment she launched into a pirouette.

"'Who is that?' asked Natalie, one of her friends, touching the edge of a wreath of flowers.

"'There he is . . . it's him . . .'

"'Is it possible? The count Arthur de V! One of the most gallant young men in the court of Charles X! . . . You certainly can't complain . . . But what's wrong? Are you anxious about a man that you see every day?'

"Judith did not hear anything—she was so happy! Arthur had just greeted her with a bow of the head, to the great scandal of the golden box in which he was seated. There was even more after the dance: at the moment when she was about to go up to her dressing room, she came across Arthur backstage, and he said in front of the gentleman of the hall, who then presided over the comings and goings of the Opera theater: 'Mademoiselle, would you permit me to accompany you?'

"'That would be a great honor to me,' mumbled Judith, trembling from head to toe, without realizing that her response had provoked the laughter of her fellow dancers.

"'All right then, when you are done, I will be waiting for you outside the theater.'

"I assure you that Judith did not take a long time to undress and change her dress; in the rush she tore her muslin sleeves and her silk pants, and Madame Bonnivet, who then worked as a chambermaid [*camarera*] (a job reserved for all the mothers and aunts of the theater), could barely keep up with her as she went down the stairs carrying the cashmere wrap her niece had forgotten.

"Arthur had remained on stage, speaking with a group of young people and with Lubert, the director, to whom he sang the praises of Mademoiselle Judith. When she arrived, he took her by the arm in front of everyone, and together they descended the stairway used by the actors. An elegant carriage waited for them at the door, and it is not possible to express the surprise and the excitement of poor Judith in finding herself seated by his side in the tight space of the carriage, which made conversation with him more intimate and sweet. Worried that Judith would get cold, he rolled up the windows. He then unfolded the cashmere wrap that she held in her hand and covered her white shoulders, her beautiful figure, and her heart, which beat at that moment with the most pleasant of all emotions. Ah! Judith was lovely and seductive, enveloped as she was in true happiness. Nevertheless, that happiness did not last long. It is such a short distance from Grange-Bateliére Street to Provence Street, and his magnificent black and white horses trotted so quickly! The carriage came to a stop; Arthur got out first, and offering his hand to his companion, he walked up the stairs to her house. When they reached the second floor, he rang the bell, paid his respects to her, and disappeared.

"Judith had another bad night. The conduct of the count seemed very strange. He easily could have paid her a visit by simply walking into the living room and sitting down. It is true that such a visit would have been somewhat awkward, but it would have been preferable to his abrupt disappearance. Lying in bed that night, all she could do was close her eyes. She got up, walked around her room, and once daylight broke, she decided to open one of her widows to breathe the pure air of the morning. But much to her surprise, the carriage of the count had stayed below all night long. The horses stamped the ground impatiently, and the driver slept in the coach box.

"Excuse me, sirs," said the notary, interrupting himself, "the next act is beginning and I don't want to miss anything; I have reserved a seat for that reason. Until the next intermission."

IV

"Very early the next morning, Judith opened one of the windows. The count's carriage was still waiting by the door. It was obvious that he sent it every night. What were his intentions? That is what she could not guess. As far as asking him for an explanation for this mystery, she would never have dared. Moreover, she saw him only on the nights of the opera, in the second box in front, which he had reserved for the whole theatrical season. He neither went backstage nor proposed to accompany her. How could she see him?

"Fortunately for her, she had just suffered an injustice . . . a violation of her rights. They had demoted her to a backup role . . . Her fellow dancers believed her to be a helpless case, and she was full of despair. She wrote to the count to tell him that she had to ask him for a favor, which was why she requested that he come to see her at her house. This letter was not easy to write—Judith took a whole day to write it, starting over again many times and finally writing more than twenty drafts. She kept copies of the drafts in her pockets, ridiculous though it may seem, and probably one of them fell out of her pocket and some curious person picked it up. That night on stage she heard some actors and audience members whispering about a misspelled letter they had discovered and passed from hand to hand. You had to hear their exclamations, their satirical commentaries, their witty remarks, and their jokes about this letter without a signature, whose author was unknown but which they hoped to include in the next day's newspaper as a model for the epistolary style of the Sévigné of dance.*

"The cause of Judith's fear and torment was not so much the conversations she had heard ridiculing her so thoroughly but rather the idea that the count would similarly belittle the ill-fated letter, which she would have given anything to take back. She was more dead than alive when Arthur entered her house the next day.

"'I am here, dear Judith; I have just received your letter, and I have come to see how I might be useful' (and he still held the disastrous letter in his hands). 'What do you want?'

"'I don't know how to tell you what I want, Monsieur count, but that note, which you have read . . . if you have been able to understand it . . .'

"'Perfectly, my girl,' answered the count with a slight smile.

"'Ah!' exclaimed Judith with desperation in her voice, 'that note proves to you that I am a poor woman, without talent and without education, who is ashamed of her ignorance, and that I would like to be able to . . . But, how can I achieve that, if you don't come to my aid with your suggestions and help!'

"'What do you mean?'

"'If you give me a teacher, you will see that I have no shortage of enthusiasm, persistence, and diligence; you will see that I will make the most of my lessons . . . if necessary, I will work day and night.'

"'Even at night?'

"'To profit from my lessons, it is important that I spend my time studying, especially since I can't sleep.'

"'What do you mean? You don't sleep? Why not?'

"'Why not?' said Judith, blushing, 'because there is an idea that ceaselessly torments me.'

"'Which idea?'

---

* The reference is to Marie de Rabutin-Chantal, marquise de Sévigné (1626–1696), called the "Queen of Letter Writers."

"'The idea that you have formed of me . . . I must have fallen in your esteem; you must see me as unworthy of yourself . . . And with reason,' she continued spiritedly, 'because I see myself that way as well . . . I know myself . . . And if that is possible, I will no longer feel embarrassed in front of your eyes and my own.'

"The count observed her with great surprise and said:

"'I will obey your wishes, my dear girl, I will do what you request.'

"The next day, Judith had a professor of orthography, history, and geography. She was deserving of his lessons and studied fervently: her intelligence and her natural talent did not require anything more than culture, and she progressed at an incredible rate.

"From Arthur's perspective, Judith loved to study. But even though Judith showed a praiseworthy perseverance in studying, she actually used that pleasant pastime to console herself and forget her personal troubles. Now she no longer went to the dance hall, nor to practices, preferring to pay the fines for her absences and instead work at home. The other dancers would say, 'Judith has her loves and her grand passions, she still isn't showing up—she will lose her position . . . It's her fault.'

"And Judith redoubled her efforts, telling herself, 'It doesn't matter, I will be worthy of him. My idea that he will very soon notice that I am capable of understanding him and that he will appreciate my progress. Vain hopes!' When the count was at her side, Judith, frozen and tremulous, lost her equanimity and forgot everything she had learned. When he asked about her studies, she faltered, and the count said to himself, 'The poor girl has a great deal of will, but little aptitude.' What she had gained from her new studies was to understand how ridiculous she could seem to her protector. This idea made her act even more timid and constricted even further the broad range of her intellectual abilities. The truth is that the count came to see her very rarely. From time to time he spent a half hour by her side; but when the bells of midnight sounded, he got up and left! Then, without reproaching him at all, Judith only asked him in a voice full of tenderness and uneasiness,

"'When will I see you again?'

"'Tomorrow I will tell you at my box.'

"And this is how it happened: Every day without fail he went to his box, in the second row in front, and when he was able to spend a few moments the following day with Judith, he pulled at the lapel of his jacket, and that meant, I will go to Provence Street. And then Judith waited for him all day. She didn't receive anyone else; she even kept her own aunt at a distance so as to be able to enjoy the sweet satisfaction of knowing that she was going to see him.

"Despite the reserve of the count, she had made a discovery: that he was devoured by some profound sorrow. What could be the source of such suffering? She did not dare ask him. Nevertheless, she would have counted herself very happy to share his pain. That happiness she neither promised to herself nor dared to possess. She was but a silent participant in the sorrows of Arthur: she suffered with the sufferings of her friend, she was sad about his sadness. The count told her many times:

"'Judith, what is wrong? What are your sorrows?'

"If she had dared, she would have replied: 'Yours!'

"One day a terrible idea seized her: and she said it to herself with a burst of emotion: He loves another! But then, why would he take a lover at the Opera? On a whim . . . to be fashionable . . . as a thing that he has bought without seeing it or knowing it . . . But then why?

Judith looked in one of the mirrors that decorated her living room: she was so young, so fresh, so beautiful! She stayed for some time submerged in the waters of her reflections. The door of the living room opened abruptly. Arthur appeared, with an unsettled look that she had never seen before.

"'Get dressed mademoiselle,' he said energetically, 'because I want to take you to the Tuileries.'

"'Really?'

"'Yes, it's beautiful outside; there is a magnificent sun. All Paris will be there.'

"'And you wish to accompany me?' exclaimed Judith, overflowing with happiness; until then the count had never gone out with her and had never taken her arm in public.

"'Certainly, there I will accompany you in front of everyone, and in the grand promenade!' The count added, in a quite agitated state, 'Please, Madame Bonnivet,' directing himself to the aunt, who at that very moment entered the living room. 'Could you dress your niece? Choose the newest, most elegant, most exquisite clothing.'

"'Thanks to God and thanks to the Monsieur count, we have no shortage of nice clothing.'

"'Good, good . . . Make haste, for we are in a hurry.'

"'Hurry, hurry, Monsieur count is in a rush,' said Madame Bonnivet, preparing to undress her niece. Judith got embarrassed and made a sign that Arthur was there.

"'What does it matter? Surely the presence of the count doesn't inconvenience us!' And before Judith could oppose her she had unfastened the bodice of her dress.

"Disturbed and beside herself, the poor girl did not know how she could evade Arthur's gaze. But poor girl! She struggled with the shame that grew out of unfounded fear. Arthur was definitely not looking at her. Entirely preoccupied with an idea that seemed to excite his anger and the most profound spite, he walked back and forth, taking long strides, with his back to Judith near the console where she kept everything necessary to arrange her hair. He mechanically took one of the crystal glasses and shattered it, reducing it to tiny pieces.

"'Oh, what bad luck,' said Judith, forgetting at that moment that she was undressed.

"'Japanese porcelain!' said the aunt, who was upset. 'It cost at least 500 francs.'*

"'It's not that: it was her keepsake!' said Judith.

"'All done? Are you ready?' asked Arthur, who had not heard that last observation.

"'In a moment. Aunt, my shawl and my gloves . . .'

"'And your cloak,' said Arthur. 'You are forgetting it, and it will be cold.'

"'I don't think so.'

"'I see why,' said the aunt, touching the hand of her niece, 'your hand is burning; perhaps you have a fever? Then you can't go out.'

"'No madame,' replied Judith quickly, 'I feel good and am all set.'

"The carriage was at the door. Judith and Arthur got in, and together they made their way through the boulevards in the middle of the day . . . Together! . . . Judith couldn't believe how happy she was; she wanted the whole world to see her . . . She reached the pinnacle of satisfaction when she encountered, on rue de la Paix, two of her friends from the Opera, whom she greeted with the grace and charm of someone who tells herself, 'I am happy!' Those two prima ballerinas were on that day traveling by foot.

"The carriage stopped at the gate on Rivoli Street, where Judith took the arm of the count, and the two walked on Printemps Street. It was not a holiday, so the wealthy and leisured population of Paris had set a date

---

* In the original this value is listed as 100 *duros*. The *peso duro* was a coin worth five *pesetas*, 22.5 grams of fine silver, or the same as five French francs in 1871. In 1850 the peso duro corresponded to 23.49 grams of fine silver. Denzel, *Handbook of World Exchange Rates*, 307–8.

for this magnificent promenade: the crowd was immense. Arthur and his companion were immediately the objects of much interest. The couple was so handsome that it was impossible for them to pass by unnoticed. They all said to themselves: 'What a beautiful young woman!'

"'That's the count Arthur of V . . .'

"'What? Did he get married?'

"Hearing this, Judith experienced an inexplicable emotion of both pleasure and pain.

"'No,' said a tall, older woman who carried in her arms a Viennese dog and was accompanied by two servants dressed in gold livery; 'no, count Arthur did not get married; his uncle would not allow it.'

"'And who is that beautiful woman that he has taken by the arm? His sister, perhaps?'

"'You do him a wrong . . . she is his girlfriend . . . a young woman from the Opera . . . that's my guess.'

"Luckily Judith did not hear the old woman's words; at that moment the Baron of Blangy, who walked behind her, said to his brother:

"'It's Judith!'

"'Arthur fell into that trap?'

"'He has lost his head . . . she will ruin him.'

"'You are right—I would like to be in his place: look how lovely she is!'

"'What an exceptional bearing! What an enchanting physiognomy!'

"'Not to mention how elegant and graceful.'

"'Watch out—you're starting to fall for her.'

"'I already have. Come on, let's get a closer look at her.'

"'If we can: there's a crowd around her.'

"And the crowd repeated similar phrases that Arthur also heard . . . Witnessing the modest bearing of Judith, the young women forgave her for being so beautiful, while the men, who observed Arthur with envy, said to themselves, 'What a lucky man!'

"For the first time, then, he looked at Judith, and he admired how truly beautiful she was. The stroll, the open air, and above all the satisfaction of hearing themselves praised had colored Judith's cheeks with a fresh charm and given her eyes an indefinably happy expression. And she was sixteen years old. She loved and believed that she was loved—all reasons for her heightened beauty. Judith's success was complete and enormous. The crowd accompanied her all the way to the avenue. But then when she saw that Arthur gave her a tender look, all the previous triumphs disappeared beside this one; after the words of praise that she had heard and the beauty of the promenade, she forgot everything, everything, once she walked into her house, telling herself, 'How happy I am!'

"The next day, when she awoke Judith received two letters. The first was from the Baron of Blangy, much wealthier than Arthur, who offered his love and fortune. Judith did not even think of showing it to Arthur nor to her aunt, nor did she think that by burning it she was making the slightest sacrifice. The second had another signature that Judith read and reread, not being able to believe her own eyes. But there was no room for doubt: it was signed, 'The Bishop of . . .' and read as follows:

"'Mademoiselle:

"'Yesterday you made an appearance in the Tuileries with my nephew, Count Arthur, creating a great scandal whose consequences are incalculable. Although as a result of the impiety of men God has permitted for everything to be turned upside down, we have a way of punishing your audacity. I therefore declare, mademoiselle, that if you don't put an end to this scandal, I have enough influence with the minister of state to make sure that you are thrown out of the Opera. If, on the other hand, you immediately leave my nephew, we offer to you, since the end sanctifies the means, a thousand louis and the complete absolution of your sins, etc., etc."

"After reading this letter, Judith was left surprised, deprived of all her courage, and she stayed for a long time in a state of stupor that one doesn't know how to explain to oneself. Later she took courage, consulted her heart, mustered all her energy, and responded.

"'Most illustrious sir,

"'Although you treat me with a great deal of cruelty, I can attest before God that I am not ashamed of anything. This is true, I swear it to you, but I do not flatter myself; if I have any merit, I owe it all to the fact that I have respected and liked myself. Yes, illustrious sir, your nephew is innocent of all the charges that you make, and if to love him with one's entire soul is to offend the heavens, then I am guilty of that crime, and I can't claim that he is my accomplice.

"'Here is the resolution that I have taken. I will tell him—the part of me that I respect would never dare to do so, so I do this for you, illustrious sir . . . the heavens will give me the strength for it . . . I will ask him, "Arthur, do you love me?" And if he says, "No Judith, I don't love you," as I believe and fear he will, then I will obey you, illustrious sir. I will go far away from him, and I will never see him again. And then I hope you will respect me

---

* The *louis* was a gold coin that circulated prior to the French Revolution (1787–99).

enough not to try to bribe me, not to add insult to injury [*no añadir al desprecio la desesperación*]—that would surely kill me.

"'But if the heavens, if my guardian angel, if the happiness of all of my life conspire so that he responds to me, "I love you!" Oh! It is terrible what I am going to tell you. You may heap insults upon me and with good reason, but in that case know, illustrious sir, that there is no power in the world that can prevent me from being with him, even if it means sacrificing my life! I would defy anything, including your anger! But what could happen to me? I could die! And why would that matter, if I had been loved?

"'Forgive me, illustrious sir, if this letter has wounded your vanity . . . It is written by a poor young woman without knowledge of the world nor of its social formulas, who believes that she would obtain some consideration in your soul through the ignorance that she confesses, through the sincerity of her heart, her profound respect for you, and above all through the great honor of being your servant.

"'Most illustrious sir, etc.'

"This is how Judith concluded her letter. She sealed it and sent it without saying a word about it to anyone, and from that moment she decided to meet her fate, waiting impatiently for the next visit of the count.

"That night there was a performance at the Opera. She was on stage very closely watching the second box in the front, waiting for the agreed-upon signal. Arthur arrived very late, and he seemed sad and worried. He neither looked toward the stage nor made any sign to Judith, who was impatient and desperate. It was necessary for her to wait until the next day.

"Indeed, that day, which was a Wednesday, he was happier. Arthur made the sign that indicated his planned visits, and Judith told herself, 'Tomorrow I will know the fate that awaits me.' That morning the count's footman showed up at Judith's house, announcing that the count would not have a moment free all day but that he would come very late at night to dine with the mademoiselle. Dine with her! That had never happened, because he always left before midnight. What did that mean? The aunt took this news in stride, but Judith could not understand it.

"Around eleven at night the dinner was ready, and Madame Bonnivet prepared a delicious and tasteful array of food. As for Judith, she neither saw nor heard anything; she waited anxiously. She waited. All the faculties of her soul, all her thoughts concentrated on that sole idea! . . . But eleven-thirty, and midnight had sounded and Arthur had not yet arrived! The whole night passed by, and he did not arrive! And she still waited. And the next day and the following days passed, and Arthur did not appear . . . She did not hear anything from him, and she did not see him again! What could explain that? What had happened?

"Sirs," added the notary, interrupting himself, "they've raised the curtain, I will continue during the next intermission."

V

"Sirs," said the notary the moment the third act of *The Huguenots* ended, "I imagine that you are impatient to find out what happened to our friend Arthur and above all to know who our hero was."

"But hadn't you already begun by telling us that?" I asked him.

"I am the curator of the exhibition; I arrange things as I please."

"In addition, the Opera is not the best place to be severe when it comes to judging exhibitions," added the professor of law. "I neither understand them nor do I ever see them."

"Which is good business for the authors of librettos," replied the notary, satisfied with the exchange that had occurred, and he continued in these terms: "Count Arthur de V was a descendant of a very old and very distinguished family from the South. His mother, who had been widowed when still very young, had not had another child; her position was not perfect, because her inheritance was small; but her brother possessed an immense fortune.

"This brother, the Abbot de V . . . , had been one of the most influential prelates in the court of Louis XVIII and then in that of Charles X, and it is said that the cleric had all the power of France at his disposal, even the army and sovereignty itself.* The Abbot de V . . . was cold and egotistical even though he was a good relative in that he wanted everything for himself and for his family. He took charge of the education of his nephew Arthur, introducing him to the court and arranging for the return of most of the property of his sister, the Countess of V . . . , which had been confiscated upon the emigration of her husband. Thus the poor countess died blessing the name of her brother, and she recommended that her son blindly obey all the commands of the abbot.

"Arthur, who adored his mother, swore on her deathbed everything that she asked of him, a promise that he was all the more able to fulfill given that from his childhood he had been terrified of his uncle and he was used

---

* Louis XVIII (1755–1824) was king of France from 1814 to 1824, followed by Charles X (1757–1836) from 1824 to 1830.

to submitting to his slightest whims without any resistance. Arthur was serious, sweet, timid, but nevertheless brave and honorable: from his earliest years he had felt a strong inclination to pursue a career as a soldier—for the uniform and for the sword—perhaps because in the residence of his uncle he saw nothing but chasubles and full-length vestments. One day he dared, albeit with misgivings, to communicate his intentions to the abbot, who was then about to be elevated to the level of bishop; the most illustrious one furrowed his brows and answered with a firm and decisive voice that he had other plans.

"Once the abbot had been named bishop, he hoped for something else. But for the time being the chapel of the cardinal was what commanded his attention. Once he had attained such a great honor, he proposed to keep his nephew always at his side with the aim of making him a member of the ecclesiastical hierarchy. In that case, the ship of his nephew's ambitions would navigate alongside his own. In other words, that Arthur should embrace the church as a career was the only plan his uncle had embraced, the only path that would quickly lead him to the pinnacle of power and honor.

"Arthur did not dare to openly resist the terrible plans of his uncle, but he had sworn to himself to never become a bishop. The bishop had already spoken to the king about his plans, and the king had approved of them. As a result, Arthur had to go to the seminary in a few months in order to fill out the forms because he was expected to follow orders immediately and pass through all of the stages of his new career without any delays.

"Arthur had not forgotten his promise to his mother on her deathbed. Everyone would have viewed it as the worst ingratitude for him to openly oppose the wishes of his uncle, his only relative and the benefactor to whom he owed his position. He therefore did not dare to openly declare war on his uncle's intentions for him to become bishop and searched for the least visible ways to oblige his uncle to spontaneously renounce those plans. Yet how could Arthur find a diplomatic way that would make him unfit to occupy the position they insisted he take?

"This was not at all easy. Perhaps because his upbringing prohibited it, or perhaps because he could not betray his own honorable principles, he would rather kill himself than agree to be a bishop. To be a libertine it is not enough to want to be one.

"He had friends with the most enviable dispositions who certainly would have taken him to their delightful orgies in order to help him. Arthur attended some public dances, some student meetings, but the recklessness he found there bothered him as much as it entertained others. His ascetic character stood in opposition to the unbridled hedonism of his companions, who ended up respecting him once they matured. Once his friends recognized that Arthur was a killjoy, he stopped going to their parties.

"Thus, and with the aim of emerging victorious in his struggle against the bishop, he thought of the women of the court. But in that court the women fled from noise and from scandal, not because there were fewer intrigues there than at other times but because they knew how to hide them better. And even if the bishop were to find his nephew involved in secret affairs, he would turn his back on them, sharing Molière's view: 'To sin in secret is no sin at all.'"

"What else could the poor young man do but run after scandal the way others run after glory without ever reaching it? One of his friends, a libertine by any measure, told him one day:

"'Take a lover among the chorus at the Opera. That theater is fashionable, and everyone attends its shows. People will know about it, will comment on it, will make noise, and you will get what you want.'

"Trembling with indignation, Arthur said, 'I would never get mixed up in such an intrigue!'

"'You will not get mixed up in it; everything will be arranged with the parents or relatives of the girl in question and end of story. It does not matter whether you are really the lover; you will seem to be the lover, and that is enough for your aims.'

"'Agreed.'

"'You will take the title of lover. You know very well that in our days there are a multitude of titles that mean nothing in practice . . . this will be one of those.'

"'Fine. Let's begin.'

"You already know about the meeting and first conversation between Arthur, Judith, and Madame Bonnivet. Everything had been arranged so that the bishop would know when the nephew had put this plan into practice. However, the bishop didn't say a word. He noticed that almost every night his nephew's carriage was parked at the door of a certain house on Provence Street. Arthur waited for days on end for his uncle to make a scene, which would have required Arthur to tell a tale of a violent passion that would make him unfit for the benevolence of his uncle. But the uncle

---

* Molière was the pen name of Jean-Baptiste Pocquelin (1622–1673), a French actor and playwright.

said nothing—not even a word—and Arthur didn't know what to make of the bishop's calm and Christian resignation.

"The calm preceding the hurricane ensued. The bishop told him one day:

"'The King is very irritated with you, but I don't know why.'

"'I can guess why.'

"'I don't want to know. His majesty has forgiven you, but I demand that you enter the seminary in two days.'

"'But uncle!'

"'That is the order of the King; you must protest to him.'

"And the bishop turned away."

VI

"Beside himself with anger and not knowing what to do, Arthur rushed over to Judith's house, took her to the Tuileries, and the night before he was to enter the seminary confessed his love to his sweetheart in front of all Paris. This time there wouldn't be any half measures. It was impossible that after such a scandal they would think that he could embark on an ecclesiastical career. This was what Arthur desired. The bishop wrote to Judith the menacing card that we have seen, and the king ordered the count to leave Paris within twenty-four hours. He had to obey. Luckily Arthur was the friend of one of Monsieur Bourmont's sons, who was leaving the next night for Algiers, where he was preparing for an important expedition.

"Arthur asked the friend to take him as a volunteer on the voyage, under the solemn promise not to say a word about it to the king or to his uncle. 'Since I am free to choose the place of my exile,' he said to himself, 'I will choose the place where I can find glory; I will go to the reign of danger and honor. Either I will be a leader or I will die trying, and when I return with a flag that shows I have conquered the enemy, we will see whether I merit the high esteem of my peers.'

"He left his uncle's house secretly and under cover of night because he knew that all his steps were watched and he feared that they would forbid his trip if they heard about it. He wrote a letter to Judith telling her that he would see her in a few days, but this letter, insignificant though it was, was intercepted and did not reach its intended destination. The chief of police was following the orders of the bishop.

"The next week, Arthur was on the open sea, and after a voyage of twenty days he arrived in Africa. One of the leaders in the attack on the emperor's stronghold, he was injured while fighting at the side of his intrepid friend Monsieur de Bourmont, who died of an injury just when they were within reach of victory. The injured Arthur was in grave danger for a long time. For two months he doubted that he would survive. While he convalesced, his fortune, as well as his hopes and those of his uncle, disappeared along with the monarchy of Charles X.*

"The bishop had not been able to resist that catastrophe: ill and full of sorrow, he sought to follow the exiled court, but this was not possible. His impatience and continual anger had agitated his brain and inflamed his blood; he began to suffer from typhoid fever, and in his state of irritation, not knowing how to avenge the Revolution of July, he victimized his nephew!†

"As soon as he had recovered from his wound, Arthur returned to Paris, and here, sirs," said the notary, raising his voice, "I begin to enter into the story. The count came to my house to get help with the negotiations for the succession since he was not in a position to personally take care of them. I had been the notary of his family for a very long time, and thus I returned to my former occupation.

"I will skip over the details of the inventory and only recount what pertains to this story. Going through the papers that I found in the files of the Bishop, I found a letter, with very fine handwriting, signed 'Judith, ballerina of the Opera.' The letter from a ballerina in the house of the Bishop! To protect the dignity of the clergyman, I would have liked to see her disappear, but Arthur had already fallen for her; and watching him grow pale as I read it, I thought for an instant that the uncle and nephew had been rivals without knowing it—may God pardon me for the uncharitable thought.

"'Poor girl! Poor girl!' said Arthur, 'What nobility! What generosity! What a treasure she is! Go on and read,' he told me, and the letter concluded with this sentence: 'If to love him with one's entire soul is to offend

---

* The mention of the ouster of King Charles X from the throne of France situates the story's main events in 1830. The French army landed near Algiers on 5 July 1830 and quickly defeated Husayn, the Algerian "emperor," or *dey*. Sutton et al., "Algeria."

† The July Revolution took place in France in the summer of 1830, only days after the French defeat of Algeria, in reaction to Charles X's ordinances violating the intent of the Charter of 1814. Protests and demonstrations turned violent by the end of the month, leading to the abdication of Charles X and the installation of Louis-Philippe as the new king on 4 August 1830. *Encyclopaedia Britannica Online*, s.v. "July Revolution," https://www.britannica.com/event/July-Revolution.

the heavens, then I am guilty of that crime, and I can't claim that he is my accomplice.'

"'It's true!' Arthur exclaimed, with tears in his eyes. 'She loved me with all of her soul, and I could not understand that, and I didn't even think about loving her. A dazzling sixteen-year-old! Oh! You don't know my friend how beautiful she was . . . She is the most beautiful woman in Paris.'

"'I do not doubt that, Count . . . But if you are willing, could we finish the inventory?'

"'As you wish.'

"And he continued reading the fragments of the letter out loud. 'But if the heavens, if my guardian angel, if the happiness of all of my life conspire so that he responds to me, "I love you!" Oh! It is terrible what I am going to tell you. You may heap insults upon me and with good reason, but in that case know, illustrious sir, that there is no power in the world that can prevent me from being with him, even if it means sacrificing my life!'

"'I have scorned that pure, innocent, and saintly treasure of love!' exclaimed Arthur. 'I am the only guilty one! . . . But I will make up for it; I will dedicate my whole life to her. I promise and swear it. Who could reproach me for this resolution? I love her. I will tell it to all the world, and all the world will envy my treasure, . . . beginning with you, Mr. Notary, as you are examining that pile of papers with such concentration without listening to me.'

"'These papers! I am looking right at the will of your uncle, the will in which he disinherits you and gives his immense fortune to hospitals and to pious organizations.'

"He said this to Arthur, who did not show the least emotion upon hearing that, and instead reread Judith's letter.

"'You will meet the most beautiful woman in the world,' he answered. 'I want you to accompany us to dinner.'

"'But the papers . . . the will . . .'

"'Those aren't worth anything,' he said, smiling. 'Luckily, Judith will love me without that . . . Goodbye, goodbye, I'm going to see her; I will gain far more at her side than all the money that I have lost.'

"And he left, radiant with hope and pleasure.

"'What an unusual young man,' I told myself, 'who can find consolation for the loss of an inheritance in a young woman!' And I worked to finish the inventory. A few hours later I had already returned to my house. As soon as I arrived, Arthur arrived in a desperate state, as if he were insane.

"'She does not exist! She does not exist! She is lost! She is lost to me!'

"'What is it? Was she unfaithful?'

"'Who told you?' he asked me, grabbing me by the neck.

"'I don't know anything.'

'Oh, thank you. I don't think I could survive such a trial. After my departure, she has been gone for three months—she has left the theater.'

"'What have her fellow dancers told you?'

"'Nothing. Some insist that she was the victim of an abduction. Another assured me, coldheartedly, that she intended to commit suicide.'

"'That is not strange, since suicide has become fashionable following the July Revolution.'

"'Oh, don't say that . . . I would lose my head. I rushed over to her place on Provence Street, and she has abandoned it without saying where she was going.'

"'What? There's not a single trace of her?'

"'The apartment is empty. No one has lived there after her.'

"'And you didn't find anything inside?'

"'I did find one thing. In her aunt's room, I found a piece of paper that had been pasted onto a bag with this address: To Madame Bonnivet in Bordeaux . . . I remember that she had been born in that city.'

"'There is always something.'

"'Take care of my business here and handle things as you see fit.'

"'What are you going to do?'

"'I am going to follow her tracks or those of her aunt . . . search for her and find her.'

"'But you are still recuperating, so it is not prudent for you to travel to Bordeaux.'

"'I cannot possibly wait until tomorrow.'

"He left that very night. And . . ."

Here was where the fourth act of *Huguenots* began, and the notary did not speak another word; he listened to the play, and for the continuation of the story we had to wait until the intermission. Monsieur Nourrit was about to jump out the window, and Mademoiselle Falcon fainted. And so the fourth act of the *Huguenots* concluded, the applause subsided, and the notary took up the thread of his tale once again in the following way:

"Arthur stayed for six months in Bordeaux, searching, inquiring, interrogating everyone about Madame Bonnivet, about whom no one knew anything. He tried to reach her via the newspapers under cover of a communication of much interest, but she did not appear. As you will see, that was not possible. The owner of a little house in which she had lived gave Arthur some leads. Madame Bonnivet had died two months earlier.

"And her niece?"

"She did not live with her, but the aunt lived well: she had 1,000 francs of life insurance."

"Why did she take out that life insurance?"

"No one knows."

"Did she speak about her niece?"

"She sometimes mentioned her name. But then she grew quiet as if she were afraid of betraying a secret that she had to keep."

"Despite all the care and interest that Arthur took in his investigations, he did not make any more progress, and he grew desperate. Since he had lost Judith, and since he considered himself forever separated from her, he had developed a true passion for her and profoundly adored her in his memory. Memories of Judith were what occupied all of his time. He remembered bitterly the moments that he had passed in her company and all her charms and love, all of which he had not fully appreciated! He could only understand the true value of his great treasure when he had lost it forever. He dedicated himself to visiting all the places where he had seen her; that is why he always attended the Opera.

"He wanted to live in the very room in which she stayed on Provence Street, but unluckily for him, a foreigner had rented it during his absence but did not live there. He tried to see it once again, but the porter did not have the keys and all the doors and windows of the room remained closed and locked.

"Once committed to reliving his memories and to finding his love, Arthur gave no thought to his finances, you understand. Working day and night to put his business affairs in order, I noticed that they had taken a turn for the worse. Disinherited by his uncle, Arthur did not possess any funds except those given to him by his mother: three thousand francs in income plus a little in change. He had spent more than half of his savings in his extravagant treatment of Judith and, later, in his thorough effort to find her.

"The smallest clue sent him scurrying in all directions and spending money hand over fist, but nothing panned out. For that reason, he kept repeating, 'She does not exist! Judith has died!' In our conversations on his business arrangements, I advised him to liquidate his assets, but he could only speak about her. I finally persuaded him of this necessity, but not without a great deal of work, because it was sensible for him to get rid of the things he had inherited from his mother. The situation demanded it: he owed around two hundred thousand francs, and with charges and taxes, that debt had consumed the rest of his fortune.

"They posted notices announcing the sale of the furniture, they purchased an insert in the newspapers, and the night before the day when the sale was supposed to take place, I received a visit from a friend that surprised me and filled me with happiness. Apparently, Arthur's was no longer a tragic destiny!

"Monsieur Courval, a man of incontestable probity who owed a great debt to Arthur's mother, proposed to pay her. The amount, including interest, reached three hundred thousand francs. Not only was it a real debt that could be recovered but my friend brought me the funds in banknotes. There was no room to doubt such a fortune. I ran to communicate the news to Arthur, but he received it with great indifference. Unless the news was about Judith, he was uninterested. I gave him the receipt for the credit to his account, and I paid his creditors without having to touch one iota of his wealth. So everything went swimmingly, save one incident that is difficult to explain.

"One day, Arthur came across this Monsieur de Courval, who had behaved so honorably with us. He usually lived in the countryside and was in Paris by coincidence. When Arthur took his hand in a show of his appreciation for his noble actions, Monsieur de Courval excused himself with great embarrassment, telling him that a number of mishaps had made it impossible for him to fulfill his obligations.

"'But just last month you paid me three hundred thousand francs, isn't that right?'

"'I did?'

"'Of course; I tore up the documents indicating that you owed me that sum.'

"'That cannot be!'

"'Go see my notary.'

"He went immediately to the house, unable to recover from the surprise his conversation with Arthur had given him.

"'It is a good thing for you, I tell you.'

"'It is better for Monsieur Arthur,' he said with an air of sadness and disappointment. 'I had already adopted my resolution... Not being able to pay is the same as not owing... and this business is not making me richer; with respect to him it is another thing... he can enjoy this happiness.'

"'But don't you know the real origin of this resolution?'

"'No sir, but I take it as a done deal. Oh, if all the bankruptcies could be resolved in this way. But frankly, in a little while . . .'

"'Does he have other debts?'

"'They are mounting to double what I have, or almost as much as what they have paid for me already: if by chance they come back for the payment of my remaining debts, please let me know.'

"'Of course I will.'

"Our surprise grew, and Arthur despaired over not being able to solve this enigma. He went to see my friend, an honorable and educated man, who did not know more than I did, you understand, about the transaction in question. They had sent him the funds, recommending that he cancel the documentation, and that was all that I could find out. He gave me the letter of remittance, and this I took to Arthur; he examined it very carefully. The letter had been sealed in Le Havre, where Monsieur Courval lived. The writing was not that of Monsieur Courval, but it looked familiar . . . But Arthur shouted out in surprise and grew paler than a cadaver upon discovering that the half-broken seal was the very one that Judith used. A long time ago he had given her a beautiful antique stone upon which there was an image of a phoenix. Rather than viewing the gift as an allusion or a tribute, Judith had considered it a symbol of sadness and had had the following phrase inscribed on it: 'Always the same.' She had never abandoned this seal, and if this seal was insignificant for others, it was so expressive of her personality that it couldn't have belonged to anyone other than her.

"'This letter is from Judith!' exclaimed Arthur. And it fell out of his trembling hands.

"'That is great! Now you can be sure not only that she lives but that she thinks about you. This must make you feel very happy and satisfied.'

"Arthur was furious with anger and despair. He would rather have been told that she had died; he asked himself, 'Why, then, would she hide herself? Because knowing where I live, she is afraid of meeting me! She feels unfit to spend time with me! She does not love me! She has forgotten me!'

"'This card,' I said, 'proves the contrary.'

"'And by what right does she humiliate me by sending me these gifts? Where does all this money come from? How dare she offer them to me? Since when does she judge me to be such a coward that I would accept them? I do not want to: I must return them, and right away.'

"'All that is well and good, but to whom should we deliver the money?'

"'That doesn't matter. I refuse them, I have only contempt for them.'

"'Fine, but the debts are paid off, and the properties no longer have liens, thanks to the three hundred thousand francs.'

"'You will immediately sell my properties, earning that sum, and you will save it as a deposit until the moment comes to return it to her.'

"'But how will it be possible for you to meet her?'

"'That does not matter to me. Since I have been so unfaithful, I will have the satisfaction of telling myself, I am ruined by Judith! But to have wealth at her cost is a humiliation that I can't tolerate.'

"And despite all of my efforts, and notwithstanding all the counterarguments I made, he stood by his words. We sold the goods and properties and made a good profit, thanks to rising prices. The first three hundred thousand francs were kept in my desk, leaving Arthur a property that produced ten thousand francs in rent as the only thing that remained of all his fortune.

"He lived like this for three years, trying to erase the memory that constantly tormented him. Somber and melancholy, he refused all pleasures and distractions; he had become incapable of dedicating himself to work or to his studies. Frankly, I acutely felt the influence of such a mournful cloud over the existence of Arthur. He came to see me almost every day, with the aim of forgetting Judith, but he always talked about her. He didn't love her, he scorned her, he said. He would have preferred to travel to the last corner of the world rather than see her again. And despite this, he mechanically went to the places that called to mind his memories of her.

"One day, or more precisely, one night, when he arrived at a masquerade ball at the Theater of the Opera, he felt his heart beating against his chest. Alone in the midst of the crowd, he walked silently through all the noise, upon the stage where he had seen her charms displayed so many times ... After losing himself in the galleries, he slowly walked up to the second box in the front, where in happier times he had spent all his nights and given the sign for his innocent trysts with Judith.

"The door to the stage was open. A woman dressed in an elegant, hooded gown of black silk was sitting on stage, submerged in profound reflections. When Arthur appeared, she got up, wanting to leave, but hesitated, as if she could barely stand up. She leaned for an instant on one of the sides of the stage and fell back into the chair. Observing the woman's distress, Arthur rushed to offer his services.

"Without saying a word, she waved him off with her hand.

"'The heat has gone to your head,' he said, as he felt an emotion he could not control, 'and if you take off your mask for a moment...'

"She refused this suggestion as well, and as if she wished to breathe more freely, she allowed her hood to fall from her forehead.

"Arthur then saw the most beautiful black hair falling here and there on the shoulders of the mask. That was the way Judith combed her hair. Her stature, her appearance, her fine and elegant figure, everything, everything looked like Judith. Here was a faithful copy of her manners; moreover, there was something absolutely captivating that dominated his whole being from the moment he saw her. Finally she stood up. Arthur cried out. Now he felt himself fainting... but recomposing himself, after a great effort, he said in a faltering voice, 'Judith! Judith! It's you!'

"She wanted to leave.

"'Please allow me one moment. At the very least you must know that I am the most unlucky man in the world, because it has taken me a long time to realize that you are worthy of all my love.'

"She trembled visibly.

"'Yes, you deserved it then. Yes, you were worthy of all homages, of the adoration of the whole world, and nevertheless, I am so foolish that I love you with all of my heart and I will love you forever even if you have been unfaithful, even if you have betrayed the purity of my feelings!'

"She wanted to reply, but the words died on her tongue, and she raised her right hand to her heart as if to justify herself.

"'And so if you have been faithful to me, then how can you explain your absence, and above all its advantages? Those advantages that I regret because I pushed you away? Yes, Judith, I don't want that, I don't accept that, I only want love; if it is true that you have not forgotten me, that you still love me, then come with me, follow me! You must love me to follow me... because now I do not have a fortune to offer you... Ah! Now you hesitate! You don't say a word! I understand your silence! Goodbye, goodbye forever!'

"He was about to leave the stage. Judith held him back.

"'Speak, Judith, please speak.'

"The poor young woman could not speak—sobs drowned her words. Arthur knelt at her feet. She had not said anything, but she cried! He believed that she was innocent.

"'So you still love me?'

"'Yes,' she answered, holding his hand.

"'And how can I trust you? What proofs will you give me?'

"'Time will show you.'

"'What must I do?'

"'Wait!'

"'And what pledge will guarantee me this love that is all of my fortune?'

"She dropped a bouquet of flowers that she carried in her hand, and when Arthur leaned down to pick it up, she sprung out of the hall and disappeared.

"Arthur followed her with his eyes for a few instants. He perceived her far away among the crowds, but he lost sight of her in waves of masks. Later he believed that he had found her . . . Yes, yes, it was she! He followed her, and at the moment that he reached the doorway, she climbed into an elegant carriage pulled by two magnificent horses that galloped off.

"Sirs," said the notary interrupting himself, "it is already quite late—I go to sleep early—and if you will permit me, I would like to leave the end of the story for the day after tomorrow."

The following Wednesday was opera day; we all met there, but the notary did not arrive. They were presenting *Robert,* a work that reminded me of my first encounter with Arthur. I could now explain to myself the sorrowful and preoccupied character of that young man, and I even thought that Meyerbeer himself, knowing what we know, would have pardoned him for the lack of attention that time he failed to listen to the sublime trio in *Robert*.

But now would Arthur find himself in a better situation to appreciate the merits of the music? Would he be happier? Had he found or lost Judith? We still didn't know the obstacles that separated them, and our impatience to know the conclusion of the story grew minute by minute during the narrator's absence. He finally arrived after the second act, and neither an esteemed actor nor a prima ballerina returning after a year's absence would have been received with such satisfaction as the notary was by us. "There he is! Good, very good! Sit down! What happened? How is it that you came so late?"

"I ate out and I prepared a contract . . . Well, I didn't officially prepare it because I no longer practice; I have sold my office, and luckily I don't owe anything to anyone."

"Except for us!"

"You owe us a courtesy!"

"The history of Judith."

"We have saved you a seat: sit here."

We all drew closer to hear the notary's account, which began in the following way: "Six months passed by, then a year, and then two. I felt compassion for Arthur, and I feared that he would one day lose his mind. The scene of the masquerade ball had affected him tremendously. Arthur was so obsessed with the details of how he had found Judith without having seen her, how she had appeared without showing him her face, that he believed himself the victim of some hallucination. Weakened from so much suffering, he persuaded himself that everything had been a dream, an illusion of the senses. And he ended up even doubting that he had ever seen or heard her. He fell gravely ill, and in the delirium of fever he imagined that Judith visited him for the last time to say goodbye. I cannot express the tender and ecstatic words that he heard from her mouth so many times while in the grips of that illness. Judith was his sole thought, his obsession. And that was the great cause for the torment that was leading him to the grave.

"I cared for him and brought him back to life, but he remained somber and melancholy. He saw no one besides me. He had not wished to make use of the money that Judith had given him, and his own money, as I told you, only amounted to 2,000 francs in income. He had spent nearly half his savings to rent a box at the Opera for the season: the second one in the front, where he had run into Judith the night of the masquerade ball. He sat there every night, hoping to see her again. Later, when he had lost that hope, he did not have the heart to go. He only came once in a while to the orchestra stalls and with great melancholy contemplated the place where Judith had worked and left saying,

"'She is not there!'

"That was his life, and with the exception of a few trips that he took from time to time, always with the hope of obtaining news about Judith or any signs of her whereabouts, he returned to live in Paris, where every night, without fail, he went to the Theater of the Opera. In order to see him more often, I subscribed to this seat for many years. Last week, he came to the Opera and was seated in an orchestra seat on the other side. That day, he was completely spiritless—he no longer had any hope, and with his back to the hall he was so immersed in his habitual reflections that he neither saw nor heard anything. The exclamations of those seated by his side shook him out of his lethargy. A young woman of singular beauty and dressed with uncommon elegance had just entered a box and was now in the crosshairs of the crowd's artillery of binoculars and lenses.

"One heard the following words:

"'How pretty she is!'

"'What a lovely face! How beautiful!'

"'What a graceful bearing!'

"'What an elegant woman!'

"'Tell me, how old do you think she is?'

"'Twenty or twenty-two years old.'

"'Be quiet—she couldn't be a day over eighteen.'

"'Do you know who she is?'

"'No sir; it is the first time that she's come to the opera. I have season tickets.'

"Other neighbors of this speaker did not know her either. However, not far from them a distinguished foreigner bowed respectfully and greeted the beautiful young woman. At that moment everyone wondered what her name was.

"'That is Lady Iggerton, the wife of a lord from England.'

"'Extraordinary. So beautiful, and so rich!'

"'And they say that at a certain point she had had nothing . . . that she was a poor girl who in a moment of desperation, out of jealousy, no doubt, had wanted to throw herself into the Seine. And that the old duke had found her, brought her to his house, and treated her like his own daughter.'

"'That is a story that belongs in a novel.'

"'Not all stories end so well. Nevertheless, the old man, who had come to care for her and couldn't walk without her, had wanted to marry her in order to leave her his immense fortune. And that is what he did.'

"'Good God, if she is a widow . . . she is a superb catch.'

"'She has already gone through mourning, and in England as in France she will belong to someone who courts her and merits her love.'

"'I believe it,' said the young man who had been speaking, and with one hand he straightened his tie while with the other he held the spectacle that never veered away from Lady Iggerton. 'I think she is looking toward me.'

"'You are deceiving yourself,' answered the stranger.

"'No, I swear it. I am not mistaken. See for yourself.'

"And she walked toward Arthur, who had just made sense of the previous dialogue, and to whom it was necessary to explain the situation. Arthur raised his eyes, and in the second box in front . . . that box that in other times had been his, he saw . . . Oh! No one dies from surprise and happiness, because Arthur was still alive when he mustered enough strength to say to himself, 'It's her! It's Judith!'

"At that moment he froze as if he were a statue; he was afraid to awake!

"'Listen sir, tell me,' said the man who sat by his side, 'do you know her?'

"Arthur did not reply, because at that moment Judith's eyes had found his, and the image of the one was reflected in the eyes of the other. He had seen in the eyes of his beloved an expression of indefinable pleasure and happiness. What was he feeling? It is impossible to say. He saw Judith's hand—that hand that was so white and so beautiful—go to her heart, imitating the signal that long ago had indicated that they were to meet, and her fingers momentarily played with the emerald buttons that Arthur had given her.

"Oh! This time he thought that he had gone crazy. He looked down, held his head between his hands, and stayed like that for a few seconds as if to convince himself that what he had just seen wasn't a dream, to repeat to himself that he still existed and that he had just seen Judith. Afterwards, when he had gathered his thoughts, he raised his eyes once again to look at her. The heavenly vision had disappeared! Judith was not in the box! She had left! A deathly cold invaded his limbs . . . An iron hand pressed against his heart. Then, remembering what he had just seen . . . and heard . . . because she had spoken to him with signs, he abandoned his seat and rushed out to the street, desiring to breathe freely and telling himself, 'This time it was no illusion. Yes, my senses have tricked me. I have fallen into error. Oh! I am losing my head. I will kill myself.'

"And deciding to kill himself, he walked dejectedly to Provence Street. He knocked at a door, they opened it mechanically, and he asked for Judith. 'The Madame is at home,' the porter replied indifferently. Not able to contain himself, Arthur cried out and steadied himself on the bannister of the stairway so that he wouldn't fall down. Walking up to the second floor, he crossed the hallway and knocked at the door of Judith's room. It had the exact same furniture as six years before. The dinner that he had ordered prior to his departure was still there; the only thing that had changed was that there were two tablecloths. And Judith, seated on a sofa, said to him the moment he entered, 'You have arrived quite late, my friend.' And she extended her hand. Arthur threw himself into Judith's arms. The two of them then gave each other the most affectionate explanations."

Here the notary paused.

"Come on, finish the story," we all said at the same time.

The notary smiled and said, "Arthur hasn't told me anything else . . . The third act of *Robert* is about to start."

"What does that matter? Keep going!"

"What more can I tell you? I just dined with them, and I signed the contract."

"They got married?"
"Yes. Judith wanted that."
"As a final surprise, perhaps?"
"It may be that she is reserving one more."
"What?" asked the professor of law excitedly.
"I don't know for sure whether this is the case," answered the notary smiling, "but there are those who swear that the old duke, her husband, called her by no other name than 'my daughter.'"

At that moment a box in the second row in front opened up, and Judith entered in a magnificent ermine overcoat, arm in arm with her lover, her husband. And in the orchestra seats one could hear the comments, "How beautiful she is! How happy they are!"

 3

Suspicions

As Federico finished the manuscript, the last lines were more a result of guesswork than of reading, since the sun's late afternoon rays had almost entirely disappeared and night slowly entered in its black cloak scattered with stars. He felt utterly stunned, noting that Eduardo did not compliment him at all, nor did he applaud, nor did he give him the smallest sign of appreciating any part of his story, which he included among his TRAVEL EPISODES. Humiliated by his friend's indifference and resentful out of self-respect, he could no longer contain himself, and without even raising his eyes to look at him, he said with distinctly icy irony: "Eduardo, I am sorry to have bored you by reading the draft of my humble novel."

Federico's tone of voice shook his friend out of the lethargy weighing him down. Eduardo turned to look off to the side of the carriage, as if to remember where he was, and without replying at all, because he hadn't understood the reason for Federico's mood, he said with surprise, "Chico, we've passed the church of Jesús del Monte. Driver, stop!" The carriage stopped. Federico moved forward to pay for the carriage and offered his arm to Eduardo, and then they began to walk back on the same path that they had taken.

"Has something happened, Eduardo? Your face looks different—are you sick?"

"I don't feel well."

"Why did you let me send away the carriage? We'll take the first one that passes by."

"No, that won't be necessary; the fresh air is clearing my mind, and this will pass."

"But what's happening?"

"Tulita doesn't love me!"

"Always the same story. That girl is going to drive you crazy. What are your reasons for doubting her affection? Isn't she happy to see you? Doesn't she prefer you to that flock of admirers who are constantly flattering her? Aren't you proud of being envied, as a happy mortal who has discovered and won the heart of the most beautiful woman?"

"My lack of confidence is so severe that at the Menocals' dance if she commits the slightest indiscretion, I will break up with her and refuse to see her again."

"You have quite a prize with the Sun of Jesús del Monte, and your girlfriend [*corteja*]* is certainly worthy of that title. But from my perspective you are becoming more jealous than a Turk."†

"I was so excited to see her, but she wasn't waiting for me on the veranda as she had said she would be! So I'm not sure if she will go to the dance, or if she is sick, . . . or if something unfortunate has happened, and that has left me feeling deflated."

Eduardo was not telling his friend the truth. Perhaps he was worried that his friend would not be discrete, so he did not confess the real reason for his torment.

"Now you will see when we pass by her house. And if not, we will go to the house of her friend the widow, where perhaps you can ask her; they typically go together to dances."

"You're right: let's walk faster, because it's already almost seven and the dance may have begun."

---

* A provincial term that means "girlfriend."—*Author*

† The Ottoman Empire was known as the "land of jealousy" in the nineteenth century because western Europeans regarded the surveillance and control of Muslim women as evidence of their alleged heightened sexuality and the men's supposed jealousy. Dadabhoy, "'Going Native,'" 52.

Meanwhile, Federico bit his lips in anger, seeing that his friend did not say one word about his novel. Increasingly bothered by Eduardo's silence, he let his notebook fall, and naturally he had to let go of his friend's arm to pick it up.

"What is that?" Eduardo asked.

"The notebook of my travels that includes the novel that I just read to you."

"To be honest, I didn't listen to anything past the introduction."

Indeed, Eduardo was preoccupied by an idea that bothered him a great deal: he was sure that Tulita was unfaithful to him, that all her attentions to him had been mere flirtatiousness and that a lucky rival had conquered her heart and would soon win her hand in marriage. This possibility had affected Eduardo so much that even a less perceptive observer could tell by his smallest movements that the passion of jealousy dominated him. It was now time for Eduardo to confirm this disturbing possibility, and the increasingly agitated young man had plunged into an abyss of conjecture, pursuing that line of inquiry typical of the man who is truly in love and believes that there is an intrigue and that he will soon taste the bitter cup of disillusionment, a line of inquiry that always results in even more reasons for distrust, because he sees with the imagination and does not perceive what has really taken place; because he translates innocent phrases into direct insults and perceives everything from the perspective of a uniquely tinted lens. So one can see why Eduardo had not been able to comprehend one single word of what Federico had just read.

"I thought that you would have taken more interest in my story," Federico continued, "but even though the test showed bad results, it couldn't be more obvious that I have just wasted my time. So I've decided that I won't try to publish it."

"Don't lose heart; I am not qualified to pass judgment on a literary work, nor have I told you, nor can I tell you, whether I like it or not. Forgive my lack of attention, and if you want to give me a chance to make things right, leave the manuscript with me, and I will read it with great pleasure."

"Chico, it can't be today; I've offered it to the widow—you know I am courting her, and I am currently passing through the testing stage [*la época de los merecimientos*] and am careful not to promise anything specific. When she returns it to me, you can read it."

"That's fine; I won't object."

In another quarter hour the two friends reached Tulita's house. They had taken the sidewalk that was closest to the covered patio of the house. The *bomba,* a kind of lantern that served to illuminate the portico, was already lit, and thanks to the reddish light that it cast, Eduardo could distinguish four people relaxing on the veranda. His heart beat violently, and the emotion that he felt when approaching prevented him from saying the phrase that he typically used for acquaintances.

"I kneel at your feet!" said Federico.

"I kiss your hand!" the three women simultaneously responded.

The man who was with them only made a slight nod of his head. Federico looked as if he took the greeting literally; he looked at his pleasantly smiling would-be girlfriend with an expressive glance. Eduardo had to lean on his friend's arm; he was suffocating in anger. Don Valentin was at Tulita's side, and Eduardo considered Don Valentin his fierce rival. As they walked by those they had just greeted, Federico looked back twice. Eduardo silently continued walking until they had turned onto Teja Street.

"You must be happy," said Federico to his friend. "They are going to the dance; the way they are dressed doesn't leave any room for doubting that is their plan. How did my little widow look?"

"Very good," Eduardo said coldly.

"Are you still dispirited? Isn't it enough to see the happy and friendly face of your girlfriend? You're selfish—you're just upset that she didn't invite you into her house, but who cares? You are the satellite of that sun, and you are lucky to be her first lover."

"I have a feeling that a very unpleasant scene will take place at the dance."

"Enough with your brilliant ideas; you are no prophet."

"We will see."

"Is it that Tulita's mother is mixed up in this business? Does she oppose your relationship?"

"No, it's not that."

"Frankly she has a sour look for a mother-in-law, but one does not go to heaven without doing penance."

"She neither opposes our relationship nor consents to it. At the last dance she was very nice to me, allowing me to accompany her, and when we reached her house she treated me with great courtesy. The next day I made my first visit, and she couldn't have been more polite and attentive. Since I have had to keep my relationship with her daughter secret, in subsequent visits to her house I have not stayed for very long, and as a result we don't have a strong bond, nor has there been an occasion for me to learn any more than what Tulita has written me: 'You have impressed mother a good deal.'"

"Well then, friend, you have navigated well. I had thought that you no longer called on her. As for me, the one I am courting is already skilled in love. It is clear that she is not happy with having been a widow for two years and that her mother wants to see her daughter well positioned in society. I am not in the running, nor do I care for the saintly bond of marriage. *Vade retro!* Time passes and *voilà tout,* as the French say.† On the other hand, when I see her she receives me well, but she complains affectionately if I go a day without seeing her."

At this point our two friends reached the front of the house where the dance was to take place. From the *pila*‡ of Horcón to the house of María Ignacia Menocal the carriages that arrived were forming a double line, waiting for their turn to go through the main entrance gate so that the women riding in them could arrive at the dance in the most comfort. Eduardo and Federico joined the group of young men who occupied the length of the lean-to, taking care to position themselves so as to be seen by the widow and Tulita upon their arrival and to offer their arms to lead them into the ballroom.

The dance had not yet begun, despite the large crowd that had invaded the house. The musicians situated under the portico entertained the crowd by alternating between waltzes by Strauss and contradanzas habaneras.§ The *bastonero,* the name given to the director of this sort of entertainment,

---

* *Vade retro* is short for *vade retro satana,* Latin for "get back, Satan."
† *Voilà tout* is French for "that's all."
‡ Fountain.—*Author*
§ Johann Strauss the Elder (1804–1849) was known as a composer of Viennese waltzes. Alejo Carpentier has argued that fugitives from the Haitian Revolution brought the contradanza to Cuba, where it become Cubanized: the contradanza was "cultivated by all the creole composers of the nineteenth century, even becoming Cuba's first musical genre to be triumphantly exported." Carpentier, *Music in Cuba,* 147. The contradanza habanera was a creolized adaptation of the French *contredanse,* which became popular in Havana in 1809. As Malena Kuss writes, "The accompanying rhythm generally conformed to what was known as 'tango rhythm' (*ritmo de tango*) and later as *ritmo de habanera* (dotted eighth-note and sixteenth, followed by two eighth-notes). [...] *Contradanzas* published in Cuba under the name of contradanzas cubanas in the nineteenth century began to be called *contradanzas habaneras* when republished abroad, or just simply habaneras. In Cuba, the idea of nationhood became identified with the paradigmatic contradanzas for piano by Manuel Saumell Robredo (1817–70) and later with the danza, based on the same model and epitomized in the exquisitely crafted and flexibly structured forty danzas by Ignacio Cervantes (1847–1905)." Kuss, "Puerto Rico," 165.

had glanced two or three times at his watch, and since it was still a few minutes shy of eight, he did not want to give the signal. For that reason, the orchestra delayed the debut of the new danza that would begin the dance; this danza was called "La Sopimpa."* Maestro Rico, the director of the orchestra, couldn't contain his delight, savoring the imminent success of the new contradanzas he had composed. As if to set up a contrast, in what he called the introduction to the dance he entertained himself by having the orchestra play very well known pieces called "La Solita," "La Piña," and "La Chancleta."

A great liveliness reigned in the ballroom. Nonetheless, not all souls were satisfied, nor did those exuberant youths all share the same desires. There was he who received an emphatic no to his romantic overtures and angrily and despairingly put on his hat to bitterly take leave of the ungrateful woman; he who was overflowing with happiness because he had won the hand of the queen of his illusions over other pretenders; he who asked for a bottle of beer in the cantina† to excite his mind and so as to be able to speak his daring thoughts with greater ease and impudence; he who vacillated because he had come across two of his love interests, both friends and both in the same room—angry at his predicament, he quickly left to elude the girls, claiming to one that he had a sudden toothache and to the other that a gravely ill relative was in his house, fearful that the third would appear and his would be the fate of the dog in the manger;‡ he who had left home in a hurry and forgotten the money he had left in the pocket of the jacket he had changed for another and then looked for a good friend from whom he could borrow a peso§ so that he could treat his date to a milk punch,¶ beer, cider, or liquor, all refreshments that he typically offered her when she was tired of dancing; and like these, so many others who experienced varied emotions and distinct ideas, plans, illusions, and hopes.

Eduardo and Federico were also quite different from each other. The first expected a breakup; the second expected a warm reception. The first

---

* *Sopimpa* refers to a series of punches in a brawl.
† A type of *botillería*.—*Author*
‡ Orihuela is referring to the Greek fable that in its shortest form reads, "El perro del hortelano no come ni deja comer" (The dog in the manger neither eats nor does it let others eat). The Spanish Golden Age playwright Lope de Vega (1562–1634) referred to the fable in his play *El perro del hortelano* (*The Gardener's Dog*), of 1618.
§ A sterling coin worth twenty *reales*.—*Author*
¶ A kind of punch that is made with egg whites, water, milk, sugar, and anise, everything perfectly mixed.—*Author*

would fall into disillusionment; the second was ready to follow a dreamy path. For the first the horizon was somber, sad, threatened by a horrible storm; while for the other it was a happy, beautiful, diaphanous scene in which rich tapestries of gold and grain decorated the palace of the sun. As soon as the orchestra director saw that the hands of his watch had reached eight o'clock, the orchestra broke out with the beautiful harmonies of the new danza, "La Sopimpa," and into the ballroom Eduardo entered arm in arm with Tulita, Federico with the widow, and Don Valentin with Tulita's mother.

 4

Playing with Two Sets of Cards

"I think that you are absolutely right."

"That's what I think," said Eduardo, lighting a cigarette. "Tonight the question will be decided. I am going to ask for Tulita's hand; my situation permits it, so that way we will join the club . . ."

"You know that the widow is more of a flirt than a fool."

"There are more fish in the sea."

"If you had been more open to conversation, I would have told you a strange thing."

"Tell me."

"Imagine, at the dance I was at the bar ordering a bottle of beer to bring to our women when I observed that Don Valentin was carrying two colossal glasses of horchata. 'Hello, Don Valentin!' 'Comrade,' he answered warmly, 'would you like another? I will pay for it.' 'No sir, thank you. That is how a man has fun?' 'Yes sir, we do what we can, and you?' 'See for yourself.' 'They say that the little widow has driven you out of your mind,' he told me. 'What do you expect?' I answered. 'It's human frailty.' 'And who is your dance partner?' 'Hombre, don't ask: we will see. In your opinion, who is the most beautiful woman here?' 'El Sol de Jesús del Monte.' 'Well she is my date.' 'Well, done, man, well done—you have good taste.'"

"Chico, is that true?" interrupted Eduardo.

"Does two plus two equal four?" Federico continued: "The craziest thing he said, and I think he said it sincerely, and with a smirk, was 'What a fool Eduardo is to let her get away,' when in fact I saw you and Tulita were in the first group of couples to begin dancing. I couldn't help but burst into laughter so loud that I caught your attention. What an ignorant, natural-born fool he is, chico!"

"Anyone would see," Eduardo added, "that Tulita was my dance partner for every song."

"Man! Did I see it? You should have heard Matilde and her mother criticizing you from the window."*

"What do you mean, Matilde? You saw her?"

"Yes, and I spoke with them for a half hour."

"Well aren't you unruffled. Why didn't you tell me earlier?"

"Sorry, but they swore me to secrecy."

"You're picking a fight with me—goodbye, then."

"You sure know how to scheme—that's how you treat all of them. With that I take leave of you. It is now eleven, the hour when you receive your clients and when I go to my office," said Federico, looking at his watch.

"Your watch is running fast," replied Eduardo. "It's a quarter to eleven: wait a little longer."

"Compadre, you know how exacting businessmen are, and my boss is not someone to be trifled with."

---

* The original reads, "Toma. ¿que si lo ví? No fué mal vestido el que te cortaron Matilde y su madre desde la ventana." Orihuela, *Sol,* 37. This sentence was not easy to translate, and I could not have done so without the help of several expert Spanish speakers. I am grateful to one of the anonymous readers of this manuscript for the Press for an earlier version of the translation of this sentence. Two participants in the WordReference.com language forums gave me additional tips: first, *toma* does not just mean "take this" or "here," as in handing something to someone, but "¡*toma!*" is instead an "expression of surprise," as in "gosh." And *cortar de vestir,* literally "to make clothing," figuratively means to criticize someone who is absent, according to the *Diccionario de la lengua española.* So in this sentence Federico engages in his typical wordplay as he tells Eduardo that Matilde and Belencita are on to him and know about Eduardo's infatuation with Tulita. As one of the WordReference forum members wrote, a literal translation could be, "It was not a bad suit fit [*no fué mal vestido*] that Matilde and her mom styled for you [*te cortaron*] from the window." Matilde and her mom have fashioned the suit to fit Eduardo perfectly because they know that he is "playing with two sets of cards," as the title of the chapter suggests and as Matilde charges. Orihuela, *Sol,* 39.

"Come on, it's early. Come with me to the Egyptian Colonnade—we'll drink a soda and then we'll spend all day at the Café de Escauriza."*

"Man, it's just that today I can't do it. I have to go see beautiful Serafina; there's going to be a big party at her house in honor of Cheita, her mother, and I've got to go."

"Ok, we'll talk later."

"I'll see you at eleven."

"Wait, let's walk out together and you can come with me to the Colonnade."

"Agreed."

The dialogue between Federico and Eduardo that we have just put to paper took place the day after María Ignacia Menocal's dance, in Eduardo's office. It was interrupted by the arrival of a client who hoped that Eduardo would accompany him as he presented a petition before the captain general, but Eduardo declined, explaining that it was forbidden for lawyers to appear before His Excellency as a proxy or representative. It was not really a pretext but rather a legitimate excuse, because that was the way things were.

"Don't forget to tell me the results of your enterprise," said Federico, as the litigant left.

"Chico, I can't tell you a word about it until tomorrow."

"That is going to be quite funny, and I am thoroughly sorry I won't be there to see it."

"I believe it. But Don Valentín is going to end up feeling disappointed [*se va á quedar con un palmo de nariz*]."

"Careful!"

"Hombre, yesterday I doubted what was most apparent; today I don't have any scruples."

"So that idiot wants to throw the cat into the water?"

"When he gets burned, I'll be the one laughing [*al freir será el reir*]."

"Are you coming, yes or no?"

"Right now."

Eduardo had an office on Obispo Street, on the corner of Mercaderes, above García's famous cigarette shop. When they went down to the street, each bought a small box of cigarettes and walked toward the Egyptian Colonnade, an establishment that served a wide variety of refreshments.

---

* The Egyptian Colonnade [La Columnata Egipciana] was founded in 1835 on Obispo Street, near the corner of Mercaderes. Quiroga, "Bitter Daiquiris," 280.

Once they started walking down the street, they returned to their conversational thread as Eduardo asked Federico, "Why is it that tonight the widow is being left out [*se queda in albis*]?"*

"My friend, obligation always comes before devotion; Serafina expects me, and that is more important than ten widows."

"Do you know that Don Valentin is going to find himself in quite a predicament? I don't envy him."

"He is going to complain like a condemned man."

"And Matilde? How will you get by?"

"Matilde will have to wait and that's to be expected [*y tres mas nueve*].† I only see her every ninth day."

"And she doesn't get angry? She doesn't demand more of you?"

"Well, she does, but she has to put up with it with a smile on her face. Isn't it too generous of her that she plays rival to the Sun of Jesús del Monte?"

"Chico, truth be told, Matilde is a mulatta who is worth a Potosí.‡ Both are women you can count on, but I don't know what to tell you. If they were mine to choose between, I would end up . . . with both of them."

"You are always joking around, Federico."

They now reached the café on Obispo Street known as the Egyptian Colonnade. The two friends ordered soda; then Federico went off to the docks, where the office of his boss was located. Eduardo walked to his office, where a black woman [*una negra*] was waiting for him.

"Well Dolores, how is niña Tulita?" asked Eduardo, recognizing the black woman as the slave of his loved one.

"Sir, I have brought a note [*esquelita*] for you."

"Good, let's see it. Come in and wait a minute."

"Niño, I can't stay; if my mistress were to find out, it would bother her."

"I will send you off right away. Here take this," he added, putting a peso in her hand. "Hire a carriage, and you will be back in the house of your masters much sooner."

"Thank you, niño, may God reward you."

---

* Although the Collins Spanish Dictionary Online translates this phrase as "to not know a thing," or for the mind to go "blank," since the Latin *albis* refers to the color white, my translation better captures the context than those other possible translations.

† *Tres más nueve* refers to something that is inevitable. It comes from the longer expression *dos por tres, seis, y tres más, nueve* (two times three equals six, plus three equals nine). Zeno Gandía, *La charca*, 9n36.

‡ Potosí, Bolivia, was the site of silver mines as well as the Spanish colonial mint. "City of Potosí."

And the black woman made a sign of the cross over the peso and carefully placed it in the pocket of her striped dress. Eduardo quickly read the note, which only contained the following lines:

"*Chino mio,** For the sake of what is most sacred in this world, be sure to come to my house tonight. Come, but arrive before seven without fail because by then it will be getting late. I anxiously await your visit. Your faithful Tula."

"Tell her that I will be there," said Eduardo, placing the note on top of his desk.

"Goodbye, niño Eduardo."

"Goodbye, Dolores."

Tulita greatly fears that I will not show up tonight, Eduardo told himself, but she can be sure that the sun would have to fail to rise in some part of the world for me not to show up at her house as the bell sounds seven o'clock. As soon as he had made this promise, two women entered his office, and he warmly offered his hand to them. The first, named Belencita, was thirty to thirty-two years old, morena, with large, black, almond-shaped eyes. Tall, portly, and elegantly dressed, she was of an agreeable appearance, somewhat loose in her manners, but courteous and unusually eloquent. The other, Matilde, the younger of the two and darker than the first, seemed to be sixteen years old. Great eyelashes shaded her beautiful Arab eyes; her naturally curly hair fell in great curls upon her breasts, and she was slender waisted, with tiny feet and hands. She conveyed a seductive charm when she smiled, the two dimples that formed in her cheeks joining two pearly lines by her lovely mouth.

Mother and daughter had come to visit Eduardo under the pretext of a consultation on settling a redhibitory action that was the concern of Belencita, but with the main aim of confronting Eduardo about his behavior the night of María Ignacia Menocal's dance.†

---

* In the version of "Cecilia Valdés" known as *La primitiva,* because it was published as a two-part short story in 1839, many years before the novel came out, Cirilo Villaverde defines *chino* as follows: "*achinado* [...] designa [...] al hijo de mulato y negra, o al contrario" (*achinado* [...] refers to [...] the son of a mulatto man and a Black woman, or the opposite). Villaverde, "La primitiva Cecilia Valdés," 243. More simply, if problematically, *chino* was popular as a term of affection, as Raúl Fernández has confirmed. Personal communication, 3 September 2017. On *chino* as a term of affection, see also Ortiz, "Chino," *Un catauro de cubanismos,* 157.

† The *OED* defines *redhibitory* as "the annulment of the sale of an article, etc., and its return to the vendor at the instigation of the buyer."

"What a lovely surprise," said Eduardo, offering his sofa to his guests.

"We are unwelcome guests," said Belencita.*

"That isn't true," replied Eduardo. "To me your presence is and will always be pleasant. And Matilde, do you have anything to say?"

"You make me feel very uncomfortable."

"OK, let's carefully consider the charge that you make. I will respond in such a manner that you will not want to leave."

"If they let you speak, they will not hang you."

"Could you please give me a glass of water, mister lawyer?" asked Belencita.

"With great pleasure."

And Eduardo, wanting to appear attentive and courteous, decided not to call his servant but instead himself went into the antechamber, took two glasses of water, and arranged them on a platter along with honeycombs, which he then presented to his guests. As he busied himself with this task, Matilde noticed a letter in a woman's handwriting on top of one of the lawsuits that was on Eduardo's desk. Since it was unfolded, out of curiosity she picked it up. Just as she had become aware of its contents, Eduardo appeared with the two glasses of water.

"If you would like beer, you'll have to wait a minute . . ."

"No, thank you," mother and daughter answered, interrupting him.

"What's wrong, Matilde?" asked Belencita, noticing her daughter blushing as she struggled with the emotions that welled up after she read the letter.

"It's nothing, mother; my corset is too tight, and I am uncomfortable."

"Wait, I will unfasten it."

"Yes, please do me that favor. I don't feel well."

"I don't like going out with you—you are too fastidious. But, girl, your corset is already loose—I don't understand."

"Since it's so hot, it's not strange that you would not feel well. Would you like me to serve you a glass of horchata?"

"Thank you! Mother, let's hurry up and go to Manuelita's house."

"Jesus, woman, how demanding you are! I don't believe we are bothering this man because we are taking up a little of his time, even though he may wish to rest, as the dance last night surely tired him out."

"To the contrary: I am honored by your presence."

---

* Here Belencita literally says, "To the person who doesn't want cabbage, offer cabbage," but this expression would undoubtedly puzzle English speakers.

Matilde got up, and under the pretext of getting some fresh air she went out to the balcony in order to more comfortably read once again the crumpled letter that she had hidden because she felt so slighted. Meanwhile, Belencita very flirtatiously began to broach the topic that interested her, interrupting Eduardo's conversation from time to time with comments in which she impugned Eduardo for having left without saying a word at the dance at Horcón. In order to successfully extricate himself from this tight spot, Eduardo confessed that the necessity of accompanying a cousin who had recently arrived from Europe meant that he had been busy at that dance.

"And the Sun of Jesús del Monte?"

"I don't understand the question."

"Come on, don't play innocent. We know that you are a lizard and a rogue and keep secrets [*picaruelo, á boca y á cangrejo*].* If I were still in my teens, I would know how to handle you. Only a fool would trust you. Matilde sure has a tough time making herself believe the lines you feed her."

"But, hija, if you don't explain . . ."†

"Let's take up another topic; this isn't worth our time. What can you say to redeem yourself?"

"I would very much like to court her."

"You have Matilde on the run. Be honest. Why are you playing with two sets of cards? You should choose one of them or fold."

"Belencita, you are so mean."

"Let us talk about my case."

"Whatever you'd like."

"I am a very bad client—isn't that true?"

---

* According to the blog *Salud Cytan*, "La boca de cangrejo es una expresión popular utilizada en la lengua portuguesa cuando alguien se compremete en mantener secreto sobre un tema determinado, cerrando la boca y no cuenta para nadie" (*La boca de cangrejo* is a popular expression in Portuguese for when someone promises to keep a secret on a particular issue, closing his or her mouth and not telling anyone). The article explains that the *siri* is a specific kind of saltwater crab that has "a very small mouth, which the naked eye cannot see" and that it uses its mouth along with its claws to hold its prey and will keep its mouth clamped onto its prey even if it dies. "Significado de Boca de siri." I am grateful to the Spanish/English *WordReference* forums, and the contributor "boroman" in particular, for this reference.

† I have retained *hija* (literally, "daughter") here because it captures the informal, playful, and flattering tone that Eduardo has adopted to throw Belencita off his scent.

"I count myself very happy to have earned the confidence of such a beautiful litigant."

"Where the hell did you learn such things? You are so fake!"

"You judge me too harshly."

"We hope that you will meet with us tonight to talk this over; get ready!"

"With great pleasure."

"Matilde! Are you ready to go?"

"Whenever you'd like, mamá."

"You are leaving so soon?"

"*Cristiano,* other clients are waiting for you and we don't want to bother you."

While on the balcony, Matilde had taken a notebook from her purse, torn off one of the pages, and with a pencil written a few words on it; when her mother called her, she had just cried involuntary tears of despair.

"Will you come tonight?" asked Belencita, as she took leave of Eduardo.

"I will make an effort to please myself and the two of you as well."

"Read this," said Matilde, pressing a note into Eduardo's hand as she left.

Eduardo noticed that something was bothering Matilde because as she said goodbye she gave him a disdainful and meaningful look. He supposed that it had to do with his inattentiveness at the dance. The note she left launched him into a sea of confusions. He faced an enigma without a solution.

 5
Quid Pro Quo

After saying goodbye to Belencita and Matilde, Eduardo read the words Matilde had written in pencil as he climbed the stairs to his office, but the paper was moist and it was difficult to decipher its content. For the time being it was absolutely impossible; he had to wait some time for the traces of tears that had fallen on the print to dry, and then, thanks to great practice that he had had in reading all kinds of handwriting, he could comprehend the half-erased words "Goodbye forever!"

"She is so jealous," said Eduardo to himself, carefully folding the piece of paper and putting it in the pocket of his jacket. He added, "I will soon make her feel better. Never trust a dog's limp or a woman's tears."

On the same day that Eduardo received the note from Tulita and the farewell from Matilde, two individuals were seated at a table in one of the most important cafes at the commercial market of Havana, appreciated for its size, its excellent service, and its location near the Plaza de Armas, on the corner of San Ignacio Street. Both were drinking coffee, and while Cubans typically do not mix coffee with any sort of liquor, one of them kept by his side a bottle of marasquino and used it from time to time to raise the level of the coffee in his cup.

"Come on, have a drink with me!"

"No thank you, I'm not accustomed to that."

"But is it possible, Federico, that having only returned from Europe eight months ago, you have forgotten to do coffee the honor of some liquor?"

"Don Valentin, it's just that in Cuba I don't dare: it is too hot in this country, and although I am criollo, I respect that a great deal."

"What, are you insulting me?"

"I don't think I am, since I accepted your invitation to have coffee."

"And what is that book that you are reading there?"

"The poetry of Villergas, that satirical writer who has arrived on the literary scene with such great promise."[*]

"Oh, I already know him. When I was in Madrid in 1842 that author was already part of the literary scene and was among the most notable writers in the republic of letters."

"He was also my very good friend, and we have enjoyed a lot of good times together. He let me see some of his poetry, and I was among the first to praise it."

"And moving to another topic," interrupted Don Valentin, "what did you think about the dance of María Ignacia?"

"It was superb; it could not have been better attended nor livelier."

"And did you make any conquests?"

---

[*] Federico refers to the Spanish comedic playwright and poet Juan Martínez Villergas (1817–1894), who lived in Cuba for several years, where he founded the periodicals *La Charanga* (1857) and *El Moro Muza* (1859–77). Villergas had written at least a dozen books by the time Orihuela published *El Sol de Jesús del Monte*. Calcagno, *Diccionario biográfico cubano*, 689–90.

"That was not an issue. I had to be the date of the little widow all night, and you have seen that she more than merited my attentions. Were you perhaps more fortunate than I was?"

"Comrade, only to a certain point. I have eyes only for the Sun of Jesús del Monte—how beautiful she was!"

"And did you court the girl?"

"With all my soul."

"And did she respond favorably?"

"Of course. I should say that I have not yet declared my love, but she is probably aware of it. Look, I see her every single day, her mother couldn't be more attentive to me, the daughter always receives me in a friendly and pleasant manner; I believe that it is a done deal."

"And don't you have a rival?"

"Oh no! I don't pay any attention to those vulgar men who have dedicated verses to her in the newspapers, who write her cards or light her cigarette on street corners; that is just foolishness . . . I get right to the point . . . Tonight at seven is the big moment . . . And in short I am resolved to marry her."

"You are getting married! You have been keeping quite a secret."

"Yes sir, I am getting married," said Don Valentin, emptying the third glass of marasquino. "I am getting married, and this liquor I am drinking is going to help me to tell Tulita face to face, and without any more beating around the bush: 'You have won my hand and my heart.' Up to now I have not dared to speak a word to her on the topic, and for two years I have silently adored her. What do you expect? She has unique charms that . . . in short, I have not dared to say 'I love you.' But that will change today."

"Well, sir, I wish you luck."

"And tell me, is it true that your friend Eduardo is involved in a romantic relationship with Tulita?"

"I have heard of that, but I am not sure."

"Well, it doesn't matter. They have told me things, but that's just talk, the gossip of envious neighbors. It is true that I have seen him at the house of Tulita on various occasions, but there is no chemistry between the two of them. In short, for me the marriage is already a done deal. Yesterday I bought the furniture, and by next week we will already be united in holy matrimony.

"If you want me to drop you somewhere, I am headed to Tulita's house," said Don Valentin, placing a peso on the table for the waiter to cover the coffee.

"I have to wait for someone under the arches of the Tacón Theater."

"Well then, come with me in my carriage and you can get off there."

"As you wish."

And both walked out of the market. We will explain to our readers the motives for the friendship between Don Valentin and the family that he hoped to join via the honest proposition of marriage, and we will take advantage of this circumstance to introduce him and the details of his life.

When Don Valentin reached the age of nineteen, he was without mother or father and working as a servant in a house owned by a man from Santander [*montañés*] who owned a wine shop on Juan de Anda Street in Cádiz, his place of birth [*su patria*].* Since the shopkeeper had been a close friend of Valentin's parents, when the boy entered his shop in despair, crying and vulnerable, the shopkeeper took him in. The shopkeeper was a friend of the captain of a brig that was about to travel from Cádiz to Havana. Perhaps because this captain felt sorry for the youngster, or perhaps because he was indispensable as a cabin boy—Valentin was smart, agile, and perfect for the job—the captain persuaded him to accept that position on his ship. Envisioning a whole horizon of opportunities, one night he disappeared from the house of the highlander without saying a word and joined the brig *La Estrella*, where they put a lantern in one hand and a mop in the other so that he could clean the deck and begin to take control of his destiny.

After forty days of hard labor and suffering, and newly muscular from operating the pumping engine and handling other tasks on board, he saluted the superb Morro Castle in the Port of Havana and set foot on the wharf with no knowledge nor recommendations other than the friendship of the sailors and the boatswain of the brig *La Estrella*. As for the captain, after giving Valentin a bag for his possessions during the voyage, placing a couple of duros in his hands, and helping him down from the prow of the brig to the small boat that headed toward the castle, he said goodbye to the boy and never saw him again.

This was not the end of the sufferings and travails of Valentin, who was overjoyed to realize his dream of traveling to America . . . No sir: the poor man realized that one did not simply find money on the streets as his grandparents had told him, yet he was certain that in Havana the old saying

---

* According to Raúl Fernández, a *montañés* is "a person from the area of northern Spain called Santander, situated between Asturias and the Basque country. Nowadays those people are called 'cántabros' because that area has been renamed Cantabria." Personal communication, 3 September 2017.

would be fulfilled: *cum sudoris vultus tuis vesceris panis.*[*] In short, after living in Havana for eight years and owning a tavern for the last two years in Hoyo Colorado, a town situated not far from the capital, Don Valentin had enough money to set up a grocery store in the city, on San Salvador de Horta Street. By the time he had reached the age of thirty, he owned his own carriage, six slaves, and 20,000 duros' worth of merchandise and cash.

Tulita's mother was accustomed to doing most of her shopping at his store. One can find the origins of the friendship that united them and provoked Chuchita's affection for him in the warm reception that Don Valentin gave her—above all when her daughter accompanied her—epitomized by the boxes of raisins and almonds that he gave her, as well as a thousand other considerate deeds and concessions, such as not charging them the full bill. Because of this, and because Don Valentin had done her a great favor once when the landlord pressed the señora for six months' rent and Don Valentin gave it to her as a loan, allowing her to gradually pay it back, they had become closer friends, and Don Valentin was received in Tulita's house as if he were a member of the family. Don Valentin was certain that he would be granted Tulita's hand in marriage because our platonic Andaluz had not found out about her secret love.

Because everything in this world must come to an end and nothing remains forever hidden under the sun, certain people did tell Don Valentin that Eduardo, the young lawyer whom we know, was courting the woman that Don Valentin called his future bride. That put spurs into Don Valentin's desire. As we have already seen, he therefore resolved to act on his plans to wed her. That day both Eduardo and Don Valentin took the same path to the house of Tulita but did not meet each other. The first wanted to decipher the mystery of the letter that Tulita had sent to him with the help of her slave Dolores. The second, speeding off in a carriage that left behind handfuls of dust in the air, was overflowing with words as he prepared with great satisfaction the speech that he would pronounce that afternoon. Both aimed to ask Tulita for her hand in marriage, and both were unaware that together they represented a *quid pro quo.*

---

[*] "Through the sweat of thy brow you shall eat your bread." *Genesis* 3:19.

 6

Hopes and Dreams

When Matilde arrived home, she locked herself in her room under the pretext of a bad headache. She ordered Belencita not to allow anyone to enter because she hoped to rest a while before eating. And since mother and daughter had the habit of sleeping during the siesta, Belencita also went to her room, warning the black cook not to interrupt her until a half hour before dinner. As soon as Matilde was alone, she reread the letter that Tulita had sent to Eduardo. Not knowing how to avenge her lover's betrayal, she grabbed his lithographed portrait, lit a match, and watched the rapid progress of the flames that consumed both the letter and the lithograph.

"I wish I could see the two of them in flames," she mumbled, full of spite, as the two sheets of paper shrank and fluttered back and forth as they fell, turning to ash. And she began to cry, unleashing the suppressed feelings that tormented her.

"To believe in a man's word! Oh! That is impossible . . . I don't want to see him again! True happiness does not exist in this world . . . Unluckily, now another woman has come between us to disturb my lovely dream. And he had promised me that he would leave her! One can see that she is white and beautiful and can aspire to his hand in marriage. I am mulatta . . . my grandmother is black. What does it matter that I am free? I can never obtain the title of his wife because this society does not permit it, and he wouldn't want to receive the sarcasm of his friends in exchange for my true love. I am not even free enough to devote myself to his love! No one will ever know what our love could have been. Unjust society!"

Thinking along these lines, poor Matilde, with tears streaming down her face, went to her wardrobe and opened the secret drawer where she kept everything that Eduardo had given her. Untying a knot of a green ribbon that held together a packet of letters that he had sent to her over seven months, she began to read them again one by one, using her fervent imagination to transport her through the various periods the letters described. Since most of the letters only contained proclamations of love, born of the various emotions her lover had experienced, she would at times forget her anger, her jealousy, and her new resolution and instead experienced moments of the most ineffable happiness, the most innocent satisfaction, sweet and lovely tranquility.

"I am crazy," she said, kissing with great enthusiasm a bouquet of dried flowers that were a reminder of the beginning of their amorous relations. "Who could read these letters and doubt Eduardo's passion? I am unjust, he loves me. Who could say so much and not feel it!"

Now that she had calmed down, she regretted burning Eduardo's portrait. She still had a miniature one in the locket of a bracelet, and she thought it was better looking than the bigger one her lover had given her. She also kissed this memento, and now completely composed, she looked in a mirror and fixed her hair.

"What did he think when he read my goodbye?" Matilde asked herself, noticing that the notebook on the table lacked the page on which she had written "Goodbye forever!" "That would not prevent him from coming to see me tonight," she added. "He does not know the motive for that resolution, and he will come to ask me for an explanation. I will pretend that I am still angry, and he will also suffer. If he only knew how much I love him!"

And either the force of habit or the need for rest obliged her to lie down in bed, but not before she scrupulously replaced all the mementoes of her relationship with Eduardo in the secret drawer of her wardrobe. It was the seven-month anniversary of the day when Matilde, full of love and enthusiasm, had accepted Eduardo's declarations of love and promises of fidelity. She had not been able to express to him her true feelings, but she did not harbor any hopes of marrying him because of the class difference between them and the prejudices [*preocupaciones*] that existed in that colony. Nevertheless, a secret impulse, more powerful than any line of thought, launched her into that sea of pleasure and happiness, of illusions and rapture, an unfathomable ocean characterized at the shore by a happy liveliness and gentle waves but further out by terrible storms.

Even though Matilde had the fortune of being beautiful and as good as an angel and had a very pleasant character and a friendly, sweet-timbred voice, she nonetheless inevitably revealed herself to be a member of the black African race, and this situated her in a very humble position in the eyes of the inhabitants of Cuba. She would have given all the valuable properties she had inherited from her father plus all her savings if she had any... she would have preferred to go from door to door begging for change if it meant she could belong to the class of white people.

"My destiny," said the unlucky woman when she thought about her social position, "my destiny could not be more cruel: I love Eduardo with all my heart; nevertheless I will have to bear the sorrow of seeing him united with another woman. I can't flatter myself by even considering the idea that one day he will belong to me as a result of the sacred bond of matrimony!"

What kinds of hopes had Matilde nurtured while devoting herself to Eduardo? Although she now was in an unenviable position, in the ardor of her youth she believed strongly that if she left Cuba with her lover, another country would welcome them. Living with the support of another country's social institutions, even if he did not marry her, at least he would never leave her, permitting her to hold the sweet title of friend in front of everyone. These were Eduardo's promises, this was the theme of their most intimate conversations. Eduardo worked constantly, she thought, in order to amass a fortune that he would share with her in Europe; and supported by this belief that she would soon have a secure financial future, day by day the sprout of affection that she nurtured in her innocent heart grew a little bit more.

We have said that Federico accompanied Don Valentin just as the Spaniard, filled with pride and satisfaction, prepared himself to ask for Tulita's hand in marriage. Knowing that to be Don Valentin's resolution, Federico thought Eduardo would be quite interested in the news, so that was why he made his way to the corner of Cuba Street, on the pretext of needing to make an important visit to the beginning of Mercaderes Street, near the Plaza de Santo Domingo.

"I will let you go now," said Don Valentin, seeing that Federico was getting ready to get down from the carriage. "Ambrosio!"

"What does the niño wish?"

"Plaza de Santo Domingo, corner of Mercaderes."

"Yes sir." The carriage driver went in that direction.

"And be careful, maestro, with the carriage, because you have already made me buy new horns this month."

Federico was highly satisfied to see that Don Valentin on his own initiative [*de motu proprio*] redirected his carriage away from Jesús del Monte to accompany him to Eduardo's house. Federico consoled himself with the idea that Eduardo, once aware of his rival's plans, would be able to take a course of action that would thwart him.

Don Valentin stopped his carriage at the corner of Mercaderes Street so that Federico could get off and then quickly directed the carriage to Jesús del Monte via Obispo Street.

Meanwhile, Federico knocked on the door of Eduardo's house.

"What can we do for you?" asked a black man who came out to receive him.

"Is Eduardo there?"

"Niño Eduardo has left."

"Do you know when he will return?"

"At eleven o'clock, as he usually does."

"I've wasted my time," said Federico to himself.

And without saying goodbye he turned his back on the black man, taking Obispo Street toward Serafina's house.

"What an impolite gentleman," said the black man, closing the door.

Eduardo had gone to Carraguao, a neighborhood not very distant from the corner of Teja, to hand over possession of a house awarded through a legal settlement to one of his clients, and since this process would not conclude until six, he had plenty of time to reach Tulita's house before seven, which she had requested. Indeed, once he had concluded the transaction, he walked toward her house. Meanwhile, in Tulita's house the following scene took place. Since her mistress had left to visit a neighbor, the slave Dolores, left alone with Tulita, had set aside her household chores for a moment to speak with her freely about the course of Tulita's hitherto secret relations with Eduardo, relations in which Dolores had taken an active part, both out of her affection for her young mistress and because the girl had offered to take her with them if she were to marry Eduardo.

"Do you think, Dolores, that Don Valentin would dare speak to my mother and ask for my hand in marriage without asking me?"

"Believe me, Mistress Tulita, what bothers me is that you are going to clash with your mother, because from what I have seen, she holds Don Valentin in great esteem."

"As far as that goes, I have a strong enough personality to refuse to allow her to sacrifice me against my will. But have you committed the indiscretion of speaking to Eduardo about Don Valentin's plans?"

"Oh! No, señora, not one word."

"Who was with him when he received my letter?"

"I don't know. I didn't see anyone."

"He must be very worried, since he didn't send me a response by letter. He is very lazy!"

"The niña knows that people who spend the whole day writing are those who are least likely to write letters. We have heard Eduardo himself say that. And how surprised he will be when he learns about Don Valentin's scheme!"

"Don Valentin will feel terrible, Dolores, because he knew me before Eduardo did. If you could go to the corner of the street to take a look and see if Eduardo is coming!"

"And if your mother comes and doesn't find me in the house?"

"I would invent an excuse for you: I would tell her that I had sent you to the pharmacy to buy a copy of the *Prensa*."

"You know what a grouch she is. I don't dare."

"Well, it's not necessary anyway. It is already six, and he will soon be here. I don't know what's wrong with me, but I can't get rid of the bad taste in my mouth."

This conversation took place in Tulita's bedroom. Anxious about what could happen given what she called the impudence of Don Valentin, there was not one moment all day long when she felt calm. Convinced that her mother would happily accept Don Valentin's proposal as a matter of course, she foresaw the nightmare that would result and its consequences for her relationship with Eduardo. At times she was sorry that Dolores had told her about Don Valentin's plans, which the slave had accidentally overheard in a conversation that morning, but at other times she was happy that she was aware of his plan, because that way she could prepare herself to resist him by all possible means. On the other hand, Doña Chuchita had already noticed the repeated visits by Eduardo; she would instantly have understood his interest in her daughter. Would she allow her daughter to forgo an advantageous union in favor of the uncomplicated relationship that Tulita had established with the lawyer?

Tulita had discreetly made the very same observation, and more than anything else she feared that in a moment of rage her mother would close the doors to her lover, that she would then use that event to force him to ask for her hand in marriage, and that he would end up despising her rather than loving her. That is why she had hastened to make this date with her lover, to prevent that from happening and use his fears to her advantage. Don Valentin always arrived after seven; if Eduardo came beforehand, then obviously she would be in a better position to let things unfold. Tulita's mother, ignorant of what was about to happen, had left that same afternoon to pay a courtesy visit to a neighbor who was sick, a visit that she did not want to make with her daughter so that she could more quickly fulfill this boring duty and return home. With this intention, she took advantage of the first chance that arose and left a quarter hour later. As it happened, the very moment that she set foot upon the front porch, Don Valentin's carriage rolled up in front of the house.

"It's better to arrive on time than to lurk about," said Don Valentin, as he respectfully greeted Chuchita.

"I come from a neighbor's house, and I'm tired of hearing her talk of poultices and mustard plasters.* To speak to sick people is a real torment!"

And they walked into the main living room. Tulita, who heard her mother's voice, headed into the living room believing that the person to whom she was talking would be Eduardo. When she recognized Don Valentin, she blushed so much that she could barely reply to his clichéd greeting.

# 7

The Two Rivals

For a long time the conversation of Don Valentin, mother, and daughter was about general and unimportant issues. Delighted that the conversation had not turned to the topic she dreaded, Tulita steered it to distract everyone's attention and to pass the time until the arrival of Eduardo, who she believed would be a strong ally against Don Valentin. Despite her efforts, the conversation began to lull and Don Valentin offered a paper cigarette to Tulita, a cigar to her mother. As he used a match to light another for himself, he said to Chuchita:

"Señora, I have to speak with you alone about a very important matter."

A lightning strike would not have so jolted the anguished soul of the young woman as the words she had just heard.

"Whenever you'd like, Don Valentin," answered the mother. "My daughter can't hear what you have to say?"

"No, señora, my business today is a matter the two of us will have to discuss."

"Well then, please come into my room," said the woman, getting up.

"Certainly," he said, giving Tulita a meaningful look. Tulita shielded her face with her fan to hide the emotion she was feeling.

---

* In the nineteenth century, the application of mustard plaster was a common medical practice. The *OED* describes it as "a poultice made with mustard, applied to the chest or other part of the body as a counterirritant."

"Dolores!" said Chuchita, calling the servant.

"What would you like?"

"Bring a light to my room."

"Right away."

"The poor girl!" the slave said to herself, having figured out what was about to happen.

Tulita recovered once she saw that a conversation separated her from the encounter that she so dreaded. While her mother and Don Valentin went to the other room, she went out to the porch to reflect on the situation, impatient for the arrival of Eduardo.

"What is this about?" asked Chuchita, feeling ill at ease because she could not understand the reason for this mysterious meeting.

"I believe, señora, that you appreciate me more than I deserve," said Don Valentin, adopting a more respectful attitude than usual, "and I believe that you are an honest person."

"I don't understand, Don Valentin. What happened? Have they come to you with some story about . . ."

"No, no señora; nothing like that . . . In short, I'll get right to the point. I am no good with flattery or circumlocution. I am Andalusian and blunt. What I would like to know is whether or not your daughter is romantically involved with Eduardo."

"By God, you had me on pins and needles. Is that it?"

"Yes and no, señora. Please answer and you will understand."

"I do not know how to answer you on that issue. I can truly say that it is not clear to me whether or not that man is in a relationship with my daughter. Up until a few days ago he frequently visited my house, but he never said a word to me. That is as much as I know."

"Well, señora, I ask you that because I have decided to marry your daughter."

"Marry!"

"Yes, señora, immediately. Do you understand? I have loved Tulita for a long time; I see how I can make myself and your daughter happy, . . . and that's all I have to say."

"Don Valentin, I would be remiss if I didn't express my gratitude for the honor that you extend to us by choosing my daughter as your wife. If you'd like to rid yourself of any doubts right now, I will call Tulita and everything will be resolved."

"If you will allow me, señora, no, that's not what I want. Since you don't know whether or not Tulita is romantically involved with Eduardo, let's do something else: you ask her and then tell me her response tomorrow when we see each other. I repeat that I am prepared to marry your daughter without any delay if she consents to that."

"Well, you will see that she consents to that. Oh, I don't have the slightest doubt about that. She appreciates you, and I am so sure that when I tell her about your intentions there will not be any obstacles that I give you my word that everything will work out according to your plan."

"We have concluded, then. Until tomorrow."

"But are you leaving so soon?"

"Yes señora, I have a lot of things to do, and I can't hold myself up any longer."

"Until tomorrow, Don Valentin."

"Señora, if by chance the result is not favorable to my wishes, and I say these words with equanimity and pride, I would be very grateful to you if you would excuse me from paying you a useless visit. You can send a note to my house instead."

"No such precautions are necessary—don't worry."

The two returned to the living room. Eduardo was seated to the left with Tulita. He stood up and nodded slightly to Don Valentin, who answered him with an insolent look as if to say "I am the king of the house" and afterwards extended his hand to him, not without telling himself that "very soon I will be free of this nightmare."

Chuchita changed her manner of speaking to Eduardo: she spoke to him in a markedly cold manner to convey that she disapproved of his presence. Don Valentin said goodbye to all for the second time, made another bow at the door, got into his carriage, and disappeared. Tulita did not dare say a word. Familiar with her mother's character, she knew how annoyed her mother would be upon meeting Eduardo, and her certainty was only reinforced by the fed-up look her mother gave her upon sitting back down on the sofa. Her friend the widow arrived to remove her from such a trying situation.

Seizing the moment, Eduardo turned to speak to Chuchita, "Would you be so good as to speak to me in private?" "Whatever you wish, señor mio," she answered. "I sure am the confessor tonight," she said to herself and got up to lead Eduardo to her room.

Tulita's heart beat violently. She had been increasingly anxious and fearful since the day Eduardo told her of his resolution to ask for her hand in marriage. They had decided that if her mother opposed the union, she would stay in a trustworthy house until they could obtain a judge's permission for the union.

"What's wrong? Why are you so quiet with me?" asked the friend, noticing that she was silent and wrapped up in her reflections.

"I will soon explain what is happening with me, my friend. I am suffering from great anxiety. How lucky you are!"

"I don't understand."

"Oh, I am suffering terribly. I find myself in the bitterest uncertainty. If you only knew the predicament I'm in." Some tears rolled down her cheeks.

"Don't you want to confide in me? Tell me, what's happening?"

"Tomorrow you will know; today I don't have the energy to tell you anything."

"If I am a nuisance," replied the widow, "I can come back later."

"My friend, nothing is further from the truth. I am sure that you don't have any reason to doubt my appreciation for you."

"Did you know that I am quarreling with Federico?"

"What has happened?" asked Tulita indifferently, preoccupied because all of her mind's energies were focused on the conversation between Eduardo and Chuchita.

"He is a man who lies scandalously. Just imagine, *china mia,* that at the dance he presented me with the manuscript of a short novel that he had entitled 'The Mysterious Theater Box,' claiming to be its author, of course.* As you know, I spend most of my time reading. When I first saw the title I wasn't suspicious—like a fool, I believed what that trickster had told me from start to finish. The next morning, as I drank my café con leche, I began to read the manuscript, and I thought that either my memory was failing me or everything that he had written was something I had already read before and now appeared only slightly changed—I didn't have the slightest doubt about that. What do you make of the young gentleman dressing himself up with the help of another's pen?"

"There are so many such authors!"

"Well, hija, you know how frank I am. As soon as he showed up, I told him very clearly that his flour was from someone else's bag. If only you could have seen how embarrassed he was!"

Although Tulita barely paid attention to what she said, the widow continued: "Girl, he held his hat in one hand and the manuscript in the other, and without another word walked away. I suppose that he will not come back and that he will take advantage of this lesson for the next attempt. If you could have seen him—the scoundrel! All the stories he used to fool me!

---

* On the term *chino/a,* see note on page 62.

If I hadn't caught him after three or four attempts, where would he have stopped? I would have fallen for his honeyed words, and he would have captured me in his net. To have faith in someone is to be a fool."

"So you can see how far he took his *bolas*,* I will tell you from start to finish [*ce por be*] what he told me at the dance. Reacting to a quarrel between two young men who vied for the same woman, he spoke about the challenges of life, and I remember that he told me the following with great solemnity: 'I traveled to New Orleans in the year '39, and I was angry at the brother of a girlfriend, who had seen me at a quarteroon [*cuarteronas*] dance where he was courting his sweetheart.† The result was that our argument got out of control: our words became deeds, and we finally challenged each other to a duel to resolve matters to our satisfaction. Since this state prohibited duels, with the punishment being the loss of citizenship rights, if one of the witnesses denounced the participants, what were we to do?'"

"Now hear the *grilla*.‡ Equipped with swords, they hired a dirigible and floated into the sky; once they reached a height at which they could not be seen, they started to fight. Our friend ended up injured but kept it together and continued to fight. By the time the dirigible began its descent, he saw that his opponent was dead, so he threw him out of the basket and redirected the downward trajectory of the dirigible. So what do you think of good Federico's schemes?"

Tulita kept quiet because she had not heard a single word of her friend's story, and her state of mind did not allow for any distractions from the powerful sensations that commanded her attention.

"I am guilty of wanting to interrupt your reflections with foolishness that doesn't interest you—let's turn the page. Eduardo appears to be having quite a conversation with your mother. Hasn't he been there for over half an hour, and with no indication that it will come to a close?"

"I didn't want to tell you anything," interrupted Tulita, as if she wished to distract herself with conversation. "I didn't want to tell you anything because I cannot tell you the details, but judge for yourself: tonight Don Valentin asked for my hand in marriage, and Eduardo has just come to see my mother with the same objective."

---

* *Embustes* (lies).—*Author*
† Pichardo defines the cuarteron as "El hijo[-a] de Mulata y Blanco o vice-versa." *Diccionario provincial*, 194.
‡ Lie.—*Author*

"The devil you say! Many will envy your good fortune. Husbands are a very scarce and typically sour fruit. And what are your thoughts?"

"That if I can't marry Eduardo, I won't marry at all."

"It's true that it's not a difficult decision. In choosing between a lawyer and a shopkeeper, I would prefer the man of letters to the guy who sells barrels of butter—I share your opinion. It is true that Don Valentin has a lot of duros, as he calls pesos, but Eduardo is a real gentleman, has a lot of talent, and is very elegant, and at his side you would be happy."

"But I don't know what my mother thinks, and that is what has me so worried."

"Oh, she is a smart woman, and she has lived through a time when parents forced their daughters to marry according to their own desires and convenience. Without interfering in what doesn't concern me, you should expect that Chuchita will ask you what you want to do."

"Tulita!" her mother called with an agitated voice.

"Coming, mamá. Will you wait for me, Lolita?"

"Be brave," the widow said, accompanying her up to the threshold between the living room and the bedroom.

"I don't know what's happening to me, but I am trembling as if I had committed a crime."

When the young woman entered the bedroom, her mother got up, walked into the living room, and speaking to the widow who was seated near the window said, "Forgive me—I'll be with you in a moment."

"Don't stand on ceremony," Lola replied.

Before Chuchita returned to the bedroom, her daughter had just enough time to ask Eduardo, "What happened?" and to hear this response: "Your mother is being evasive."

"I have called you, my daughter, because we need to address a very serious question, and you will be the judge. Isn't that right, Señor Eduardo?"

"Yes, señora."

"Good. Don Valentin and this gentleman hope to win your hand in marriage; and from my perspective both merit my respect and praise. Tell me, if you will, whom you choose, and then I will take action. Think carefully about this, because it is your fate that you will decide."

"Mamá, since you give me your permission, I will tell you my heart's desire. The one I love is Eduardo, and for that reason I don't need to reflect at all, because I will give my hand in marriage to the one who has won my heart."

This innocent response, the child of the pure sentiments that Tulita nurtured, apparently did not fully satisfy her mother, because Tulita noticed something in Chuchita's appearance, notwithstanding the care her mother took to hide her displeasure.

"Well, please return to your friend and allow me a moment to say a few words to Eduardo."

Tulita had been anxious before going into her mother's room, where she had expected to speak her mind. Afterwards she felt as if she had relieved herself of a great burden. However, she was no less dejected and melancholy upon returning to the living room, because she had looked deep into Chuchita's eyes hoping to understand the effect of her words on her mother. Her mother's look made it plain to her that not only did Chuchita disagree with her views but she would never accept them.

This young woman was quite accustomed to observing her mother's countenance to discover her most hidden thoughts, and Tulita perfectly comprehended what Chuchita was trying to say with that look. Nevertheless, whether her imagination misled her or whether her desires painted a more optimistic picture, Tulita ended up erasing that impression from her mind when she saw her mother return to the living room with Eduardo and join the conversation with a show of great satisfaction. That night Chuchita was more talkative than usual, Tulita completely regained her composure, Eduardo seemed very pleased, and the widow was more loquacious than ever.

At eleven at night Eduardo said goodbye, using for the very first time the following phrase: "See you tomorrow!"

When she heard that, Tulita asked him, "How did it go?"

"Perfectly! I'll tell you tomorrow."

A bit later the widow took her leave, and Dolores seized the moment by accompanying her out the door.

"Lola, do you know what's happening with Tulita?"

"She's going to marry Eduardo."

"I'm so happy."

The poor slave, thinking that she would have a new master and mistress in Tulita and Eduardo, was so happy that she didn't sleep at all that night.

 8

Secret Meeting

Two days passed in absolute tranquility, without anything occurring to distract the two lovers, Tulita and Eduardo, from their romance. At night, from seven to eight, when Eduardo typically arrived, Tulita felt a sort of vertigo of pleasure and hope, which enlivened the play of emotions on her face, making her even more beautiful. Eduardo was endowed with an ardent, enthusiastic, and exalted imagination, with sound judgment, a just spirit, a resolute character, and an education that he had achieved by his own efforts. His aims and intentions in his relationship with his loved one were noble, elevated, and pure.

Relishing his feelings of satisfaction during the hours of sweet pleasure that he spent with Tulita, Eduardo completely forgot Matilde, who believed in the existence of love because she felt it and expressed it in everything she did. No longer able to silently suffer the pain caused by the sudden indifference of her lover, Matilde confided to Belencita that she had been shocked to find in his office a note from Tulita and as a result had left a note for him on a page torn out of her notebook.

Mother and daughter agreed that the true motive for Eduardo's inattention was the "Goodbye forever!" Matilde had traced with her pencil. Nevertheless, after many conversations and much reflection, the mother ended up guessing the object of his love and told her daughter, having arrived at the belief that the true cause and only motive for the absence of Eduardo could not be anyone other than . . .

The Sun of Jesús del Monte!

"Listen," Belencita said, moving close to Matilde, "I know how much you have suffered for some time, and I sympathize with you in my soul, but cheer up and don't pay any attention to men. Your father had the same personality as Eduardo—unpredictable and capricious . . . If you only knew how much he made me suffer!" Staying still and keeping very quiet, Matilde listened to her mother.

"You will be avenged without realizing it."

"What do you intend to do?" asked Matilde with a grave and sad tone.

"I don't intend to do anything now, but because, as far as I know, Eduardo's love for *that woman* . . . ," and she pronounced that word with disdain and contempt, "will be a fire that burns itself out. You have resisted your impulse to leave him—perhaps you are not capable of doing so. But his love will burn out, and then nothing will remain at the bottom of his heart but sorrow and regret."

"That must be true!" Having said this, Matilde, as if searching for any object to distract her from errant thoughts, set her hands on the keyboard of the piano and played the prelude to her favorite ballad, which Eduardo had always appreciated. Then she went to sit down again next to her mother.

"That music doesn't express anything other than sweet and agreeable sentiment. Instead it should express a hurricane of anger."

Belencita sighed and did not respond.

Matilde returned to the piano, and expressing her yearning through the pedals, she played like a madwoman, creating a discordant and unusual noise that at one point mimicked the sound of thunder. Poor Matilde! In only three days of being separate from him, she had deteriorated hour by hour, devoured by a cruel torment. She still was thinking of how it would be possible to avenge the bad treatment she had suffered at the hands of her unfaithful Eduardo.

"If at least he had answered me! He neither visited me nor wrote a word! He is not sick, I know him all too well... If only he were sick—then I would not feel guilty and anxious and want to blame him."

At times the unhappy woman toyed with the idea of sending Eduardo some objects that reminded her of him and asking her ex-lover to return her letters, but she didn't dare turn such thoughts into reality... She still had some hope yet was so fearful of losing him forever! At other times, Matilde took up her pen and wrote down some complaints that seemed so lifeless that she stopped, erased them, reread her letter, and began again...

To never finish...

Belencita, a woman with experience in love and more knowledgeable about the world than her daughter, adored Matilde to the point that she obliged her every whim because the mother had no other reminder of her abiding love for her former husband. As a result of this affection, Belencita set into motion her scheme without saying a word. Further on we will have the opportunity to persuade you that her plan was not fruitless.

Around the time when these events took place, the topic of all conversations in Cuba was a conspiracy that the local government of the island warned was about to break out. The conspiracy's aim was to overturn the government of the country and seize the reins of power for the black race, thereby destroying the white race.* The common people [*el vulgo*] saw things differently. The military commission followed the trail of suspected rebels, jails filled with captives, a large number of people expired in prison cells and on scaffolds, and many fled, abandoning everything that was dear to their hearts ... Many took their own lives ... and what is even worse, an extraordinary number of hapless blacks, their declarations beaten out of them with the lash, died victims of cruel torture ... Even such measures failed to produce evidence that the conspiracy actually took place. Blood flowed like rivers in the *tendales* of the sugar plantations of Cuba!† ... On the *cafetales* [coffee plantations] the poor blacks suffered on the ladders of punishment, in the presence of their implacable executioners! ... We must cast a veil over such monstrous deeds; someday an impartial and severe history will set the record straight. We provide this brief context so that one might understand the true state of the souls of slaves and masters [*señores*].

The conversation between Belencita and Matilde seamlessly turned to the horrors afflicting the colored race [*raza de color*], an issue that cut them to the quick.‡ Matilde contributed to the conversation somewhat indifferently, preoccupied as she was with what more directly concerned her at the moment, while Belencita forcefully expressed high humanitarian ideals. The arrival of one of their acquaintances interrupted their conversation.

"Hi Federico," said Belencita, altering her tone. "What's going on?"

"A melancholy event that has stirred up emotions and affects every soul today."

"Well, what happened?"

"Did you know Plácido?"

"The poet!" said Matilde, growing interested in the conversation.

"Yes, señora." And Federico added, "Well then, this poor man ..."—he didn't dare say *mulatto* for fear that mother and daughter would feel humiliated—"was just executed ..."

---

* In this paragraph the narrator refers to the Ladder Conspiracy of 1843–44, discussed in the introduction.
† A place where they set the sugar out to dry.—*Author*
‡ Since *Afro-Cuban* was not an available term in the nineteenth century, those of African descent were collectively known either as *negros* (Blacks) or as *la raza de color*. When Belencita and Matilde discuss the *raza de color*, they are implicitly refusing the contemporary distinction between *pardos* and *pardas* (light-skinned mulattoes such as Plácido) and *morenos* and *morenas* (those with darker skin).

"Executed!" exclaimed the two, registering surprise and compassion on their faces.

"Yes, señoras, executed, and nevertheless he swore that he was innocent. If you allow me, I will read you the detailed account of this terrible drama, which I just received in the mail from Matanzas from a friend who was an eyewitness." Matilde and Belencita moved their chairs closer to where Federico was seated. He took out a letter from the pocket of his frock coat and began to read:

"Final hours of the Cuban poet
GABRIEL DE LA CONCEPCIÓN VALDÉS (PLÁCIDO)[*]

"On Thursday, June 27, 1844, at around four in the morning, they called this famous victim to the door of the jail cell in which he was locked up, alerting him through the bars that he should get ready to go. Plácido woke up, and despite the narrow size of the side door, the poet recognized the leader of New Town, Don Antonio Solís, and exclaimed, 'It's all over now, they are taking us to die!' He immediately dressed himself without hurrying, with the composure of a hero, and as he noticed that Jorge López, one of his companions of misfortune, was gathering all his clothes to bring them with him, he said, 'The voyage that we are going to take is short: we will soon live in another warmer clime, where clothes aren't necessary.'

"With a steady step and a serene expression, Plácido left the jail and with characteristic equanimity reached the Hospital of Saint Isabel, whose chapel was to be the last juncture of the unfortunate man. They paused in the patio of the building in order to read the sentence to him and the other accused. Noting where they were going to place the handcuffs, he turned to his comrades and said:

"'Men, we tread on the first step of the scaffold.'

"After they had weighed down the first man with chains, a soldier dropped the handcuffs that he was carrying, and noticing this, Plácido added:

"'Even slaves resist the oppression of innocence!...'

---

[*] I have examined the holograph manuscript edition of Orihuela's account of the death of Plácido that the Houghton Library of Harvard University holds in its José Augusto Escoto history and literature collection. Orihuela, "Últimas horas." Although the Escoto collection attributes the manuscript to Orihuela, he copied it from a pamphlet by José María Salinero, the owner of the printing house La Aurora de Yumurí, who published it in Veracruz, Mexico, in 1844. Morales y Morales, *Iniciadores*, 171n1.

"Plácido listened to the sentence that condemned him to be executed like the rest with a serene brow and peaceful soul, while his comrades could not master the terrible emotions they felt. The mulatto Plácido, unshakably calm as if he weren't one of the victims, began to encourage them, making sound and rational reflections on the uncertainties, miseries, and disappointments of life. He sought to persuade them that it was preferable to die young, before one reached a sad old age through a thousand sufferings and martyrdoms; that the certainty of the impending arrival of one's final hour should matter nothing to a man; that individual dignity dictated that they await death with valor and strength; that many men now enjoyed immortal fame because, shielded by innocence, they had died with bravery and could have accomplished more in life; and finally, that it was preferable to die from the lead of a bullet rather than to languish in bed with a long and painful illness.

"With such reflections he succeeded in encouraging them and infusing them with the heroic resignation that never failed him. Upon entering the narrow space of the chapel, Plácido said, 'I will die singing, like a Cuban mockingbird.'

"And he then recited the ode to the celebrated Spanish poet Don Manuel José Quintana, which is on the FUNERAL WREATH of the Most Excellent Señora Duchess de Frías.* When he saw the prosecutor of his case, Don Ramón González, Plácido asked him:

"'Which one among the criminals is José de la O, who played the odious role of false informer?'

"And after the prosecutor pointed him out, Plácido spoke to him, asking him in a loud voice: Where had he met him? Had he ever spoken to him? What kind of relationship did they have? And since José de la O replied that he had never met him, nor spoken to him, nor ever been his friend, nor had they had any sort of relationship, he said, 'I forgive you all the same.' Plácido then added, 'I know that nothing will change my fate, but I have taken this step, Señor González, so that you will be convinced of the injustice that you have committed against me.'

"He spent the whole morning exhorting his ten companions in misfortune with energetic, persuasive, and at times truly sublime arguments.

---

* The narrator refers to the *Corona fúnebre en honor de la Exma. Sra. doña Maria de la Piedad Roca de Togores* (1830). Orihuela held Manuel José Quintana in very high esteem, as evidenced by the fact that he opened his collection *Poetas españoles y americanos del siglo XIX* (1851) with a selection from Quintana's verse.

When one of his companions began to lose hope, Plácido called on him to follow his own example: he would unfailingly remain steadfast and serene until the last moment of his life. Observing that Santiago Pimienta was very moved by the reflections of the mournful poet in that moment of anguish, Plácido approached him, and affectionately placing his hand on his shoulder, he improvised a poetic composition of which I have only been able to recall the following lines:*

> Open your heart's wide veins.
> May my blood flow to console your pains.

"And he concluded by adding:
"'They raise the Creoles like children and they educate them like women, but they know how to die like men!'
"For the rest of the day he was happy at times and serious at other times. At one moment he was talking to the priest who was helping them, asking him for explanations about certain mysteries of our religion; at another moment he was consoling the others, inspired by the sublime inspiration that accompanied him until his final moments, and then he was directing short epigrammatic songs at the curious who visited him. Late in the night, he asked for a pen and paper, and wrote the following verses:

GOODBYE TO MY LYRE

> Not within the filthy dungeon's grime
> Crowned by lilies and laurels sublime
> Rests the inspired lyre that would sing
> The glories of Isabel and Cristina;
> That which was offered by the sempervivum
> To the swan of Granada with graceful aplomb.
> Everlasting Lord. God of great compassion,

---

* Santiago Pimienta was a free mulatto who owned slaves and the ranch La Paciencia in Matanzas province. He was the brother-in-law of Andrés Dodge. According to the testimony of Félix Ponce, a free pardo carpenter, Pimienta "was disposed to sacrifice all his wealth for the liberty of slaves and to constitute this Island into a Republic equal to that in Santo Domingo [meaning Haiti]." Paquette, *Sugar Is Made with Blood*, 255. Pimienta's mother, Desideria Pimienta, hosted many of her son's associates at dinners but claimed to authorities that she knew nothing about the conspiracy. Finch, *Rethinking Slave Rebellion in Cuba*, 122.

Grant this, Lord; that it was not
Some luminous instrument celestial
With which Thou praised the glorious angel,
Nor is it the prostituted lute
Of a perverse and bloody criminality:
Thine was its brilliant luminosity
Thine it will be, Lord; no more profane melody
My fertile and melodic inspiration
Ay! I carry in my head a world
A world of regret and deception,
A world very different from this dream,
From this lethargic and deep dream,
A den, perhaps, for a furious genius,
I dream only of tears and bitterness.
A world of pure glory
Of justice and heroism
That is not for nihilism
To portend, a world divine
That men don't comprehend,
That the angels have seen,
And even after having my dream
I cannot understand.
Perhaps, in a short period of time
When I discern the empyrean realms
Kneeling before Thy throne
I will witness my dreams fulfilled.
And then, casting Thine eyes
On this mansion of crimes
Thou will give me grace infinite
For having left it,
Meanwhile, may the cause of my torment
Hang on a branch sacrosanct
That Thou made divine.
Goodbye my Lyre . . . thou are entrusted to God
From today on. Goodbye! . . . I bless you . . .
For thee the serene and inspired soul
Scorns the cruelty of the enemy fate;
Men will see thee there consecrate,
May God and my final goodbye accompany thee,

> Between God and the tomb one doesn't lie . . .
> Goodbye, I am going to die . . . I am innocent!

"He then wrote the following card to his wife:

> My love:
>
> Goodbye! . . . At least you may console yourself to know that my final wishes are for the peace and happiness of Cuba, and I divide my remaining belongings equally among my mother, Rafaela, and Gila.
>
> Your Gabriel.

"Later, unleashing his creativity, he wrote the following sonnet around midnight:

> **GOODBYE TO MY MOTHER—SONNET**
> The appointed lot has come upon me, mother,
> The mournful ending of my years of strife;
> This changing world I leave, and to another,
> In blood and terror, goes my spirit's life.
> But thou, grief-smitten, cease thy mortal weeping,
> And let thy soul her wonted peace regain,
> I fall for right, and thoughts of thee are sweeping
> Across my lyre, to wake its dying strain,—
> A strain of joy and gladness, free, unfailing,
> All-glorious and holy, pure, divine,
> And innocent, unconscious as the wailing
> I uttered at my birth; and I resign
> Even now, my life; even now, descending slowly,
> Faith's mantle folds me to my slumbers holy.
> Mother, farewell! God keep thee, and forever!
> —The Pilgrim.[*]

"The décima that I include below was also written by Plácido on that night:[†]

---

[*] Translated by William H. Hurlburt in his "The Poetry of Spanish America," 148.
[†] The décima is a popular improvisational form of verse put to song. See López Lemus, *La décima constante: Las tradiciones oral y escrita*.

TO JUSTICE—PLATONIC LOVE

In the soul, like the evening star
Resplendent, itinerant,
I hold the divine portrait
Of the deity that I venerate:
In vain do I hope to find
This ideal beauty
And I long to search for
The celestial mansion
Because I do not think
The original exists on earth.

"And he finished playing his lyre by offering the following poem:

ENTREATY TO GOD

God of unbounded love and power eternal,
To Thee I turn in darkness and despair!
Stretch forth Thine arm, and from the brow infernal
Of Calumny the veil of Justice tear;
And from the forehead of my honest fame
Pluck the world's brand of infamy and shame!

O King of kings!—my fathers' God!—who only
Art strong to save, by whom all is controlled,
Who givest the sea its waves, the dark and lonely
Abyss of heaven its light, the North its cold,
The air its currents, the warm sun its beams,
Life to the flowers, and motion to the streams!

All things obey Thee, dying or reviving
As thou commandest; all, apart from Thee
From Thee alone their life and power deriving,
Sink and are lost in vast eternity!
Yet doth the void obey thee; since from naught
This marvelous being by Thy hand was wrought.

O merciful God! I cannot shun Thy presence,
For through its veil of flesh Thy piercing eye

Looketh upon my spirit's unsoiled essence,
As through the pure transparence of the sky;
Let not the oppressor clap his bloody hands,
As o'er my prostrate innocence he stands!

But if, alas, it seemeth good to Thee
That I should perish as the guilty dies,
And that in death my foes should gaze on me
With hateful malice and exulting eyes,
Speak Thou the word, and bid them shed my blood,
Fully in me Thy will be done, O God!
 In the chapel of Santa Isabel at one in the morning on June 27, 1844.
 GABRIEL de la CONCEPCIÓN VALDÉS.*

"At two in the morning he began to write his testament with a steady and secure hand, as he had written his previous poetic compositions, which one can verify by observing his penmanship. At about three thirty he called for a scrivener to authorize his final instructions. After completing these formalities, he conversed for a long time with this public functionary. A few moments after five in the morning he approached the scrivener again and in a low voice but with surprising insight told him:

"'I have finished sweating out the malign and vicious fever. Until this moment I had not truly known all the bitterness and terror of the fatal crisis I face, but my heart is still inspired, it is whole and functions with all of its natural energy; with that same resolve you will see me seated on the bench.'

"At a quarter to six, as he descended the final steps of the entrance to the hospital, he began to recite the verses of the ENTREATY, troubling the priest, who worried about the words of the poet without being able to silence him, words that inspired the other conspirators and the immense crowd assembled to bid farewell to him on the scaffold, who were keenly interested in the popular victim. The celebrated poet Plácido surprised them all by courageously draining such a bitter cup.

"He walked with a steady and measured step to the beat of the drum and reached the place of punishment. Upon arriving, while they chained his comrades to their respective benches, he turned toward the immense crowd that had gathered close to the scene and raising the crucifix that he held in

---

* Translated by the poet John Greenleaf Whittier in "Placido, the Slave Poet."

his hands, he said in a loud, clear, and distinct voice, 'Goodbye, beloved nation! . . . I ask for the pardon of all. Pray for me.' He paused and then continued: 'I indict Don Francisco Hernández Morejón and Don Ramón González for all eternity.'" They immediately ordered him to sit down, and when they fastened his hands to the stake projecting out from behind the bench, he said very clearly, 'Don't tie me down. I always keep my head lifted up.' Nevertheless, the soldier, complying with his dismal duty, tied his hands firmly. Once the signal was given, the priests left the scene, the order was given to fire, and the detonation was terrible to hear!"

When he reached this part of the account, Federico took out his handkerchief and dabbed his tears. Matilde and Belencita had not stopped crying since he began reading. Returning to the story, Federico said, "Every moment of the life of such a singular man was extraordinary until its very end; he offers an example perhaps without precedent in the annals of humanity. One could say that even the bullets respected him, because once the smoke of the gunfire had dissipated, he was the only one left who not only showed signs of life but lifted up his head and turned to the people shouting:

"'Goodbye world! Don't you pity me? Fire away!'

"At that moment three bullets pierced his body. A second discharge ended the days of the unfortunate and extraordinary poet, a man certainly worthy of another, nobler end. His final moments portray him just as he was, revealing all the passion and nobility of his brave soul. Plácido had died innocent, and the stain of this crime would have to fall on the head of someone, and this individual would have to live under the burden of a life of regret.

"But is the conscience of a tyrant capable of regret? . . ."

Federico put the manuscript away; taking leave of Matilde and Belencita, he urged them to be silent and discrete.

---

* Francisco Hernández Morejón was named captain of the rural militia of Sabanilla, near Matanzas. Ramón González was a prosecutor who has been dubbed the "murderer of Plácido." On Hernández Morejón, see Morales y Morales, *Iniciadores,* 158. On González, see Bachiller y Morales, "Plácido," 555, 559.

 9

The Disappearance

"Has her mother treated you well, Eduardo?" asked Federico, having run into his friend at the Tacón Theater four days after Eduardo obtained permission to continue in his amorous relations with Tulita.

"Things couldn't be better, chico."

"So Don Valentin has been left in the lurch [*ha quedado á la luna de Valencia*]."*

"Neither more nor less than the saints of France, with their pale, blind eyes."

"When is the big day?"

"My wedding day? That is a bigger deal. Within six months—I need to get to know my fiancé and see whether things work out."

"And you won't change your mind in the meantime?"

"Like you, I'm a gem of a guy and I live by my principles."

"Do you say that because of my courtship of the widow?"

"Precisely."

"Oh, what a joke!"

"What do you mean?"

"Well, it's obvious."

"I don't understand."

"You don't?"

"Not in the least."

"Ha, ha!"

"You laugh?"

"That's the only thing I can do."

"As you wish."

"But man, if you play the lover, with so much vanity and pretension, then truly I believe that will deliver a good result."

"And what is that?"

"That you will get married."

---

* According to the online *Diccionario de la lengua española* of the Real Academia Española, to be left "a la luna de Valencia" (literally, "on the moon of Valencia") means to be discouraged in one's aspirations.

"Get married? Have you lost your mind?"
"So..."
"So..."
"It's only an amusement, right?"
"Obviously."
"My friend [*Calavera*]!"*
"Chico, I have not been able to forget the customs of France."
"What, to fall in love and be happy?"
"That's how the world turns!"
"Not I," said Eduardo, with a more serious look. "I am going to get married. I've given my word and it is a done deal."
"And poor Matilde?"
"That love affair has been a pastime; I don't have two bodies, and between Tulita and her..."
"The thinnest thing always severs a rope. In Switzerland one time I was involved with three women, and they were sisters, and if you only knew how much work it was for me to get out of that mess. There was a brother as well, a captain, who proposed to divide me in two with one slice, but fortunately I got out of there just in time, and not because I was afraid."
"Enough."

---

* See Orihuela's note on page 123. *Calavera* literally means "skull" or "skeleton," but here it is a corrupted form of *carabela* or *caravela*, which scholars have frequently misunderstood. Pichardo argues that African-born slaves used the term *carabela* to express solidarity with one another: "This is a very common word among African-born slaves [*negros bozales*] who are somewhat assimilated, signifying a compatriot who came from Africa in the same boat." *Diccionario provincial*, 140. However, Fernando Ortiz has shown that there was a more specific meaning for *carabela* rooted in the practices of a secret society of Congo witchdoctors: "*Kindembo*, or *Ki-ndembo*, is the name of an ancient secret brotherhood of African Congo witchdoctors that had some influence in Cuba. [...] It is from this society that the term *caravela* emerges, a term that was very common in Cuba during the times of slavery. Many have understood this term to mean 'fellow slave brought to Cuba in the same slaver,' but this was the mistaken etymology of the Spanish speaker, who believed that the word meant 'brought in the same carabela.' By the time the slave trade had become a larger-scale operation, *carabelas* no longer existed in the ocean. The African word *caravela* was a Congo word. It indicated a certain company that one kept, but this was that of having been initiated along with others into the fraternity of the Ndembo. *Caravela* meant in Congo *kala*, 'perennial and irrevocable condition or being a sworn life member,' and *vela*, the 'secret place where the sworn initiation of the Ndembo took place.'" Ortiz, *Los instrumentos de la música afrocubana*, 3:423. I am indebted to Raúl Fernández for this source.

"It was not fear that drove me away: it was a precautionary measure, because I was in up to my neck in another much more interesting labyrinth."

"Strange things always happen to you."

"Oh man, don't say anything—the episode made me suffer a long time. You see, in Brussels I was engaged to an employee in a tobacco shop, lovely like love itself and blonde like gold. The girl, knowing that I lived in Bern, where the three sisters lived, meddled in my affairs all day long and discovered me reading a letter from my presumed triple father-in-law challenging me to a duel. She cried and yelled at me, and I allowed her to ask a judge to prevent the duel. The judge gave me a clear choice: either they would throw me into jail or I would return with her to Belgium. When night fell, I didn't show up as agreed but left a letter daring my foe to follow me to Brussels, explaining the motives for my sudden disappearance."

"What a con man," Eduardo said to himself, as he offered Federico a box of paper cigars.

"You smoke Mendozas?"

"It's the factory I've been using for years."

"Well thanks—mine are made by García, 'my fame crosses the globe.' It's the brand that I like best."

"It's six o'clock," said Eduardo, consulting his watch.

"One doesn't have to ask where you are going tonight."

"Well frankly, I don't know what's wrong with me: I was about to not go to Tulita's house and instead go over and give some satisfaction to poor Matilde."

"Man, don't be cruel: leave well enough alone [*lo que no has de comer déjalo bien cocer*]. How can you let that unhappy creature, who suffers so much from the humble social position she occupies, experience ill-treatment in addition to adversity?"

"You are right. So I will take the bus [*guagua*] to the corner of Teja Street, then in a hop, skip, and a jump I'll be at Tulita's house."

"Would you forbid her to be called the Sun of Jesús del Monte once you had received the nuptial benediction?"

"Of course, that would be the end of that nickname."

"But you are going to go there later. Would you like to go to Escauriza to drink a soda?"

"I just drank a coffee."

"Well let's walk on the avenue toward the Castillo de la Punta."

"Hell [*Diablo*], that would be too far; instead we could see the most beautiful women walking toward Carlos III."

Both began to walk on the tree-lined street that runs next to the botanical garden, now the site of the rail station called the Villanueva stop.

"And your Serafina?" asked Eduardo, returning to the earlier conversation.

"She is also water under the bridge."

"What?"

"Done for [*Tronitis*]!"*

"So soon!"

"I was already bored."

"Bored?"

"I'm not made to be a babysitter."

"I don't understand."

"I don't like educating little girls."

"Is she that young?"

"Thirteen years."

"And so what was she like?"

"*Bocato cardinali.*"†

"And you are leaving her?"

"I'll tell you, she is the spoiled daughter of a scrivener, and I don't want any dealings with those Pharisees."

"So you fear the courts, eh?"

"Do I fear them? I'm in an absolute panic! . . . *Vade retro . . .*"‡

"Ah, you are finally coming to your senses."

"Because of my fear of tribunals?"

"No, because of how suddenly you gave up on your pursuit of the widow and Serafina."

---

* I could only find rough approximations for *tronitis*, which sounds vaguely like a word in Latin. The closest word in Latin is *thronus*, which means "lamentation," "dirge," "song of mourning," or "elegy." The closest word in Spanish would be *tronido*, which literally refers to a thunderclap and figuratively refers to a disaster or fiasco. Given Federico's linguistic playfulness, I think *tronitis* connotes the finality and suddenness of his breakup with Serafina.

† Federico is referring to what Spanish speakers imagine to be the Italian expression *bocatto or bocato di cardinale*, meaning "a cardinal's mouthful," or food fit for a cardinal. However, Italians don't use that phrase; instead, it is a rough translation into incorrect Italian of the Spanish phrase *bocado de cardenal*. In Italian a mouthful is a *boccone* or *bocconata*, not a *boccatto* or *boccato*. So the phrase is what the blog *Fraseomanía* calls "a phrase made in false Italian—an uncommon linguistic fake." Rafa, "Bocato di Cardinale."

‡ See note on page 56.

"Well, that is not even the best news; it's that in good times I'll be a living example of the vulgar ditty

> I am alone, I was born alone,
> My mother gave birth to me alone,
> Alone I must go,
> Like the arrow in the sky."

"I envy your good humor."
"And I envy you for your woman."
"Do you want her?"
"I have nothing to give you for her. Would you like a jacket made from fine linen and a white pique waistcoat?"
"You joker!"
"Well it's not as if I am the first to make such a proposition."
"You always have something to say. What are you saving for when you are old?"
"There will be a storehouse of stories, you'll see."
"Come on, tell me, because you entertain me a great deal with your tales, and today I'm so upset that I can't stand myself."
"Then listen. While I was in Madrid, living on Fuencarral Street, there was a Sevillana with black eyes—in short, she was gorgeous and embodied the spirit of Andalusia [*con toda la sal de Andalucia*]. She lived in the room next to mine, and since the grille of her door faced the main resting area of the stairway, whenever I used the stairs I checked whether the grille was locked or not. That woman—and it goes without mention that anyone who says the word *woman* implies someone who is curious—most of the time left the little door either open or unlocked, so that she effortlessly fulfilled the role of the sentinel of the house. This meant that she saw me sometimes in amorous relations with a woman and followed me all the way to the entrance of my room. So when I flirted with her, she reminded me of all my philandering. Although at first I preferred to be a martyr rather than a confessor, there was no way out; I proposed to exchange my girl, as well as an overcoat and a pair of boots, for her."
"To whom?"
"To her father, or to the first who would accept my proposal, as long as she would accept me as her boyfriend."
"And how did she reply?"

"She laughed like a crazy person and closed her door in my face. Nevertheless, two months later we were walking arm in arm on El Prado, we ate breakfast in front of the Castellana Fountain, and we went to drink a lovely moscatel accompanied by grilled chestnuts at both the upper and the lower Caravanchel."

"She was definitely wife material [*Eso merece cuarentena*].*"

"Seeing is believing."

"To change the subject," said Eduardo, "have you seen Don Valentin?"

"No."

"What do you think he is up to?"

"He probably walks around feeling rejected."

"And he was so open in his pursuit of Tulita."

"That's a bad sign."

"Why do you say that it's a bad sign?"

"Because I have observed that for one to be successful in such endeavors, one must be carefree."

"That's what you think."

"Oh, if we were walking more slowly I would tell you a long story in which in order to flatter a woman I came across like the black man in the sermon, with my hands on my head and cold feet."

"I won't delay my visit any longer," said Eduardo. "That's the end of the story for today. Driver! Driver!"

"Well, chico, send my best regards to Tulita."

"Goodbye."

"Bye."

Eduardo had entered the bus that was headed to San Salvador de la Prensa and therefore passed by the corner of Teja.

"Are you headed to Cerro, attorney?"† asked one of his clients, a *guajiro*,‡ the only person whom he encountered upon entering the carriage.

"No sir," Eduardo answered. "I'm getting off at the corner of Teja."

"So is it true that they have killed the mulatto Plácido with four shots?"

---

* *Cuarentena,* which derives from the word *cuarenta,* "forty," refers both to a quarantine and to the Latin American tradition of helping the mother of a newborn for the forty days after pregnancy by caring for both her and her child. Parker-Pope, "How to Mother a Mother." This period often involves a prohibition of sex. Tuhus-Dubrow, "Why Won't This New Mom Wash Her Hair?"

† Although now Cerro is a *municipio,* or borough, of Havana, it was founded as a town in 1803. "Cerro (La Habana)."

‡ A laborer in the countryside of Cuba. —*Author*

"Yes sir. The military commission has ruled that the unfortunate man is one of the leaders of the conspiracy."

"Those mulattoes are so evil! I have not yet run across a good one, Mr. Attorney [*señor Licenciado*]."

"There is everything in the vineyard of the Lord."*

"I am horrified by the sight of those raisins."†

"That is prejudiced!"

"You may say what you wish. I am not well read, nor do I write well as you do, but I have seen so much in the coffee plantations on which I have worked as overseer [*mayoral*] that I swear by the Virgin that nothing good comes from Guinea."‡

"Well, friend, I do not have slaves, nor have I ever owned them, since I emancipated those who fell under my control as a result of the death of my father. I hire servants, and they could not serve me more to my liking."

"You are too good, Mr. Attorney, and you use your heart to judge others. One must treat blacks like soldiers, with food and a stick, with bread in one hand and a lash in the other. I own a little fourteen-year-old black girl. When she came under my control nine months ago, she was worse than Aponte, but today she is as tame as a ewe.§ I would like you to see her: in short, if you won our argument, I would give her to you."

"I greatly appreciate the offer, but I am sorry that I must tell you that I cannot accept it. As I've said, I have never wanted to own slaves."

---

* This saying makes reference to the following passage in Isaiah 5:7 in the Old Testament of the Bible: "The vineyard of the Lord of hosts is the house of Israel."

† The curly hair of people of color.—*Author*

‡ Here *Guinea* is a metonym for the continent of Africa.

§ For another use of this phrase in a nineteenth-century Cuban novel, see Villaverde, *Cecilia Valdés, or El Angel Hill,* 90. The Aponte Conspiracy was an antislavery rebellion involving free people of color and slaves in Havana in March 1812 that was spearheaded by Afro-Cuban *cabildos,* or mutual-aid societies. On 14 March 1812, spurred on by rumors that military leaders from the Haitian Revolution were offering to spread their revolution to Cuba, a group of free Afro-Cubans and slaves burned down the Peñas-Altas plantation and killed the whites there, and on subsequent days the rebellion spread to three nearby plantations. The insurgents then hid in the countryside, and the Cuban army spent months hunting them down. The presumed leader of these rebels, José Antonio Aponte, was a free Afro-Cuban sculptor who was a member of the Batallón de Morenos (Free Black Militia), and according to some scholars he was also a member of the Cabildo Shango Tedum. Aponte had hosted meetings of the rebels at his house and a tavern, and he had written a letter to plantation slaves asking them to participate in the insurrection. Childs, *1812 Aponte Rebellion,* 122, 140–44.

"But one can't refuse such an offer, Mr. Attorney. I will write up the bill of sale and you may sell her to someone else."

"No, my friend, I cannot engage in acts of domination over other people. What can I do? It's in my character."

"What a strange thing!"

"It's my practice [*costumbre*]. Moreover, wherever one finds abuse, wherever one finds wrongdoing, there I will go to seek justice."

"But, my dear Christian, how is it wrong for me to buy and sell a slave?"

"It is indeed a great wrong, my friend. Because I have a generous heart, I will always side with the oppressed. I believe strongly that oppression is never just; tell me, given this principle, do we have the right to oppress our fellow men?"

"I understand, Mr. Attorney, and you are absolutely right. Right now [*ahora mesisimo*] I am falling into something I don't understand; attorneys are such devils.* Truly, as for me, I would not like to find myself mixed up with blacks."

"Well, you yourself give the reason without the need for further commentary: blacks are men just as we are; they are endowed with intelligence, with reasoning, and with the same aptitudes that you and I have. What, then, gives us the right to sell them and treat them as if they were irrational animals? Do you think it would be right for me to place you in servitude, to punish you cruelly whenever I wish, to speculate with the sweat of your brow, and even to kill you with impunity for a few gold coins?"

"You speak like a book, Mr. Attorney [*señor letrado*], and now I will say, as do many men such as yourself, that blacks may as well be happy and earn salaries because they would have many benefactors. From this moment, I renounce my job as an overseer because I am just as Christian as the next guy, and as for getting rid of my fellow men, sir, I do not want that. If you would be so good as to educate me during your idle hours, I would spend many profitable hours at your side with my mouth wide open [*con un palmo de boca abierta*]."†

"Any time you want, my friend, you will find me ready to tell you what I consider to be just, based upon my humble opinion."

"Mr. Attorney [*señor licenciado*], I love humanity very much, just as I care about my oxen and my farm."

---

* The guajiro's phrase "ahora mesisimo" marks him as uneducated.
† A *palmo* was a unit of measurement equivalent to twenty centimeters.

"Well, I desire your well-being and success as I desire my own. Whoever loves his country and oppresses those outside it loves neither liberty nor his fellow men and is selfish, a man unworthy of what counts among good men."

"If I had only had a teacher like you. I used to ask the priest how to count to five, but the priest spoke Latin and said so many things at once that I ended up being confused. Would you believe that last Lent he prohibited us from playing the *tiple?*"*

"That is not strange to me in a country in which there is no . . ." And when Eduardo said the last word in his ear, the poor guajiro opened his eyes wide. "And this follows: when you come to my house to consult, you must speak not only about the dispute but also about any doubts you may have so that I will be in the best position to clarify things to your liking."

"We have arrived at the drinking fountain of Horcón, and there is still a ways to go to reach the corner of Teja, so would you be kind enough to explain something to me?"

"Sure."

"I have heard people use the word *patria,* and I understand that to mean the land where I was born—am I mistaken?"†

"To a certain extent. The real nation is the world; that sentiment that men call nationalism is a complete lie. Where there are no social virtues there is no nation. Anyone who suffers is a brother, and we must help him; whether a man is born in France or in England, he is still our brother. It is a lie to call the Spaniard a Spaniard and a criollo, criollo. No, sir, we are all brothers; our true nation is the world. You see, I was born in Africa, but nevertheless if you need me I am your brother, and wherever the oppressed can be found, there I will be to help them, to the extent that it is possible."

"Good, very good. I am happy to the depths of my soul that this conversation has helped me to open my eyes." The guajiro added, shaking Eduardo's hand, "I appreciate it with all my heart." Changing his tone of voice, he said, "Would you please do me a favor?"

"Whatever you want."

"When you get off at the corner of Teja, I am going to get off as well."

"So?"

---

* A kind of guitar whose body one generally makes with a fruit of this country that is called the *guira.*—*Author*
† *Patria* literally means "fatherland"; "nation" is a rough equivalent.

"I have here," and he pointed to the pocket of his pants, "four reales that my woman doesn't know about, and we are going to drink some beer."

It is the custom to accept such an offer from a guajiro because when a group of people are so traditional in their customs, to reject such a spontaneous invitation would create a very disagreeable scene. Knowing this, Eduardo did not reject the friendly invitation.

Indeed, once they reached the corner of Teja, the litigant and his client got off, and the two entered the tavern at the corner of Jesús del Monte Street.

"Waiter," said the *montero*, "one of your best bottles of beer!"*

"The one that goes by the name of pé pé," added Eduardo.

At the counter of the bar, Eduardo and the guajiro clinked glasses and then drank.

"To your health, Mr. Attorney!"

"To the health of us both, my friend!"

A bit later, the guajiro continued walking along Del Monte Street, reflecting on the words his lawyer had spoken. Eduardo walked up Jesús del Monte toward Tulita's house. It was already past 7:00 at night. Although on the island of Cuba the sun rises at 5:30 in the morning, it usually sets at 6:15 or 6:30, making artificial light necessary at that hour. Since Eduardo was walking on Jesús del Monte Street at six, all the porticoes and roofs had streetlamps guiding pedestrians, thereby avoiding the fine that was imposed on residents who did not abide by that law.

Eduardo felt confused when he couldn't see the light on Tulita's portico, which should already have been on, but it often happens that because the servants are involved in other tasks or are forgetful, they are late at lighting the lamps. Continuing his walk, he said to himself, "That is a rare negligence on the part of Chuchita. It would be a miracle if the head of the neighborhood [*capitán del barrio*] did not force them to pay the fine specified in the proclamation of good government." Eduardo grew even more surprised when he reached the front door and could not see the faintest glimmer of an interior light. "That is very strange," he said to himself. "They must be busy in the inner bedrooms." In many houses in Havana and beyond the city walls [*extramuros*], it is common for people to light the lamps in the inner rooms and leave the main living room in complete darkness,

---

* In general, *montero* refers to a man who makes his living by hunting in the mountains. But in the context of Cuba, *montero* is a rough equivalent to *guajiro*.

thereby avoiding heating up the house with artificial light. They tend to light the lamps in the living room only when entertaining guests.

"I've never seen the likes of this before," continued Eduardo, his mind racing. "But either someone is ill in Tulita's house tonight or it is very hot. We are in the last days of the month of June, and that wouldn't be strange." However, when he reached the porch he noticed that the door and the window were both shut tight. "Perhaps they suddenly moved and didn't have time to notify me—let's see." And he knocked at the neighbor's door.

"Señora," said Eduardo to an elderly lady who opened the door, still unsure of what was happening, "could you tell me where the neighbors in number fifteen have gone?"

"I couldn't tell you because I don't know. I don't think the other neighbors know either."

Eduardo was left dumbfounded. He knocked on the door of number 15 two or three times. That family had disappeared.

 10

Treachery

Havana's general appearance is odd. The foreigner or traveler who visits the city is typically surprised because although many of its streets run in a straight line, this principle of regularity is not always strictly observed in the city itself. Standing before a magnificent building such as the house the Most Excellent Señor Don Joaquín Gómez inhabits, one can find right next to it a tiny one-story house, and the most modern, tasteful, and elegant building can stand next to the soggy walls of a convent or the crumbling adobe of a hut, the miserable refuge of a pauper.*

On San Salvador de Horta Street, as we believe we have said, Don Valentin kept his general store. Although the house he owned had two stories,

---

* Joaquín Gómez was "the most important businessman of the decade of 1830" in Cuba. Born in Cádiz, Spain, Gómez was a cofounder of the first bank in Havana. Thomas, *Cuba*, 141–42.

the second was actually a shrunken mezzanine that was so narrow and dark that a person couldn't stay there for long—it was a garret [*zaquizamí*] of sorts. Since one couldn't open the windows, or more accurately, the bars of that small prison, one who dared to stay in that room for a quarter of an hour could easily asphyxiate.

Next to that house, which was a constant insult to those beside it, existed two magnificent and opulent buildings, true palaces compared with that ill-begotten place, which was a monument to either the fantasies or the poverty of the owner. In the humblest of the three houses one could find Don Valentin, and since he was always on the watch for anyone wishing to purchase one of those indispensable goods that he made available to the public, he chose for his bedroom the dingy mezzanine. The small man frequently went out in his carriage to show off its silver trimmings. He kept the carriage in the garage of an old acquaintance of his, who because he was his compatriot charged him double the typical rent. This was a detail that this good Andalusian had not noticed since he was so obsessed with his carriage.

It would not be necessary to point out that Don Valentin, who was instructing his driver to set up the carriage, believed that on special days every decent person must display his carriage. And it was equally obvious that Don Valentin would never expose his carriage to the curious public on rainy days, because there was an astounding abundance of mud on the streets and it was not pleasant to soil the mahogany of one's carriage. The day in question was stormy: the mud forced everyone [*cada quisque*] to stay home; nevertheless, Don Valentin had gone out, so the errand must have been urgent. The clock at the Convent of San Francisco had sounded seven o'clock when Don Valentin arrived home, covered in mud from head to toe and angrier than a gambler who has lost his last coin.

"What happened, Don Valentin?" asked the head porter of the office, seeing him enter so splattered with mud.

"Man, don't say a word. I had just gone out, you see, to buy something at Plaza Vieja, and I had not quite reached the corner of San Ignacio street, when zás . . . a rogue of a black carriage driver goes by—and look at what he has done to me."

"You are covered in mud up to your ears."

"My soul is probably all muddy too, and may the person who invented mud be damned."

"And you are coming to get changed?"

"If only that mangy dog of a driver would do the same! I would like him to change his skin just as I am going to change my shirt . . . I have never given anyone such a delightful beating in all my life."

"And your cane is missing its handle."

"No handle?"

"Yes, sir. Look," and the porter showed him the cane.

"I am just sorry that the handle was made of gold, but it's all the same given the state I'm in. That drunkard couldn't have chosen a better time. I left him rolling in the mud. From the first blow he jumped from his horse like a flying fish [*lisa*],* and before he fell I hit him with more wood than a mule could carry."

"I hope his owner doesn't show up and ask for damages!"

"Let him come, as long as he doesn't carry a bigger stick than his slave."

"And if they initiate a *sumario* against you in court?"†

"The shoemaker of the captain general is my buddy; just yesterday we dined together. Let the scribes and Pharisees come and try to take things away from me, just as the best chemist can try to melt down diamonds to get gold."

"Do you know who has taken the place of the owner of the flower shop?"

"Who?"

"The guy who opened a secondhand shop a few days ago at the entrance to the Portals of Alfaro."

"No, so?"

"He is unbelievable," said the employee, placing his pen behind his ear. "You are going to see how stupid he is."

"You may have heard of that swindler [*tripili trapala*] of a lawyer Juan B . . . , who by all measures is a mulatto. Well, his scrivener was penniless [*estaba como suele decirse á la cuarta pregunta*], and having consulted with him, he indicated the way forward: twenty ounces of gold. The scrivener gave him such good instructions that you will be surprised how he attained that sum."

"The fact is that that morning he showed up at the secondhand shop to buy some scissors to cut paper."

"Yes, yes, I understand: but clean me up here . . ."

"Where?" said the employee, wanting to please his boss.

---

* A type of fish that is quite popular in Havana.—*Author*
† Criminal proceedings.—*Author*

"No, look man, don't be so stupid! Clean my eye: it's splashed with mud and it's hurting me."

The employee took out a cambric handkerchief, and as he did as Don Valentin had asked, he continued:

"Standing in front of the owner, he asked for scissors."

"That's fine," said Don Valentin to the man who was holding his handkerchief and who had just stained his shirt with the mud he had removed from his boss's right eyelash.

"So, as I was saying, the poor man showed him the scissors, and the other simply asked him the price. 'Six reales,' answered the shopkeeper. 'Six reales!' exclaimed the customer, incredulously. 'Six reales and not one *chico** less,' answered the shopkeeper. Then the customer went right up to the shopkeeper's ear and said to him something very offensive. 'You are insolent,' said the shopkeeper out loud. 'What insolence?' the customer asked. 'You insult me.' And he once again whispered in his ear, 'Go to the devil, you scoundrel!' '*You* are the impudent scoundrel.' Finally things came to a head: the shopkeeper raised his measuring rod, and not only did he strike the ribs of the insolent customer but he also left a two-inch wound on his head."

"Very well done," replied Don Valentin. "I would have done the same."

"But what happened next is that the wounded man yelled, 'Help!' . . . Witnesses testified, and since no one had heard his provocations, all the employees of the neighboring shops believed in good faith that it was the result of the outrageous behavior and cruelty on the part of the owner of the flower shop."

"There you have what things are like in this country."

"Well, as you heard, everyone sided with the astute customer, and two hours later the justice system had confiscated everything. They had made an inventory of everything: knives, scissors, pins, rolls of string, everything was strewn on the ground. You will note that the person who headed that procedure was the lawyer Juan. . . . What is certain is that they did not leave the poor insulted man with more than thirty *borregas;*† and right now he is languishing in jail while the proceedings that should have absolved him are costing him his entire savings."

"Such outrages happen in Havana," said Don Valentin, "and then these Creoles complain about the rectitude of the captain general. If I were the

---

* One quarter of a *medio real*. —*Author*

† Coins of gold worth 17 pesos. —*Author*

captain general, I would straighten everything out in an instant. The honorable men of Captain General Tacón are missed dearly."*

"Excuse me, sir, but I don't agree with you on that point. Tacón was far too cruel; he may have done good things, but he did many bad things."

"If I were the Spanish government," said another employee, who was copying various letters of correspondence belonging to Don Valentin, "rather than giving all the captains general a place to live when they return to the coasts of Spain, which is the customary way that the government signals approval of their service, I would order them to be shot with four bullets."

"I hope," said the main employee, speaking to Don Valentin, "that the caning you gave that carriage driver won't backfire on you."

"I have more than enough money in my cash register," answered Don Valentin, already ascending the twisted stairway leading to his mezzanine.

And as he climbed up the winding stairway that led to his bedroom, taking a look at his white pants, more splattered with mud than a beautiful night with shining stars, he cursed the carriage driver once again and entered his room. Despite his practice in finding the matches that he kept in a little stamped tin box in a particular spot, as he went up the stairs in darkness he knocked his knee against a *butaca* that he had absentmindedly left in the middle of the room.† He exploded into another round of curses. A little later, when he found the box of matches, he lit a gas lamp, and he amused himself for a long time by changing his clothes. Why did he take up the old cloak, the gift of a countryman, that he had accepted as a token of affection and would wear once or twice a year? We still don't know, and his main employee didn't guess the reason either, nor did the other employee who worked on the other side of the desk in copying the correspondence.

The fact is that he went out with the cloak over his shoulders and everyone in his house noticed this. He had also traded his typical beaver hat for a bowler hat made of felt that looked shabby and ridiculous given its state of deterioration. Wearing this strange outfit, he asked for a carriage [volanta] for hire and got ready to go.

---

* Miguel Tacón (1775–1855) served as captain general of Cuba from 1834 until 1838. He fought against Latin American revolutionaries in Nueva Granada in 1810 and 1811. José Antonio Saco called him a "horrifying [...] tyrant," and María de las Mercedes Santa Cruz y Montalvo, the Condesa de Merlín, called him "odious." Calcagno, *Diccionario biográfico cubano,* 610, 611, 613.
† A kind of leather armchair.—*Author*

"It looks like Don Valentin doesn't want to change his clothes again, given the getup he's wearing," said the main employee to the second one, who was sitting next to him at the desk.

"And he has ample reason to do so," the second employee answered. "The night is quite dark, there is a great deal of mud, and it would not be surprising if there were another downpour before ten."

"Damn, in this city the rain is punishment."

"September is the worst."

"And that month is not far off. As sure as vespers call forth saints, we are going to turn into frogs."

"I certainly think so."

Don Valentin took care not to give orders to the carriage driver as he walked out of his house so that his employees couldn't figure out where he was headed. Under such circumstances, the men in his office stayed quiet and kept working on the tasks in front of them until they received new orders. The driver directed the rented carriage toward Santa Teresa Street, which is also called Teniente-Rey Street, and reaching the wall, he took a left turn and went through the corresponding gate. Once in the outskirts of Havana, it turned to the left and took Del Monte Road; it passed the ceiba tree where Maloja Street comes up, and nevertheless it continued forward on the road.

Once it reached Chávez Bridge, where Horqueta Street leads to Carraguo, and continued on the road to the left, it seemed to the carriage driver that he had already gone past the intended destination. He worried that the man in the cloak had fallen asleep, as often suddenly happens with his passengers. In this case, the driver was worried for two reasons: first, because of the passenger's odd clothes, and second, because he had not indicated the final address. So the driver pulled to a stop and asked, "Where are you headed, sir?"

"To the fountain of Horcón," answered Don Valentin, bothered because the black man's question had distracted him from the matter that had taken hold of his imagination. The carriage driver whipped the miserable, worn-out horse that pulled the carriage and continued on his path, further down Del Monte Road.

Eduardo's surprise at finding that Tulita and her mother had suddenly disappeared was even greater when that same night he went to see the widow, who either dissembled perfectly—because she was not less astonished than he was—or indeed knew nothing about what had happened.

Eduardo continued to search for his lover until two in the morning. When he returned to his house that night he ran a great risk of having to pay a fine of half an onza since the government does not allow anyone to travel the streets of the city after eleven at night under that penalty, which one can also pay by spending eight days in prison. There was not one person in the neighborhood he hadn't asked in one way or another, including the servants of the nearby houses and the captaincy of the neighborhood, to see if they had filled out forms to establish themselves in some new place.

That night all his efforts came to naught.

This experience released floodgates of conjecture and worry, but he wasn't able to figure out why they had gone away. "Even tomorrow," he told himself, "it is possible that I will not know where they are hiding. If this is Don Valentin's doing, I swear that I will avenge myself as necessary. Matilde . . . loves me too much to have taken part in this conspiracy."

The next day, as Don Valentin was headed toward the fountain of Horcón, Eduardo could not leave his office until eight at night. Eduardo was so gravely worried that he undertook new investigations in the neighborhood to try to discovered some fact that would help him make sense of Tulita's strange disappearance.

Eduardo cut through the Estancia del Rey [King's Estate] in order to more quickly reach the house of the widow, hoping that she could give him some sort of news, as he had asked her to find out where Tulita lived. All of a sudden, someone who had been spying on him from the corner of the street approached him in an ambush and shot him point blank. Eduardo fell, rolling in his own blood . . . and the assassin disappeared.

 11

Sailing

"Take in the topgallantsail!
   "Get that fore sheet!"
   "Tie a reef in the topsails!"
   "Gather the mainsail!

"Tie another reef in the topsails!"

"Captain," said one of the sailors who was manning the helm, "that rascal often fails to work his shifts, and he rarely obeys."

"We have prepared it well for the night," answered the captain, giving the sailor a sharp look to see whether he was telling the truth. "It's true," he murmured. "Quickly," he added. "Two men to the pump! Take in the reefs again! Grab the jib rope! Hoist and pull!"

The sailors had swiftly completed all of their duties so the brig *Joven Emilio* could survive the violent storm that was about to strike. It was two in the morning. The sky was covered with gathering clouds that were casting an ever-darker shadow over the area where they were sailing. The wind gained strength, lightning shot back and forth across the sky, and the captain, experienced with the storms of the Gulf of Mexico, assured the pilot, who had tied himself to the side of ship right next to him, that in fifty-three round trips from Havana to Veracruz and vice versa, he had never seen such an ominous and frightening sky as in the current storm.

Every so often, the wind would whip the rain into huge sheets of water that rose to the height of sixty meters and unleashed their fury against the poop of the boat, forcing the naked masts to cross one another and wail in throes of agony. A surge of the sea ended up dislodging the kitchen, as the receding water swept away great shards of the hull. "Foreman," shouted the captain, using the megaphone, "have the men prepare the ropes and jettison the boxes of sugar that are on board! The ship doesn't obey the rudder. The water is unpredictable; it doesn't respect rank!" And so in less than half an hour boats, life preservers, cables, barrels, and around thirty boxes of sugar were floating in the waves and the deck was open and unencumbered.

"What's happening with the pump, boys?" the foreman, full of anxiety, asked the two sailors who were incessantly emptying the water that kept swamping the brig.

"Just look," said one. "The water keeps flowing in, and if the storm doesn't subside, the pump will not be enough."

"Wait a minute while I use the probe."

And the foreman checked how many inches of water still remained.

"Still nine inches!" he said, growing pale. And he stepped aside to speak alone with the captain.

Before reaching the spot where the captain had tied himself down, a blow from a wave tumbled the foreman toward the entrance of the poop cabin, and if he had lacked the presence of mind to grab one of the henhouses along the flank with all of his strength, he would have ended up a meal for sharks.

"Tie yourself up!" the pilot called.

"Boys," the captain shouted, turning to look at the rudder, "throw everything overboard, everything you can."

And before he could finish the sentence, a huge sheet of water, entering from the poop and passing over the deck with lightning speed, bathed everyone from head to toe. The foreman had been leaning against the portside railing, supporting himself by grabbing one of the ropes, when the wave drenched him up to his waist. The storm raged at full strength for fourteen hours. Then, from two in the morning until six, the storm gradually calmed down, and finally the sky cleared up completely. At four, the captain was already in his cabin, resting for a while; by then everything was silent. At six in the morning, the powerful sun of the tropics cast rays of the most resplendent light onto the tranquil sea, which resembled the sleeping waters of a lake. The sky was clear and beautiful. All the sailors, following the orders of the foreman, busied themselves with repairing the damage the storm had caused, and even the pilot, to gain the gratitude of the captain, worked just as diligently, fabricating a large round patch.

"The mother and daughter must have been frightened to death," said the pilot to the foreman.

"Well, we've suffered a fright ourselves as well."

"In the Gulf of Mexico, one can never breathe easily. If we had not reacted quickly last night, I fear that we would have taken in even more water."

"The boat will not be very thirsty today."

"Nine inches of water!"

"I counted twelve, and it wasn't even one in the morning."

"And the pump is working?"

"Oh, now it is," said the foreman, placing a bit of chewing tobacco into his mouth. "Today it is as dry as a bone."

"And the one-eyed man?"

"His majesty has not yet appeared."

"I will call him," said the pilot, "because if he does not come out to breathe some fresh air, he will never recover from seasickness."

"That guy is such a chicken. Three days into the voyage and he has not come on deck. It's fine that women don't come up, but he should . . . If I had power over him, I would have tied him to the foremast and given him a couple of dozen lashings to fortify him."

"Don't wake him up," the foreman added, pushing down the coattails of his overcoat. "It is better that he remain in bed. He can only open one eye because the devil took the other eye, so let him sleep, it's less of an effort. Give him broth and let him snore like a convict until we get to Veracruz."

"No, no. I'm going to call him."

"You devil, you want to catch a glimpse of the little mulatta . . . Out with it, we know that you're a sinner. Well, frankly, I like the mother more than the daughter. Later, the young one won't do anything but whine . . . But the mother . . . she is the type—Jaime," he interrupted himself, "watch that cord! . . . And you, foul mouth, give it more rope and don't waste so much tar."

Even as the foreman was saying this, the pilot was already calling to the passenger in one of the cabins. The curtains of the women's cabin were drawn, so he couldn't tell whether they were sleeping or not.

"Hello, who is it?" the man whom the pilot awoke said in a weak voice.

"Do you feel better?"

"I feel a bit better, but I had a dreadful night."

"Did you hear the storm?"

"So much that I couldn't sleep at all. Does it look like the weather has changed?"

"It is a gorgeous day."

"My sister and my niece? . . ."

"They still aren't up."

"They must have been so scared!"

"If you don't know the danger, you don't fear it so much. If you could have seen what the weather and the sea were like, you would still be trembling. Are you getting up? Come on, let's go on deck, and you will see that soon you will regain your bearings and you'll no longer feel sick."

"I don't feel well enough."

"Would you like to drink a glass of Jamaican rum and we'll go up?"

"I accept the glass of rum with great pleasure."

"Just a moment."

While the pilot went to the storeroom to get the rum, someone pulled open a curtain, and the person in that cabin asked the captain, "Has the storm ended?"

"Completely, señora, don't worry." Lifting the latch of the storeroom door, he descended, humming a danza habanera.*

---

* On the *contradanza habanera,* see note on page 56.

"Ay, what a terrible night! Mamerto!"

"What, Belencita?"

"How are you?"

"Better. And you?"

"Brother, I've got an extraordinary headache. What a night! Did you feel the hurricane's strength?"

"Yes—I wasn't able to sleep soundly until this morning. What terrible lurching we suffered!"

"I thought we were going to drown," said another voice from inside the adjoining cabin.

"I made a promise to Our Lady of Belén that I must fulfill when I reach land. I have worried so much about you, Matilde!"

"Well, it would have made no difference to me had I died," said Matilde.

"Jesus, girl, don't say such blasphemies. *Vaya,* you take things too far. You know that such comments annoy me, and you must like to upset me. I have patiently endured everything, and I would endure even worse trials as long as I could save my brother."

"As far as that goes, I cannot deny it," replied Matilde. "My uncle knows what a sacrifice this voyage has been for me." And looking at the portrait of Eduardo that she always kept with her, Matilde cried bitterly.

The pilot brought the rum, and since he found the three passengers in conversation, he happily took part in it and with the utmost courtesy offered two generous glasses of wine to Belencita and Matilde. A little later they were all on deck breathing the pure air of the seas, which revived them a great deal. When the captain got up, he was so pleased to see his brig traveling five miles an hour thanks to the light breeze that he ordered biscuits, an excellent tea, and a bottle of *perfecto amor* and with his passengers drank a toast to the success of the voyage.

The trip Belencita and Matilde were taking was unavoidable. Julio, Belencita's only brother, was fleeing for his life. Having had to sell all their possessions at rock-bottom prices, Belencita and Matilde, through great sacrifice, persistence, expense, and inconvenience, had been able to free Julio from a threatened prison sentence and from the scaffold on which he would have expired. His only crime was that he was a man of color; the rising persecution against that poor race had reached an extraordinary

---

* Parfait Amour, a popular liquor in the nineteenth century and still made in France, is a purple-colored liquor with a base of curaçao and flavored with rose petals, vanilla and almonds. "Parfait amor (licor)."

intensity. Matilde had no other desire than to speak with her Eduardo, whose portrait she had removed from her bracelet and placed in a medallion in a necklace to preserve it as if it were the holiest of relics.

Belencita cried at first as she watched the gorgeous beaches of Cuba recede: she thought of her childhood friends, the impossibility of returning, and the necessity of seeking refuge in a strange place. Belencita had recognized the cruel necessity of not saying one word to anyone about the voyage because of the risk to Julio's life. Therefore, the worries and suffering of the three passengers were all the more overpowering during the first days of the voyage, especially as the storm threatened to strike.

Julio had been living in the town of Altemisa, sixteen leagues from Havana.* As the only tailor in town, he had opened an establishment that earned him enough to live a peaceful and comfortable life. His attentiveness to the needs of his clients had won him a great number of friends. Although as a humble mulatto he was not able to socialize with his white acquaintances, Master Julio, as he was called, was nonetheless welcome in the homes of the coffee plantations and pastures near his town. The marquis or count would not think twice about dealing directly with him, entrusting him with the uniforms of their carriage drivers and any other items of clothing they might need. And since their bills mounted and Julio could not be demanding with such men of high rank, they received him in a friendlier manner than did the whites employed in the service of the plantation. He felt honored by this treatment, even if his bills took longer to pay off and he had to write off more than one in his record book under the category "unrecoverable." Nevertheless, that highly recommended him to his clients and was undoubtedly the reason why many whites, among them the occasional marquis or count, took his hand and greeted him affectionately, which pleased Master Julio more than earning money for his work.

In this way, Belencita's brother had created an independent position in society. Single, despite being 40 years old, he was happy and content. But since in life no one lacks enemies, and luck doesn't last, Master Julio also had ups and downs, and for that reason we have witnessed him sailing aboard the brig *Joven Emilio* heading to Veracruz.

---

* *Altemisa* appears to be a misspelling. Artemisa is a town to the southwest of Havana. By Orihuela's estimation, it is approximately 55 miles from Havana, but a search on Google Maps shows that the trip from the Plaza de Armas in Havana to Artemisa is now 44 miles.

In the same town of Altemisa, there was a discharged soldier who had served for many years under the military commander. Although he boarded for free in the house of his former superior, this man, somewhat knowledgeable in the tailor's craft, thought it would harm his dignity if he were to ask for work in Master Julio's shop. As he said to someone who gave him advice, "A white man should never subordinate himself to a mulatto." Such folly and pride led him to prefer a thousand privations and even humiliations from whites, whom he considered to be of his class, to honorably earning his living by working with Master Julio. In addition, he must have envied that hardworking and honorable man who kept his business in strong shape and maintained good credit.

"If I were able to find someone to lend me thirty coins," said the white man, speaking with the barber of the town one day, "that one-eyed man would not be able to sew a stitch."

"Why?"

"Look, because I would go to the city, bringing along five or six little black apprentices [*negritos aprendices*], and steal the shirts off their backs, making them work day and night, placing a top-quality shop right next to his, and if the one-eyed man didn't close his business within a month, I would go to work picking fruit."

"But, my friend, why are you so angry at poor Master Julio? The poor guy works to earn his living, and that is his only crime; why don't you do the same?"

"What? A poor guy! . . . No, no . . . What that dog does is take bread away from whites . . . If I were a political leader, I would kick him out of my jurisdiction with his boxes still unpacked. Why don't I do that, and why don't I buy some irons and start my own shop?"

"And can't the military commander help you in some way?"

"The commander is a good person, but he is poorer than poverty itself."

This conversation, a light brushstroke that sufficiently characterizes the envy of Julio's enemy, makes us understand that this individual would not let one opportunity slip by in plotting the ruin of the poor tailor. That aim soon became the obsession of the soldier as soon he found someone to lend him some money, which he used to compete with the tailor, at first without success. However, the soldier saw his big opportunity when they began to charge the class of color with having conspired against the whites: without any qualms he devised the barbarous plan of actually finishing off this hapless man, accusing him of being one of the ringleaders of the revolution.

Fortunately for Julio, the barber of the town, a good friend, gave the tailor advance warning of the ambush the soldier was preparing. Julio abandoned his business and showed up at the house of his sister Belencita. Having learned of the danger her brother faced, danger that also threatened her, Belencita thought it best to hide him while she sold everything they owned and planned their trip to Veracruz, with the aim of living there for a while until the bloody persecutions of those times had ceased.

This incident took place on the same day that Eduardo, disconsolate, set out to try to discover where Tulita lived. Matilde would not have been able to see Eduardo even if her mother had permitted her, because their delicate predicament could have become worse. Resigned to neither see nor communicate with anyone, only on the day of departure did she write a letter to Eduardo explaining what had happened. Even though Belencita had already written him with all the details, Matilde repeated everything so that she could devote all of her last night in Havana saying farewell to her lover.

After a voyage of thirteen days, the brig *Joven Emilio* dropped anchor between the Castle of San Juan de Ulúa and the city of Veracruz. When Belencita, Matilde, and Julio disembarked, their first errand was to go to the Church of San Francisco to distribute alms among the poor who begged at its doors. Belencita fulfilled her promise to her namesake virgin in gratitude for the three of them being now safe from danger.*

# 12

The Boulder of Guachinango

Not far from the town of San Antonio Abad, on the island of Cuba, there is a cafetal known by the name La Reunión (The Reunion or The Gathering).† Properties dedicated to the cultivation of coffee typically assume the form of whimsical gardens, with broad and level streets lined with palms,

---

* "Her namesake virgin" refers to la Virgen de Belén (the Virgin of Bethlehem).
† Orihuela unconventionally writes the name of the town as "San-Antonio Abad," with a hyphen, which I omit. San Antonio Abad is another name for San Antonio de los Baños.

mangoes, and orange trees, and within their grounds one can spot gorgeous Alexandria roses, which emit their delicate perfume in competition with the aromas of other plants surrounding them, including the numerous coffee plants, which respect a most curious symmetry.

At the highest and most central point of this country estate, the original owners erected as an ensemble their own dwelling [*casa de vivienda*], the overseer's house, the granary, the *barracones*,* the infirmary, and the milling house. These buildings, arranged in the order in which they were erected, formed a beautiful circular plaza where the four main tree-lined streets of the plantation converged. The cafetal La Reunión marked out its boundaries with a stone fence a vara and a half high, and the *tranquera*, or gate, led to the only main road running between Alquízar and San Antonio Abad.†

Inside the stone fence, and close to the main gate, there was a sort of sentry post, a humble bohío, which was a kind of hut formed from *yaguas*‡ and branches of coconut trees, that was the dwelling of *taita* Pio, an octogenarian slave who since he could no longer work in the fields now worked as watchman [*guardiero*], charged with placing or removing the large beams of wood that blocked the entrance in order to allow passage to the people, carriages, and horses that arrived; he therefore served as a sort of permanent gatekeeper. *Taita* Pio's typical outfit was limited to a coarse red wool cap, which contrasted with his snow-white curly hair and the ebony color of his face, a piece of cotton tied with rope at the hip, like a woman's tattered petticoat, and a wool blanket thrown over his shoulders. The interior of his bohío had no furnishings other than a platform bed and a wooden bowl.

On a dark and humid night in the month of December, two individuals traveled from the village of San Antonio Abad to the cafetal La Reunión. Despite the darkness, one could tell that they were master and slave because the elegantly dressed one, in front, was on a spirited sorrel, while the other, galloping on a mule a respectful distance behind, was holding in his hands the enormous brim of a *sombrero de yarey*, in a sign of respect that he employed whenever speaking to the master. And indeed, Eduardo was

---
* The slaves' dormitory.—*Author*
† A vara is a unit of length equal to just under 3 feet.
‡ According to the *Diccionario de la lengua española*, a *yagua* is "a palm tree that serves as produce and is used for roofs for the huts of Indians and to make containers, hats, and rope." http://dle.rae.es/?id=c8iXqbU. However, according to Raúl Fernández, "[A] 'yagua' is not a palm tree, [a] yagua is a board, a plank cut out from the trunk of the palm tree to build a country hut, *una casa de yaguas*." Personal communication, 3 September 2017.

returning to the cafetal along with *el negro* Mariano, slave to the owner of the plantation.*

"Are we near the Boulder of Guachinango?"

"No, sir, we are still somewhat far away."

"What a dark night! Mariano, take out your machete!"

The slave obediently took out the steel machete that he kept on his belt just as Eduardo was releasing the safety of his pistol.

"The place we are about to pass," he said, "has frequently been the site of robberies and murders, so it is prudent for us to be prepared."

"You are right, and especially now that it is Easter, it is harvest time for criminals."

"Mariano, as soon as you see a figure heading for us, cut him off from the side if he comes from the right, take the left, or vice versa; but if he insists on approaching from the front, you already know your duty..."

"Oh, yes sir! Don't worry, you already know, sir, that I am well prepared."

At that moment, our travelers heard the gallop of other horses coming from the opposite direction, and as they approached, they could distinctly hear the monotonous song of one of the men, who let his inspiration run free in a *zapateo,* a provincial dance tune from the island of Cuba:†

> A mulatta died on me
> No one can take her from me now
> And no one will be left alive
> If they don't capture who killed her.

---

* *Negro* is the term for Black in Spanish. In Cuba, the term also served as a synonym for slave.

† The *zapateo* is a rural Cuban dance that reached the height of its popularity around the middle of the nineteenth century. In this dance, the partners dance facing each other but without holding hands. The woman holds her skirt with both hands, and the man leans forward, with his arms crossed behind his back. The man circles around the woman, who tries not to turn her back to him. "Zapateo cubano." The zapateo dates from the early eighteenth century, when guajiros—Black, mulatto, and white rural workers in Cuba—"had developed a creolized song form derived from the traditions of Spain which came to be called the *punto guajiro*. [...] The punto guajiro is an art of *repentismo,* or poetic improvisation, to the accompaniment of a plucked stringed instrument, which might be a *bandurria* (a small, oval-shaped plectrum instrument) or, in the nineteenth century, the small, high-pitched, four-string guitar known as the *tiple.*" Sublette, *Cuba and its Music,* 91. Cuban writers claimed that the zapateo dance was "the national dance." Sublette, *Cuba and its Music,* 93.

When they reached the travelers, Eduardo and Mariano took the left side of the road, as they had agreed, leaving the right side to the others, and in keeping with the country's customs, all greeted one another simultaneously in their different accents:

"Good evening, gentlemen!"

Despite the many voices that took part in the greeting, Eduardo recognized that of his friend Federico, as Federico did Eduardo's, and for that reason they came to a stop. While their traveling companions offered one another cigars [*puros*], which they smoked with pleasure, the two friends conversed.

"You are returning to the cafetal so soon, Eduardo?"

"It is already after midnight, Federico, and since it is somewhat humid, the wound on my arm is already bothering me."

"Oh, I thought you were entirely healed."

"Yes, I am healed, but wounds incurred during the rainy season grow sore when the temperature changes, and tonight bad weather threatens. And the dance at San Antonio, rather than entertaining me, saddened me even further. What do you expect? I can't get Tulita out of my mind!"*

"The Sun of Jesús del Monte is deeply rooted in your heart. I had begun to believe that in the six months since her disappearance the wound that man gave you would begin to heal, but you are a model of constancy, chico.† As for me, frankly I was not cut out to imitate the lovers of Teruel."‡

"And what are you doing?"

---

* Here, in an example of the uneven orthography in Orihuela's text, he spells San Antonio without a hyphen, in contrast to his earlier mention of the town.
† For the meaning of *chico,* see note on page 12.
‡ Literary historians argue that the story of the lovers of Teruel first appeared in Spanish literature ca. 1555 with the publication of Pedro Alventosa's *Historia lastimosa y sentida de los dos tiernos amantes Marcilla y Segura, naturales de Teruel.* An important early Spanish version of the play was Andrés Rey de Artieda's *Los amantes* (1581), whose plot D. W. Cruickshank describes as follows: "The play opens with the return of the hero Marcilla to Teruel after seven years' absence, but Isabel has been married that day. When he manages to see her alone later the same evening, she denies him a farewell kiss, and he dies of grief. To prevent suspicion from falling on them, Isabel and her new husband leave Marcilla's body on his father's doorstep, but Isabel, belatedly grief-stricken, goes to the funeral to give Marcilla's body the kiss she had refused, and dies." Tirso de Molina's play *Los amantes de Teruel* appeared in 1635. Juan Pérez de Montalbán's play *Los amantes de Teruel* (1635) was a popular adaptation of the Teruel story: twenty-eight editions of it appeared between 1635 and 1800. There were many other versions of the play from the sixteenth century through the nineteenth. Juan Eugenio

"Chico, tonight I am returning to San Antonio even though I have only been a guest at my uncle's house in Vereda Nueva for a week.* Since country folk are so trustworthy, and since the dance that you have just left should last until daybreak, I think I will stay there until five in the morning and then return."

"But will you go to the little dance that they will have at the cafetal La Reunión?"

"As two and two make four."

"You are unstoppable."

"That's how I am."

"Well, chico, see you tomorrow. I feel some raindrops, and I still have more than a half league to travel."†

"Why don't you come back to San Antonio tonight and we'll return together to the cafetal tomorrow?"

"No, thank you, Federico, I am out of sorts, and it would bother me even more. Above all my arm bothers me."

"Well, goodbye."

"Give me a match."

Federico made his horse approach that of Eduardo, who lit his friend's cigarette. They gave each other a handshake, and once again they heard the phrase,

"Cheers, *caballeros* [gentlemen]!"

Mariano returned to take his respectful position behind Eduardo, and they continued their trip without being able to hear each other since the horses were trotting and large drops of rain were beginning to fall.

"Mariano, do you have any matches?"

"Yes sir, niño Eduardo."

"Well let's wait for this downpour to stop under this ceiba tree, and in the meantime I will light a cigar since I don't feel like a cigarette. Do you smoke?" he asked, taking out a box of cigars.

"Niño . . . but in front of your *mercé* . . ."‡

"That's no big deal. Take it."

Hartzenbusch's version of the play first appeared on the stage in January 1837. Cruickshank, "Lovers of Teruel," 881–82, plot summary on 882.

* Vereda Nueva is 6.7 miles west of San Antonio de los Baños. Here Orihuela misspells it as "Verada nueva."
† A half league is 1.7 miles.
‡ *Mercé* is a shortened form of *merced,* which is a respectful form of address. See note on page 7.

"Eduardo gave a cigar to Mariano, and the two sat under a corpulent ceiba tree, which sheltered them with its branches from the by now torrential rain.

"My right arm hurts so badly!" mumbled Eduardo.

"Does the niño want to put on the overcoat that I am carrying in my bag?"

"Give it to me because the humidity makes me suffer a lot."

"What happened, sir?"

"A wound I received around six months ago on a rainy night like this one."

"Was it a duel, niño?"

"No, it was an act of treachery that the villain must now pay back a thousandfold."

"There are such bad people in the world!"

"He was a rival of mine, a man named Don Valentin, who was envious because I was the choice of the woman that he loved in silence. One night, full of anxiety as a result of the disappearance of my girlfriend, I was walking through the neighborhood inquiring as to her whereabouts. He followed my steps. Just when I was crossing a type of *placer** between Jesús del Monte Street and a cluster of houses on the left, entering from the corner of Teja and adjacent to the Estancia del Rey, the coward approached me with a pistol in his hand, and I had no time to react. When the bullet passed through my forearm and the pain was so strong that it numbed me, I fell down, thinking that he had killed me. At that point, understanding the full horror of his crime, he prepared to commit suicide. But right when he cocked the trigger of his other pistol, he fell into the hands of justice, which prevented him from playing it out."

"And you, sir?"

"When I came to, I found myself in my home, under the care of a neighbor and my servants. It took me three months to recover because the wound failed to heal, and I had to undergo a second operation. I was about to lose my arm, but fortunately Doctor Le Riverend, a celebrated French doctor, supervised my recuperation, and thanks to his knowledge and care, I am now perfectly healed. Nevertheless, whenever there is a change in the weather it bothers me somewhat."†

---

* An uninhabited expanse of land.—*Author*
† Here Eduardo refers to Julio Jacinto Le Riverend (1794–1864), a French national who emigrated to Cuba in 1824. Le Riverend worked as chair of anatomy and surgery at the

"And did they hang Don Valentin?" asked Mariano, full of admiration for Eduardo.

"They did not precisely hang him, no, but no one will release him from jail. Nonetheless, I forgave him the personal offence, refusing to take part in the judicial proceedings."

"That was generous of you, niño, but that criminal, that traitor who tried to murder you, doesn't deserve it."

The rain began to subside, and impatient to arrive, Eduardo set his horse off at a gallop. The black man followed silently for a while. Ten minutes into their trip, the Boulder of Guachinango came into view.

"It seems to me, niño Eduardo," said Mariano fearfully, "that along the pathway [*vereda*] to the left of the boulder I see a figure that appears to be a man. If the niño wishes, we can take the path on the right."

"Is your machete ready? Well, then, don't worry, I'm also prepared. Nevertheless, let's take the path to the right."

The Boulder of Guachinango is a great rock that arises in the middle of the road that Eduardo and Mariano were taking, creating a kind of cave. The terrain there is quite uneven and divides the road into two pathways, one lower and the other three meters high, with a length of around fifty steps, and in the center of this sort of isolated mountain one can find this concave rock that has often served as a refuge for bandits. When Eduardo arrived at the incline, a whistle sounded loud and clear. The black man heard it and deemed it prudent not to say a word about it. Kicking his spurs into the mule, he rode to the left of Eduardo to be in a better position to defend him if necessary.

"Halt!" Six men suddenly appeared with rifles.

Recognizing the thieves' advantage, Eduardo dropped his pistol as a man tried to force Mariano to drop his machete. The pistol discharged as it hit the ground, and the surprised bandits asked one another, "What? What is that?" And they looked at one another without realizing where the shot had come from.

"Tell that dog," said the man who had approached Mariano, "that he needs to let go of the machete or we will shoot your brains out."

University of Havana in the 1850s and was editor of *El observador habanero: periódico de medicina y de cirujía práctica* (1844–48) and the *Revista médica de la Habana* (1854–57). He was also the author of the book *Memoria sobre la leche* (1849). Palmer, "From the Plantation to the Academy," 65, 67.

"Mariano, give him the machete," Eduardo said calmly. "Sirs, do you want the money that we've got?"

"Soon, and with few words."

The black man obeyed, full of anger, because the bandits had the upper hand and wouldn't let him get away with even just one *machetazo* [strike of the machete].

Fortunately, while the six highwaymen were busy disarming the travelers, a company of soldiers were walking from the town of Alquízar toward the village of San Antonio Abad, and since they were close enough to hear the detonation of the shot, they hurried their step, so that before the thieves could realize it, they found themselves surrounded by rifles as if caught in a spell. The bandits immediately fled. Four of those who dropped their rifles fell into the hands of the troops, since they no longer posed a danger to anyone. Two were able to escape thanks to the speed of their horses. The official in charge sent a sergeant with ten men in pursuit of the fugitives and four men to accompany Eduardo and Mariano to the cafetal La Reunión. They took the other thieves to the jail in San Antonio Abad since it was the closest town. Eduardo took his leave of the official, thanking him for his service and recovering his personal effects. When he reached the cafetal, he gave a duro to each soldier and two to the head official so that they could have a drink in his name.

When *taita* Pio was wakened so he could open the gate to allow those who called him to enter, he vacillated for a few minutes about whether to do so since Eduardo came accompanied by soldiers.

"Open it, sir—there is no need to be afraid." Eduardo said.

"*Ño* Pio, don't you recognize me?"*

"Ah! You are a *calavera*?† Yes, right away."

"Take this, sir, to buy cigarettes," said Eduardo, giving *taita* Pio a peseta, while the slave closed the gate.

"Thank you, sir [*su mercé*], thank you," and the black man kissed his hand with great affection to demonstrate his gratitude.

---

* The word *ño* is an abbreviated form of *señor*.
† Among blacks this word means compatriot.—*Author*

 13

A Dance in the Countryside

The Baron of C . . . , owner of the coffee plantation La Reunión, had left the capital for a few days to enjoy the upcoming Easter holiday. Together with his wife and his nine-year-old daughter, their only offspring, he was enjoying the innocent pleasures that country life offers, spending his days hunting and his nights going to parties and dances in the nearby towns of San Marcos, Alquízar, Las Cañas, Quira de Melena, San Antonio Abad, and Vereda Nueva. He attended cockfights and took trips to neighboring sugar plantations, which were bustling with the sugarcane harvest. He also engaged in other amusements that were no less pleasurable—even if country life is boring for those who live there year-round, such forms of entertainment are poetic and pleasant for those who enjoy them only from time to time.

Eduardo, a consultant, proxy, and counsel in legal questions to the baron, had earned the family's regard and respect and was not only their lawyer but also a close friend. That was why when his doctor recommended that he move to a place with fresh air, he followed his advice, deciding to stay at the coffee plantation La Reunión to recuperate from the wound that Don Valentin had inflicted on him and to allow the melancholy that had seized his soul after the disappearance of Tulita to dissipate.

Until the owners of the farm showed up, Eduardo's companions were limited to the overseer, the family of the *mayordomo* [caretaker], the cowherd, and the doctor who was trusted with the duty of caring for *la negrada* [the slaves].* For this reason, the tranquility of the monotonous life that he lived in the countryside did not cure him of his demoralized state but instead made him suffer more deeply and thoroughly. Nothing could distract him from the passion in his soul, his obsession. At times he regretted abandoning the labyrinth of legal work, while at other times he wanted to

---

* Although the *mayordomo* typically worked as a bookkeeper or accountant, as Aisha Finch has explained, in this case the *mayordomo* performs a role closer to that of the *administrador,* or the supervisor of the slave population, which I have rendered here as "caretaker." Finch, *Rethinking Slave Rebellion in Cuba,* 39. The *mayordomo* should not be confused with the *mayoral* [overseer].

immediately set off for the city to live next to the house where Tulita had lived in order to derive pleasure from walking past the very same porch where she, the most beautiful rose in the garden of Cuba, had spent her afternoons. He lacked purpose in his life: before he could put one plan into action, he had already begun to prefer another direction, and in that state of indecision he spent his days, finding neither equanimity of soul nor peace of spirit.

At six in the morning he typically walked along the *guarda-rayas** of the coffee plantation, entertaining himself by reading the works of Rousseau or Voltaire, both of whom he most enthusiastically admired; or he would take out his notebook and pencil to write some poetic compositions, in which he portrayed his own situation in the gloomiest colors; or with a penknife he would trace on the trunks of bamboo plants or orange trees or lemon trees the same poems he had written in his notebook. These were the activities that took up his mornings until the hour of lunch.

Many afternoons from just after lunch until the sun stopped shining on the fields, he would observe that sad tableau of the slaves busy at work and think about the miserable situation of those unfortunate people. He had many humanitarian and philosophical thoughts! He shed so many tears of compassion after witnessing a hundred individuals of both sexes, nearly nude, uprooting the undergrowth of the forest to prepare for the sowing of the coffee seeds. Their backs, full of scars and wounds, were reinjured day after day by the stinging whip of the driver [*contra-mayoral*]! . . .

The life of the field slave is more bitter than that of a prisoner in imperial Russia.†

---

* Tree-lined streets.—*Author*
† Russia engaged in an aggressive project of expansion by conquering all of northern Asia, the territory of Siberia, which it had firmly under its control by the mid-sixteenth century. From the mid-sixteenth century on, Russia used Siberia as a penal colony, sending convicts, political prisoners, and prisoners of war there. It was not until 1763 that Tsarina Catherine II, known as Catherine the Great, sought to partially abolish torture in Russia. Her grandson Alexander I abolished the slitting of nostrils in 1817 but continued to allow the branding [*kleimenie*] of criminals. As Erika Kriukelyte writes, "The serfs had not been affected by these reforms and it was only in 1845 that the power of estate owners to inflict capital punishment upon their serfs was restricted by the state in the penal code. Finally, in 1863, most remaining corporal punishments were abolished." Russia sent 772,979 exiles to Siberia from 1823 to 1887. A portion of these were hard-labor convicts (*ktorzhniki*) and hard-labor colonists (*poselentsi*), who were deprived of all civil rights and had to remain in Siberia for life. Depending on the decision of the Bureau of Exiles, these convicts worked in forced labor in the mines, in

In addition to this spectacle, which he witnessed every single day, the slaves offered another on Sunday afternoons near their barracoon: a kind of savage dance set to the beat of a drum, which keeps a mournful cadence, accompanied by an instrument they call the *marino bola*.* They use another instrument consisting of a bow and a string pulled tight, moving one end close to the mouth while they beat the string with a stick, making a sad and monotonous sound, accompanied by a chorus in their nation's African language. Viewed from a distance, given the clamor [*algázara*] their music makes and their strange dance moves, they seemed more like wild beasts fighting over their prey, eager to satiate their ravenous hunger, than rational beings. And this preferred entertainment of the blacks so intoxicates them that they forget the trials of their miserable existence in their moments of pleasure.

Taking turns with the instruments are the *mandingas*, the *congos*, the *carabalíes papá*, the *carabalíes viví*, the *lucumíes*, and individuals from numerous other nations with their characteristic dances, their gestures and rude pantomimes, which are impossible to describe, and their loud, grotesque, and infernal music.† When the bell of the *batey*

---

chain gangs on the highways, in agriculture, or in workhouses. The maximum sentence for forced labor was twenty years, after which the convict could work in agriculture under police surveillance. Kriukelyte, "Creation of Modern Prisons," 5, 7, 11, 12, 16, quotation on 12.

* Raúl Fernández has informed me that *marino bola* refers to the *marímbula* (Cuba) or *marímbola* (Puerto Rico). Personal communication, 11 January 2018. The *marímbula* is known as the "Cuban thumb piano" and can be "used harmonically as well as rhythmically." Griffin, "Marímbula." According to the National Museum of American History website, "The *marímbula*, (also *marímbola*), is an African-derived folk instrument found across the Caribbean. Large enough for its player to sit on, this instrument consists of a large, resonating box with metal strips that are plucked to provide a simple bass accompaniment." "Marímbula."

† As Aisha Finch has argued, "Researchers have overwhelmingly shown that these nation names should be understood primarily as geographic identifiers; that is, as indications of where on the African coast the captives embarked, rather than precise indicators of ethnic, linguistic or cultural backgrounds." *Rethinking Slave Rebellion in Cuba*, 25. The Mandingas embarked from Sierra Leone and Gambia. The Congos came from West-Central Africa, which encompasses parts of present-day Gabon and all of Congo and Angola. The Carabalí came from the Bight of Biafra, which includes parts of contemporary Nigeria, Cameroon, Equatorial Guinea, and Gabon. The Lucumí people came from the Bight of Benin, which extends from Ghana to Nigeria. All these putative ethnicities included a wide range of ethnic and linguistic groups. Finch, *Rethinking Slave Rebellion in Cuba*, 25–27. However, Jorge and Isabel

sounds, after the sun has set, they return exhausted and covered with sweat to their respective rooms, only to get up at dawn and return to the heavy chores of the workweek. Their breakfast is boiled yam, a piece of salty beef jerky, and roasted plantains, and they eat the same food at lunch. Those two meals provide them with their only respite from work until six at night, when they return to the barracoon.

Eduardo's compassionate character emerged more and more as he witnessed all of this. Many times he used his influence to support some poor slave who for a slight infraction was condemned to suffer a *bocabajo* or to die under the horrible torment of a *novenario!*† On one occasion, he willingly walked three miles to come to the aid of a hapless pregnant black woman, already far along, who asked him to intercede with her owner because she had escaped to elude punishment. They had already opened the iron collar to fasten around her waist and ordered four of her fellow slaves to tie her down and give her one hundred lashings for the simple reason that on her way from the kitchen to her owners' dinner table she had broken a platter!

The slaves of the coffee plantation La Reunión gathered together to greet Eduardo upon his arrival. While he was there, the slaves did not suffer the *novenario* or the *bocabajo,* although they did suffer some punishments that were less harsh, and never in his presence. This was the first condition that Eduardo demanded from the owners upon accepting their offer for him to stay on their farm for his convalescence and recovery, a condition

---

Castellanos have shown not only that many of these nation names did in fact refer to broad (if not precise) geographical areas of origin for slaves but also that many slaves used these terms themselves, often turning them into compound names that made the nation names more specific: "many Cuban slaves called themselves Lucumí, and the Cuban Gangá called themselves 'Gangá-cramo, Gangá-fay, Gangá-conó, Gangá-quisí, etc.' which correspond to the Kissi, Gola, Vai, Kono, Kran, Toma, and Mende people of southern Sierra Leone and northern Liberia." Castellanos and Castellanos, "Geographic, Ethnologic, and Linguistic Roots," 97, 98.

* A *batey* is the plaza in the middle of the slaves' dwellings. The *Diccionario de la lengua española* of the Real Academia Española defines *batey* as follows: "In the sugar plantations and other farms of the Antillean countryside, a place occupied by the living quarters, boiler, mill, slave dormitories and warehouses, etc."

† This [novenario] is the term for the barbarous punishment of one hundred lashes daily for nine consecutive days, which the overseers, or those charged with the management of the coffee plantations, sugar plantations, pastures, small farms, and haciendas, tend to impose on the poor slaves without any regard to sex.—*Author.* On the bocabajo (which elsewhere Orihuela spells "boca-bajo"), see the author's note on page 8.

that the Baron de C... accepted and delivered in the form of an order in a letter written in his own hand to the caretaker: that as long as Eduardo was at the coffee plantation, the lash shouldn't be used against any of the slaves. According to Eduardo, this was an order that was followed to the letter.

The arrival of the owners of the plantation, along with the happy and ebullient character of the baron, combined to transform Eduardo's experience of rural life. As a result of the nudging of the baron and the suggestions of the baroness, Eduardo went to the dance at the town of San Antonio Abad, from which we have seen him return accompanied by the slave Mariano. Even if he had not decided to stay until morning, as the hosts had urged him to do, the dance did succeed in distracting him from all the sorrow that had kept him down in the dumps.

The baron and his wife were sorry about Eduardo's unpleasant encounter with the bandits, an incident that was the topic of commentaries and conversation throughout the following day. All the guests at the coffee plantation heard about the episode, a story that made the rounds of neighboring farms and accrued new details, becoming distorted to such an extent that if someone had told the story to Eduardo, he would not have recognized himself as the hero of the tale. The next day Federico arrived at the cafetal. The caretaker, who was walking through the garden that circled that main house, was the first to greet him.

"And Eduardo?" he asked, giving his horse to one of the slaves who appeared when he dismounted.

"He's in the infirmary," said the caretaker. As he was somewhat knowledgeable about medicine, he added with an ironic smile, "It appears that you like to see cataplasms and mustard plaster. Would you like a coffee?"

"No, thank you."

"Although it is four o'clock, it will be another half hour before lunch is served. Would you like to join us?"

"No, no, my friend, the trip from Vereda Nueva was stifling. And the head of the house?"

"The baron is playing a game of ombre [*tresillo*] with his wife and the doctor."

"Well, I will go see Eduardo."*

"Do you know what happened last night?"

"What happened?"

---

* Here the original text mistakenly uses Federico's name rather than Eduardo's.

"They robbed him at the Boulder of Guachinango, and he miraculously saved himself."

"As he was on his way to the coffee plantation?"

"Exactly."

"You're kidding!"

"What do you mean?"

"But . . . No, no! I don't believe you."

"If it's not true, they can kill and bury me."

"Lovely oath."

"What?"

"They can kill and bury me! . . . Please!"

"Comrade, I'm not joking [*no hablo de chirigota*]."

"Can it be true?"

"Ask anyone."

"But I was just talking with him, a few hundred steps away from the Boulder of Guachinango."

"Well, friend, right there six delinquents approached him and robbed him, and at that very moment by coincidence a company of soldiers headed to San Antonio were passing by."

"Well, sir, if that happened to me I would want to free myself too."

"He will tell you the story better than I can."

"Let's go see him. But let me first say hello to the baron . . . What is the meaning of those little colored lanterns placed around the house?"

"Don't you know that tonight there is going to be a party [*jaleo*]?"

"Oh, that's right. Today is the baroness's birthday. There are going to be beautiful women here tonight."

"Is that true?"

"Above all the Sun of Güira de Melena."*

"She is indeed lovely."

"Without a doubt, friend."

"And who is the happy mortal who is with her?"

"She is still single."

"What? She is not yet engaged, so one could simply . . ."

"As good as gold [*oro molido que fuera*]," said the caretaker, satisfied with having been able to use his favorite phrase.

"Is it really true that Yoyó is single?"

---

* Güira de Melena was a town in the Province of Havana. It is now part of the Province of Artemisa.

"Go see for yourself. Tell me, sir, to continue in that vein, did you know that girlfriend that Eduardo had?"

"Who, Matilde?"

"No, sir, the one they say disappeared."

"Ah, of course: the Sun of Jesús del Monte!"

"Exactly. Well done. Was she really so beautiful?"

"I think so."

"More so than the Sun of la Güira?"

"That is a question of taste; I prefer her to la Yoyó."

"Comrade, I have heard people speak about Tulita as a stunning woman, but I have met la Yoyó, and I don't think that there is as angelic or beautiful a woman anywhere else on earth."

"I think she looks like the queen of Spain."

"Like Isabel Segunda?"*

"I mean in her majestic and svelte figure; as far as her face, la Yoyó has no rival."

"And tell me, Federico, have you seen the queen herself?"

"Just as I see you before me."

"In the flesh?"

"What do you mean, in the flesh?"

"I mean," said the caretaker, a bit embarrassed, "in flesh and blood."

"Of course, man, I was talking to her."

"Amazing. What dresses! So much jewelry! She lives in such luxury! What a crown! Does she talk as we do?"

Federico could not contain his laughter upon hearing the ignorance of the poor man from the country [*pobre campesino*]; the caretaker smiled without understanding the reason for Federico's laughter. Federico and the caretaker entered the living room, where the baron was playing the game ombre. While Federico greeted the owners of the cafetal, Eduardo came in. Inviting Federico to walk through the shady grounds of the cafetal as the lunch hour approached, Eduardo began to recount in great detail the surprise that had been waiting for him at the Boulder of Guachinango.

"I also have news for you."

"What is it?" asked Eduardo.

"I found out today in Vereda Nueva that they condemned that scoundrel Don Valentin to five years in prison."

---

* Isabel II (1830–1904) was queen of Spain from 1833 to 1868 but acted as ruler from 1843 to 1868.

"Is that true?"

"You heard right."

"So who..."

"I read a letter to my uncle from the official who was involved with the case and who now has the rank of lieutenant."

"The prison is on the island of Cuba?"

"No, it's in Ceuta."*

"Well, chico, I am sorry that man has fallen into disgrace."

"The punishment fits the crime!"

"It was a moment of error... It's not my fault; I was obsessed with saving him."

"That's not right."

"No, your friendship with me makes you see things that way, but his crime was one of passion."

"And if you had been in my place?" interrupted Federico, adding, "What do you expect, friend? I can't stand criminals. When they robbed me on the route from Barcelona to Madrid, between Bellpuig and Mollerusa, they didn't do anything but threaten me after cleaning out my pockets, since there were eight passengers besides me in the coach. All told, I assure you that if you had told me that on such and such a day they were to be hung, I would happily have gone to watch them kick away at the air. And to move on to another topic, have you heard from your girlfriend?"

"Absolutely nothing."

"So the story that she took a trip to Jamaica was false."

"That's what I think: the letter the captain of the port sent me doesn't leave a doubt. I suspect that they have gone to Veracruz; I am trying to verify that right now."

"It would be good for you to reunite with Matilde."

"I've overturned every rock on the island looking for her."

"But man, they don't even know whether they have left at the neighborhood political office or at the captaincy? Say what you want, but I think they're still in Havana."

"I would have heard by now. One of my acquaintances has trying to discover Tulita's whereabouts for more than six months, to no avail. How she must be suffering, the poor thing!"

---

* Since 1580, Ceuta has been an autonomous Spanish city on the border with Morocco on the African continent, at the Mediterranean entrance to the Strait of Gibraltar.

"That Chuchita is such an atrocious character. To be capable of shutting her up and not allowing her to see anybody."

"What I don't understand," said Eduardo, shedding a few tears, "is that she has not written me a single world."

"Clearly, it's that she hasn't had an opportunity to do so."

"It's a mystery, and I'm suffering extraordinary anxiety just thinking about her."

"There is nothing hidden under the sun, and when you least expect it you will see how everything will be resolved."

"That is the hope that sustains me."

"Take heart and try to distract yourself."

This was their conversation as they returned to the walkway of the *batey*. The musicians the baron had found in San Antonio for the party that night had just dismounted their horses, and guests from the neighboring farms were beginning to arrive. When Federico and Eduardo entered the living room, they found a large party under way. Some guests were singing, accompanied by a guitar, as the baroness played the piano and her daughter gracefully and coquettishly danced the zapateo.

Eduardo's friends surrounded him, annoying him with questions about what had happened the previous night, some in order to verify what they already knew, others to discover more details so that they could further embellish the story when they found an opportunity to tell it to friends, and still others to show their regret that this unfortunate event had taken place. A few moments later lunch was announced, and everyone walked over to a temporary gazebo that had been constructed in the middle of the *batey*. The meal was splendid and quite lively. Eduardo made various toasts in verse to the baroness, congratulating her on her birthday, and he made other toasts to the guests. For his part, Federico took turns with other improvisers in making ¡*bombas!*—loud and exaggerated jokes woven out of nonsense, absurdity, and laughter that grew more and more boisterous.

At eight o'clock the guests were still at the table. As coffee was served, the baroness sat down at the piano and played the overture to the *Semiramis* in order to please her friends.* When she had finished that lovely composition, all the guests erupted in applause and bravos that were interrupted by the

---

* *Semiramis* refers to *La Tragédie de Sémiramis* (Paris, 1749), by Voltaire (1694–1778), which inspired Giacomo Meyerbeer's opera *Semiramide riconosciuta* (Turin, 1819) and the opera *Semiramide* (Venice, 1823), by Gioachino Rossini (1792–1868). It's not clear which overture the baroness chose to play.

arrival of a new guest. The Sun of Güira de Melena walked into the living room, attracting the attention of everyone.

"How beautiful!" said some.

"Arrogant girl!" said others.

"Those are fifteen well utilized years!" remarked Federico.

"The dance begins!"

A little later, you could hear the rhythmical measures of the danza cubana. Eduardo danced with the baroness, Federico with la Yoyó. The first did it purely as a courtesy, the second because he was infatuated with that lovely child.

# 14

Unexpected Encounter

Federico was the only guest who spent the night at La Reunión coffee plantation, even though the dance ended at two in the morning. Café con leche was brought to his bedside precisely at eight in the morning. The black man who served him the coffee said, "Niño Eduardo is waiting for you in the living room, sir."

"Good. Tell him that I'll be there soon."

Federico quickly got dressed and went to meet Eduardo, holding in his hands the cup of coffee, which he had not yet finished because it was so hot.

"Hi, chico, what's up? You must have rested well."

"As you saw, I went to bed at midnight, but I slept barely an hour."

"Chico, you missed the best part. The dance was brilliant. La Yoyó is a superb *hembrota* [female specimen]!"

"She is indeed quite pretty."

"If I lived in Güira, I would court her. But right after Christmas I have to return to my office . . . It must be done!"

"But you didn't tell her anything? She is green, right? Remember the one about the fox . . ."

"I think that there may be some little cousin of hers who will end up taking advantage of her."

"Who? Ángel?"

"He's the one. It's also true that if I lived in Güira or its environs, that would not present any obstacle to my repeating to her, 'I love you! I idolize you!'"

"If this is how let passion dominate you, you will never lead a life of moderation..."

"Well, who falls in love in such an old-fashioned way in this century as you do? Tell me, would you like to come to Vereda Nueva to have lunch with me?"

"I'm not even in the mood to take my daily walk."

"Get out of your funk," said Federico, giving him a little box of paper cigarettes. "Afterwards we will play a game of billiards and then return to eat at the coffee plantation."

"All right, I'll go with you."

"The baron's family is still sleeping, from what I can tell, so whenever you want we can leave."

"Then I'll get them to saddle up the horses."

Eduardo called the caretaker, gave the necessary orders, and ten minutes later the horses were already there, poking at the gate with their hooves in excited anticipation of the trip. When the friends got ready to mount the horses, the caretaker appeared again, bringing another horse. "Where are you headed?" he asked.

"To Vereda Nueva," answered Federico.

"I am going to San Antonio. I will accompany you until the fork in the road if you will allow me to do so."

"With great pleasure," answered Eduardo.

And the three mounted their horses and took off at a gallop. As they trotted down the principal avenue that served as the entrance to the cafetal, they were far from one another, but once they reached the main road, the mud forced them to continue on very close to one another for a long time. That was when Federico took out some cigars and offered them to Eduardo and the caretaker to pass the time more pleasurably.

"Are you headed to San Antonio to see some woman?" Federico asked the caretaker.

"Oh no, sir. I am going to the house of the black witchdoctor [*negro brujo*]."

"A witchdoctor! What do you mean?" asked Eduardo, surprised by the formal tone with which the caretaker spoke to him.

"Yes, sir, to the witchdoctor," he replied.

"We have witchdoctors, and at this hour," said Federico, smiling maliciously.

"What, you two don't know *taita* Juan?"*

"Who is *taita* Juan?" asked Eduardo.

"The miracle of the jurisdiction."

"The miracle!"

"Yes, sir, the miracle."

"Let's see, let's find out if that's true," said Federico.

"What detestable roads!" said Eduardo, spurring his horse, which had sunk into the mud nearly up to the strap of the saddle.

"To the left!" warned the caretaker. "The path is quite narrow."

"I avoided it well," said Federico, joining the other two, who had gone ahead. "Continue on, mister caretaker."

"As I was saying, *taita* Juan is a miracle; he is a black man who knows all the devil's arts."

"What? And do you believe that? . . ." asked Eduardo, interrupting him, as Federico suppressed the laughter that was bubbling up.

"Do I believe? As if I hadn't seen certain things with my own eyes."

"Certain things!"

"Come on, explain yourself," said Federico, curious to hear the story about *taita* Juan.

"Well, you two are going to be surprised."

"Tell us!"

"All right. Before telling you my reasons for putting my faith in the witchdoctor's words, I am going to refer to some incidents in his life."

"Perfect," said Eduardo.

"Approved," said Federico.

"Well, sir," began the caretaker, "*taita* Juan is a *negro* Lucumí whom they brought from some expeditions to Guinea when he was still *un mulequito*;† and the great-grandfather of the Baron of C . . . bought him for twelve ounces of gold in the *barracones* . . .‡ His masters kept him in service at their

---

* Two entries related to *taita* in the *Diccionario de la lengua española* are relevant here: "1. n. A term that children use to signify father. [. . .] 3. n. Cuba and the Dominican Republic. A form of address often used in speaking to elderly black people."

† African-born slaves who have not reached fourteen years of age are called *muleques*. —*Author*

‡ An old market where slaves were publicly sold, established outside the walls of Havana in the neighborhood that today they call Colón.—*Author*

home in Havana for two years, a period in which an old mulatta, a wet nurse who served the grandfather of the current baron, was charged with teaching him Christian doctrine and preparing him to receive baptism. After one year of instruction, *taita* Juan already spoke Spanish as well as we do, but neither barefoot friars nor God himself could turn him into a believer."

"He didn't want them to shave his head," interrupted Federico.

"He didn't want to risk it," said the caretaker.

"Go on, go on," said Eduardo.

"Let's get to the point," said the caretaker, now assuming the tone of someone who is going to recount an extraordinary tale. "Just between me and you, the black man did not get baptized, because each time that he showed up the priest didn't want to baptize him."

"The priest didn't want to baptize him?" asked Federico.

"Since the devil of a black didn't know how to pray," answered the caretaker, "it was not until the final time that he appeared at the church that the priest allowed him to be Christian, and from then on Juan was his name."*

"All that is good," Eduardo said, "but let's get to the most important question: how is it that he became a witchdoctor?"

"How did he become a brujo? The devil was already in him while he was in his mother's womb. The thing is that he began to do sorcery [*brujería*] on his own when he reached the age of two years, and the devil himself, who can never remain quiet, intervened, and you will see what came of it. One day *taita* Juan approached a very young child, and according to legend, he employed conjuring and turned him into a *berraco*."†

"Are you out of your mind?" interrupted Eduardo.

"A pig!" repeated Federico, bursting into laughter.

"Exactly. You may laugh, but it was just as real as the fact that the three of us are standing here."

"And is it possible that you believe that ridiculous story about that guy?" asked Eduardo with a teasing smile.

"Ridiculous, huh? Ridiculous? To see is to believe, but there's more to tell. *Taita* Juan also did other things that were no less strange and was sent

---

* As Matthew Pettway has pointed out in an analysis of the catechism of the Diocese of Havana, *Explicación de la doctrina Cristiana acomodada a la capacidad de los negros bozales* (Explication of Christian doctrine adapted to the aptitude of non-Hispanized Blacks) (1796, rpt. 1823), to the Catholic church "blackness was a somatic sign of moral depravity." Pettway, *Cuban Literature*, 54.

† A pig.—*Author*

to the baron's sugar mill as a punishment. There he remained until the age of eighty, when he became useless as a field laborer, so the baron allowed him to hold the office of watchman. To recount all the work of the devil that he performed afterwards would be a never-ending tale. He finally made a contribution to the government and to society not many years ago."

"And what was that?" asked Federico.

"If it were not for *taita* Juan, a large number of individuals would have passed on to the other life, and Chávez Bridge would not have served as a scene of spectacle featuring the head of a bandit in an iron cage."

"It was not long ago that we saw the head of Pelao, the famous bandit."

"So," said Eduardo, "what does that have to do with the witchcraft of *taita* Juan?"

"Everything," answered the caretaker. "The person who discovered the hideout of the bandit's gang, who had committed horrible assassinations, was that black man."

"So by that account, he did not employ all his knowledge to do damage?" asked Eduardo.

"Oh no, sir. And frankly, since that time we have reconciled with him. If that had not happened, he would be in jail serving as a midwife for all the little mulattoes [*chinitos*] or he would have had to leave the island."

"Let us hear more details about his important contributions," said Federico.

"We will," continued the caretaker, "but let me eat a couple of guavas, because the ones in that tree look good."

"They look as if they're from Peru," said Eduardo.

"We'll eat some as well," added Federico. "Since we are on the topic of guavas, let's not miss a chance to taste them."

Indeed, the three approached a tree whose branches were so full of guavas that they fell off the branches and rolled off the farm's property. After eating a few and continuing on their voyage, the caretaker again spoke up: "You must have heard about some of the robberies and murders committed by the group of highwaymen led by Pelao."

"Yes, sir," answered Federico and Eduardo at the same time.

"Well, among the worst crimes perpetrated by that monster and his accomplices in the jurisdiction of Matanzas would have to be the one that I will now recount to you. So many unlucky travelers reaching the crossroads

---

* There is no mention of Pelao in the two-volume *El bandolerismo in Cuba,* nor does the name appear in Calcagno's *Diccionario biográfico cubano.*

called Buey-Vaca* not only lost their possessions but also suffered the cruelest treatment: the bandits confined them in the most remote area of the mountain, tying them to trees with strong ropes so that they couldn't move at all, and then abandoned them to die of hunger and thirst so that they would end up being a meal for stray dogs. Facing the horrible sight of the piles of cadavers scattered in the forest, and not brave enough to face the terrible agony that awaited them, the unfortunate victims pleaded with the bandits to kill them then and there. With insolent jokes and raucous laughter, the ferocious thieves granted their wish, as they divided up the spoils of their barbarous enterprise with impunity.

"One day I was working on the finances of the administration of the farm in the baron's house in Havana when *taita* Juan walked into the living room. I had already heard about the black man, so I was surprised to see him and couldn't explain the reason for his visit, because when I had left the coffee plantation the slave had remained there to work.

"'What is this, *taita* Juan!' said the baron, no less surprised than I was. 'What is happening at the farm?' And while he asked this question, he looked at me as if wanting to read in my appearance the explanation for the mystery.

"'Sir, please give me your blessing,' *taita* Juan said, kneeling down. 'I come to you, sir, because there is a terrible thing happening at the crossroads of Buey-Vaca.'

"'What is this dog saying?' asked the baron, upset by the black man's words. 'Caretaker,' he said to me, 'go and find out what is happening while I put these finances in order.' I left with the black man, asking myself, 'What does Buey-Vaca have to do with the cafetal La Reunión? Why has *taita* Juan walked so far to talk to his master?' Well, sir, the case was indeed frightening. He told me that there were more than fifty cadavers in the middle of the forest at the hideout of the gang of bandits, and there was clear and precise evidence of where the thieves were hiding and where they harbored the stolen goods. After I told the baron what *taita* Juan had told me, he notified the captain general. At the moment that the troops surprised the bandits, following the instructions left by the black man, there was still time to save an unlucky woman who was tied to a large ceiba tree and menaced by wild dogs in the middle of the stretch of the forest littered with skeletons. You must understand that since *taita* Juan had never traveled between the district of San Antonio and the jurisdiction of Matanzas, because of his

---

* *Buey* means "ox," and *vaca* means "cow."

knowing the way with the precision that was evident in his instructions, it was obvious that he was a witchdoctor—through the arts of the devil he knows everything. The fact is that no one had heard of the hideout until he sounded the alarm. But let's move on with our story.

"As a result of this, the baron emancipated him, and from that time he has lived on the banks of the Ariguanabo,* which flows out of the town of San Antonio on the west side."

"I don't see anything extraordinary in that story," said Eduardo. "It's possible that *taita* Juan heard about the atrocities that they were committing in Matanzas and just kept quiet about his source."

"Oh, no, sir!" answered the caretaker. "If I have not said enough for you to be persuaded that the black man is a witchdoctor or a prophet, whatever you might call it, I'm going to tell you what I have seen with my own eyes."

"Well, that's an entirely different matter," said Federico, winking at Eduardo in order to poke fun at the caretaker's credibility.

"I am not your gossipy aunt, and what I have seen can't be taken back. Either believe or walk away."

"Go ahead, explain yourself," said Eduardo, watching Federico as he spoke.

"Sirs, this is not a *jarana*,"† answered the caretaker. "I can tell by your faces that you are mocking me, and that makes me doubt your friendship."

"I suppose that is true," answered Eduardo.

"Back to the story," said Federico.

"Well, sir," said the caretaker, "more or less about three months later in the pasture of the first elected mayor of the village of San Antonio, they stole a spotted Arabian horse that would easily be worth twenty ounces of gold, and the thief left in its place a bad, tired mare and a bag of clothes that contained three striped shirts and a cotton handkerchief.

"The son of the mayor, an alderman of the municipal government, came to see me that very evening, asking me to accompany him on a visit to the black witchdoctor to discover the whereabouts of the horse. I accepted, curious to see and hear *taita* Juan, whose history I knew. At around eleven at night we reached the hut [*choza*] where he lives. It was raining cats and dogs when we knocked on his door, and the night was darker than the mouth of a wolf.

"'Who goes there?' asked *taita* Juan, opening the door in a bad mood.

---

* A river that flanks the village of San Antonio Abad.—*Author*
† Joke.—*Author*

"'We come in peace,' answered the alderman.

"'Show yourself, Pablo,' replied the black man, addressing him as if he knew him and had trusted him his whole life."

"But he didn't know him!" remarked Federico, amazed.

"At some point they had seen each other," answered the caretaker. "We dismounted and entered the small space of the hut.

"'You have come to discover the whereabouts of an animal with four paws,' the black man said to us after tracing several circles in the ground, and he began to whisper some prayers. Don Pablo, surprised, looked at me, and I was equally astonished. A little later, he opened several holes within the lines that he had just traced and without deigning to raise his eyes he continued by interrupting his cabalistic prayers with the following command:

"'Pablo, first throw a little bit of money into these holes, and then more and more coins . . .'

"And Don Pablo mechanically obeyed the order of the black man. Once *taita* Juan got him to fill all the holes with pesetas and reales, he began to prophesize more than we had hoped he would. And—much to our astonishment—the devil even revealed the color of the men's shirts."

"And did you find the horse?" asked Eduardo.

"Tied to a caimito tree on the property of the Count of B . . . , just as the brujo had told us."*

"How strange!" said Federico.

"It is very strange," answered the caretaker. "And even though they stole a herd of oxen from our house two days ago, I am so certain of recovering them that I am not in the least bit worried. It is true that I will have to pay *taita* Juan four or five pesos in compensation, but he will tell me where to find the oxen."

"Well, friend," said Eduardo, "what do you want me to tell you? If I were to be frank, I am absolutely certain that *taita* Juan does not prophesy; from my perspective, all these things are nonsense and tall tales [*embustes*] to ensnare the guileless."

"Everyone may believe as he pleases," said the caretaker, "so I bid you bon voyage."

"Go forth and prosper."

They had reached the place where the road to Vereda Nueva begins. Eduardo and Federico continued commenting on what they had just heard

---

* *Pouteria caimito* is the scientific name for the the tropical fruit tree known as the abiu, or yellow sapote.

from the credulous caretaker, who mumbled to himself, "When young men from Havana come to the countryside, they think they know everything and want to give us lessons on things that we have experienced at first hand. They don't believe what happened to me! Forget about it, forget about it."

"What do you think about what the caretaker has told us?" Federico asked Eduardo.

"It's all very clear." Federico answered. "Perhaps this *taita* Juan is associated with some thieves who have established a system of pilfering from their neighbors with the least possible risk."

"But what about his knowledge of even the names of those involved?"

"That is very easy to understand: when they transfer the stolen objects from one point to another, they send as many signals as they need to *taita* Juan, and this is why he can perfectly play the role of clairvoyant [*adivino*]. There is no other explanation."

"Now I understand—you're right. But I am still amazed that they haven't prosecuted the black man, since he creates so many troubles by abusing the ignorance of the poor guajiros."*

"Perhaps someone is protecting him."

"Rogues have all the luck."

"What time is it?" Eduardo asked Federico.

"Ten twenty."

"Well, my watch says exactly eleven."

"The devil! Judging by my stomach, your watch runs better than mine, because I have an extraordinary appetite. You know, I think we are lost!"

"What do you mean, lost?"

"This does not seem to be the road that I have taken on other trips to Vereda Nueva."

"Man, then we are lost."

"Let's find out whether we are or not," said Federico.

"Let's ask at this farm [*estancia*]."

"All right."

Federico stepped forward to consult with a guajiro who was scattering feed for some chickens under the overhang of the living quarters. Eduardo awaited the return of his friend, and when he had returned he said,

---

* See note on page 98 for Orihuela's definition of *guajiro*.

"We are on the right track: I don't have a good sense of direction, but if we stay to the left whenever the road divides, we will reach our destination, and there is only a quarter of a league left to go."

They resumed at a trot, but they had not gone forward twenty paces when Eduardo heard a familiar voice call his name. Turning around, Federico and Eduardo recognized the black woman who was running after them.

"Niño Eduardo!"

"What a surprise!" he exclaimed.

"What luck that I saw you pass by!"

Eduardo took her hand with the greatest joy. The black woman was none other than Dolores, Tulita's slave.

Eduardo asked her so many questions that the poor woman grew embarrassed and, crying out of happiness, didn't know which question to answer first.

"Tulita is going to be so happy when she finds out that I have spoken to you . . . She is very skinny, niño Eduardo . . . Have you received any letters from the girl?"

"If I could only see just one of her letters!"

"She has written so many of them! . . . That is all she does. Oh, you don't know how many tears the girl has cried and continues to cry since they forced her to come to her cousin Don Sebastián's farm. She spent three months on the brink of death . . . I thought she would die . . . If you could only see, niño Eduardo, how she has suffered, you would feel sorry for her. I have been her only comfort during your absence."

"What, am I to believe that she hasn't forgotten me?"

"Forgotten you! It is true that she harbors many complaints . . . Your amorous relations with Matilde . . . Not having written her."

"Have I known her whereabouts before today? I made so many fruitless attempts to find out where she was. If it had not been for this odd, chance encounter, who knows when I would have heard anything about her. Poor thing!"

Eduardo cried tears of happiness.

"I assure you that niña Tulita is so in love with you that I am afraid to tell her the news that I met you."

"As far as that goes, don't tell her a word. I will tell you what we need to do."

"Do you know that a few days ago niña Lola came out to stay with niña Tulita?"

"Lola?" asked Eduardo, without being able to remember who that person was.

"The girl Lola. Have you forgotten her?"

"I don't remember her."

"The friend of my mistress."

"The little widow," said Federico.

"Ah, yes!"

"She has been a great comfort to niña Tulita. All day long all Tulita does is talk to her about you. After lunch, they go out on an afternoon walk together and talk some more. When they return at night it is only to continue the same conversation."

"But can you explain the reason for this sudden trip?"

"Ah! It's true, you have asked me two or three times already. You know, the third day after the mother had agreed to give her daughter away in marriage, she received a letter that Doña Belencita, the mother of Doña Matilde, had sent her, declaring that you were romantically involved with her daughter at the same time as with the niña Tulita. So since she is such a jealous person, she became furious, scolded her daughter all day long, and swiftly arranged everything without telling her a word. The next day she woke us up very early in the morning, put us into two-person carriages, and left for the farm of Don Sebastián, where we have stayed for nearly six months."

"Chico, your future mother-in-law sure has a strong character," said Federico.

"Niña Chuchita," replied the slave, "is more stubborn than a bull, and you should have seen how vigilant the mother was in attempting to prevent her daughter from communicating with anyone and how the mother struggled to persuade the girl to marry Don Valentin. But niña Tulita is extremely resolute, and so constant in her devotion to you that no one has been able to change her mind."

While Dolores was speaking, Eduardo, his mind racing, was trying to devise a plan for how he might have his first meeting with Tulita.

"All right," he said, after a period of silence. "You say that she spends all her afternoons with the widow?"

"Yes, sir."

"And the mother?"

"Sometimes she goes out with the girls, and sometimes with Don Sebastián."

"Wait a minute. Lend me your pencil, Federico."

Federico took out his notebook and gave it to Eduardo. Eduardo wrote a few lines on one of the pages, tore it out, folded it, and as he gave it to Dolores he said, "Be very careful that no one sees you when you give this note to Tulita. Tell her that I will be at the place I wrote down at five o'clock sharp."

"All right, niño Eduardo. I'm going to leave now because they might miss me, and you know what my mistress is like." And Eduardo and Federico continued down the road to Vereda Nueva after taking leave of Dolores, but not without asking her to keep quiet and to follow the instructions carefully.

 15

The Meeting

"Yes, I am the most unfortunate woman!"

"Do you think, dear friend, that Eduardo, a young man of good conduct, after taking the step of asking for your hand in marriage, would abandon you and walk away from his promises, a man who has fought so hard for you and without a doubt is passionately in love with you?"

"I don't know what to tell you, Lolita, but I can't get the name of that mulatta out of my mind . . . To engage in amorous relations with a woman of color at the moment when he was asking for my hand in marriage! Oh! That is an affront! To prefer that Matilde! I would never have believed it."

"Don't give so much importance to a youthful folly . . . That would never have any effect on the happiness that awaits you."

"Happiness!" said Tulita, swallowing a sigh. "Happiness, when my mother opposes the union so openly! And Eduardo has completely forgotten me . . . He doesn't respond to my letters . . . I've written him so many and not even a word . . . Men! What right do they have to deceive a poor woman? And it is my fault for having loved him so much! Just a few months ago I was so happy! He doesn't love me!"

"And do you know if those letters have reached him?"

"I suppose so."

"To whom did you give them?"

"To the slave who goes to San Antonio to buy provisions."

"Do you trust that black man?"

"I've given him a peso for every letter I've given him, but I don't know anything more. He assures me that he has placed all twenty letters in the mail."

"Well, I am going to tell you a secret if you promise to be discreet," said Lolita.

"Tell me whatever you want."

"Those letters . . ."

"What?"

"Those letters are in the possession of your mother."

"Is that possible?" asked Tulita.

"I'm telling you the truth. For her to have confided that to me, I have had to pretend to be on her side about everything, and for that reason last night she told me that she had intercepted your correspondence by using the clever method of offering the slaves of Don Sebastián an impressive sum if they were able to obtain all the letters you write and deliver them to her."

"Now you see how cruelly my mother treats me! And my only crime is to love Eduardo. Thank you, my friend. I was unjust when I blamed him for not answering me."

"And as for Matilde, I have heard that she has gone away to the Mexican republic with her mother and uncle because he was involved in the black conspiracy, so you can rest assured that she has completely disappeared."

"Good, very good . . . That soothes me, but how is it possible that you have neither seen nor heard anything about Eduardo?"

"What do you expect? He is naturally occupied with the duties of his profession."

"Well, give me the letter that I gave you yesterday . . . Today I will write him one that is not so strident."

"As you wish."

"You say that you can deliver my letters into his hands without fail?"

"You can count on it."

"Oh! I would be grateful for that favor all my life. Mother is taking her afternoon nap; you be on the lookout while I write another letter for Eduardo."

"Take the one that you gave me yesterday."

"No, no, I've changed my mind. I want the two letters to go together: yesterday's letter and the one that I will write today, in which I will make amends for the first.

Tulita sat down to write while the widow lifted the curtain to warn her friend in the case that Chuchita were to wake up, ensuring that Tulita wouldn't be surprised in flagrante. This scene took place in the living quarters of Don Sebastián's cattle ranch the same day that the slave Dolores bumped into Eduardo. By coincidence, Chuchita had sent Dolores to a small neighboring farm to buy a basket of tamarinds, and when Eduardo and Federico passed by on the road, she saw them and recognized Eduardo.

Happier than someone who has just found a great treasure, Dolores returned to the cattle ranch. Unfortunately for her, it was the day when she had to help the other slaves in the harvest of a load of coffee [*una punta de café*], a small planting that Don Sebastián had made in the cattle ranch, to contribute to the provisions of coffee that his household drank all year long. So it wasn't possible for her to deliver the letter to her mistress as soon as she wished. She did all she could to finish as soon as possible, and indeed, when Tulita finished writing the last word of her letter to Eduardo, the black woman cautiously approached her.

"Jesus, Dolores, you scared me!"

"What's going on?" asked the widow.

"I bring good news," said Dolores, with an air of satisfaction and an extremely happy expression.

"About what?" asked the two friends.

"About niño Eduardo."

"About Eduardo?" both women asked, both surprised and anxious.

"Have you heard something?" asked Tulita, making a sign to the widow to make sure that Chuchita wasn't waking up.

"Yes, mistress . . . That is, no, mistress."

"Explain yourself? Where have you been?"

"I have spoken to a friend of his."

"To a friend? And what did he tell you? Is he all right? Does he love me?"

"Oh yes, mistress . . . he always talks about you."

"But who told you about my Eduardo?"

"He did," said Dolores, no longer able to resist the temptation of telling Tulita everything.

"He did? Eduardo? When? Where did you see him?"

"Very close by."

"Is he coming to see me? Do you know where he is? Oh, I am so happy. But what if my mother hears about it?"

"Take this: he gave me this little note this morning."

"See," said the widow, curious to find out what Eduardo would say. "And you doubted the affection of your lover?"

"I need you to help me sort through my thoughts," answered Tulita, after reading for a third time the lines Eduardo had written. "I would like to see him . . . but I don't dare; or rather, I don't know what I would like nor how to figure it out! Please give me some advice!"

"Dear friend, you're acting like a little girl—calm down . . . Let's see what he has written, and then I will tell you what I think."

"Yes, I am a little girl . . . it's true . . . it's the happiness that I feel . . ."

So the widow took the little note and read the following words:

"My life and soul, if I still merit a place in your heart, if you would like to make me the happiest of mortals, be at the gate that leads to the main road at five o'clock this afternoon, where you will find your faithful, EDUARDO."

"Congratulations."

"What time is it?"

"I don't know," answered the widow, "but it must be past four o'clock."

"Wow!" said Dolores, who had positioned herself in such a way that she could avoid being seen by Chuchita if she were to wake up.

"Let's go for a walk," said Tulita, taking the arm of her friend. "I'm impatient to see Eduardo."

And the two friends headed over to the meeting place.

"Dolores, it is your job to come to warn us in case mother comes over here," said Tulita.

"Don't worry, I will keep two steps ahead of the señora."

While Tulita and the widow were walking to the meeting place, it would be good for the reader to accompany us to the coffee plantation La Reunión, where Eduardo and Federico had returned at three in the afternoon that same day. The two friends were seated at the table enjoying a frugal meal that Eduardo threw together quickly because he wanted to set off for the cattle ranch of Don Sebastián a half hour before five. The baron was about to go hunting—they didn't expect him to return until nighttime—and the baroness had gone with her girl to pay a visit to family friends in the village of San Antonio.

"Eduardo, I envy how happy you have been since you found Tulita."

"Oh! You can't imagine how anxious I was and how many ideas passed through my head after I saw Dolores."

"And how will you make up with the mother?"

"I don't even want to see her. I hate that woman with all of my five senses. She had some gall to run off with my love and deprive me of the consolation of speaking to her! Oh! I assure you that I will never forgive her as long as she lives."

"But chico, you are also being unfair: your affair with Matilde gave her the opportunity to take that course of action."

"Nevertheless, she has condemned me without listening to me. Even if I did have that affair, did she stop to consider what effect her actions would have on our happiness?"

"Women, compadre, have a more exquisite sensibility than we do, and they are more imaginative, which is to say that she will stubbornly insist that you would not have changed your troublesome behavior, and since jealousy is an essential ingredient to domestic tranquility, she has preferred to attack the evil at its roots rather than allow the cancer to reach the heart. Moreover, the real guilty party in this whole affair is Belencita."

"That's true. Belencita is no less guilty, to be sure; she betrayed me in a way that I will never forget, even though she could not have suspected all the consequences of her revelation."

"In intrigues of this nature, women are one of a kind."

"Did I show you the two letters that Matilde and Belencita wrote me the day of their departure for Veracruz?"

"Yes, I remember them."

"I was weak enough to reach an agreement with those poor women: rather than living more independently, and therefore more comfortably, I would take them to Europe, where I would share my fortune with Matilde and, shielded by different social institutions, I would marry her. But this did not go beyond simple promises, and as a result our love was only a pastime. As you have seen in those letters, not only are they waiting for me in Veracruz, counting on me to come and help them to realize their dreams, but Belencita had the audacity to reveal everything to Chuchita."

"And you are surprised that your would-be mother-in-law would begin to take on the role that she would surely play in the drama of your marriage?"

"But it was a very violent and stupid step to take."

"Your mother-in-law is such a scoundrel! Chico, I have decided that if I am to enter into the sacred union of matrimony, it must be with a woman who is an orphan, without mother or father."

"She will always have other relatives."

"Oh, that does not matter. I do not recognize any relatives other than molars and other teeth."

"The result of this is that since you are getting married in Cuba, you will never be free, even if your wife is free, because someone will always show up claiming the vague title of relative."

"Well, let them come, because they will have to reach into their pockets [*rascarse pelo arriba*] and pay up [*tres mas nueve*].* I have seen so many arguments in marriages as a result of the stupidity of husbands who allow in their own home those parasitic plants with the properties of the *guaguao*, which burns all those who brush against them!† As for me, I know that if I were to commit the crime of getting married, I would have to prevail over all difficulties [*he de matar el gato*] from the first day that I bore the title of husband."‡

"If I get married to Tulita, I assure you that we will have to live entirely alone."

"And you will have done the right thing a thousand times over. Who is capable of resisting the terrible struggle against relatives who become spies and censors of the husband's conduct? If you treat them well, it is bad, and if you treat them bad, it is worse. There is nothing to do except to be alone, and quite alone."

"It is already four o'clock," said Eduardo, looking at his watch. "Will you accompany me?"

"Where?"

"What do you mean, where? To the meeting."

"But there is still time."

"I don't want to be the first to wait."

"Right, so didn't you tell her to come at five?"

"Well, we have to walk . . ."

---

* *Rascarse pelo arriba* means "to take money out of one's pocket" (F. V. and M. B., *Colección*, 477).

† According to Esteban Pichardo, the *guaguao* is a kind of *ají*, or pepper: "The guaguao [is a plant with] small leaves and with a fruit the size of a [green] pepper, which is red or yellow when it matures and is very spicy and used primarily in Tierradentro." *Diccionario provincial*, 41.

‡ "Matarle a uno el gato, ó Matar uno el gato, son frases figs y fams. que significan entre nosotros vencer la dificultad ó impedimento, real o aparente" (Matarle a uno el gato, or matar uno el gato, is a figurative and common phrase that among us mean to overcome a real or apparent difficulty or impediment). Román, *Diccionario de chilenismos*, 3:582.

"You can do that in ten minutes."

"Agreed, but I would like to be there a half hour early."

"All right, let me drink another cup of coffee and we will leave."

"Hurry up, then."

"I'll be ready in a minute."

As soon as Federico downed his cup of coffee, the two friends mounted their horses and took the road to Vereda Nueva. Full of love and hope, Eduardo rushed toward the encounter with the woman who reigned over his mind. Seconds felt like centuries in his feverish impatience, and he even felt that the distance that separated them was greater than it actually was. These thoughts grew out of his impatience to once again gaze at the captivating face of his love.

 16

Plans

"I'd like to know, maestro, can you give me a carriage [*volanta*] with a good pair of horses?"*

"Where are you going, sir?"

"To Havana."

"We will need to stop to change the team."

"Fine."

"We can do that, if the gentleman agrees, in the city of Santiago."†

"Agreed. There are two things I want to know: if you can get everything ready by tomorrow night at ten, and how much it costs."

---

* *Maestro* literally means "master" or "teacher," but in this case it refers to the expertise of Eduardo's interlocutor as a master horse trainer. However, English speakers would not use *master* as part of a phrase unless referring to particular professions or a specific expertise, such as a master of capoeira or karate. In this case, the maestro is what English speakers call a horse trainer.

† Here the *maestro* refers to the town of Santiago de Las Vegas, which is currently 10.9 miles from San Antonio de los Baños along the most direct route and approximately 13.9 miles from Old Havana.

"The first is difficult, because everything depends on whether the gentleman is generous. As far as the second one goes, you may offer me what you please and I will arrange everything."

"None of that: I want a clear price. And I will pay you in advance."

"If you would like, I will drive the carriage myself."

"No, I have a good driver."

"Then the gentleman will pay me forty pesos."

"I will give you three ounces of gold, but only on the condition that the carriage be ready to be delivered to my driver at ten at night."

"You can count on that."

"Well and good. Take the three ounces."

"Rest assured that everything will be set."

"As we agreed. Until tomorrow."

"What does your driver look like?"

"Don't worry about that. When a black man comes and mentions my name, give him the carriage."

"Would you like to choose among the carriages to find one most to your liking? Please come and see, sir."

"That is not necessary: whichever one, as long as it is good."

"The niño will take one of our very finest."

"I trust your words, maestro."

"Do not worry, sir, the sun will fail to rise before I betray my word."

When Eduardo left the showroom of the man who rents carriages, with whom he had the preceding conversation, he met with Federico, who had just gone swimming.

"Hola, chico!" said Federico, "To see you in San Antonio and so early in the morning!"

"I had to run an early errand, and I have completed it. I'm very happy to see you."

"Are you going to return to La Reunión?"

"Yes, but at noon."

"It's nine o'clock now. What will you be doing in the meantime?"

"I need to take care of another matter; I hope you can help me."

"Tell me—whatever you'd like."

"Where are you headed?"

"I was going to the Gonzálezes' house to spend some time chatting before eating lunch."

"Come with me, then. We'll walk by the edge of Ariguanabo and talk business."

"Let's go, then."

"You can help me," said Eduardo, offering his arm to Federico and walking at a leisurely pace, "by finding a trustworthy black man who can serve as my driver for a couple of days."

"Compadre, I am just as much a stranger to the countryside as you are. I am sorry to say that I do not have enough contacts to immediately satisfy your need."

"That doesn't matter."

"It doesn't matter?"

"Exactly."

"I don't understand you."

"Listen to me."

"Please explain."

"Find out if someone in the town can rent out his driver."

"That is another matter."

"And then immediately hire him without worrying about the price and let me know."

"And it must be today?"

"Each minute of waiting is like a century for me and pains me."

"May I ask why?"

"I don't keep any secrets from you."

"Tell me, then."

"I want to take Tulita away from her mother."

"How does that involve the black carriage driver?"

"You don't understand me."

"No, I don't."

"Well, it's what I don't have: I already have a carriage and horses, but I didn't want to hire as my carriage driver the maestro who rented out the carriage and the horses, because I'd like to keep things secret."

"I get it, and I'll be quiet."

"So when?"

"Tomorrow at ten at night I need to drive the carriage to a spot close to the cattle ranch where Tulita is staying. I see her every night at ten, and tomorrow I am prepared to take her with me to Havana."

"And of course she has agreed to this?"

"I have not spoken a word to her about it, but she will not oppose it."

"Good, good. I will speak to some friends in town today, and I will hire the carriage driver."

"I can count on you."
"For..."
"For this task."
"Don't worry about it."
"Do you have money?"
"I've got six onzas left. Tomorrow is the last day of the Easter holiday, and it will be enough."
"Good, take three onzas so that you have enough for your expenses, and above all so that price is not an obstacle."
"Man, keep your money. My uncle is in San Antonio de los Baños, and in case I'm short..."
"Nevertheless."
"No, it won't be necessary."
"As you wish. The essential thing is that the black or mulatto man be intelligent in his dealings with horses and that he know the road well."
"And where can I send word?"
"Send it to me at the coffee plantation La Reunión as soon as you have found him."
"Good. But have you thought about the alarms that will sound after you have kidnapped that girl?"
"Don't worry about it. I'll marry her right away, and everything will be done. There may be some rumors, but you know that I'm not worried and I don't pay attention to the pettiness of most people [*del vulgo*]."
"And the widow is still at the cattle ranch?"
"Tomorrow morning she returns to the city."
"She hasn't spoken to you about me?"
"Not one word."
"I had already thrown her into the dustbin of history."
"It's your fault. If you had shown up to my first meeting with Tulita, she was with my girl, and perhaps you could have salvaged your relationship with her, and you would have helped me a great deal."
"Why?"
"Because you would have entertained her while I explained myself to Tulita."
"Leave that for a fortune-teller. You know that I stayed away from your rendezvous because I didn't want to bother you. Moreover, Lola is a flirtatious and run-down woman who has fully lived her thirty years."
"Nonetheless, she has a pair of eyes that shine like diamonds."

"That is her only good quality. On the other hand, her mother is too fond of gossiping with everyone, and I don't like spending time with people like that."

"You have become quite ethical."

"Well, since you are staying in San Antonio until midday, let's have lunch together, and then I will immediately go take care of your errand."

"I accept."

"I will tell you about a scene that I witnessed yesterday at a *timba*.*"

"And what is that?"

"An exquisite disappointment."

"I'm all ears."

"It was three in the morning; I had already lost five onzas, which fortunately was the only money that I carried with me, and I was stunned to see that even though I won a point once in a while, that was offset by the fact that they were cleaning out my pocketbook one duro at a time from the beginning of the game. When we wrapped up the game, we noticed that Dr. N . . . , an untiring aficionado of the vice of gambling, and always the first and last of the players at the card tables, had fallen asleep and was snoring loud enough to wake the dead as he leaned against one of the corners of the table. The fellow who had served as the *gurrupié*,† a funny man, then proposed:

"'Señores, do you want to play a mean trick on the doctor?'

"'What do you have in mind?' asked those of us who were disposed to play along.

"'A joke,' he answered.

"'Explain what you mean,' one of us asked.

"'Since everything is already finished, and that man is sleeping like a hog,' he continued, 'let's turn off the lights as if we're still playing, and I'll touch him on the elbow and we'll all have a good laugh.'

"Chico, sure enough, that's what happened. The doctor woke up, and all of us had to chew our handkerchiefs to keep from cracking up. As soon as the poor old man rubbed his eyes, the *gurrupié* played his role perfectly. 'Whose turn is it? These ten duros? And he moved some of the money. The jack is knocking at the door! Those two onzas? Let's see, señores . . . Are you . . . is that the king or the horse? No more bets can be placed.'

---

* A card game.—*Author*
† The head card player.—*Author*

"You can't imagine the torture the doctor experienced at that moment. He first began to ask in a disconsolate tone,

"'What's wrong with my eyes?'

"'Don't play the fool,' one person said. 'You're distracting me. Here, let me see those ten *duros!*'

"'My friend,' continued the doctor, 'can you tell me what's with my eyes?'

"'Buddy, could you be quiet?'

"'Señores, wait . . . I'm blind!' And he began to cry bitterly.

"What a prank! Finally, when we saw that he was convinced that he had gone blind, they turned on a light and everyone erupted into laughter. The doctor was as furious as a man about to face a firing squad."

"Buddy that prank was horrible."

"We thought it was delicious."

"At his expense."

"Perhaps, but he is vice personified. Let's change the subject. How will Chuchita react when she finds out that her daughter has been kidnapped?"

"She will scream."

"One expects that, but will you tell her?"

"Tell her? I won't tell her one word. To the contrary, I would like for her not to know where her daughter is for a long time so that she can taste the bitterness that has made me so anxious."

"And don't you think that her daughter will object to that?"

"I would assume that the affection she has professed for me and her desire for us to get married would lead her to overlook the sorrows that would torment her mother."

"My friend, you are now a happy man. But let's get lunch, because my stomach is at the point of begging for scraps."

"Let's go."

"The two friends walked into a nearby eatery, at the platform of the train station, and after dining splendidly, they took leave of each other, Eduardo leaving Federico in charge of the driver [*calesero*]. As Eduardo was returning to the coffee plantation La Reunión, he was thinking to himself:

"To be loved brings such happiness! . . . Everyone says this, everyone believes this; nevertheless, if the person is frank with himself, he will have to confess that it also results in great anxieties . . . All of us must confront hurdles, restlessness, worries, sorrow and tears, anguish, and even regret—true tempests of life that come along with this sweet happiness. To inspire a pure, sincere, noble, and delicate love is the dream of the generous and honorable soul. One begins to live at the very instant when such a sweet vertigo paralyzes our faculties. It is from that moment that we can begin to trace our most delightful memories; we seek glory, wealth, social standing—everything just so we might be loved.

"To be loved, is to be understood, is to be blessed, consoled and happy, . . . it is to have a guide, a northern star in the tortuous path of life; it is to have a wise counselor who is able to appreciate the qualities and true worth of a person, a judge who is invested in the case, who is severe out of pride but indulgent out of tenderness, who dreams of the potential of one's perfection . . . it is to have a friend who guesses what is happening in the bottom of one's heart, with whom one can be honest to allow one's soul to grow, who consoles us in misfortune; it is to offer intimacy for intimacy, affection for affection, pleasure for pleasure . . . And when one has fully enjoyed the extent of that state we call the height of supreme happiness, when there is nothing beyond that, neither for the spirit nor for the physical existence that is its sublime emanation, then there is restlessness, anguish, disenchantment, and society—nay, the whole world—is at once a cradle and grave!

"Tulita is an angel that I have encountered in the desert of life: her sweet apparition before my eyes has transported me to a new world of dreams of glory, of unlimited delight . . . Will those dreams last? I don't know, but I am sure that matrimony is the grave of love . . . Nevertheless, an irresistible power is dragging me to the edge of that grave, which they call the perfection of one's social position, so let us enter. Dreams fly by with the velocity of thought, and a dream is perhaps the happiness that awaits me . . . let us enjoy that dream!"

As he concluded these reflections, Eduardo reached the coffee plantation. When he dismounted his horse, the caretaker came to greet him.

"Did you know that I found the herd of oxen?" he asked with irony in his voice.

"The herd of oxen!" answered Eduardo, without understanding what he had just heard.

"Yes, sir, and you don't believe in prophets!"

"I know, I know."

"But look, sir, right where *taita* Juan said: there are the poor animals that have not eaten in thirty hours, dead from hunger and thirst."

"Dead?"

"No, sir; I mean to say with a hunger that consumes them."

Then Eduardo described the simple way that one could pass oneself off as a witch or a prophet and explained that the caretaker's beliefs were the product of *taita* Juan's methods.

Surprised, the caretaker answered, "Now I am inclined to believe that the dog actually has been fooling us."

"Would you like to see proof of that with your own eyes?"

"I would be very grateful for such evidence."

"Well, I am going to take the watch that you have in your bedroom. Immediately go and consult with the witchdoctor, and if he is able to guess that I have it, by my word of honor I will give you twenty onzas of gold."

"Really?"

"You heard right. But if he doesn't guess correctly, will you buy me a beer?"

"My friend, that is not expensive. But I will do this only to persuade myself of what you are telling me."

"Could you get me some coconuts?"

"Are you thirsty, sir?"

"Yes, I feel a bit fatigued."

"Julian! Julian!" yelled the caretaker.

"What would you like, sir?" answered a slave who immediately appeared.

"Get the rope ladder [*trepadera*] and cut off some coconuts and bring them to the gentleman."

"Yes, sir."

Julian went to follow the orders the caretaker had just given him, and as he headed down the main path to find the coconut grove, he came across another black man, who attracted his attention because he wasn't from the coffee plantation.

"Good day, *paisano* [compatriot]."

"Good day, *calavera*."*

"Is niño Eduardo at the coffee plantation?"

"He just arrived a little while ago."

"I have a letter for the gentleman."

"Well, he is in the house speaking to the caretaker."

"Many thanks!"

"No problem."

The slave who had asked these questions of Julian was the driver whom Federico had sent with a letter explaining exactly how he had performed his duty.

---

* See Orihuela's definition of this term in note on page 123. See also note on page 94.

 17

Paying a Visit

Once Federico had fulfilled his obligation by hiring a driver for the trip Eduardo was planning, he went to pay a visit at the house of the mayor of the village of San Antonio, where the most distinguished people met every night.

The mayor, a man of mediocre intelligence and quite a joker, had grown close to Federico because as the mayor's right-hand man, Federico was the bookkeeper [*refaccionista*] for the eleven farms the mayor owned.* Since Federico was not his inferior in life experiences, notwithstanding their difference in age—the mayor was approaching fifty—they sympathized with each other and got along swimmingly.

"You have arrived late today," said the mayor when he saw Federico enter.

"It's better to arrive on time than to wait the whole year," Federico answered the mayor, who was eating cookies with his coffee.

"Would you like a coffee?"

"Yes."

"Hey, Manuel! A cup of coffee for the gentleman!" the mayor called to one of his servants. Squeezing Federico's hand as a sign of appreciation, he asked, "What's new?"

"The same old story." And Federico settled into a magnificent lounge chair that the mayor very attentively offered him.

"I'm going to show you a very curious document."

"Let's see—what does it concern?"

"Although you don't want to believe in malignant spirits, you are going to be convinced that even if they don't exist today, they did in other times."

"Really!" said Federico. "It's not just a rumor?"

---

* Orihuela italicizes the term *refaccionista* in this sentence, possibly because it was a neologism: it doesn't appear in the *Diccionario de la lengua española*. However, the *Diccionario* does include as the sixth meaning of *refacción* the following entry: "*Cuba*. An expense that the owner incurs for the maintenance of an *ingenio* [sugar plantation] or other farm." I have therefore translated *refaccionista* as "bookkeeper" since Federico apparently manages the finances of the mayor's eleven farms.

"No, man, see for yourself," and he gave him a book that was on a side table.

Then Federico read on the title page "Account of the Ecclesiastical Visit of the Most Illustrious Mr. Morel."

"And what is the purpose of doing me this favor?"

"Read, read it, and then you will tell me what you think."

Then Federico read aloud:

"I certify, attest, and offer my true testimony to those assembled, I Bartolomé del Castillo, the public notary of the ecclesiastical jurisdiction of the village of San Juan de los Remedios del Cayo, today being the fourth of September at nine or ten o'clock in the morning, in the sacred parochial church of said village; those present are José González de la Cruz, rector and priest of the parish of this village, the vicar and ecclesiastical judge of the commissary of the Sacred Office of the Inquisition, and the commissary of the Saint on the Cross, exorcising a demon . . ." (Federico grimaced.)

"Please continue," said the mayor. "Now the good part starts."

Federico continued, "Exorcising a demon that many have said possessed a black creole woman from this village named Leonarda, who lived close to the village; the demon called himself Lucifer, and he and thirty-five legions had taken control of the body of the woman, whom the priest required to take an oath that is as follows . . ."

And upon concluding this paragraph, Federico stood up and in an indignant tone said,

"But is it possible that human ingenuity [*la invención humana*] could be so abusive of the simplemindedness of men?"

"Please continue," said the mayor, "because that's not all."

Federico continued, "I, Lucifer, swear to Omnipotent God and to the saintly Virgin Mary, to Saint Michael and to all the saints of the sky, that I will obey you in everything that the ministers of God order in his name, in the name of his honor and liberty, and if by chance I break this pledge, I would like Satan to be my tormentor and my sufferings to increase by seventy times more than I would like, amen. San Juan de los Remedios on the fourth of September, 1682. Witnessed by the mayors Rojas, Monteagudo, and others."

"What do you say to that, my friend?" asked the mayor.

"That the priest of San Juan de los Remedios, José González de la Cruz, was the haughtiest and most dishonest rogue of those who have exploited humanity just to wear a gown and pray."

"Don't be so severe, man."

"I can't tolerate men of the church,"* replied Federico. "Those crows with the talons of vultures have done more damage to society than all the plagues that the world has suffered up to now."

"Well, I tell you, if I were single like yourself, I would become a monk without wasting any time."

"Undoubtedly, it is the career in which one can improve one's position, and monks profit at the expense of those fools who tolerate them. They live on the country, they commit all sorts of crimes under the mantle of hypocrisy that covers them, and they live a luxurious and independent life; but despite that, I'm not the type of person to contribute to such a farce that allows those people to carry in their hands the rope to strangle the poor apostolic Roman Catholic."

"How is it that you don't believe that Lucifer made that statement?"

"They can't administer communion to me with the wheels of a mill. I am absolutely amazed by the fact that a most illustrious bishop would authorize such idiocies and permit them to come out in public."

"Well, friend," said the mayor. "I have spoken today with the very priest who lent me that book; he is a broad-minded man. Do you know what he told me?"

"What?"

"That the event certainly and positively did take place."

"I would say to you that if it is really so certain and true, then wolves do not bite one another. Rather than contributing to the flourishing of Christian religion, those Sardanapaluses turn it into an object of ridicule.† And frankly, now that I have read it with my own eyes, I greatly distrust the man who believes in superior beings, whether one or many, in supernatural beings, who supposedly direct everything that takes place on earth, as if they

---

* Here Federico says "la gente de corona" (men of the crown) instead of "la gente de la iglesia" (men of the church), but given the context of the quote, I think Orihuela meant to say the latter, not the former.

† Sardanapalus was a mythical king of Assyria who was a composite figure of three kings who suffered tragic fates. He modeled his speech, dress, and behavior on that of women, which is perhaps why Federico likens priests, whose dress-like vestments resemble women's clothing, to Sardanapalus. Arbaces's army of Medes Persians and Babylonians defeated Assyria when Sardanapalus abandoned the fight and burned himself to death in a reaction to a flood in his capital city that had apparently fulfilled prophecy. *Encyclopaedia Britannica Online,* s.v. "Sardanapalus," https://www.britannica.com/topic/Sardanapalus-legendary-king-of-Assyria.

created it, and other such rumors, because in the belief that if they repent at the hour of their death they will be saved, they commit all kinds of crimes with a cold stoicism."

"Let's turn the page and talk about something else because my wife is coming, and if she hears you espousing such doctrines you will fall in her eyes."

Then the wife of the mayor appeared, savoring one of the large cigars that are called *vegueros*. Federico greeted her cordially, and after responding in kind, she sat down beside her husband.

"Easter has been quite cold this year. Isn't that right, Federico?"

"Señora, those of us who live in the capital regard the countryside as always very pleasant even if it isn't as lively this time of year as the city."

"When do you plan to return to Havana?" asked the mayor.

"The day after tomorrow."

"So soon?" asked the mayor's wife.

"For those of us who have serious jobs, it is not possible to indulge our fondest desires all the time. I would happily stay in San Antonio for much longer, but that isn't possible."

"What was your impression of the school dances?" asked the woman.

"They were ordinary. My only observation is that there is a very particular custom in this village: when one young woman gets up and leaves the dance, all the other young women follow her lead and desert the dance hall even if it is not yet midnight."

"Of course," answered the mayor, "women are very petty with each other: none of them wants to be seen as inferior to another, and since it is prestigious to disdain even the most innocent pleasures, above all in public, you will have noticed that if the first woman to leave the dance is a person of some importance, all those who value status will follow her without any delay."

"What would you like to do tonight?" asked the wife of the mayor, wanting to change the topic because she didn't want to hear about the foibles of her sex.

"Let's play cards, if Señor Federico will agree to be the third player."

"With great pleasure," he answered.

"But we're going to play for a real," said the señora.*

"As you wish," answered Federico.

---

* The real was in use from the fourteenth century until 1864. Eight reales were equivalent to one silver peso. TePaske and Klein, *Royal Treasuries,* xvi.

Then the slave Manuel, who had heard the whole conversation with crossed arms, waiting for Federico to return the cup when he had finished drinking coffee, carried in a little card table, and the three interlocutors sat down to begin the game of ombre.

 18

Hours of Anguish

The landscape of the Cuban countryside is rich, fertile, and beautiful. The European who is fortunate enough to visit Cuba will marvel at its stunning and spectacular scenes of virgin nature. Its coffee plantations, sugar plantations, and cattle ranches are lovely gardens. It abounds with scattered and abandoned banana trees, their broad leaves stretching forth at random, the curved coconut tree, the bamboo, sugar cane, coffee plants, and so many other fragrant plants that shed their brown leaves only to grow back again. The observer who has abandoned the city and explores the rural roads of this gorgeous country will witness great verdant savannahs that are just marvelous. In those parts, there are only two seasons in the year, spring and autumn, and if it is true that the sun of the tropics is too hot, it is also true that light breezes come to soften the intensity of its rays. If one adds to this the patriarchal life of the *guagiros*,* the simplicity of their customs, their sweet character, the hospitality they extend to guests, and the pleasures they enjoy both in the estate of the planter and in the hut of the laborer, it will seem that only adventure, peace, and happiness can be found in Cuba's broad expanses.

Nevertheless, there one can find sad souls, one can hear complaints that strike to the core of one's heart, there one can find abundant tears of bitterness, there they irrigate the fields with human blood, there one can find spectacles that only take place in the most barbarous countries on earth, because there slavery reigns!!! What a terrible degradation of humanity!

It seems impossible that in the nineteenth century there still exist racial differences among humans in the world.

---

* Here Orihuela uses an alternative spelling for *guajiros*.

The whites of Cuba believe themselves to be superior to blacks, mulattoes, and anyone whose mixture includes black African blood, and despite this, some of the proudest families of the country have a fraction of blood from the race they consider to be degraded.* Who has given them the right to classify themselves as superior? And even if we were to accept the hypothesis that blacks are inferior, why is it necessary to tear so many poor souls away from their native lands only to treat them like savage beasts and condemn them to suffer under the lash of a tyrant for the rest of their lives? Isn't it time for this barbarous commerce in human blood to end? The scoundrels! ... The crime that they commit against the oppressed race of Africans—whom the vile merchants of the Spanish Antilles steal from their countries of origin and weigh down with chains—is unpardonable before the eyes of reason and before the intimate sentiment of one's conscience.

If in Cuba this degrading tendency ceased to exist, if its system of government were more in harmony with nature's, if in Cuba man could retain his dignity as man and if the despotism that has led to exploitation and the omnipresence of death were to end, if this country were to reform itself—perhaps that solemn day is not far away—and if all its masses could enjoy civilization and liberty, then it would be one of the most enviable countries on earth.

Two days after sending the coachman to Eduardo, Federico had to return to Havana. The Christmas holiday was over, and he returned to the city's labyrinth of financial dealings. However, he had left a pair of borrowed silver spurs at La Reunión coffee plantation. He returned there to retrieve the spurs and take them back to Havana in order to return them to a colleague in the commercial house where he worked, who had lent them to him.

---

* The Spanish-language original reads, "Los blancos de Cuba créense superiores a los negros y a los mulatos, a todo lo que tiene mezcla de sangre Africana y á pesar de esto algunas de las mas orgullosas familias del pais tienen que lamentar el participio de esa que estiman raza degradada." Orihuela, *Sol,* 98. The word *participio* presented a puzzle to me because it is a grammatical term meaning "participle," as in "the present participle of *to run* is *running.*" The Latin *participium* has the same grammatical meaning, but it also means "sharing," deriving as it does from the Latin verb *participare,* "to share," which is *participar* in Spanish. *Oxford Dictionary of English,* s.v. "participle." Given that derivation of the term *participio,* one could translate the sentence as referring to what the proudest, allegedly white families of Cuba share with Blacks and mulattoes: *sangre Africana* (African blood). My translation is not a literal one, but it captures this meaning of the original.

For that reason, once he reached the *batey* of the coffee plantation, he asked for the caretaker.

"He has gone out," answered the slave Julián, whom he found watering the beautiful flowerpots that adorned the front of the house.

"And the overseer?"

"He has left on his rounds of supervision of field work."

"Who is inside the house?"

"Niño Eduardo."

"Eduardo?"

"Yes, sir."

"Well, inform him of my arrival."

"Come, sir, and you will find him walking in the path by the avocado trees."

"Take me there."

As soon as they had taken fifty steps, Julián pointed toward the area where Eduardo was walking, and he returned to his house chores.

"Chico!" said Federico, giving Eduardo a hug. "You're still here?"

"You're looking at me."

"And Tulita?"

"She is at the cattle ranch."

"But what happened? Have you changed your plans?"

"No, I am determined to see things through."

"Well, what a surprise! I thought that you and your woman would already be in Havana like two lovebirds."

"It's not possible to do everything you want."

"I already had reason to doubt that it would be so easy to persuade her to follow your plan."

"Oh! That's for sure."

"And so, why do I still find you here?"

"We're going to leave tonight."

"Tell me, what did she say when you explained your plans? She has quite a temper."

"I will tell you. The carriage was parked twenty steps from the cattle ranch on the highway, and, full of love and hope, I went to tell Tulita about my scheme. As always, she was lovely, obliging, and seductive. But something in my appearance or in my conversation alerted her that I was not as calm as usual.

"'What's wrong with you?' she asked, 'you seem sad and restless.'

"'I am not happy,' I replied.

"'What's happening?'

"'I'm just not happy.'

"'You're not happy? Do you doubt my love?'

"'Would you be able to give me real proof of your affection?'

"'Doesn't my heart already belong only to you?' "'Then tonight you will come to me.'

"'To speak to mother? Oh, that is pointless... You know...' Interrupting her, I told her my idea. She grew pale and her eyes filled with tears.

"'Take pity on me,' she said. 'How could I abandon my mother like that!'

"'Until you are my wife, I cannot find peace.'

"'Speak to my mother,' she answered. 'That is the prudent thing to do.'

"'But you just told me that it would be fruitless to do so.'

"Placing her delicate hand on my mouth, she interrupted me, saying, 'Let's talk about something else... This was just a joke, right?' I blew my whistle, and the carriage appeared. 'You see,' I told her, 'the carriage is waiting for us.' We then argued about it, but she eventually prevailed. I love her so much! The following night I found her to be more willing. At one point, I regretted not having the carriage close by. But now it's all decided, and tonight we will leave."

"Well, sir, it was a good outcome. I have to take the train that leaves from San Antonio at noon, and I will be at my home by four in the afternoon. What a dream I had last night!"

"A pleasant one?"

"To the contrary. I will tell you about it because it was so extraordinary. I thought I was on my way to Madrid, staying at an inn in Arganda, and I was following the tracks of Palmita, a woman with whom I had a relationship in Spain long ago. On the night of my arrival at the inn, the woman was preparing to continue her journey at three in the morning, with the aim of arriving at Madrid by ten. That was when four cavalrymen [*húsares*] appeared *de hospite in salutato*;* they walked into the inn, and at the very moment when I was about to tell the woman my intentions to join her in the same carriage, they grabbed me and tied me to a mattress with strong ropes, placing me in front of a window so that I could see what was about to happen. My smothered calls for help were in vain, as you will see. I could see that they dragged the woman over to the fireplace, where she was on her knees, pleading for her life to the soldier who was threatening her with his pistol in his left hand and a dagger in his right. Another cavalryman was

---

* Without greeting the host.

slashing the owner's wife across the forehead with a dagger. Meanwhile, the other cavalrymen shoved the innkeeper inside the kitchen chimney, tied his hands and feet, and hoisted him up the chimney. While the muleteer pulled the rope to adjust its height, a cavalryman poked at the fire, while another contented himself with watching the facial contortions of the innkeeper. That scene horrified me so much that with great effort I broke free of the ropes, but bam! I fell to the ground."

"Did you just make that up this very instant?"

"Make it up!" said Federico, showing Eduardo his right arm—"Look."

"That is a superb bruise!"

"Well, then you can decide whether that would be the result of the blow that I took."

"Didn't you say that it was a dream?"

"Yes, it was a dream, but I woke up just as I fell out of my hammock. I almost broke my arm."

"Now I understand."

"Time flies, and I still have to make haste to reach the train on time, so congratulations. I have to get the spurs that I left in the caretaker's room."

"Have a good trip. Don't forget to come see me; tomorrow I will be back home."

"Chico, and the coachman?"

"No need to worry at all; I will pay him well, and I will send him to your house after our trip."

"Bye."

"Bye."

Federico went to the caretaker's house, where he found him balancing debits and credits in his ledger. Federico then put on his spurs and mounted his horse to return to San Antonio.

Eduardo spent the whole day preparing for his trip. He returned to pack his bags and explained to the coachman everything he required regarding the carriage and the horses. When night fell, he bid farewell to the baron and the baroness, who asked him in vain to stay until Kings' Day so that they could all travel together to the city.* Eduardo declined as grace-

---

* In Cuba, King's Day (el Día de los Reyes) was a Catholic celebration on January 6 in honor of the Adoration of the Magi Kings. On that day, slaveholders allowed slaves to circulate without restrictions. Some slaves donned the clothes of the master, others wore African garb, and still others dressed up in the manner of Parisian figurines. The slaves then assembled in *cabildos,* or mutual-aid societies, and roamed the city dancing,

fully as he could, speaking of his need to resume work on the legal documents that he had entrusted to a colleague and of the grave consequences that would result if he delayed any longer. The caretaker refused to allow him to get into his carriage until he had drunk a bottle of beer with him.

"Perhaps another time," answered Eduardo, who was so anxious to reach Tulita's side that the minutes seemed to last centuries.

"Don't insult me," replied the caretaker. "I am very formal. I have lost the bet, and the attorney will allow me the pleasure."

"Which bet?"

"Have you forgotten?"

"Frankly I don't remember, but get to the point if you want us to drink a beer."

"You have taught me a lesson that I will never forget."

"A lesson?"

"If I were able to do it, I would not hesitate to give him a good *boca-bajo*."

"To whom?" asked Eduardo, without understanding one word of what the caretaker was saying.

"To the black witchdoctor."

"Ah! So you are finally convinced?"

"He is a rogue through and through."

"How did you prove it?"

"You were absolutely right. Who would have guessed that he would be such a rat? As you might imagine, I went to ask him where to find the machete that I had left in the herdsman's cabin. Frankly, its disappearance had left me out of sorts, because I had gone for two days before I realized it was missing. Well, after *taita* Juan got two pesos out of me, I left like the slave of the sermon, with cold feet and a hot head."

"I am glad that you are now disillusioned with him."

---

playing music, and asking for the New Year's gift [*Aguinaldo*]. White Cuban creoles referred to the participants as *diablitos* (little devils) in a pointed expression of their dislike of the license granted to slaves. Ortiz, "La fiesta afrocubana del Día de Reyes." Eric Sundquist has pointed out that in 1838 the King's Day festivities resulted in a rebellion in the Trinidad Valley. Sundquist, *To Wake the Nations,* 212–13. Philip Howard has shown that the *cabildos* of Cuban people of color both enslaved and free played an instrumental role in planning and enacting several slave rebellions, including the Aponte Controversy (1812) and the Conspiracy of La Escalera (1843–44). *Cabildos* offered assistance during illness, subsidized the cost of funerals and burials, bought the freedom of some enslaved members, sustained African cultural practices and languages, and served as centers for social life, as Howard has shown. Howard, *Changing History,* 27, 49–51.

"To your health," said the caretaker, as they clinked their glasses of beer.

"To everyone's health!" said Eduardo.

The slaves of the coffee plantation were very sorry to see Eduardo go. They missed him because once again they heard the crack of the whip in all corners of the property, and now no one cared about their sufferings. The baron himself, his wife, and his daughter were indifferent to the punishments meted out to the poor blacks. As a result, some slaves took to the hills after committing the slightest offense, rightly preferring hunger and the discomfort of wandering to the painful torment of punishments. The *cimarrón** can at the very least console himself with breathing freely on those days when he can evade his masters' searches.

But so few can escape!

Since the poor slave who travels through the countryside needs written permission from the overseer or the master, which must in turn be authorized by the head [*capitán pedáneo*] of the jurisdiction to which the plantation belongs,† and since any person who apprehends a fugitive slave wins a prize of four duros, it is very rare indeed for the slave who runs away not to be back under the power of his master within a few days. In the capital there are even more ways for slaves to hide, but they are not more fortunate for that reason. If in the countryside they content themselves with punishing the *cimarrón* with a few more lashes, in the city they place chains on one of his feet, which they attach to a large block of wood to make movement more difficult. They typically shave slave women's hair to make the penalty more severe and to expose them to ridicule. As for the block of wood, it often stays attached to the chain on the foot for a whole year. It is only taken off when a pleasant event takes place in the family, such as a successful birth, or the master's birthday, or the miraculous cure of a person whose life the doctors had written off, or the wedding of one of their children! . . .

What a sad degradation of humanity!

When Eduardo reached the cattle ranch of Tulita's cousin, it was eight at night. The entrance to this ranch was to be found on one of the flanks of the property along the highway of Vereda Nueva that faced a narrow *serventía*,‡ so the carriage went down that path. Tulita waited for the carriage every

---

* The slave who flees.—*Author*
† The *capitán pedáneo* is the head of a jurisdiction that is subordinate to a municipality.
‡ Path.—*Author*

night under the branches of a colossal mamey [*mamey de Santo Domingo*],* which was one hundred steps from the entrance to the cattle ranch. The main house was located a great distance away in a small forest formed by a double row of mango trees. Although in a single glance one could take in the full expanse of the rest of the ranch's terrain, which was dedicated to pastures for livestock and was stripped of trees and instead covered with grass, the lovers were able to engage in their intimate conversations without being seen. The slave Dolores served as a lookout to make sure that they weren't surprised and that her mistress wouldn't find out about their trysts.

Since his desires were about to be fulfilled, and since he was certain that Tulita would no longer delay their departure, Eduardo trembled with pleasure. From that night forward, no one would be able to compete for Tulita's affection, because once they reached Havana they would get married in secret, as they had agreed. He headed toward their usual meeting place.

As usual, he cautiously whistled to warn her of his pending arrival, and since she did not answer his signal, he whistled again, but without any results. He waited for a moment, but no one interrupted the eternal silence of the night. "Surely she has prepared some kind of surprise for me," Eduardo thought, and he quickened his pace. When he reached the mamey, Tulita was not there, so he waited a bit longer. Impatiently struggling with the doubts that were overtaking his imagination, he went to look one final time: he lit a match and investigated around the trunk of the tree but did not find the agreed-upon mark.

"Perhaps she arrived ahead of time," he told himself, when already the last vestige of hope was abandoning his heart. He glanced at his watch: it was ten after eight. Then he lost himself in his thoughts for a moment. As both lovers had agreed, their conversations usually began at eight o'clock and lasted until ten. When for some reason she did not show up at the agreed-upon time, she sent her slave Dolores to make a groove near the trunk of the tree, and this served as a sign to Eduardo that he should wait for her. But that night neither his lover nor the sign appeared.

---

* "Botanically, it [the mamey] is identified as *Mammea americana* L., of the family Guttiferae, and therefore related to the mangosteen, q.v. Among alternative names in English are mammee, mammee apple, St. Domingo apricot and South American apricot. To Spanish-speaking people, it is known as *mamey de Santo Domingo, mamey amarillo, mamey de Cartagena, mata serrano, zapote mamey,* or *zapote de Santo Domingo.* [. . .] This species is often confused with the sapote, or *mamey colorado, Pouteria sapota,* q.v., which is commonly called *mamey* in Cuba." Morton, "Mamey."

What powerful obstacle had disrupted Eduardo's plan a second time? Had Tulita changed her mind? Would she fail to fulfill her promise to accompany him to the city that night? A thousand doubts, conjectures, and fears took hold of his feverish imagination for some time.

19

In Prison

The island of Cuba is the Spanish colony with the most inflated aristocracy. There the white European, no matter how humble his birth, is the personification of Don Quixote of Cervantes—albeit an impoverished version—an attribution that, even if we do not take into account the actual story in the novel, gives him a reputation that is at once exaggerated and illegitimate.* There, with a few notable exceptions, as soon as the most liberal men of the Old World arrive, they become insolent and fanatical advocates of absolutism. In general, the white class of this country are those who until very recently filled the archives of the Spanish ministries with petitions for titles of Castille, crosses, special consideration, honors, and official privileges. And since the aspirants aren't content with presenting accounts of either legitimate or false merit based on grandparents who either did nor did not exist, they exchange obscene amounts of money gained by dint of great sacrifice to obtain coats of arms, shields, and livery adorned with silver and gold. Such titles constitute a hierarchy within monarchical states and are actually a form of slavery, because in essence all those titles of counts, marquises, barons, viscounts, and so on, created under these systems are none other than halters slipped around the necks of those who are foolish enough to try to decorate themselves in recognition and support of their lord—nay, their *master*—the king, for whom they are nothing more than miserable, exploited dogs who are obligated to grovel, even if some

---

* *Don Quijote* appears with a *j* rather than an *x* in the original.

of them have a sense of personal dignity that would otherwise reject veneration and servility.*

Now that the light of education reaches the lowest classes [*las clases mas inferiores*], there is growing resentment toward the great commerce in titles established by the royalty, and the creoles of the Antilles no longer purchase them to the extraordinary extent that they did before. Nevertheless, it would be good to note in passing that this ambition and this misunderstood aristocracy, the bitter fruit of society's tree, having originated and developed among the Europeans, maintains such a visible and demonstrable presence that one may observe that those with the most interest in demanding honors and distinctions are those who least deserve them; they are the people who have needed to cover up crime and immorality with that useless tinsel.

Don Valentin, the young man from Andalusia whom we have seen in front of his general store on San Salvador de Horta Street, may have had an ordinary income but nonetheless fell ill from this sickness, and when he noticed that his accounting books showed that he had made more than twenty thousand pesos, he set his sights on obtaining a cross. So as soon as possible, he went to one of the agents in the ministries of Madrid and wrote a check for five thousand duros in the name of one of the businessmen in the capital of the Spanish monarchy. He also wrote a letter of instruction to his agent in which he said that "on the day when the government *Gazette* publishes notice that it has awarded me with the cross of a Gentleman of the Order of Carlos the Third, to which I aspire, you may present yourself at the house of the businessman Don N., who is instructed by my orders to give you five thousand duros under the conditions that I have specified." With great dedication, the commissioned man in Madrid climbed the stairs of the ministry, penetrating antechambers, paying courtesies, and making offers, and within six months, Don Valentin had obtained the title of *caballero* [knight].

From that moment on, he would never go anywhere, even in his own house, without wearing the little ribbon in the buttonhole of his jacket. And on the days when he took his regular carriage rides on the Alameda,

---

* Cuban *costumbrista* writers often criticized the craze for obtaining titles of nobility. Portuondo, "Landaluze y el costumbrismo," 364. One of the leading *costumbristas,* José María Cárdenas y Rodríguez, known by his pen name, Jeremías de Docaransa, did so in his "Un título," in his *Colección de artículos satíricos y costumbres* (1847), 105–14.

he would wear the gold cross hanging from a kind of ring attached to the brotherhood's ribbon. Many times when he was alone in front of the mirror admiring the cross, he would tell himself:

"This decoration is beautiful but . . . (and here he would breathe a deep sigh) it has cost me six thousand duros, or in other terms, six thousand beads of sweat . . . It is also certain that I am a knight, and . . . yes sir, a knight." And he contented himself with that.

We have seen how this man, envious because Eduardo had been chosen as the suitor of the Sun of Jesús del Monte—whom Don Valentin wanted to marry more out of vanity than out of love—in a fit of jealousy had masterminded the treacherous crime of committing a homicide, and at the very moment when he had been surprised in flagrante* was prepared to commit suicide once he was certain that his rival had died. Let us continue now, if the reader wishes to accompany us, narrating the following events that are woven into the fabric of this story.

Don Valentin was immediately taken to jail, where he was held incommunicado for twenty-four hours. They then took his statement for the investigation. They seized the entire inventory of his general store, threw his employees out onto the street, boarded up the doors of the establishment, and executed the judicial process to its conclusion, resulting in a sentence of imprisonment in Ceuta, confirmed by the court of law.†

Did Don Valentin's Cross of the Order of Carlos III help in any way to ameliorate his stay in prison? No, sir. Instead, what worked was the pesos he slipped into various pockets. And that was why they permitted him to stay in the ground-floor room to the left of the entrance and near the main square of the jail and the chapel, a room that was no less humid and no cleaner than the other rooms and cells of the building but nevertheless allowed him to receive guests during the appointed hours and to be free of the vile society of thieves and murderers who populated the rest of the rooms. He lived in the company of a scrivener, imprisoned for falsifying various documents and for his excessive greed for money. Nevertheless, the scrivener was a man of distinguished education and had very good friends whom he put at the disposal of his jail companion. Since they spent six to eight months in the same cell, they sought to stay as healthy as possible, but

---

* Here the original reads "in fragranti," which is Orihuela's corrupted version of the Latin phrase *in flagrante delicto* (in the heat of the crime). The Spanish for *in flagrante* is *en flagrante*.

† See note on page 131.

Don Valentin had already begun to complain of rheumatism as a result of the cell's extraordinarily humid air.

Don Valentin left the jail cell in which he had been isolated for twenty-four hours and moved to this room; and just as he undoubtedly had felt great terror when he experienced the nightmare of being deprived of liberty, now he felt great delight in finding himself in the company of a decent, well-behaved person. Even so, many times he lost courage when he contemplated those large and austere walls, the thick bars on the cells, the iron door that creaked haltingly on its hinges every so often to allow the exit of some victim, who left either radiant with happiness, destined to soon forget the troubles of prison, or shedding bitter tears because he was about to suffer his prison sentence or to pay for his crime on the scaffold. On the other hand, the entrance of new prisoners was always a somber spectacle for those who suffered in that melancholy mansion, and Don Valentin was beginning to understand the full horror that the condemned experienced. He bemoaned the fate of those who were tossed into those filthy cells because of some disgrace or excess of passion. The monotonous and mournful songs of the prisoners and the somber sound of the ocean, which reached him clearly and distinctly in the silence of the night, contributed no less to the sadness that he began to feel.

The jail in the capital that housed Don Valentin was a modern building erected outside the walls of Havana, by the seashore. It reminded one of the numerous abominations the leader himself had ordered his successors and underlings to erect.* Some eighty steps from the Castillo de la Punta is a broad plain where scaffolds are usually erected. Since the whole building is made of masonry stone, taken from the roads along the seashore, the saltpeter in the stone, which is constantly decomposing into liquid, makes the building very humid and unhealthy.

When the scrivener and Don Valentin found themselves alone during the hours when visits were not permitted, they entertained themselves with various games to kill time, which tended to pass very slowly. Soon they began to get to know each other and grow close, and the new arrival slowly grew accustomed to the sad life of the incarcerated. After they had spent four months residing in this terrible place, Don Valentin lost patience and hatched a plan for exacting revenge. As he reflected on the source of his disgrace, all the love that he had professed for the Sun of Jesús del Monte

---

* Orihuela is referring to Leopoldo O'Donnell (1809–1867), who served as captain general of Cuba from 1844 to 1848.

changed into hate. Even if Don Valentin knew that Eduardo had not acted with great generosity, he forgave him in light of the fact that Eduardo had spontaneously refused to take part in the case against him. Don Valentin decided in the deepest part of his soul to use all the means at his disposal to disturb Tulita's peace since she was the sole reason for his ruin and sufferings.

"Do you know, sir," said Don Valentin one day to the scrivener, "that my case is taking a very bad turn?"

"Why?"

"The official in charge told me yesterday that the judge is building a case against me, and it appears to him that they will condemn me to two years..."

"Of house arrest?" asked the scrivener, surprised that the sentence was so light.

"No sir, in the penitentiary."

"That is bad!"

"What do you think I should do?"

"If I were in your place, my friend [camarada], I would discretely offer one hundred onzas to the judge, fifty to the prosecutor, and a dozen to the official in charge of the case, and surely they will regard your time in prison as sufficient to pay for the crime."

"I'm not good with those kinds of negotiations, and I can't access that much money right now."

"No?"

"Not even half. My lawyer told me that it was necessary to grease the wheels so that the carriage would go forward, but since I have no money, they are abandoning me once and for all."

"Compadre, it is better to pay a little at the appropriate time than to pay a lot when it is not necessary. I am speaking from my own experience. In Havana, to deal with a dispute it is indispensable to have the following: in civil proceedings, pesos, patience, justice, knowing how to ask, . . . and hoping that they want to give; and in criminal cases, money, money, and more money."

"My wallet is just as you have always seen it—always open."

"But, my friend, when the most urgent time comes and it is empty, what do you expect? That's the way the legal system is . . . you can only wait patiently."

"Oh, if only I had the six thousand duros that I gave for this miserable piece of ribbon!"

"Six thousand duros?"

"Six thousand duros, peso after peso."

"They robbed you."

"A friend bought the same cross for seven thousand."

"It doesn't surprise me. When one wishes to throw money away, anything is possible."

"Well, you heard right: six thousand duros that I will cry over my whole life."

"As far as I'm concerned," said the scrivener, "it would be better to nail that sum to the hooves of a horse than to give it away to the thieves who take those bribes."

"Everyone makes stupid mistakes."

"Who got you mixed up in that mess?"

"What do you mean by mess?"

"Well, I mean to say, who advised you to get involved in that foolishness?"

"A compatriot who made a fortune on the island merely by selling coal for spare change [*por chicos y cuartillos*].*"

"Well, you should be grateful to him."

"I have observed that a man in this country gets no respect unless he is distinctive in some way. A minor government official or a deputy or any policeman will enter homes and stir up a scandal, charging four or five duros on the pretext that the inhabitants violated the laws of the 'proclamation of good government'; such officials neither recognize nor respect the dignity of the people unless they see some sort of medal on their jackets. That is why I and many others like me sacrifice the fruit of our labor for these miserable decorations."

"Friend, but the remedy is worse than the illness."

"I have come to understand that, but unfortunately it is too late."

"Is it true that they have picked you clean, as they say?"

"They have picked me so clean that the day they give me my liberty, I will find myself with my hands tied."

"That's life."

"Oh, but I will exact revenge," Don Valentin mumbled, full of rage.

"Be careful, comrade, to not make another mistake that will get you locked up in this place again."

"Locked up? I assure you, Mr. Scrivener, that even if it costs me my life, I will not return to a jail like this."

---

* According to Pichardo, a *cuartillo* is a coin that is "half of a *medio* or a quarter of a *real sevillano* or *sencillo*, which contains two *chicos*." *Diccionario provincial*, 194.

"In truth," he answered, taking a look at the walls of the prison cell, "rather than being a detention, this is a punishment *corporis aflictica* [causing harm to the body], and it is very harmful indeed. Nevertheless, when one leaves this horrible cell an innocent man, they don't make any amends or compensation other than writing on an official document that he is innocent, and they don't pay him for the time spent in prison. Oh, men are none other than tyrants to their fellow men!"

"That is the truth."

"Well, friend, make an effort, a sacrifice, and see if you can scrape together the funds to get yourself out of this predicament."

"My friends, my only remaining option, are strictly superficial. Today I am certain that if I were to ask for a favor—even a small favor—they would turn their backs on me."

"The same thing has happened to me, and I have very good relationships."

"Now, that has happened to me as well, and consider this: those whom I have injured have done more for me than those whom I have helped."

"Such are the disillusionments of life."

When the two reached this point in their conversation, the jailers called on Don Valentin to appear in the deposition room in front of a witness. While Don Valentin was on his way there, accompanied by the jailer, he was telling himself, "If one day I find myself free, I will be completely ruined and lost, so there is no other option: all the troubles I am experiencing today will fall on her head."

Not knowing how to entertain himself while Don Valentin was away, the scrivener took up a newspaper and read a section that contained the following article:

I. CHRISTMAS EVE[*]

"Waiter, bring me a punch . . . with a lot of rum . . . nice and hot! What do you want? I like to watch the blue flames of the punch dance; I see in them sprites that smile at me with their roguish eyes, that open their arms to me, that make signs to me and float among the flames like little waves among the big ones."

---

[*] The story that follows is by Víctor Balaguer and appeared by the same title, "Veladas de Navidad," in *Junto al hogar: Misceláneas literarias,* 1:5–32. Orihuela praises Balaguer in his prologue and attributes the following stories to Balaguer at the end of the chapter.

"You're crazy!"

"Crazy? Who is calling me crazy?... Well, then, you don't think that I see sprites in the punch? Of course I do! Just as I see you, Enrique... Paganini was always accompanied by an intimate demon who sometimes took the form of a dog and on other occasions took the form of the deceased George Harris; Napoleon saw a man in the flesh every time an important event was about to take place; I can't remember which race of kings of Germany, since Germany has so many kings, saw a mermaid in the year... I don't remember which year... in the year... Do you know, Enrique?"*

"I don't know anything."

"Well, it doesn't matter—some year. Even Socrates had his devil, and I have my sprite, my sprite named Azucena... A beautiful name, right? Her eyes shine like two fireflies, and every day I see her enveloped in her vapors the color of fire when I shine the light on the rum and convert the punch bowl into the mouth of hell. Waiter, waiter! *Señor le serviteur,* and the punch? The punch!"

"Adolfo, Adolfo, you're crazy, you're delirious—you scare me."

"Enrique, either shut up or I'll send you on a walk. Tonight is Christmas Eve. I want to savor my anticipation of the turkey stuffed with cherries, raisins, pine nuts, etc., etc. Bravo! The punch has arrived! Magnificent! It is a delicious punch! When I think that in this container of porcelain—because this is at the end of the day a container... when I think that in this container and in this small flask, inspiration, life, and glory all swim.... And the sprites! Enrique, drink! Tonight is Christmas Eve. Let us drink, let us drink, and to the clinking of the cups, let us sing praise to God about love while intoxicated, as the song says. I like songs, especially the ones... Why aren't you drinking, Enrique? I tell you it's an especially delicious punch... Waiter, waiter! Come here, give me your hand... Squeeze it, you so and so! Like that! You are a good looking guy, and you have served us a punch that not even... that is beyond compare... Thank you! Enrique, tonight is Christmas Eve, so drink, drink and... what the devil! The sprite hasn't

---

* Niccoló Paganini (1782–1840) was an Italian composer and violin virtuoso. Once he had attained fame in Europe, rumors circulated that he was in league with the devil. *Encyclopaedia Britannica Online,* s.v. "Niccoló Paganini," https://www.britannica.com/biography/Niccolo-Paganini. The narrator also refers to George Harris, 1st Baron and British general (1746–1829). From the 1770s through the 1790s, Harris served in the American War of Independence, in Ireland, and also in India. *1911 Encyclopaedia Britannica,* vol. 13, s.v. "Harris, George, 1st Baron," reprinted in Wikisource, https://en.wikisource.org/wiki/1911_Encyclopædia_Britannica/Harris,_George,_1st_Baron.

arrived. Azucena? Azucena? No response. Where the hell has she gone? Tonight is Christmas Eve. You know a ballad with that title. Go on, sing it while Azucena arrives. Sing, poet, sing! It is a strong punch, I tell you. Let's see, won't you begin? . . . Sing and drink!"

II. THE BALLAD

"The Montseny shakes its white head to let its snowy hair fall down to its feet like a mountain girl when she undoes the gold comb that pins up her flowing hair.*

"The nightingales sing in the trees without leaves, the insects dart around among the plants without flowers, and love bubbles up in the heart. My heart is tranquil, and the sky is blue. Faith courses through my heart like precious gold in a mine's depths. A very black cloud that appeared in a spot on the horizon has burst open like an overripe pomegranate. From behind it the moon appears. This is how the flower grows out of the calyx.

"Isn't it true, Virgin of Llobregat, you who sleep with the window cracked open so that the rays of the moon come to visit you, isn't it true that you hear in your chaste dreams the stream murmuring over a bed of pebbles that crosses the fields of my patria like a nimble deer?† Isn't it true that the breeze tosses the lily and jasmine; isn't it true that the breath skips among the skeletons of trees; isn't it true that the zephyr howls, hidden within the fallen branch of a willow; isn't it true that it slips into the bed of you who repose and sings in your ear the mysterious ballad of the night, sweet like the first beat of love in a chaste heart?

"What is this? At the first light of aurora the Colossus of Memnon lets sound his sonorous voice: at the ringing of this bell an indefinite murmur came out of the forests.‡ Montseny stirs and greets the night with its white head; the moon soon illuminates seas of green, the emblem of hope. In the middle of the night, nature revives in an instantaneous spring. Everything breathes, everything bursts into life. The trees swing, luxurious with foliage; the flowers bend forward, rich with perfume; the rivers unroll their

---

* The Montseny is a mountain range to the northwest of Barcelona.
† The Llobregat is a river in the state of Catalonia, Spain.
‡ The Greek mythological figure Memnon, king of the Ethiopians, was the son of Tithonus and Eos. Achilles killed Memnon after Memnon joined his uncle Priam, the last king of Troy, in battle against the Greeks. *Encyclopaedia Britannica Online*, s.v. "Memnon," https://www.britannica.com/topic/Memnon-Greek-mythology.

ribbons of silver; the seas move in agitation . . . and the white clouds cross the sky, winged messengers of love and hope.

"Men do not see all this, because men are blind.

"The angel that appears in the skies, above the fields, above the water, is our Savior. That is why everything is dressed to the nines; that is why everything is covered in green.

"And in the middle of the night! In the middle of the night, the angels sing in the valley to the young and innocent shepherds who gaze at the bright stars. The angels fly by and cross the light of the moon and say, 'The Savior is born of Mary's womb; sing, shepherds!' The flowers cry pearls of dew. Baby Jesus lifts his tiny infant's hands to the sky and nevertheless is tied to the earth by chains of roses. His breath is the wind, his crib the grass, his eyes the blue of the sky. Go to Bethlehem, shepherds! Try to persuade cold and hardened souls; tell them to go down to the valley to see the baby in his bed of straw so that his voice and his smile lift their mundane thoughts to the skies. They say that as the angels fly toward their celestial patria the shepherds go to Bethlehem and tell of what is happening, and the people make fun of their words. So the shepherds immediately return to the valley, kneel before the baby, and believe in God.

"The star shines in the vault of the sky, shines in the eyes of the kings of the Orient; the kings walk forward in a group, respectfully bowing their heads, and bless the Savior, who rests in the arms of his mother. From the depths of the earth, looking like flowers of purple and gold, beautiful spirits rise, candid and joyful, rise to the skies and fall and take in their arms cups of gold that emit fragrant perfumes of myrrh and incense. Angelic harmonies fill the air. A universal chorus, a chorus of melodious voices, lifts up from the land proclaiming: the Savior is born! And everyone takes heart, everyone repeats the same words, everyone leans forward, everyone whispers, everyone sings!"

III

"Enrique, Enrique, you've made me cry. I no longer want punch. Your ballad consoles me like a day of sun. I like these somber colors, the fantastic hues that you have used. Enrique, your song has given birth to a multitude of ideas in my mind. Waiter! Waiter! Take away the punch. I no longer want to drink. I am no longer thirsty. Enrique, I understand that we should have spent the night in the valley, at the foot of a tree, alone, face to face with nature and with the memories of our infancy. Do you remember, Enrique?

When we were children, do you remember? We met at the home of a nice old lady who told us extraordinary stories, marvelous fairy tales, popular legends. Ay! You are a poet, and nevertheless you have forgotten. I have not forgotten; I keep those memories alive in my heart just as a woman keeps the flowers that her first lover gave her. Stop that, Enrique! You are an ingrate! . . . That poor old woman! I remember her so well! I could draw her . . . and our neighborhood as well . . . that neighborhood in which we lived the first years of our lives together . . . Move your head! Do you think that you remember as well as I do? Yes? As I do? I bet that you don't. Let's see, which history did the good woman tell us on Christmas night the last year that we spent by her side? Eh? You see how you grow quiet? . . . Do you see how you don't answer? Are you convinced now that you are an ingrate? Well, as your punishment, I will tell it to you. It is better for you to drink punch so that you will spend the night with sprites, and with the blue flames, and with Azucenas, and with all those visionary dreams of a romantic imagination. I am crazy, isn't it true, Enrique?"

"That's possible."

"You are right . . . Thank you for your ballad. It has cured me. Would you like me to tell you a story?"

"Oh yes, yes! I like to remember those days from a different period of my life on special days like this one."

"My story will help you to remember them. Your old heart will go back to the time when it was young. May I begin?"

"Begin."

"Then listen."

The Branch of the Elm

I. ISA

The young Count of Entenza left his castle one day and went down to the edge of the river to take a walk. He was a noble gentleman. He noticed a sad and pensive young woman at the foot of the elm. There are women—almost all of them from the race of the South [*de la raza del mediodía*]—women whose soul is revealed with one look. The delicacy of their shapes, the virginal purity of their profiles, the elegance of their bearing, and the intelligence of their expressions combine in these women to reveal beings born to love; in these women the fleeting and fanciful thoughts apparent in the visage allow one to penetrate, as if through a veil, the depths of the soul, since innocence has nothing to hide. The young woman that the count noticed was such a woman. In the first flowering of adolescence, her dazzling beauty harmonized with her face. The count approached her. "Lovely woman, there by the foot of the elm," he said, "what's wrong? Why are you sad?"

As she raised her eyes to the gentleman, the young woman answered with a voice as sweet as the murmur of a stream, "I am like a bird; I have neither a father nor a mother."

"What happened to your father?"

"One night, as a storm roared in the distance, the ocean tossed a ship up onto the reefs of my country and spit out onto the sand planks of wood along with dead bodies. After sunset, I left our hut with my mother, and by the light of the moon we came across the motionless body of my father."

"What happened to your mother?"

"My mother died at daybreak. All that night the bells rang for the dead. Isn't it true, sir, that it is very sad to hear the bells sound for the dead?"

The count threw some gold bracelets onto her lap and asked her, "Will you be my love?"

"Pick up your bracelets, sir. On the day when I am ready to love, I will only ask for the heart of my husband."

"Listen," insisted the count, "if you want to love me, I will give you a white horse with a golden saddle."

"Neither the white horse nor the golden saddle will be enough to buy my affection."

"Listen, if you will love me, I will give you a crown of pearls to make you beautiful."

"The day when I wish to be beautiful, sir, it will be enough to give myself a crown of flowers."

"Listen, if you wish to be mine, I will give you this cross that my mother wore on her breast. I swore on her deathbed not to give it to anyone but my wife."

"If you give me that cross and you make me your wife, I swear to love you forever, sir. But first listen to this: I was born as the rooster crowed. The old women of my town whispered into my mother's ear: 'It is a good omen, old Magdalena; the girl who is born while the rooster crows will be happy and fortunate. Your daughter will have someone who loves her, and perhaps a gentleman will unsheathe his sword for her, but ay! Hide her husband the first Christmas night after her wedding. Those who are born when the rooster crows bring bad luck to their husband the first night of the birth of Jesus that they spend together.' That is what the old women of my town told my mother."

The count laughed out loud and asked, "What is your name?"

"Isa, sir."

"Well, then, come, Isa, come to my castle. I will make you my wife. I am Roger de Entenza; the other knights have nicknamed me the morning star.* My hand is strong in combat, I lead the life of a knight. When I throw myself into the field of battle, men fall from the blow of my morning star, like shafts of wheat falling at the blades of the reaper. What, then, do I fear? Come, Isa, come with me. You are my wife."

"Wait a minute, sir. I want to take a branch of the elm tree beneath which I was seated when you saw me."

II. ZELISKA

Upon seeing Roger enter the castle accompanied by a stranger, and a beautiful stranger at that, Zeliska trembled from head to toe, and her eyes sparkled the way two glowing lumps of coal do when they are hit by a ray of light. Zeliska was a daughter of Nubia.† One day Roger had made her a slave.

---

* To the best of my knowledge, the name Roger de Entenza is a reference to the historical figure Ruggiero (Roger) di Lauria (1245–1305), known as Roger de Llúria in Catalan, an Italian soldier who served the Crown of Aragon as an admiral in Sicily, Naples, and Calabria. He then went to Catalonia to defeat the French fleet in 1285. He also defeated the forces of Frederick III, the king of Sicily, in Ponza in 1300. Agustí, *Los almogávares*, 30, 38. His second wife was Saurina, or Angarina, de Entenza, the daughter of Berenguer de Entenza. However, as Enrique later informs Adolfo, "The Entenza family, that constellation of Titan gentleman warriors, have lent their name to many heroes of stories and legends," so it may be that the fictional Roger de Entenza is entirely the stuff of myth. The Almogávares had originally been shepherds who lived in the Pyrenees on what is today the border between Spain and France. They faced the loss of their livelihood when their lands were invaded by those they called Saracens, a name for Muslims, in the thirteenth century. They therefore formed armies to repulse the invaders, who named them *al-mugavar* (those who start riots). They then fought during the Reconquista in southern Italy and in expeditions to the Byzantine Empire in the fourteenth century. See Iguacel, "Almogobars/Almogávares." On Roger de Lauria and the Almogávares, see also Agustí, *Los almogávares*, esp. 26–38. Here Balaguer is recovering early Catalonian history as a literary resource. See his *Bellezas de la historia de Cataluña*, vol. 2 (1853), for his discussions of Berenguer de Entenza and Roger de la Flor. The morning star is a spiked, club-like weapon.

† Here the original text contained the misspelling "Nucia." I take Orihuela to mean Nubia because later the text refers to Zeliska as "la hija de la Nubia." Nubia was the "ancient region in northeastern Africa, extending approximately from the Nile River Valley [. . .] eastward to the shores of the Red Sea, southward to about Khartoum

"Zeliska," Roger told her with a commanding look, "this young woman is your mistress. Honor and love her."

Zeliska felt that her lips, red as a pomegranate, began to grow pale; she felt as if she had taken a blow to her heart; she felt as if a hand of iron was squeezing her throat. Nevertheless, she bowed and placed her lips on the tips of the young woman's fingers. "Blessed be the stranger," she said with a tremulous voice, "that my master gives me as my mistress. I kiss the tips of your fingers because from this day they shall press upon my slave's forehead; and I kiss the dust on your shoes so that I might turn myself into dust when you are angry."

Poor Isa immediately turned pale even as she blushed. She couldn't quite understand it. These words struck her as incredible. The count took her by the hand and walked off, telling the daughter of Nubia, "Such is your duty, Zeliska, thank you!" And he immediately introduced Isa to all his vassals, who paid their respects and honored her as their mistress and sovereign. The next night the windows of the castle were resplendent with light, the country folk danced in the field, gentlemen filled the salons, and happiness shone from every face. Isa, the daughter of the elm, was now the wife of the noble Count of Entenza, famed for his morning star.

III. THE SLAVE

When the noblemen had left, when the merriment of the country folk no longer resonated throughout the valley, when the lights flickered out, Isa saw Zeliska, walking lightly like a shadow down the hallway. Isa followed the slave. As quickly as a deer that flees from a hunter, the daughter of Nubia crossed the corridor, walked up and down two or three stairways, and reached the armory. Isa soon joined her.

Zeliska walked toward a man of athletic stature who was leaning against a column. The young wife hid behind a collection of weapons. The slave whispered a few words to the athletic man, who was a black slave. After listening in a respectful way to what Zeliska said, he left. Since she was now alone, she took out a handkerchief, tore it into two, and went to throw it out the two windows of the room. One of the windows faced east, the other west. It was true: Zeliska loved the noble count.

(in what is now Sudan), and westward to the Libyan Desert." *Encyclopedia Britannica Online*, s.v. "Nubia," https://www.britannica.com/place/Nubia.

IV. THE TORN HANDKERCHIEF

Yes, she loved him. That is why she waited until the night of his wedding to follow the custom of her country and tear the handkerchief into two pieces, throwing one to the wind of the East and the other to the wind of the West. From then on, every tie was broken between the man and the slave. Now Zeliska could hate him with all her soul. Nothing in her conscience held her back. The woman had broken the chains of slavery.

V. THE GOLDEN NECKLACE

Christmas night approached. Now, during the days of the birth of Christ a peculiar custom was followed among the Entenza people [*raza*]. To signify that he was the slave of the Savior, on certain days at a given hour the count appeared to his vassals with a necklace of gold, a sign of slavery. This only took place during Christmas and Easter, and no one could remember a time when an Entenza had failed to perform this traditional practice. Roger readied himself to do what had been done so many times. The ceremony was prepared, but the necklace of gold that his ancestors had used in previous years had gone missing. How, then, to proceed?

"Sir," Zeliska said to Roger, "your slave Hagen is an artisan of great merit. Entrust him with fashioning a necklace of gold, and he will not let you down."

Zeliska's words made Isa lift her head and take notice; she was sewing a tapestry and took her eyes off her work to fix them on the slave. Roger gave the necklace to Hagen, who promised to finish it by Christmas Day.

"Sir," Isa said to her husband, "when you elevated me from being a poor and simple orphan to the level of your wife, I told you that there was in my town a particular tradition; allow me to remind you of it. It is common belief that every woman born when the rooster crows brings bad luck to her husband on the first Christmas night after their union. There is only one way to ward off this bad luck: the wife must keep any object that was present at the first romantic encounter that she had with her husband. Now do you remember, sir? The day that you first saw me, I was seated by an old elm, from which, following custom, I broke off a branch. Promise me that this branch will not be separated from us during the first day of Christmas. God is good and just, sir, and he will do with this branch what suits him."

"Do what you wish, Isa," said the count, smiling.

That day came, and with it the hour of the ceremony. The vassals were in the armory. The count, seated in a chair, was ready to begin. Isa was at his side, and at her feet a page sat an elm branch in his hand. Zeliska stood behind the husband and wife, and the way she looked at them... Oh! Her looks were frightening.

The door to the hall opened, and Hagen, the black slave, entered with a firm step, carrying in his hands a cushion of velvet, upon which one saw a brilliant gold necklace. He walked toward the count and kneeled before him, presenting him with the cushion. Standing up, the count reached out to take the necklace and fasten it around his neck. At that moment, the page made a movement and dropped the elm branch, which fell on the cushion and the gold necklace that Hagen had given to his master.

Isa stood up. "Sir, sir," she called out, "do not touch the necklace; the elm branch has fallen on top of it. You must examine it before putting it around your neck."

Hagen was disturbed. Zeliska's eyes shot forth flames. He examined the necklace. By means of a diabolical mechanism, the necklace was tightening little by little, reducing its circumference to a tight circle. Zeliska had seduced Hagen and asked him to manufacture this necklace so that it would choke the count before he could take it off. Zeliska and Hagen were expelled from Roger's lands, and from then on the noble couple Roger Entenza and Isa lived happily, and not even a shadow of unhappiness appeared to disturb their union.

VI

"Do you see, Enrique? Do you see how I was able to remember it? Are you convinced now? Furthermore, I remembered it as vividly as if I had heard it just a moment ago. The good old woman concluded by saying, 'My children, the hand of God was revealed in this event. God wanted to reward both spouses for their commitment to each other.' Poor old woman! Yes, that is exactly what she said. Do you see, Enrique?"

"But Adolfo, that is not just an old woman's tale, because such stories are truly children of the poetry and simplicity of older times. And furthermore, the Entenza family, that constellation of Titan gentleman warriors, have lent their name to many heroes of stories and legends. Popular imagination has delighted in dressing them up with a certain adventurousness characteristic of novels that suits them very well; they are exactly like the stories of the Moncadas.* In which field of battle did the sword of a Moncada or the mace of an Entenza not conquer all? Moreover, in which fable, story, or tale does a Moncada not appear as a mysterious, manly, dramatic figure, which is the exact popular image of an Entenza? I know a story about one of the Entenzas..."

"A story? Tell it to me—I'm dying to hear one. Please begin, but first... Waiter! Waiter! Come and bring me a punch. The devil! That lovely story has made me so thirsty. Poor old woman! You say they are old maids' tales? What does it matter? What's important is that they are entertaining. Let us hear, then, your story, Enrique.† And here is the punch. Magnificent! I will drink while you tell the story. Begin. I am all ears."

A Shroud with Its Braids

I

Like the migrant bird that returns after winter to visit its patria and nest, Berenguer de Entenza returns to Greece, to the Greece that is the theater of his exploits and witness to his glories.‡

---

* George Ticknor has identified Francisco de Moncada (1586–1635) as a Spanish nobleman connected by family to both Valencia and Catalonia who was governor of the Low Countries and commander in chief of its armies. His father, Gastón de Moncada, was viceroy of Sardinia and then of Aragon. Moncada defeated two hostile armies in 1635. In 1623 he published his *Expedition of the Catalans and Aragonese against the Turks and Greeks,* and in 1635 he published *The History of the Catalan Expedition,* which tells of the mercenaries under the command of Roger de Flor. Ticknor, *History of Spanish Literature,* 3:159. However, this text may be referring to an earlier Moncada.

† In this sentence Orihuela writes "Henrique." Balaguer, however, uses "Enrique," and I follow him here.

‡ Berenguer VI de Entenza (d. 1307) was a noble of the Crown of Aragon and a commander of the Almogávares. He was also a friend and comrade of Roger de Flor (1267–1305), a half German and half Italian man born in Brindisi who served in the navy of the king of Sicily. Agustí, *Los almogávares,* 40. Roger de Flor traveled to Genoa and "became the commander of a force of almogávares (Spanish mercenaries) in service to the Aragonese king of Sicily, Frederick II, who was warring with the house of Anjou." *Encyclopaedia Britannica Online,* s.v. "Roger de Flor," http://www.britannica.com/biography/Roger-de-Flor. Roger de Flor eventually became the vice admiral of Sicily and was therefore was the highest official in charge of Sicily's troops. Agustí, *Los almogávares,* 41. In 1304, Berenguer joined the Catalan expedition to the East after it had expelled the Turks from the Anatolian Peninsula and reached Constantinople (later to be known as Istanbul). Upon Roger de Flor's death in 1304, Berenguer took over as the head of the campaign and led

Look at him! There he goes; he walks on that galley in which the oarsmen row indolently, cutting the water and provoking prolonged moans from the ocean waves of his patria. Look at him! There he goes! He takes leave even as he longs for his old, flowered neighborhood; he abandons the old holm oaks that cover his parents' castle with shade, he leaves the mountains that echoed the sound of his trumpet, the banks of the river that offered welcome solace for his childlike play, the hallways of the palaces that trembled when the Berenguer clan paced them armed from head to toe.

There goes Berenguer! Far beyond the seas there is a country that smiles and waits for the Catalan adventurer. A country with a blue sky and snowless mountains that with its horizon salutes the winged swallow, just as beyond the tomb there is another immortal land, golden with the rays of an eternal sun, that invites the elect and just to rest in its orchards. There goes Berenguer! In that ship that loses itself in the immensity of the ocean just as the eagle loses itself in the sky; in that ship that tosses on the shoulders of the turbulent ocean and brushes up against the menacing crests of waves, much as a black cloud harboring in its belly a lightning bolt passes through the air, scraping the soaring peaks of mountains. And just as the cloud carries a lightning bolt, so the ship carries in its hollow three hundred soldiers [*almogávares*], which is to say, three hundred heroes.

Hurrah, Berenguer de Entenza! Hurrah, the dashing leader [*adalid*]! Fly to that seductive land of Greece, where with slow deception Odoardo Doria, the ill-begotten admiral, will capture you; return to that land where at the foot of the cedars your brother in arms Roger de Flor, the brave adventurer, sleeps with dreams of death; return to Gallipoli, your dwelling place and your court, where the men are your servants and the women your slaves.* Hurrah, Berenguer! Reunite with your brave Catalans, wave your banner on the plains of Andrianople, call out the first savage "Fire!" in the heat of the battle, as you inspire your soldiers and Turcopoles,

---

his troops against Greece and Gallipoli. Wikipedia, s.v. "Berenguer VI de Entenza," https://es.wikipedia.org/wiki/Berenguer_VI_de_Entenza. On Roger de Flor, see Agustí, *Los almogávares*, 39–41, 72–75. On Berenguer de Entenza, see also Agustí, *Los almogávares*, 72–95.

* Odoardo Doria was an admiral in the navy of Genoa in the fourteenth century. Malleson, *Studies from Genoese History*, 180). Gallipoli is located in northwestern Turkey.

waving your terrible mace back and forth and letting loose without pity or mercy. Hail to the Catalan warriors! Hurrah, hurrah, Berenguer!*

When the rays of the moon play upon the ship of the Almogavars like the flight of pleasant ideas that enter the mind of the bard of the forests, its opal light illuminates a group of pilgrims.† A warrior with a sunburned face rests his head in the skirt of the beautiful Leila. Leila is the maid of Salónica, whose mind is like a light butterfly that flies from flower to flower but whose soul is as devoted to the military leader of Entenza as the handle of a Greek's dagger is to its blade.‡

The moon shines in the rows of sequins, the gold rings, and the clusters of pearls scattered in her braids, which rest on her shoulders, shoulders that are white like the snow in the mountains or like the immaculate swan in the lakes. Berenguer points his finger toward a far-off white ribbon that seems to encircle the horizon. "That is your patria, Leila," he tells her. "There are the gardens, there is the family's cedar tree under whose shade you swore your eternal love to the Catalan leader." Leila's eyes sparkle with happiness upon seeing the white ribbon indicated by Berenguer's finger. It is the fog that envelops her town.

"Leila, I am sad. Why am I sad? I don't know. I am more powerful than anyone else. I have left my patria to fly to a country in which a brave army awaits me; I have conquered peoples and cities; there are plains that I call my own; if I wish to, I can wrap myself in the mantle of Caesar, I can seat myself on the throne of Constantinople; like the ancient God, I need only open my hand to let peace or war fall upon a town. Why, then, am I sad, Leila?"

"Leila will explain why. You have a premonition."

"Oh! Yes, it presses against my heart."

"Leila will tell you if it is based in reality," says the young woman in a sweet voice. And taking up a rose that was tucked into her blouse, she adds, "I am going to pluck this flower, and I am going to throw its petals into the ocean. If the wind pushes the petals away, happiness awaits you; but if the petals fall into the water, adversity will be your lot. If, alternatively, the wind sends them back to us, fear death."

---

* Adrianople is the historical name of Edirne, a city in northwestern Turkey.

† I have corrected inconsistencies in tense in the original, using the present tense for the remainder of the tale.

‡ Salonica and Thessalonica are historical names for present-day Thessaloníki, Greece, which is approximately 310 miles north of Athens.

Leila lifts her arms and throws a handful of rose petals off the ship. The wind suddenly blows violently. Not one falls into the ocean, not one gets lost; all return to the shelter of the ship. Leila lets her arms drop to her side, and she tries to hide her feelings by closing her eyes, but in one of her eyelashes a tear trembles like a dewdrop.

"Leila," said Berenguer, "if I die, you must make me a shroud from your thick hair."

The ship reaches shore. Poor Berenguer! During his absence, Rocafort, ambitious Rocafort, had captivated the soul of the troops with lies.* Berenguer de Entenza thought that he would find loyal hearts; instead he found only cold warriors. Nevertheless, many came to join his forces. "You are the one who accompanied Roger de Flor when he guided us into battle," they said. "You are our leader [*gefe*]. You are the one who has shared with us the laurels and spoils of victory; you are our leader [*caudillo*]. You are the one who after the death of Roger avenged his killing by carpeting the plains and the rocks at the seaside with blood; you are our leader [*adalid*]."

The Almogavars ended up dividing into two groups. One had Berenguer de Entenza as its leader; the other, Berenguer de Rocafort. Rocafort was devoured by envy and jealousy. And those were not his only vices. One day, passing in front of Berenguer's tent, he said, "Leila is very beautiful." And after taking a few more steps, he looked back and said, "Yes, Leila is very beautiful!" And he went away mumbling, "Oh, yes, Leila is very beautiful!"

O night of Christmas! A sad night! O night of mourning and blood! Is it possible that while the bells of all Christian people were welcoming the birth of Jesus, the echoes of Charadjilarkir were repeating the cries and moans of the dying leader? O Berenguer! Why did you cross the salty ocean? O Leila! Leila, why did you allow him to leave your arms? Berenguer, brave Berenguer de Entenza, the bards who have so often sung of you only know the site of your tomb and send with their canticles the farewell tribute to your memory.

Berenguer crosses the blue waves in the arms of hope and of his Leila, who is more beautiful than a handful of stars. Berenguer reaches Greece.

---

* Like Berenguer de Entenza, Berenguer de Rocafort, or Bernat de Rocafort (1271–1309), was a commander of the Almogávar soldiers who participated in the Catalan Campaign of the East. Rocafort refused to recognize Berenguer de Entenza as leader of the campaign, leading to tensions that culminated in the supposedly accidental killing of Berenguer de Entenza by Gilbert Rocafort, the brother of Bernat de Rocafort, and their uncle, Dalmau de San Martín. Wikipedia, s.v. "Bernat de Rocafort," https://es.wikipedia.org/wiki/Bernat_de_Rocafort.

May God watch you, Berenguer! You will fall on the plains of Charadjilarkir. It is night, the moon shines ... its color is blood. The Almogavars advance toward Christopolis and have already reached the mouth of the Karasu River.* There they set up their tents. Tired, Berenguer takes off his armor and lies down at the feet of Leila. O Christmas night. O sad night! The Almogavars in Rocafort's camp have started a fight with those in Entenza's camp. "Wake up, Berenguer," Leila shouts. "Wake up, my love! I hear gunshots. Wake up, Berenguer, and fly to the sound of combat."

Entenza stands up, erect like a tree. He jumps onto his horse without any hesitation, then puts on his armor and his helmet. He ties his sword with a single ribbon, and with one hand holds a spear. The night breeze tosses his black hair to and fro. Berenguer and Jilberto de Rocafort, the two brothers, and Dalmao de San Martin, their uncle, cross over with their horses concealed among the ranks of their soldiers.

"Onward, onward!" yells the first Rocafort. "Injure, kill, exterminate!" At this precise moment Berenguer de Entenza arrives. "May dishonor fall upon those who have pronounced such sacrilegious words among the sons of the same land!" yells the noble and generous leader. The two brothers Rocafort and Dalmao de San Martin, armed to the teeth, attack Berenguer, the same way three ravens attack their prey.

Piercing him with a lance, Jilberto says, "For me!" Stabbing him with a dagger, Dalmao says, "For us!" Berenguer de Rocafort finishes him off by hurling his spear and mumbles, "For Leila!" Torrents of blood escape from the open wounds on the body of the noble Entenza. A shout of exquisite agony, a shout that sounds like a name, cuts through the air and reaches Leila's tent. O Christmas night! O sad night! The winged wind carries the groan of her loved one to her ears. Leila rushes to the place where Berenguer de Entenza has fallen and embraces his body. In a moment, she has loosened her braids. Sequins, pearls, and rings of gold roll away on the ground. A sea of hair covers the shoulders of the young woman. "Leila promised to make you a shroud out of her hair, O my love!" Her hair is so long that it nearly hides Berenguer's corpse. Leila is stretched over the body. The battle continues with even more fury. The combatants approach one another. They battle only two steps away from the lovers. Soon they battle over them.

---

* Christopolis is the historical name of Kavala, a city in northeastern Greece. In 1302 the Catalans were unsuccessful in their attempt to conquer Christopolis.

Horses trample Leila, but she refuses to let go of her lover's body. And so she dies.

O sad night! O Berenguer, why did you cross the blue waves? Hurrah, hurrah, Berenguer, noble leader! May God watch over you, Berenguer! You have fallen on the plains of Charadjilarkir. Only the night wind and the bards' song know where one must go to pay tribute to the bodies of the lovers and to seed with flowers and tears the rocks that cover them.

"An epic intonation, a somber color, a mysterious tint... *Arma virumque cano* [I sing of arms and the man]... Not bad, Enrique. Drink some punch; you must have a dry throat. Drink, my son."

"I am not thirsty."

"Bad luck for you. It seems that your story has left you sad. Well, in tribute to it, or to my old wives' tale, as you call it, I don't know... well, don't you want to drink?"

"No."

"Not even to talk?"

"No."

"Not even to laugh?"

"No."

"What brevity. And do you intend to spend much time without speaking? Because look, I don't like mute people or those who speak only in monosyllables. I am going to lie down in this chair to dream about Berenguer and Leila. What, you don't want to drink? Nor talk? Are you sure? Then listen, Enrique, when you are no longer angry, wake me up. Good night."—V. BALAGUER.

 20

Gossip and Troubles

With an embrace and a kiss for Chuchita and Tulita, the widow Lolita left for Havana and reached her house that very day. At the invitation of Tulita's mother, she had been a guest at the cattle ranch. Still sympathizing with Tulita, she now worried about the nightmares that were troubling her friend. Lolita had spent Easter in the company of her friend Tulita, but it had not been a happy time for her, since she had been unable to go to dances and was isolated from society and all kinds of get-togethers. Her trip to the countryside had effectively been a sacrifice for the friendship rather than a vacation. Lolita's mother, for her part, had seen her daughter's trip as a way for her to satisfy her curiosity about the life of that family, and that is why she had accepted Chuchita's invitation to her daughter. She had hoped to learn every single detail of the events leading to their sudden decision to move away.

"Good, good," the widow's mother said in her typically anxious voice, seeing her daughter walk in. "Tell me, Lolita, what's happening in the lives of those people?"

"Mamá, take my jacket and put my clothes in the closet. How have you been?"

After a tight embrace, mother and daughter kissed each other on the cheeks.

"Not as well as you," the mother replied, "because I have not been able to have as much fun as you've had."

"Fun!" said a discouraged Lolita. "It was surely great fun to be penned up behind stone walls day and night."

"What do you mean, penned up?"

"Mother, you know Chuchita's character."

"I know her well."

"So my whole vacation in the countryside was only privation and monotony: as you can see, I never even put on the pink and celeste dresses."

"That's too bad. Well then, weren't there any dances nearby?"

"Of course there weren't any."

"You didn't go to any?"

"Not even once."

"Then those people only went away to be caged up. What a bright idea!"

"And there was nothing else; we didn't set foot outside the cattle ranch a single day."

"You'll never go there again. Come on, why did they go to such lengths to invite you? And what do they talk about? What's happening?"

"Oh! It's a long story."

"Come on, tell me, because I'm dying to find out."

"It was all a result of Chuchita's eccentricity. A few minutes after my arrival, she kept reading a letter that a mulatta had sent her."

"A mulatta!"

"Yes, a mulatta who passes for white."*

"And?"

"This mulatta is the mother of a girl that Eduardo was courting [*llevaba amores*]."

"Really?"

"Yes, señora. But that is of little importance..."

"What do you mean, of little importance?"

"Well it's obvious: do you think a relationship with the daughter of a mulatta would entail any obligation whatsoever?"

"Well, that's obvious, but we'll see..."

"So this letter is the reason for such a sudden trip. The funny thing is that Chuchita sought to use the trip to cut off all relations between her daughter and Eduardo, but mother, now I will tell you a secret."

"Yes, yes," said the mother, becoming all ears, as Lolita asked her not to tell a soul.

"Eduardo discovered the hideout of the family, and he met with Tulita every night."

"So Chuchita knows nothing about this?"

"She is not even in the least bit suspicious."

"It is very difficult to protect a woman."

"Very difficult indeed."

"I remember that back in my days...," and then the mother of the widow looked at herself in the mirror that she kept in the front of the house and tidied her hair somewhat coquettishly. "I remember very well," she continued, "that your grandmother—may she rest in peace—watched me like a hawk. I was fifteen and in a relationship with your father. We were living in the town of Guanajay. By the way, they put him in prison on the supposition that he had participated in the conspiracy called the Soles de Bolívar.† For that reason, your grandmother was completely pacified and gave me more freedom than ever before, quite satisfied that I would not face any kind of danger. Well, one morning, according to plan, I escaped from

---

* Lolita's description of Matilde's mother Belencita as a mulatta who can pass for white contradicts the narrator's earlier description of Belencita as *morena,* or a dark-skinned mulatta. Either the narrator is playing fast and loose with his descriptions or Lolita is misinformed.

† Lolita's mother is referring to the conspiracy known as the Soles y Rayos de Bolívar (Suns and Rays of Bolivar), an abortive anticolonial rebellion in Cuba in 1822 in which whites, Blacks, and mulattoes attempted to establish the independent republic of Cubanacán. On this conspiracy, see Pérez Guzmán, "Cuba bolivariana."

home, and then I watched as he broke out of prison, and finally we ran away together."

"Well, as for me, it will be a happy day for Tulita when she doesn't wake up at the cattle ranch."

"And she will have done the right thing. Since Chuchita is already older than fifty and beginning to lose her memory, she has forgotten that young women need to find husbands."

"And a better partner than Eduardo would be very difficult to find."

"That woman is so strict!"

"It's as if her whole purpose is to make Tulita settle for Don Valentin."

Then Lolita told her mother the story of the treachery of Eduardo's rival and how Eduardo had recovered completely from the wound.

"It was a surge of jealousy that overcame Don Valentin," said the widow's mother. "But does Chuchita know the details of the incident?"

"The daughter didn't dare utter a word about it."

"Now I understand: that is why she has fallen for the story that Eduardo and her daughter were in league together."

"Of course."

"And aren't they considering returning to Havana?"

"They aren't just considering it: Chuchita asked me to maintain a strict secrecy about where she was hiding because she was afraid that Eduardo would find out about it."

"Yes, but *tarde piace* [to be late is pleasing], as the Italians say."*

"Chuchita smelled a fish."

"So how did Eduardo discover where Tulita was staying?"

"The slave Dolores told him when she encountered him on the way to Vereda Nueva with Federico."

"That clown is also running around over there?"

"I am happy that I have not seen him; he is a real drag, although I hear everyone celebrate him for being a nice guy."

"A nice guy! More like a ton of lead."

"I am so glad to have swatted away that fly."

---

* In Italian, *essere tardi piace* means "to be late is pleasing," but the *Diccionario de la lengua española* gives an alternative origin for the phrase in Spain: "From the Gallego. Tarde piache, 'tarde piaste,' a phrase that tradition attributes to a soldier who, having eaten an egg that had been incubating, heard the chick peep." In the Spanish version of the origin of the phrase, then, *piace* or *piache* derives not from the Italian *piacere,* "to please," but rather from the Spanish *piar,* which means "to cheep." I thank Raúl Fernández for telling me of hearing this phrase in Spanish as a child in Cuba.

"Well, Lolita, I also have to tell you about some things that have happened while you were away."

"Go ahead."

"In the first place, the pharmacist gave birth."

"Really?"

"But luckily the baby drowned soon afterward."

"It drowned?"

"Or they drowned it."

"And the family?"

"The parents of the pharmacist? They live in Belén with the shepherds."

"Didn't the parents know what happened?"

"Too much so . . . but they act dumb. Judge for yourself whether they would know that the girl they wanted to send to Guanabacoa under the pretext of bathing in the mineral waters of Santa Rita was pregnant. The doctor told them to wait until she was at least forty days pregnant before sending her on such a trip."*

"She disguised the pregnancy very well."

"As was necessary—a single girl, and what would people have said? But they are quiet as can be; today if you were to ask about her, they would say that she has a cold and a fever."

"That's no fever. I wonder how many people go through such ordeals."

"Do you know who died?"

"Who?"

"The monk."

"The monk! I don't believe it . . ."

"Woman, have you forgotten him?"

"Ah! Let's see—Picua?"

"That's him."

"Poor fellow!"

"He died like a man condemned."

"Like a man condemned?"

"There was no remedy."

---

* Natural springs abound around Guanabacoa, an indigenous word that literally means "village of the waters." In the nineteenth century, "its proximity to the capital, and the reputation of its waters and its mineral baths has made it a popular destination for Habaneros, whether for reasons of health or pleasure." *La Reina de las Antillas.* By 1956, 11 of the 27 brands of mineral water sold in Cuba were from Guanabacoa. "Las ruinas de La Cotorra en Guanabacoa."

"Why?"
"He didn't want to confess."
"So?"
"You don't think that's important?"
"I'm not saying that . . ."
"Since he was spending all day in Our Lady of the Pillar Church [*la iglesia del Pilar*]* helping with Mass, he grew so familiar with the vestments and the rituals with wine that he grew tired of them."
"Do you know who got married?"
"Who?"
"Cecilia Valdés."†
"Chica!"
"Yes."
"With Mariano?"
"With Mariano."
"Well, didn't that guy say that he would not marry an orphan [*hija de la cuna*]?"‡
"They ensnared him in the gambling house."
"I'm glad!"
"Why?"
"Well, because that way they taught him a good lesson."
"Who?"
"Mariano. Imagine—he was overflowing with pride, and yet he ended up marrying an orphan."
"But the girl also has a good education."§
"Money covers up everything. And marriage and death fall from the sky."
"And that's the truth."
"I believe it."
"Well, listen do you know who has ended up being disappointed? Lusita."

---

* The reference is to the Iglesia Nuestra Señora del Pilar in Havana.
† The surname Valdés was often used for orphans. Many critics regard the 1882 version of Cirilo Villaverde's novel *Cecilia Valdés* as the most important nineteenth-century Cuban novel. Fischer, introduction to *Cecilia Valdés*, xi. However, thirteen years before the publication of Orihuela's *El Sol de Jesús del Monte,* Villaverde published earlier versions of the same story: the two-part short story in the magazine *La Siempreviva* and the first version of the novel, both published in Havana in 1839. Luis, *Literary Bondage*, 100; Villaverde, *Cecilia Valdés*, ed. Ivan Schulman, 579.
‡ An abandoned girl.—*Author*
§ Good education here figuratively means that she has a lot of money.—*Author*

"Which Lusita?"

"The shoemaker."

"How did that happen?"

"The man who asked for her hand in marriage made her spend a lot of money on the preparations. He had her sew twelve sheets, twelve shirts, twelve vests, twelve sets of underwear, and he even had her embroider initials on twelve pairs of socks. When she had given everything to him, he took off, and I don't remember whether she ever saw him again."

"Really?"

"You heard me right."

"What a lovely hoax. And where did he go?"

"Some say to his father's sugar plantation, and others are certain that he left for New Orleans."

"Then he must have taken a steamboat."

"What really stings is the innocence of Margarita."

"Margarita?"

"Yes, the daughter of the melon woman."

"So what happened to her?"

"Upon entering school the other day, the teacher said, 'Tell me, child, is it true that your mother has just given birth to a little brother even though the father has been in Spain for three years?' 'Yes,' answered the girl; 'but father writes to mother every time the mail comes.'"

"So all those letters gave birth to the infant."

"So one would imagine. And you should have seen it: what a wonderful baptism."

"Yes, yes!"

"They say that he was father, godfather, and sponsor."

"Then he was the shopkeeper on the corner..."

"The shopkeeper on the corner, who was the godfather, spared no expense on that day. I attended, of course, and what champagne! What succulent hams! What beer! What wonderful desserts! And on the way from the church of Carraguao to his house, he even tossed around forty pesos in medios reales to the boys on the street."

"That is why there was a long chant of '¡Juye pepe! Juye que te Juye!'"*

---

* There is a strikingly similar scene in the *costumbrista* sketch "Chucho Malatobo" (1846), by José Victoriano Betancourt, in which after the title character's baptism his godfather throws coins to the street urchins who follow the family, as the children chant in unison, "Juye que te juye, juye Pepe." Betancourt, "Chucho Malatobo," 65. I

"They were unfair to him when they shouted, 'Cheap godfather!'"
"Now, that's clear."
"You know who won the big lottery? Juanillo, the one they worked to death."
"The big one?"
"One hundred thousand pesos."
"What a prize!"
"And they came at him like a rock flying toward the eye of a pharmacist."
"He was very unlucky."
"Well, now you will see how he passes his days like a big shot, with a new carriage [*quitrín*] and a large bank account; he now wears scarves and a well-fitted coat that resembles the top of a Milord carriage."
"He will soon put on airs."
"He is already courting one of the daughters of the captain."
"So soon?"
"And the girl thinks he is a likely suitor."
"Don Dinero (Mr. Money) can do many things."
"As Quevedo said, 'Don Dinero is a powerful gentleman.'"*

---

suspect that Orihuela took his passage straight out of Betancourt's sketch, changing a word here and there. I'm somewhat confused by the phrase "Juye Pepe," especially since *juye* sounds like the Spanish *judío* (Jew). "Juye Pepe" probably means "Run, José," since *juye* is a corruption of the word *huye*, which means "run away," and Pepe is a nickname for José. As Stephen Silverstein wrote to me in an email of 24 January 2021, "Betancourt's text, I find, borrows from the picaresque genre, and more specifically from Quevedo's *El buscón*, whose protagonist is a *converso* [Jewish convert to Christianity]." See Quevedo y Villegas, *Historia de la vida del Buscon*. Silverstein has also found a similar scene and phrase in *El fatalista: Novela cubana* (1866), by Estéban Pichardo y Tapia. See Pichardo, *El fatalista*, 76. In Orihuela's case, given the mention of the stinginess of the shopkeeper, I suspect that this passage invokes the specter of what Silverstein terms the "notional Jew" in anti-Semitic discourse as opposed to "empirical Jews." Silverstein, *Merchant of Havana*, 2. As Silverstein writes in his email of 24 January, there are "a few elements here that when added together conjure Jewishness: the age-old smear of greed, the connection with the converso, and the parallel sounds in juye and judío."

* Francisco de Quevedo y Villegas (1580–1645) was a Spanish Golden Age poet and satirist. Along with his poetry, he is known for his picaresque novel *La vida del buscón* (1626) (*The Life and Adventures of Buscon, the witty Spaniard*), *Encyclopaedia Britannica Online*, s.v. "Francisco Gómez de Quevedo y Villegas," https://www.britannica.com/biography/Francisco-Gomez-de-Quevedo-y-Villegas.

"Look, look," said Lolita, interrupting her mother and pointing at a person who was walking toward their house. "Do you see how that man resembles Don Valentin?"

"Girl, do you think it's him?"

"He would have gotten out . . ."

"Well, if it isn't Don Valentin!"

"Ladies, my respects. How are you?"

"Please come in."

Don Valentin entered the house of the widow, making it appear as if his planned visit were actually a chance encounter.

 21

Revenge

Eduardo remained petrified for a long time, incapable of explaining why Tulita was not there to meet him. Fear, hope, suspicion, and doubt fought in his mind, and he couldn't settle on just one feeling. His head was a volcano.

"Has she changed her mind?" he asked himself without daring to believe that was true. "Oh, that is impossible! She gave me her word and I cannot doubt that promise . . . Nevertheless, what reason could have been so powerful as to make her not only miss our meeting on such an important night but also fail to even tell me to wait? That is a cruel joke! Let down once again. Oh, it cannot be! Calm down . . . my imagination is overactive . . . Let's wait some more . . . perhaps Dolores has forgotten to send me the signal, or she wasn't able to do so. Let's wait!"

More than a half hour passed, and still a sepulchral silence reigned. Finally, full of desperation and anger, he took a few mechanical steps toward the road that leads to the house of the cattle ranch, and the ringing of distant bells reached his ears. Eduardo looked all around, and thanks to a bright moon, he perceived the shadows of various blacks who were running in a great hurry to the stand of mango trees. He hesitated for a moment, not daring to walk forward; the bells were now silent.

"Something extraordinary is happening at the cattle ranch . . . ," Eduardo said to himself. "Have the slaves revolted? Do they want to kill the whites?"

"Oh no, that can't be," he later reasoned. "The bells aren't ringing..." Eduardo wanted to run into someone who would relieve him of the doubts that tormented him, but without risking the success of his plan. That hope was in vain: no one came to free him from the terrible uncertainty of his predicament. It is impossible to describe the level of anguish that took hold of his imagination, as when some horrible nightmare takes us by surprise. Finally facing up to the challenge, he went off in the same direction as the blacks. Little by little he was able to make out the objects in front of him. Eduardo noticed different groups of blacks in a state of great agitation, and no longer doubting that some strange accident had occurred at the ranch, he ran with great anxiety, wanting to find out why everyone was so alarmed.

It was not possible that the blacks were starting a revolution against the whites, because they were showing signs of fear and terror... Nevertheless, it was nine in the evening, which is the hour when when they lock the slaves in their dormitories until the sun rises the following day. What could be happening? Full of anxiety, Eduardo continued to run. He was nearly exhausted when a greatly fatigued Don Sebastián approached him, soaked in copious amounts of sweat.

"What is this? What's going on?" Eduardo asked Tulita's cousin. He could not understand the response, since the man mumbled his reply, but when he followed Sebastián's gaze through the two rows of mango trees, he observed a reddish glow that definitively explained the reason for Don Sebastián's terror. A voracious fire had engulfed the house of the cattle ranch. He then made a supreme effort to gather all his strength and raced off in search of the object of his affections.

"Tulita! Tulita!" were the only words he heard.

"At that moment, the terrified slave Dolores snatched Chuchita from among the flames and dragged her to safety. When Chuchita had escaped from danger she cried, 'My daughter! Save my daughter!' and then fainted.

At the very moment that Eduardo was about to plunge into the flames, by a happy coincidence he witnessed the scene in which Chuchita was saved. Understanding the imminent risk to his loved one, he bolted into the flames as fast as lightning and disappeared. The fire had begun in one of the inner bedrooms of the house. It had therefore gone unnoticed for a long time and continued to spread until it nearly engulfed the whole house. Since the house of the cattle ranch was built of adobe and had a roof of guano, the fire was able to spread with extraordinary speed.

The same day, Chuchita—meddling more than usual—had scolded her daughter for writing a letter to the widow in which she spoke of Eduardo, a letter whose content made the mother suspect that he had discovered Tulita's whereabouts and returned to rekindle their relationship. As a result, Tulita fell ill with a very strong fever at four in the afternoon, since her soul was preoccupied with the escape that she was going to make that very night. Tulita was also reeling from the way Chuchita had unleashed her anger by making cruel remarks to the slave Dolores, whom Chuchita suspected of acting as an accomplice.

Unable to resist the power of the fever, which had become so severe that it left her in a state of delirium, poor Tulita had to go to bed. Dolores could not leave her young mistress's bedside for an instant, applying mustard plasters, bathing her feet, and doing whatever was needed for her care. Chuchita's vexation increased with the revelations Tulita made in her delirium. Although she only spoke in incoherent phrases, those were sufficient to confirm her mother's suspicions not only that Eduardo and Tulita were in correspondence with one another but that they had seen and spoken to each other, and this behind her back, which in her severe judgment was the worst crime her daughter could have committed. This explains both why Tulita could not meet with Eduardo and why Dolores could not go there to at least explain what was happening. The room in which Tulita was recuperating was next to the one that first burst into flames. Don Sebastián had been enjoying the breeze in the opposite room, and the six slaves that he had put to work at his ranch had been locked up at nightfall.

The fire had begun at eight thirty at night. The first to see it was Don Sebastián. Once the flame had consumed the roof, it burned with such golden brilliance that it made him get up to find out why the sky was so radiant. Convinced that it was a sizeable fire, he ran to the barracoon and let all the slaves out so that they could come and help put out the flames. He rang the bells in the courtyard to request help from nearby farms, but quickly losing hope of saving the house from the fire, he didn't have time to explain to the slaves the danger threatening Chuchita and her daughter. He feared that they were already victims of the blaze, since the flames covered more than half the house, exactly where the two rooms were located.

Dolores and Chuchita were powerless, enveloped by the flames before they knew it. But when one of the flaming rafters fell next to the bed in which Tulita was recovering, it fortunately dragged a good portion of the wall with it, and that is when they realized the extent of the danger they faced. Despite her surprise, Dolores had sufficient presence of mind to save herself, dragging along with her Chuchita, who was struggling to catch her breath and looked as if a lightning bolt had struck her.

An instant later Eduardo burst out of the flames, carrying Tulita in his arms.

Dolores had left her mistress lying on the ground on a blanket that covered part of her head to go to a nearby well to bring a bit of water to sprinkle on her forehead, hoping to wake her mistress from the stupor that had paralyzed her. For his part, Eduardo was busy trying to help Tulita. In the meantime, a man hidden behind one of the mango trees was enjoying the terror that his fire had provoked. When he saw Dolores pass by just after leaving Chuchita's side, he walked steadily and serenely to the place where she was still lying senseless. As he approached her, he said in a stentorian voice: "You are not mine, but you won't belong to someone else either! . . ." And he buried his dagger up to its handle in Chuchita's chest three times.

As she made convulsive movements in her death throes, the assassin realized that he had made a mistake. "Oh! Damn it," he exclaimed and then laughed and added, "Tulita will be a victim of the fire! Good, I am avenged!" And he threw himself into the flames.

"Get that killer!" cried Dolores.

"What?" said a panicked Eduardo, taking his dagger out of its sheath.

"Niño Eduardo! Niño Eduardo! That man has just assassinated my mistress!"

"That poor soul who just threw himself into the fire?"

"Yes sir!"

"He has already paid for his crime!"

"Do you know who he is?

"Do you know him, by chance?"

"Yes, sir."

"Who is he?

"Don Valentin!"

"That vile man!"

At that very moment there was a frightening explosion: the main roof of the house collapsed in flames. Within two hours even the rubble had been reduced to ashes.

The Final Chapter
Tears

"Miss, the doctor is waiting."

"Tell him to come in."

A tall, skinny person passed into a well-appointed living room. He had white hair, was dressed in black, and held a tortoiseshell cane from which two tassels of silk hung near its gold handle, signifying his social rank.

"Tell us the truth, doctor," said the woman who received him in the living room. "Please tell us if there is any hope that the patient will be saved."

"Let us go see her," he answered. "She was in very serious condition yesterday, and if the antidote doesn't work and the illness remains tenacious, science will have nothing left to help her."

"The poor thing!"

The doctor and the woman walked into the adjoining bedroom. Belencita was in her sickbed. Belencita and Matilde had lived in Veracruz for exactly seven months; now Belencita was on the verge of dying as a consequence of a slow and painful illness. Her brother Julio had left on a business trip to Acapulco, and from there he he had planned to take a ship to Canton, so when the terrible sickness brought Belencita to the last hours of her life, Matilde and some women in the neighborhood were the only ones to attend to Belencita at her bedside. Belencita had already suffered three nights of agony, and Matilde could not rest for an instant because her mother's condition worsened every day. As a result of her abiding love for Eduardo, when she had a free moment to herself she took out the locket containing his portrait, which rested on her chest, and consoled herself by contemplating the expressive face of her lover.

"If only he had received my letter!" a disconsolate Matilde told herself many times. "Is it possible that he, the one man who is capable of making me happy in this world, has forgotten me so soon?" And then releasing a deep sigh and resigning herself to her fate, she added, "I hope he is happy, because for me happiness doesn't exist."

The doctor's examination of the patient lasted for a quarter of an hour. Judging by his face as he left the room, he was not at all satisfied with the results of the medicine that he had prescribed. Belencita had fallen into such an extremely delicate state that she had lost her ability to speak, and her life was flickering out, as the light of a candle does when the oil that feeds the flame dwindles down.

"How does she look to you?" Matilde very anxiously asked the man with the tortoiseshell cane, at the same time wiping away the tears that clouded her beautiful eyes.

"We must wait: illnesses suddenly descend on us yet go away too slowly. Moreover, this is a very delicate case; I'm very sorry to tell you that you will have to resign yourself to whatever fate decides."

Since the doctor's tone of voice revealed to poor Matilde more than she had wanted to know, she sat down abruptly to give free rein to her tears, already anticipating the state of absolute orphanhood in which she would find herself. The neighbor who had earlier shown the physician into Belencita's room left to accompany him to the door to the street, and as they descended the stairs she asked him, "So there is no remedy?"

"Please send for the scrivener to take her final testament and tell her to get ready to receive the sacraments, because it is very possible that by the time the moon rises tonight she will have left this world."

Without daring to walk into her mother's room, Matilde, full of sorrow, asked the neighbor who had just entered the house not to leave Belencita's bedside for even an instant. Matilde told her to alert her to any new developments, because she was about to try to get some sleep on the sofa. The fears that besieged Matilde made it impossible for her to get the rest she needed. In her state of constant anxiety, it seemed that her mother was receiving the last rites at every moment, and this nightmare preoccupied her so much that she didn't have the strength to bear the weight of the terrible misfortune that hung over her.

It is so sweet to enjoy the caresses of a mother! Nevertheless, happiness is so fleeting that it arises and disappears like storms in the sky. The pleasure and pain of life don't pass beyond the narrow confines of earth, and we pass through small mounds of dust on earth to return with our atoms to constitute other beings subject to the same emotions and the same immutable law of decomposition. Matilde was absorbed in meditating on the future that awaited her once she was alone, entirely alone amid the hazards of life. A servant snapped her out of her sad reflections by announcing the visit of a gentleman.

"Federico!" cried Matilde upon seeing the individual who had just arrived, throwing herself into the arms of her visitor and bursting into abundant tears.

"Matilde, what has happened?"

"You're about to witness the worst of my misfortunes."

"Well, what has happened?"

"Mother is dying."

"Really?"

"She has been bedridden for a month. You will not recognize her today. She is on her way out."

"How terrible... Well, you must try to console yourself and brace yourself to endure the difficulties of this world."

"When did you arrive?"

"Yesterday. My business partner asked me to arrange for the shipment of some bales of tobacco with the bank that holds Belencita's savings, and it was from that bank that I found out where you live. You have no idea how sorry I am to find you in such dire circumstances. If I can help in any way, you know that I have always held you in high esteem, and I would be delighted to serve you."

"Many thanks, Federico."

"I speak sincerely."

"You have traveled from Havana?"

"That's correct."

"And Eduardo?" asked Matilde, unable to contain a sigh.

"It is a long story."

"Is it a good story?"

"Yes."

"Has he spoken or written to you about me?"

"Yes, he has spoken to me many times. As far as writing, he did not give me letters to give to anyone in Veracruz. I thought you had already forgotten him."

"He certainly deserves it—the ingrate!"

"I agree with you. Eduardo has not loved you as you deserve."

"I was weak to have believed in him. And tell me, the Sun of Jesús del Monte?"

"I am sorry that I can't give you hopeful news."

"Well, what's happening?"

Then, lowering his voice, Federico whispered a word into Matilde's ear that had more of an effect than a lightning bolt. "Could it be?" she exclaimed, and unable to hold herself up, she swayed to one side and finally fell like lead onto the sofa. She made no other response, as her betrayed love absolutely dominated her feelings. She listened with great indifference to the entire story Federico told her about the Don Valentin's treachery, Tulita's disappearance, and all the other events the reader is already aware of.

"And there is no doubt that Don Valentin was Chuchita's killer?"

"Dolores clearly recognized him," said Federico.

"Isn't it true that they had condemned him to five years in the penitentiary in Ceuta?"

"That's true, but he was able to escape and then return to fulfill his destiny because he bribed his jailer with a large sum. Finding himself completely ruined and already in prison, he had conceived the project of exacting revenge on Tulita. Once he had escaped, nothing entered his mind besides finding that girl. One afternoon he appeared at the house of Lolita."

"Which Lolita?"

"The widow, a family friend. He made it seem as if he had served his time for attempting to kill Eduardo in a fit of passion and was especially keen to see Chuchita. By chance, the widow had just returned from the cattle ranch where she had spent Christmas with her friend, so she told him that the mother and daughter were in the countryside. He wrote down the precise directions, and that's how he was able to murder Tulita's mother."

"So much has happened in seven months!"

"What are you doing, Matilde?"

"Nothing. This memento bothers me, and I will destroy it."

At that moment Matilde tore into tiny pieces the portrait of Eduardo that she kept in her locket.

"May I see Belencita?" asked Federico, wishing to relieve Matilde of her embarrassment by changing the subject.

"She is so fragile!"

"Then if you will permit me, I will come to visit you tonight."

"I would not dare to ask it of you, but I would appreciate that a great deal."

"I am sorry that I must attend to some matters I cannot avoid. I can only remain in Veracruz for a few days, and I must make the most of my stay."

"When do you leave?"

"In fifteen days."

"So soon?"

"It's not a vacation for me. If it were up to me, I would stay longer, but I am working under strict guidelines, and I can't ignore the instructions that have been given to me."

"Where are you staying?"

"In the residence of Mr. Bell, a stagecoach inn."
Federico got up and grabbed his hat, getting ready to leave.
"So you will stop by tonight?"
"I will not make you wait."
"Goodbye, Federico!"
"Goodbye, Matilde! I hope that Belencita recovers as soon as possible."
"Thank you, many thanks, my friend."
"Matilde is so pretty and interesting!" Federico said to himself as he descended the stairs. "If it were not for the prejudices one finds in Cuba, I would court her and . . . no, not so much to get married . . . not that . . . In my opinion, as I have always said, marriage is the worst form of servitude . . . Only when free can the ox lick itself clean."

At seven that night, when he arrived at the house where Matilde lived, Belencita had already been dead for two hours.

After the terrible incident of the murder that Don Valentin committed, Eduardo, having returned to Havana in the company of Don Sebastián and Tulita, married her. Enjoying this moment of great happiness, the widow and her mother both attended, and Federico was there along with other friends, all of whom continued to witness the happiness of the newlyweds.

Returning from his trip to Veracruz, Federico told Eduardo about Belencita's death and Matilde's good fortune in marrying a rich businessman from that city soon after finding herself in complete orphanhood. As for the Sun of Jesús del Monte, since Eduardo's wife had stopped going by that name, it was not long before another young woman, who lived quite near the house where the heroine of this novel had resided, began to use the nickname as if she were its rightful owner. This young woman combines an unusual beauty with candor, innocence, virtue, and talent, very distinguished attributes that merit the great esteem of all those who have the satisfaction of knowing her.

THE END

Afterword

The Problems of Slavery and Racial Equality in Early Cuban Narrative

In August 1844, Domingo Del Monte, one of the main proponents of literary Americanism in Cuba and the organizer of the *tertulia* (literary gathering) that produced the founding texts of Cuban literature and antislavery narrative, wrote to the editor of the *Globe* of Paris from that same city in an effort "defender mi nombre de la fea mancha de traidor" (to defend my name of the ugly stain of traitor) for supposedly having been the "principal instigador de los negros esclavos y de los hombre libres de color para que se rebelasen contra el orden establecido" (main instigator of the Black slaves and the free men of color so that they would rebel against the established order) in the Conspiración de la Escalera (The Ladder Rebellion, 1843–44).[1] In his defense, Del Monte argued that not only did his parents own a sugar plantation near Cárdenas with one hundred slaves but his father-in-law's sugar plantation produced two thousand boxes [*cajas*] of sugar a year.[2] To have supported the Ladder Rebellion, he claims, he would have had to harbor "un odio tan reconcentrado a mi propia raza, [y] a la suerte futura de la isla de Cuba" (an intense hatred for my own race [and] for the future of the island of Cuba).[3] He could not have made common cause with Black people, because he regarded them as "un ramo tan salvaje de la familia humana" (such a savage branch of the human family) and hoped that Cuba would become "el más brillante foco de la civilización de la raza caucásica en el mundo hispano americano" (the brightest beacon of the civilization of the Caucasian race in the Hispanic American world).[4] Del Monte characterizes the Ladder Rebellion's aims in the following way:

> El plan de la conspiración, según los mismos negros declarantes [. . .] se reducía, en ultimo resultado, a destruir con el incendio los ingenios y demás fincas de campo y destruir con el puñal y el veneno a todos los hombres blancos, para gozar impunemente de sus hijas y mujeres, constituyendo después en la isla una república negra, como la de Haití, bajo la protección de Inglaterra.[5]

The plan of the conspiracy, according to the Black witnesses themselves [...] ultimately boiled down to setting fire to the sugar plantations and other farms, destroying them, and killing all white men with dagger blows and poison so as to enjoy with impunity their daughters and women, later establishing on the island a Black republic, like that of Haiti, under the protection of England.

In sum, Del Monte defended himself by claiming (1) that his entire family owned slaves, (2) that Black people were savages and that Cuba would be better off without them, and (3) that the Black rebels of the Conspiración de la Escalera sought to kill all white men, burn their sugar plantations and farms, and rape their wives and daughters in order to turn Cuba into a second Black republic modeled after Haiti. Del Monte managed to fuse the figure of the Black antislavery revolutionary with the figure of the alleged Black rapist, thereby creating a figment of the white Cuban creole imagination, which disrespected the legacy of Black diasporic resistance in the Americas.

Eight years later, another white Cuban exile in Paris, Andrés Avelino de Orihuela, wrote a searing indictment of racial discourses and white Cuban privilege in *El Sol de Jesús del Monte*. A few chapters prior to the denouement of the novel, the narrator angrily denounces slavery, claims of white superiority, and even race itself:

> Allí [en Cuba . . .] se riegan los campos con sangre humana, allí pasan escenas propias de los pueblos mas bárbaros de la tierra, por ultimo allí hay esclavitud!!! ¡Terrible degradacion de la humanidad! Parece imposible que en el siglo diez y nueve existan todavía en el mundo differencia de razas en el género humano. Los blancos de Cuba créense superiores á los negros y á los mulatos, á todo lo que tiene mezcla de sangre africana, y á pesar de esto algunas de las mas orgullosas familias del país tienen que lamenter el participio de esa que estiman raza degradada. ¿Quién les ha dado el derecho de clasificarse superiores?[6]

> There [in Cuba . . .] they irrigate the fields with human blood; there one can find spectacles that only take place in the most barbarous countries on earth, because there slavery reigns!!! What a terrible degradation of humanity! It seems impossible that in the nineteenth century there still exist racial differences among humans in the world. The whites of Cuba believe themselves to be superior to Blacks, mulattoes, and anyone whose mixture includes Black African blood, even though some of the proudest families of the country have

a fraction of blood from the race that they consider to be degraded. Who has given them the right to classify themselves as superior?

Both Del Monte and Orihuela opposed slavery, but there the similarity ends, because their views on Black people and race could not have been more different. Whereas Del Monte opposed slavery because he hoped to rid Cuba of Black people, Orihuela opposed slavery because he opposed notions of white superiority, the supposition of racial differences and hierarchies, and even the notion of race itself. Whereas Del Monte was defending himself from accusations of having participated in La Escalera, Orihuela featured the conspiracy in his novel as epitomizing the unjust oppression of slaves and free people of color in Cuba, thereby upholding La Escalera as a model for Cuban identity. And by featuring La Escalera as a model of Cuban identity, Orihuela implicitly called into question the widespread tendency among white Cubans to vilify the Haitian Revolution as the wrong kind of republicanism because it was Black republicanism. Orihuela exposed the hypocrisy of whites of Cuba who claimed superiority to African-descended people based on their alleged purity of blood yet were themselves descendants of forgotten or concealed mixed-race unions.

What, then, is Orihuela's distinct contribution to the canon of novels on race and slavery in the Americas? By claiming Harriet Beecher Stowe and Gustave de Beaumont as his main literary models in his prologue to his translation of Stowe's novel, *La cabaña del tío Tom* (Paris, 1852), Orihuela explicitly refused to frame his own work in relation to the Del Monte circle of writers, who wrote the founding texts of Cuban literature and circulated them clandestinely. He instead insisted on claiming his place within a broader hemispheric and transatlantic antislavery literary tradition. However, since Orihuela attended the same college as many of the Del Monte circle writers and published in some of the same journals that they did, and since they wrote the canonical fiction on race and slavery in nineteenth-century Cuba, this afterword explores the extent to which they moved in the same social and cultural circles, how their work may have been in conversation, and their differing approaches to questions of race and slavery.

If for many of the Del Monte circle writers slaveholding and racism were ironically compatible with putatively antislavery writings, for Orihuela antiracism was an essential component of his antislavery views and sets him apart from the Del Monte circle. And although the narrator of his novel takes a dim view of slave culture, his ostensibly white character Eduardo adamantly opposes the racism of one of his legal clients and expresses pride in being an "African" who was born in the Canary Islands.[7] Moreover, Orihuela's narrator condemns discourses of what he terms "white superiority" and argues that racial hierarchies and even the concept of race itself are incompatible with nineteenth-century notions of civilization and progress.[8] The advantage of Orihuela's focus on the population of free Blacks and mulattoes in relation to the Ladder Rebellion and his distinct contribution to nineteenth-century Cuban literature is to link the problem of slavery to the question of racial equality, a question the Del Monte circle writers tended to ignore when focusing on slavery, as was the case with Suárez and Tanco, or when emphasizing the alleged moral depravity of mulattas, as in the case of Villaverde's early fiction.

The Del Monte Circle and the Problem of Race

Domingo del Monte was one of the most influential promoters of Americanism in Cuban literature from as early as 1826, when he called on José María Heredia (1803–1839) to move beyond his frequent references to Greek literature and instead produce content more directly relevant to the Americas.[9] Del Monte had become an important proponent of an incipient Cuban creole nationalism by the early 1830s: he sought to establish free rural schools and gain political representation for Cuban creoles, penned antislavery poetry that drew the ire of colonial censors, wrote influential literary criticism, and fought for the ill-fated Cuban academy of literature.[10] Del Monte and other creoles found the colonial government to be intransigent on a variety of fronts: in 1824 a censorship law prohibited any writings on politics and required the prior review of publications; the government increasingly cracked down on meetings of more than two people in an effort to short-circuit anticolonial conspiracies; and in 1834 it shut down the proposed Cuban academy of literature before it could even get under way.[11] Saco's essay in defense of the planned academy resulted in his banishment from Cuba in 1834 and his exile in what Moreno Fraginals has called the "fierce suppression of *criollismo*"—*criollismo* here referring to Cuban creole nationalism—by Miguel Tacón, the captain general of Cuba from 1834 to 1838.[12]

Facing the intransigence of the colonial regime, Del Monte turned to private literary gatherings in his own home. The clandestine meetings began in Del Monte's hometown of Matanzas in 1834 and moved to Havana in 1835; they continued there until 1843.[13] The participants included

Gaspar Betancourt Cisneros, Emilio Blanchet, José Antonio Echeverría, José Zacarías González del Valle, José Jacinto Milanés, Ramón de Palma, Felipe Poey, Anselmo Suárez y Romero, Félix Tanco, Cirilo Villaverde, and Juan Francisco Manzano, among others. Del Monte encouraged the writers to portray the evils of slavery and to write a more realistic type of literature.[14] Del Monte commissioned the following antislavery narratives: Manzano's *Autobiografía* (written in 1835, published in 1840), Suárez y Romero's *Francisco* (written in 1839, published in 1880), and Tanco y Bosmeniel's *Escenas de la vida privada en la isla de Cuba* (written 1838, published in 1925), which included "Petrona y Rosalía" and "Un niño en la Habana" (written in 1837).[15] An additional antislavery novel published during this period was *Sab* (1841), by Gertrudis Gómez de Avellaneda, who did not participate in the Del Monte circle.

The emergence of Del Monte's literary circle exposes two key features of the relationship between colonialism and Cuban literary production in the late 1830s and afterwards. First, colonialism in Cuba resulted in the partial privatization of literary production, creating a split between the condemnation of slavery in novels, which often did not get published in Cuba until a generation later, and the more implicit imaginings of creole nationalism in articles, short stories, and *costumbrista* sketches that newspapers were able to publish. Second, since the colonial state sought to monopolize the terrain of what it considered to be political writing by forbidding it, struggles over colonialism took place on the more informally political terrain of culture, whether in the Del Monte *tertulia* or in periodical writings.

The colonial government did allow the publication of cultural and scientific newspapers, as long as they were not overtly "political."[16] The members of the Del Monte circle published in a number of such newspapers, including the *Noticioso y Lucero* (1832–44), a daily that counted Orihuela among its contributors.[17] I have found two poems that Orihuela published in the *Noticioso y Lucero* in 1838: "La flor de muerto sobre el sepulcro de mi amada" and "El mendigo."[18] Other contributors included Plácido and the *delmontinos* Betancourt Cisneros, Suárez, and Milanés.[19] Del Monte circle writers also published in *El Aguinaldo Habanero* (1837–38), which de Palma and Echeverría edited. Del Monte, Milanés, Manzano, and de Palma contributed to this paper.[20] De Palma also edited the *Álbum* (1838–39) beginning in November 1838.[21] Its contributors included Echeverría, González del Valle, the slave poet Juan Francisco Manzano, Milanés, Súarez, José Quintín Suzarte, and Villaverde.[22] Villaverde published his stories "Una cruz negra" and "La joven de la flecha de oro" in *La Cartera Cubana* (1838–40).[23] *El*

Diario de la Habana (1810–48) counted among its contributors Betancourt, Gómez de Avellaneda, de Palma, Poey, and Miguel Teurbe Tolón.[24] Villaverde served as one of the several editors of *El Faro Industrial de la Habana* (1841–51). Orihuela's character Eduardo is a contributor to *El Faro*.[25] De Palma and Echeverría collaborated as directors of *El Plantel* (1838–39), a literary newspaper. Its contributors included Echeverría, González del Valle, Milanés, Poey, and Villaverde.[26] Del Monte did not serve as the editor of these publications, but members of his *tertulia* did. Together, these newspapers constituted an infrastructure for the writings of the Del Monte circle. Orihuela's contributions to the *Noticioso y Lucero* and his mention of *El Faro Industrial* in his novel show that his writings appeared alongside those of some of the leading lights of the Del Monte circle and that he was aware of their work. In addition, in 1838 Orihuela graduated from the Seminario de San Carlos, as did many of the members of the Del Monte circle in the mid to late 1830s, including Villaverde, who graduated in 1834, González del Valle, who earned degrees in 1834, 1837, and 1838, de Palma, who graduated in either 1836 or 1837, and Suárez, who graduated in 1837.[27] The *delmontinos* who preceded Orihuela at the Seminario included Poey, who graduated in 1820, and Del Monte, who graduated in 1821.[28] Tanco was also an alumnus.[29]

The Colegio-Seminario de San Carlos, founded in 1772, became the key institution for the formation of creole consciousness in nineteenth-century Cuba and was an incubator for antiracist thought in Cuba.[30] The college underwent a series of curricular reforms under Obispo (Bishop) Juan José Díaz de Espada (1756–1832), known as Obispo Espada, who established chairs in chemistry, botany, and physics after he assumed control over the college in February 1802.[31] By the early nineteenth century the college was the most important school in Cuba.[32] Its students would include some of the leading lights of nineteenth-century Cuban literature: José Antonio Saco, Rafael María de Mendive, José de la Luz y Caballero, Cirilo Villaverde, and of cours, the lesser-known but talented Orihuela himself. Obispo Espada modernized the curriculum, shifting it away from Scholasticism and toward more contemporary, post-Enlightenment forms of philosophical and scientific inquiry. As early as 1808 Obispo Espada vocally opposed both the slave trade and slavery in an effort to reform Spanish colonial policy. He later called for racial equality for free mulatto and Black people.[33] Obispo Espada served as one of the intellectual mentors of Félix Varela, whose studies at the Colegio-Seminario de San Carlos and then at the University of Havana gained him so much esteem that Obispo Espada named him deacon in December 1810 and then professor of philosophy in 1811, when he was just twenty-three.[34] Varela "completely revolutionized the method and content of the instruction of philosophy" at the Colegio de San Carlos.[35] Like Obispo, Varela opposed slavery and the slave trade and even espoused racial equality, arguing in his *Lecciones de filosofía* (1818–20) that Blacks and mulattoes were Cubans and should be regarded as the equals of whites under the law.[36] Thus the racial views of Espanda and Varela strongly resemble those of Orihuela's narrator in *El Sol*. In 1821, Espada named Varela professor of constitutional law, and Varela lectured on "the theoretical foundations for sovereignty, liberty [. . .] and the concept of *patria*."[37] In 1821, Obispo Espada sent Varela to Spain to serve as the head of the Cuban delegation to the Cortes during a brief period of constitutional rather than monarchical rule in Spain. In 1822, while serving in the Cortes, Varela wrote "Memoria que demuestra la necesidad de extinguir la esclavitud" (Report that demonstrates the necessity of extinguishing slavery), in which he argued for the extinction of slavery, and not its abolition, which he regarded as a British model that would bring the planters to financial ruin.[38] The list of Varela's students reads like a who's who of nineteenth-century Cuban intellectuals and writers: Saco, Luz y Caballero, the poet José María Heredia, Domingo del Monte, José Teurbe Tolón, Gaspar Betancourt Cisneros. Although the racial views of these writers varied to some extent, all worked within (and at times against) the antislavery and antiracist legacy of Obispo Espada and Varela.

Although the Del Monte group purchased the freedom of Manzano, and although Plácido wrote in some of the newspapers that counted Del Monte circle writers as collaborators, its writers called for banning the slave trade rather than slavery itself, expressed hostility toward Blacks, and even included some slaveholders among its members.[39] In fact, Del Monte's family owned the Ceres sugar plantation, with one hundred slaves, and Suárez y Romero and his brother were the owners and operators of the *ingenio* Surinam, his family's sugar plantation, while he wrote his antislavery novel *Francisco*, which has led Moreno Fraginals to condemn him as practicing a contradictory "slaveholding antislavery."[40] Villaverde spent seven of his first eleven years at the *ingenio* Santiago in San Diego de Nuñez, where his father worked as a doctor caring for slaves.[41] According to Urbano Martínez Carmenate, the members of the Del Monte circle weren't antiracist: "they were only worried about moral infractions, the extreme harshness of punishments, and the slaves' exposure to subhuman work conditions."[42] In addition to having vilified Plácido in the *Globe* of Paris, Del Monte characterized slaves as "despicable, stupid, immoral" and accepted racial hierarchies as part of divine Providence's plan for the world.[43] Even Tanco, whom critics have regarded to be as astute as Avellaneda in his antislavery critique—Benítez Rojo argues that he was the "most radical" antislavery advocate in the Del Monte circle—combined "human compassion for the slave [and] contempt for their culture and dark skin," as Ivan Schulman has argued.[44] Such negrophobia has led critics like Alberto Abreu Arcia to condemn what he has called the "moral and discursive duplicity" of the Del Monte circle.[45] In addition to the "slaveholding antislavery" (Moreno Fraginals) that marred the writings of Del Monte and Suárez, I want to emphasize the *racist antislavery* of Del Monte and Tanco and the *racist reformism* of Villaverde.[46]

It is reasonable to assume that in addition to moving in some of the same social circles as the *delmontinos,* the voracious Orihuela had read either Villaverde's "Cecilia Valdés," which was published in its "Primitiva" edition in the Havana-based magazine *La Siempreviva* in 1839, or the first short version of the novel *Cecilia Valdés,* published in 1839. Orihuela's critique of racial discourses and whiteness outstrips those of his contemporaries in Cuban narrative by explicitly rejecting the racial theories that Del Monte, Tanco, and Villaverde deployed in their stories and letters in the 1830s and 1840s. Race was an unresolved problem for these three, who in their fiction decried the victimization of slaves (Del Monte and Tanco) or free mulattas (Villaverde) yet maligned African-descended peoples as racially inferior.

Whereas other white Cuban creoles included Blacks and mulattoes in Cuban nationality only when they regarded them as "negros buenos" and/or exceptional in their talent or intelligence, Orihuela regarded mulattoes and Blacks as essential to the culture, history, and social fabric of Cuba.[47] Here I differ with William Luis, who has argued that "for Del Monte and antislavery writers, the Cuban nationality also included blacks."[48] This may be true in the most minimal sense, but what were the terms of that "inclusion"? Del Monte, Suárez y Romero, and Tanco all called for an end to the slave trade and perhaps even a gradual end to slavery, but they also regarded African-descended people as racially inferior to them and equated the health of the future Cuban nation as dependent upon the degree to which Cuba could whiten itself by encouraging European immigration. Moreover, scholars have recently argued that Suárez actually didn't call for an end to slavery itself but rather for a milder form of slavery that he equated with a form of slaveholder paternalism that he and his contemporaries called *buen tratamiento,* or the good treatment of slaves.[49]

Orihuela, by contrast, explicitly condemns racism as incompatible with discourses of progress and even rejects racial discourse in general, in an unprecedented move by a white Cuban in the nineteenth century. By explicitly rejecting racial discourse and racism, Orihuela makes the most unequivocal case by a white Cuban writer of the 1830s through the 1850s for the full recognition of the personhood of mulatto and Black Cubans and the utter inadequacy of racial discourse. By focusing on the damaging effects of the repression of the Conspiracy of La Escalera on both famous free people of color like Plácido, a historical figure, and ordinary free people of color like the characters Matilde, her uncle Julio, and her mother, Belencita, Orihuela departs from the "noble slave" logic of exceptionality that marred the erstwhile critiques of racism in Gómez de Avellaneda's *Sab* and Suárez y Romero's *Francisco*. The persecution of Plácido foreshadows the fate of Matilde's uncle Julio, a mulatto tailor, who narrowly eludes the crackdown on suspected insurgents. In order to save Julio, Matilde and her mother flee with him to Mexico. As Orihuela's narrator remarks, in a clear condemnation of the racism that propelled the repression of free people of color during La Escalera, Julio's "only crime was that he was a man of color."[50] Moreover, Orihuela makes slave rebellion central to the discourse on nation and race at a time when the legacy of the Haitian Revolution was anathema to white Cuba creoles. As Rafael Rojas has shown, Cuban antislavery writings stopped short of advocating full equality for African-descended peoples because *delmontinos* feared that Cuba would become another Haiti.[51] Del Monte, Saco, and Tanco all portrayed slave rebellions—and Black and mulatto majority societies—as threats to white people and their property. By contrast, Orihuela implicitly compels white Cuban creoles to confront their long-standing fears of a repeat of the Haitian Revolution on Cuban soil by thinking through the implications of the Ladder Rebellion.

Félix Tanco y Bosmeniel and the Limits of Racist Antislavery Thought

As a resident of Havana, Orihuela may not have known Tanco, who was born in 1797 in Colombia, came to Cuba in 1808, and worked as a postmaster in Matanzas from 1828 until authorities charged him with having participated in La Escalera in 1844.[52] However, it was quite possible that Orihuela knew *of* Tanco. As a poet who would later become the editor of

Poetas españoles y americanos del siglo XIX (1851), Orihuela may have been familiar with Tanco's poetry, a selection of which was published in the collection *Rimas Americanas* (1833). "Petrona y Rosalía," which Tanco later entitled "El niño Fernando," formed the first part of Tanco's trilogy on slavery in Cuba, which circulated clandestinely in the Del Monte circle; the other two stories were "El hombre misterioso"/"El cura" and "Un niño en La Habana."[53] In "Petrona y Rosalía," Tanco attacks the immorality of Cuban slaveholders—and in his prologue he argues that Cuban *costumbrismo* must critically address the issue of slavery and the relations between whites and Blacks and that such a critique does not mean that he is an enemy of Cuba.[54] In "Petrona y Rosalía" Tanco shows that the Cuban slaveocracy is anything but a meritocracy as don Antonio, doña Concepción, and their son, Fernando, monopolize the rewards of a colonial slaveholding society—the luxurious carriages, the opulent houses, the gold watches, and the slaves, who signify and also produce wealth and power, work unremittingly, and suffer implied rape and brutal punishments. Tanco's story shows that slaveholders rule by oppression, immorality, and deception. A transplant from Colombia and therefore without loyalty to the Cuban slave regime—much like Orihuela, a transplant from the Canary Islands—Tanco indicts Cuba's slaveholding society.

Tanco and Orihuela both deploy *costumbrismo*'s moral critique of Cuban culture. Tanco, Orihuela, and Villaverde all set up a contrast and/or connection between a corrupt and immoral white Cuban man who epitomizes the vices and racism of white Cuban society—Fernando in "Petrona y Rosalía," Eduardo in *El Sol* and Leocadio in "Cecilia Valdés"—and a woman of color, whether free or enslaved. However, whereas Villaverde's narrator emphasizes the moral vices of Cecilia Valdés and therefore the alleged dangers of mulatta sexuality, Tanco's narrator emphasizes Rosalía's virtue in "Petrona y Rosalía": "Niguna coquetería ni desenvoltura en sus movimientos fáciles y seductores. Rosalía ignoraba estas artes de la corrupción y del ejemplo de la sociedad" (There was no coquetry or flippancy in Rosalía's easy and seductive movements. She knew not such arts of corruption, lacking society's bad example).[55] Thus Orihuela's emphasis on Matilde's virtue resembles Tanco's portrayal of Rosalía and contrasts with Villaverde's portrayal of Cecilia Valdés as consumed by passion and vice.

However, Orihuela's approach to questions of race is substantially different from Tanco's. First, Tanco combines "humanitarian compassion for slaves and scorn for their dark skin and culture," according to Ivan Schulman.[56] Tanco wrote to Domingo del Monte, "Los negros ensucian [. . .] a esa sociedad" (Blacks sully [...] this society).[57] Whereas both Tanco and Del Monte uphold racial hierarchies, betraying their investment in whiteness as an ideal, Orihuela engages in an extended critique of whiteness and its constitutive racist discourses in *El Sol*. Orihuela did not share the racist views of Del Monte and Tanco; instead, the narrator of *El Sol* condemns racial thinking as incompatible with the advances of the nineteenth century.

Orihuela's narrator not only calls into question the validity of racial differences—which antislavery and proslavery advocates alike took for granted—but also undermines discourses of white superiority by arguing that a mixture of African blood is present not only among Blacks and *mulatos/as* in Cuba but also among whites, particularly "some of the proudest families of the country."[58] Moreover, by exposing the contradictions of the character Eduardo, who chooses a white woman over a mulatta yet professes racial egalitarianism—Eduardo says that Black people have "las mismas facultades" (the same capabilities) as white people and opposes racial domination—Orihuela implicitly exposes the racist antislavery thought of the Del Monte circle writers, implicitly calling for a new, antiracist vein of antislavery work.[59]

Orihuela's novel goes well beyond a critique of slaveholding society that would ultimately rehabilitate whiteness, as in Tanco's thought. In Tanco, the representation of antiracism relies on the discourse of shared humanity that emerges in the exchange between a white woman and the five-year-old son of a slaveholding couple in "Un niño en la Habana." The boy has "already conditioned himself according to the racist mentality that characterizes his father as a master of slaves," as Adriana Méndez Rodenas has argued.[60] At one point in this sketch the white woman, the boy's interlocutor, states that "los negros son lo mismo que tú" (Blacks are the same as you). The boy responds, "No señora, los negros no son los mismos que yo sino como los bueyes y los cochinos, y siempre es menester estarlos sobando" (No, ma'am, Blacks are not the same as I am, but rather like the oxen and pigs, and it is always necessary to whip them).[61] Given Tanco's comments alleging the racial inferiority of Africans, the boy's belief in racial hierarchies is most likely not the object of critique here. Instead, rather than faulting discourses of racial inferiority in themselves, Tanco may be suggesting that he opposes their use in rationalizing plantation violence. In that case, it is likely that Tanco joins Suárez in implicitly advocating an ameliorative *buen tratamiento* of slaves rather than an immediate end to slavery.

Anselmo Suárez y Romero and the Slave as Romantic Racialist Victim

Suárez completed *Francisco* in 1839 at the request of Del Monte, whose literary salon he attended; the novel was posthumously published in New York in 1880.[62] Suárez based the novel on his observations of his family's sugar plantation, Surinam, where he "served, along with his brother Miguel, as the administrator of the family's sugar mill."[63] The censors of Cuba rejected a portion of *Francisco* that Suárez attempted to publish in his *Colección de artículos* (1859).[64] Many critics have termed *Francisco* an antislavery novel, but Stephen Silverstein, building on the work of Karim Ghorbal, has argued that Suárez, along with José Antonio Saco, actually did not advocate an end to slavery but rather the *buen tratamiento* of slaves, a policy that was intended to prolong slavery in the face of slave revolts, high slave mortality, constraints on the slave trade, and higher prices for slaves.[65]

Francisco tells the tale of a slave who is "negro y de nación" (Black and born in Africa), whose story of repeated torture at the hands of his slaveholder bears some similarities to that of the slave poet Francisco Manzano and, of course, owes its title to his name. Employed in the city as a *calesero* (chaise driver), Francisco runs afoul of his mistress, Señora Mendizábal, when he asks for the hand of her favorite slave, Dorotea, a tailor.[66] Since he is an *esclavo de nación* (slave born in Africa) with a "tez de azabache" (jet-black face), Francisco's proposed marriage to Dorotea, a nearly white *esclava criolla* (slave born in Cuba), would lower her status and reflect negatively on her mistress.[67] Moreover, Dorotea has had a daughter named Lutgarda with Francisco without the mistress's permission.

Both *El Sol* and *Francisco* are organized around love triangles. In *El Sol*, two differing immigrants from Spain to Cuba, Eduardo and Don Valentin, fight for the title character, the white woman Tulita; for this love triangle to occur, Eduardo must dispense with the earlier love triangle involving him, the mulatta Matilde, and Tulita. Once he is no longer involved with Matilde, he can seriously pursue Tulita. *Francisco* pits Ricardo, the immoral slaveholding son, against the Black slave Francisco in a contest for the love of Dorotea. These love triangles are allegorical: each character represents broader collectivities. The ultimate resolution of the love triangles is the imagined resolution (or lack of resolution) of the problem of racial hierarchies in Cuba in the case of *El Sol* and of slavery in the case of *Francisco*.

As in Tanco's stories and Orihuela's novel, *costumbrismo* is a potent mode of social critique in *Francisco*. In a manner similar to Tanco's representation of Fernando and Orihuela's portrayal of Eduardo and Federico, Suárez deploys the common *costumbrista* figure of the spoiled and immoral son in his portrayal of Ricardo as an indictment of the slaveholding regime. Suárez speaks of "la perdición" of Ricardo: since his father died when he was only a few months old, his mother spoiled him; her aim was "no oponerse en lo más mínimo" (to not oppose him at all). As a result, Ricardo is characterized by "las costumbres desarregladas, la desnudez absoluta de principios morales" (disordered customs and the absolute lack of moral principles).[68] And again, much like Tanco and Orihuela, Suárez emphasizes the racism of elite white creoles. Ricardo persecutes Francisco in an effort to win Dorotea for himself but also out of a conviction that Blacks are inferior. Speaking of Blacks, Ricardo says, "Ellos descienden de los monos" (They descend from monkeys).[69] Ricardo buys the argument of contemporary ethnologists that Blacks are members of an inferior, ape-like species. As in Tanco, in Súarez the critique of racism is at the same time a critique of the alleged excess of violence on slave plantations and also a call for *buen tratamiento,* a call for the amelioration of slavery but also for its prolongation.

There are significant differences between *Francisco* and *El Sol*. The most glaringly obvious difference is that by valuing Francisco for his Christian resignation, Suárez emphasizes the victimhood of slaves, turning them into an object of compassion for whites rather than foregrounding their own ongoing struggles to end slavery, as does Orihuela in *El Sol* with the novel's historical grounding in La Escalera and the martyrdom of Plácido. And whereas Orihuela's narrator explicitly rejects racial discourse as an explanation of differences among humans, Suárez constructs Francisco's character as a textbook example of the discursive tradition of romantic racialism later popularized in the United States by Stowe. Stowe's romantic racialist theory held that Black people were more artistic, emotionally responsive, and nonviolent than white people and thus more Christian in their temperament.[70] Indeed, Suárez represents Francisco in romantic racialist terms as the ideal Christian, a martyr of the faith:

> Su genio apacible se hermaneaba perfectamente con la resignación de un cristiano, con el sufrimiento de los estoicos, indicio de una alma grande que permanece serena en medio de los infortunios que la abruman. Por eso aquel tinte lúgubre de su rostro que cautivaba y seducía; aquel tinte con que son representados los mártires de la fe.[71]

His mild-mannered character was perfectly compatible with Christian resignation, with the suffering of the Stoics, the sign of a great soul that remains serene in the midst of misfortunes that weigh him down. For that reason, that melancholy cast of his countenance, which was so captivating and appealing, was the same as that which characterized the appearance of the martyrs of the faith.

Moreover, much as Gómez de Avellaneda represents Sab, the narrator repeatedly refers to Francisco as a "noble" man with an "alma grande" (great soul), deploying the logic of the exceptional slave.[72] Suárez admits as much in a letter to Del Monte dated April 11, 1839: "Francisco es un fenómeno, una escepcion muy singular, no el hombre sujeto á las tristes consecuencias de la esclavitud" (Francisco is a phenomenon, a very unique exception, not a man subject to the sad consequences of slavery).[73] The problem with this Cuban variant of romantic racialism is that it portrays noble slaves as exceptional when compared with the vast majority of slaves, thereby failing to join Orihuela in challenging prevailing racial discourses.

Cirilo Villaverde and the Mulatta's "Stained Blood"

Since Villaverde published the definitive version of *Cecilia Valdés* in New York in 1882, thirty years after the publication of *El Sol* and forty-three years after the writing of *Francisco,* I will confine myself to an analysis of the first of the two early versions of Villaverde's tale, both of which appeared in print in 1839. The two early versions of "Cecilia Valdés" represented Villaverde's fullest narrative on race in Cuba prior to the Ladder Rebellion. The first version, the story deemed "La Primitiva," refers to slavery only implicitly, as the historical backdrop to a narrative that faults whites and mulattoes alike for an alleged moral depravity that the narrator represents as stemming from the racially mixed lower social strata of Havana, cross-racial desire, and the stark contrast between privileged whites and economically, socially, and sexually vulnerable mulattoes and Blacks.

Cecilia is a mulatta who allegedly exemplifies the dangers of too much democracy—of allowing what Villaverde calls "la plebe" to consort with one another across ethnic and class boundaries with too much freedom and too few social controls in what he describes as "escenas populares" (popular scenes).[74] He introduces Cecilia as exemplifying the social problem of the existence of orphans. Villaverde as social reformist writer acts *in loco parentis* in relation to the orphan Cecilia and society at large, condemning whites and Blacks alike for the alleged immorality of racial intermixture.

The narrator follows Cecilia from the time when, as a student of philosophy in 1826, he first encountered her as a spirited ten-year-old girl running around unsupervised in the streets of Havana to her subsequent fall from innocence at the age of fourteen. In the first part of the story, two sisters spot Cecilia passing by the windows of their house and, taking a liking to her, ask her to come inside. Cecilia amuses the sisters, but readers clue into the possibility of incest when the sisters remark that Cecilia resembles them, their brother Leocadio, and their father. For her part, Cecilia recognizes the sisters' father as a man whom she has seen in the company of her grandmother, and she recognizes Leocadio as the student who often follows her and flirts with her.

In part 2, Cecilia describes her encounter with the Gamboa family to her grandmother *ña* Chepa, who warns her that they are "bad people," calls Leocadio "perverse," and claims that one day, when Cecilia least expects it, they will cut off her hair.[75] The grandmother then tells Cecilia a cautionary tale about a girl named Narcisa, who, drawn by the distant strains of a violin, steals away to a dance while her grandmother is praying. A handsome young man appears and asks her where she is headed at that hour of the night and then offers to take her to the dance. As he walks with her he turns into the devil, grabs her by the throat, carries her up the Torre de Angel, and throws her into a deep well. Despite her grandmother's numerous warnings, Cecilia follows what the narrator terms "el camino de la perdición" (the road to ruin) when she runs away with Leocadio and never returns.[76]

Although the narrator adopts a posture of social reform in telling the story of the orphan Cecilia, much as do the French writers he decries, he is as much a part of the problem as he is part of the solution. The narrator repeatedly verbally caresses the body of the young girl, commenting on the successive stages of her body's development, on the color of her skin—she is known as *la virgencita de bronce* (the little bronze virgin)—and on her beauty. At one point, the narrator remarks that "verdaderamente el rostro de esta niña singular era un modelo acabado de belleza" (truly the face of this singular girl was the perfect model of beauty).[77] Cecilia's beauty is a curse because it is inextricably bound to what the narrator calls her "sangre [...] manchada" (stained blood).[78] Drawing on the theory of the inheritance of acquired characteristics that Jean-Baptiste Larmarck (1744–1829) developed in his *Philosophie zoologique* (1809), Villaverde writes that "la infeliz Cecilia, hechura del crimen, su estrella la arrastraba al pecado por el mismo camino que arrastró a su madre, herencia o vínculo que frecuentemente vemos trasmitirse de padres e hijos hasta la *quinta* generación" (unhappy Cecilia, the product of crime; fate dragged her toward sin along the very same path that it dragged her mother, an inheritance or link that we frequently see parents transmit to their children all the way to the fifth generation).[79]

There are several commonalities between "Cecilia Valdés" and *El Sol*. Both deploy the literary form of *costumbrismo* for the purposes of social critique; both focus on mulattas from Havana, whom they characterize as beautiful—Villaverde's Cecilia is initially ten years old; Orihuela's Matilde is sixteen; and both foreground the figure of the morally dissolute young white Cuban male Leocadio in the early versions of "Cecilia Valdés," Eduardo and Federico in *El Sol*. However, there are significant differences between the two tales. Both Villaverde in "Cecilia Valdés" and Orihuela in *El Sol* write in the vein of a social reformist *costumbrismo*, but with conflicting aims: Villaverde focuses on the moral reform of "la plebe."[80] Orihuela differs from Villaverde by portraying the plight of free people of color not as a result of their flawed moral character, "stained blood," or as a degraded class but rather as a result of the racism of white creoles, as Orihuela makes clear in his portrayals of Matilde and her uncle Julio and in the account of the martyrdom of Plácido.

Whereas Villaverde constructs a pedagogical relationship between narrator and youthful protagonist, Orihuela's mulattas are older and wiser than Cecilia. And whereas the narrator of "Cecilia Valdés" is the voice of social critique, in *El Sol* the mulattas Matilde and her mother, Belencita, join the narrator in that role. The discourse of blood is only present in Orihuela insofar as the narrator states that mixed blood characterizes people of all classes and colors in Cuba, from Blacks and mulattoes to "the proudest [white] families."[81] By contrast, Villaverde's narrator is obsessed with the contamination of stained blood. Villaverde's narrator assigns some of the responsibility for Cecilia's "perdition" to Leocadio but places much of the blame on Cecilia herself, whom he describes in highly racialized and sexualized terms as an ardent and passionate mulatta.[82] In florid prose, Villaverde describes how Cecilia's passion for music grows indistinguishable from her sexual passion, which ends up driving her crazy with desire and into the arms of the feckless Leocadio: "Otro día tocó el arpa y cantó y otro, y otro; hasta que sus cantos y los sonidos melancólicos de su instrumento se perdieron confusos y apagados en el torbellino de su pasión, que le brotaba por todos los poros del cuerpo, al extremo de enloquecerla y llevarla humilde como un cordero a los pies de su sacrificador" (She played her harp and sang day after day after day until her singing and the melancholic sounds of her instrument faded, confused and lost in the whirlwind of her passion, which sprouted from all her body's pores, to the point of driving her crazy and leading her tamely like a lamb to the feet of the man who would sacrifice her).[83] Both Cecilia and Matilde are the victims of white men. But while Villaverde's narrator portrays Cecilia as raised in the streets and therefore prone to lasciviousness herself, Orihuela's narrator does not point out any moral shortcomings in Matilde; instead the narrator points to the shortcomings of Eduardo, who cynically plays with "two sets of cards," as Matilde's mother, Belencita, points out, until he ultimately chooses a white woman over Matilde.[84] Whereas in Villaverde the narrator articulates the moral critique of white and mulatta characters, in Orihuela the mulatta characters themselves voice a critique of racist and sexist behavior and legal structures.

Cecilia Valdés embodies a social problem: the lack of social and moral safeguards to regulate interactions between what the narrator calls "la plebe" (the common people) and "la raza ilustrada" (the enlightened race), the second of which the narrator equates with whites.[85] She and Leocadio embody two sides of the problem of social customs in Cuba: on the one hand, the unchecked sexuality of mulattas; on the other, the immorality of privileged white creole men. "Cecilia Valdés" figures their potential union as contaminating the imagined community of Cuba with racial mixture, sexual depravity, and immorality. Unlike "Cecilia Valdés," Orihuela's novel does not blame the mulatta victim of the white man's predations. Instead, Orihuela's Matilde both embodies and articulates how whiteness poses a series of social problems resulting in the excess privilege of white people and the vilification of Black people and mulattoes like Matilde's uncle Julio. Whereas in Villaverde's "Cecilia Valdés" a mulatta is the title character, in Orihuela the title character is Tulita, a white creole woman, as if to suggest that Cuba's problems revolve around the power and prestige of whiteness, power and prestige that make the union between Tulita and Eduardo and his tragic abandonment of Matilde a fait accompli. But Orihuela's character Matilde does not just offer a cautionary tale about the damaging effects of racism; she also invites a reflection on potential racially mixed futures for Latin America.

El Sol de Jesús del Monte's Place in Cuban Literature

Orihuela, Suárez, Tanco, and Villaverde all wrote in the *costumbrista* mode, emphasizing the Cuban vernacular and criticizing local customs and vices with the aim of social reform. Orihuela did not represent Cuban slavery with the chilling detail that characterized the narratives of Suárez and Tanco. And Villaverde's nightmarish portrayal of Leocadio as an overprivileged white man is perhaps more memorable than Orihuela's ambivalent and nuanced portrayal of Eduardo. Orihuela's Eduardo is an antihero who expresses antiracist and antislavery views yet acts in a racist manner when he betrays his *mulata* girlfriend, Matilde, by refusing to regard her as a serious rival to the title character, the white Tulita, precisely because Matilde is not white. Orihuela's distinct contribution to Cuban letters makes a different set of moves: *El Sol de Jesús del Monte* makes La Escalera, an antislavery and anticolonial revolt, the centerpiece of a critique aiming to dismantle Cuban racial hierarchies, slavery, and even the idea of race itself. It thereby surpasses the reformist critiques of Suárez, Tanco and Villaverde. *El Sol de Jesús del Monte* is therefore the most radical novelistic critique of race in Cuba through the 1850s.

Why, one might ask, was Orihuela able to more fully criticize racial discourse than his contemporaries in Cuba? What made him special? The answer may lie with Orihuela's *isleño* origins as a Canary Islander. Orihuela emphasizes the racial ambiguity and ideological dissent of his semiautobiographical character Eduardo, who, like Orihuela himself, was born in the Canary Islands but raised in Cuba. In his conversation with his *guajiro* client, Eduardo racializes his own Canary Island ancestry as only ambiguously white when he claims that he was born in Africa; Tulita refers to Eduardo as "Chino mío," which is a term of endearment with possible racial overtones of referring to a person of mixed African ancestry; and the narrator describes him as having a "tez morena" (brown face).[86] Tulita's use of the word *chino* could be simply as a term of affection, which was one possible use of the term, but the term also invoked the light brown skin of mixed-race people and in the context of Cuba's multiple denominations of skin color indicated more specifically "the son or daughter of a mulatto man and a black woman, or vice versa."[87] What accounts for this abundance of racially ambiguous referents attached to Eduardo? Despite his racial blind spots, with his claim of African birth Eduardo openly, if implicitly, acknowledges the *mestizaje* that historians have identified as a defining characteristic of the population of the Canary Islands.[88] And on Cuban soil, "the Canary

Islander is 'barely white' [*blanco de orilla*] and lives among the lower social sectors. [. . .] The vague accusation that *isleños* were *pardos* or mulattoes was common among the American social elite."[89] In the 1840s, white Cubans who opposed the increased Africanization of the island through the clandestine slave trade ironically called for the immigration of Canary Islanders to Cuba to "whiten" the island.[90] Indeed, Gaspar Betancourt Cisneros brought Canary Islanders to work on his cattle ranch. He remarked, "They work alongside my black slaves, performing the same tasks without distinction," thereby, no doubt, undermining their claim to whiteness in the eyes of many Cubans.[91] Perhaps Eduardo's racial ambiguity reveals a hidden historical affinity with the *mulata* Matilde, her family, and even Plácido himself, the martyr of La Escalera, one that Eduardo himself does not recognize but that the novel takes pains to make legible. Indeed, it is no coincidence that the only white man that colonial officials executed in connection to La Escalera was a Canary Island immigrant, Antonio Marrero. Twelve witnesses accused Marrero of taking part in the conspiracy by fomenting revolt among the slaves at the Buena Esperanza coffee estate in Matanzas.[92] Perhaps the ultimate importance of *El Sol de Jesús del Monte* is that it threw discourses of race into crisis at a time when they shaped the global economy and everyday interactions in the Americas.

Notes

Introduction

1. To my knowledge, there were two translations of *Uncle Tom's Cabin* into Spanish in 1852, Orihuela's and one by Wenceslao Ayguals de Izco. This is in keeping with Surwillo's findings ("Representing the Slave Trader," 780–81). Ayguals's preface is dated 7 December 1852, whereas Orihuela's is dated 12 October 1852. This evidence supports Orihuela's claim that his was the first translation of *Uncle Tom's Cabin* into Spanish, although this is certainly splitting hairs. See Ayguals de Izco, "Advertencia preliminar," 4; and Orihuela, *La cabaña del tío Tom* (1852), 5. For an analysis of Orihuela's choices as a translator of *Uncle Tom's Cabin*, see Chaar-Pérez, "Bonds of Translation."
2. See "Romantic Racialism in the North," in Fredrickson, *Black Image in the White Mind*, 97–129.
3. Orihuela, *Dos palabras*, 3. On Plácido, see Bueno, *Acerca de Plácido*; Cué Fernández, *Plácido*; Fischer, *Modernity Disavowed*, chap. 3; Lugo-Ortiz, "Notas en torno a Plácido"; Nwankwo, *Black Cosmopolitanism*, chaps. 1–3; and Pettway, *Cuban Literature*, chaps. 1, 3, 5, and 6.
4. Orihuela, "Carta del traductor," 3. Unless stated otherwise, all translations are my own. Unbracketed ellipsis points were present in the original. Bracketed ellipsis points represent omissions by me.
5. Marianne Noble has defined the "sentimental wound" as "a bodily experience of anguish caused by identification with the pain of another." "Ecstasies of Sentimental Wounding," 295.
6. Sánchez-Eppler, *Touching Liberty*, 26; Hendler, *Public Sentiments*, 2–3; Howard, "What Is Sentimentality?," 70.
7. Orihuela, *Sol*, 98.
8. Williams, *Playing the Race Card*, 55.
9. Williams, *Playing the Race Card*, 55.
10. Here *creole* refers to a person of any ethnicity born in the Americas, not necessarily to a person of mixed race. See Anderson, *Imagined Communities*, 47.
11. Unlike Delany's Plácido, Orihuela's Plácido is only a historical personage rather than also serving as a character in the novel and doesn't play any role in the plot of the novel other than appearing in a purported eyewitness account that was published prior to the novel in a pamphlet and compelling three characters to shed tears.
12. Williams, *Playing the Race Card*, 28–40.
13. Williams, *Playing the Race Card*, 15.

14. Williams, *Playing the Race Card*, 11.
15. Tompkins, *Sensational Designs*, chap. 7, "'But Is It Any Good?' The Institutionalization of Literary Value," 186–202.
16. Tompkins, "Sentimental Power," 554–76.
17. Thomas Elsaesser, qtd. in Williams, *Playing the Race Card*, 29.
18. The Spanish colonial regime in Cuba prohibited any mention of Plácido for decades after his death. Paquette, *Sugar Is Made With Blood*, 260.
19. Agamben, "Bartleby," 267.
20. Gillman and Gruesz, "Worlding America," 228.
21. Gillman and Gruesz, "Worlding America," 231.
22. Latour, *Reassembling the Social*, 217.
23. On the Del Monte literary circle, see Benítez Rojo, "¿Como narrar la nación?," 104; Fischer, *Modernity Disavowed*, 107–30; Martínez Carmenate, *Domingo del Monte*; Moreno Fraginals, "Definiendo una política"; and Luis, *Literary Bondage*. On the understudied topic of Cuban exiles in Europe prior to the Ten Years' War, see Domingo Acebrón, "Reformistas cubanos en París."
24. As Kahlil Chaar-Pérez has suggested, Orihuela was not an abolitionist, because he endorsed a gradual approach to ending slavery. "Bonds of Translation," 150.
25. Jesús del Monte was the neighborhood with the highest concentration of Canary Islanders in Havana between 1801 and 1850, at 79.78% of residents. Hernández González, "Emigración Canaria," 78–79.
26. Sommer, *Foundational Fictions*, 6.
27. Sommer, *Foundational Fictions*, 5.
28. Horkheimer and Adorno, *Dialectic of Enlightenment*, 10.
29. Horkheimer and Adorno, *Dialectic of Enlightenment*, 93.
30. Horkheimer and Adorno, *Dialectic of Enlightenment*, 95.
31. J. Cornejo Polar, *Costumbrismo*, 14.
32. Escobar, "Costumbrismo," 123; Mestre, "SOL," 298.
33. Daylet Domínguez has pointed to scholarly "inattention" to *costumbrismo* in "Cuadros de costumbres," 135; José Escobar mentions Montesinos's assessment in "Costumbrismo," 119–20. See also Ocasio, *Afro-Cuban Costumbrismo*, 59.
34. Escobar, "Costumbrismo," 119.
35. Domínguez, "Cuadros de costumbres," 135–36; Lane, *Blackface Cuba*, 21; Poblete, "Lectura de la sociabilidad," 12; Schwab, "Social Observation," 206–8.
36. J. Cornejo Polar, *Costumbrismo*, 20; Escobar "Costumbrismo," 118; Iarocci, "Romantic Prose," 386–87; Lane, *Blackface Cuba*, 21; Ocasio, *Afro-Cuban Costumbrismo*, 4–5.
37. Dominguez, "Cuadros de costumbres"; Lane, *Blackface Cuba*; Poblete, "Lectura de la sociabilidad"; Schwab, "Social Observation."
38. Vuelta Abajo is the westernmost region in the Pinar del Río Province of Cuba.
39. On the novel's importance, see Fischer, Introduction, xi.
40. Orihuela, *Sol*, 117.

41. The Cortes de Cádiz had taken a prominent role in the resistance to the French invasion and occupation of Spain beginning in 1808. That year, Napoleon had made his brother king of Spain. The Central Junta of Seville, which ruled in the place of the ousted royal government, established General and Extraordinary Courts that first convened in Cádiz on September 24, 1810. The Constitution of 1812, drawn up by the Cortes, became the blueprint for liberalism in Spain and Spanish America: it constituted a limited monarchy subject to parliamentary control and established proportional representation for the colonies but denied people of African ancestry political representation. Once Spain had ousted the French and Fernando VII regained the Spanish throne in 1814, the king of Spain refused to recognize the Spanish Constitution of 1812 and dissolved the Cortes. However, as a result of a military coup by Lieutenant Colonel Rafael de Riego against Ferdinand VII, the Cortes reconvened beginning in 1820, beginning the period known as the Trienio Liberal (1820–23). During this period the Spanish American representatives in the Cortes unsuccessfully sought to establish a more decentralized model of colonial organization that was more attuned to the specific needs of the colonies and gave local elites a greater role in decision making. On Spanish American representation in the Cortes from 1810 to 1812, see Rodríguez O., "'Equality!'" On the Trienio Liberal, see Sánchez Andrés, "La Búsqueda." On the Soles y Rayos de Bolívar movement, see Pérez Guzmán, "Cuba bolivariana," 11.
42. Fernández Madrid, Tanco, Miralla, and Rocafuerte met one another while in exile in Cuba from late in the second decade of the nineteenth century to early in the third decade. Fernández Madrid served as president of the United Provinces of New Granada from 5 October 1814 to 21 January 1815 and president of the Republic of Colombia from 14 March to 22 June 1816. Rocafuerte was the president of Ecuador from 1835 to 1839. "Fernández Madrid de Castro, José."
43. I have been unable to discover the dates of Lemus's birth and death. Calcagno includes an entry on Lemus under "Lemos (José Francisco)" in his *Diccionario biográfico cubano*, 369–70.
44. Pérez Guzmán, "Cuba bolivariana," 13.
45. Pérez Guzmán, "Cuba bolivariana," 15.
46. Pérez Guzmán, "Cuba bolivariana," 16, 18.
47. Johnson, *Fear of French Negroes*, xx.
48. Orihuela, *Sol*, 87, 89.
49. Williams, *Playing the Race Card*, 32.
50. Paul Ryer has persuasively argued that although English-language scholarly work frequently uses the term *Afro-Cuban*, "as a term to describe Cuban people, the imported expression presupposes that which must first be ethnographically demonstrated. Not only is it not in common use among the population, but it is often resisted by those it purports to describe." *Beyond Cuban Waters*, 108. I agree with Ryer that *Afro-Cuban* is a vexed term, and that is why

I have sought to find evidence of representations of solidarity among *pardos/as* and *morenos/as*. However, the terms *pardo/a, mulato/a,* and *moreno/a* are similarly vexed in that they artificially divide up the population of free people of color according to skin color. Moreover, as Marlene Daut has pointed out in a different geographical and historical context, in the aftermath of the Haitian Revolution *mulatto* was by no means a neutral descriptor but was instead a demeaning term. Daut, *Tropics of Haiti,* 17. Daut argues that in cultural and historical analyses of Haiti—and her comments apply to the Caribbean more generally—"the term 'mulatto,' which absolutely reeks of the pseudo-science of slavery, must be subjected at every turn to interpretive scrutiny." *Tropics of Haiti,* 129. However, in the interest of erring on the cautious side, and recognizing the persuasiveness of the evidence that Ryer has cited of popular opposition to the term *Afro-Cuban* by Cubans on the island, I use the terms *pardo/a, mulato/a, moreno/a,* and *negro/a* in order to capture their distinct meanings in the Cuban colonial context.

51. As Matthew Pettway has argued, "Plácido published revolutionary poetry that defined liberty as the divine right of Cubans, and he assailed the queen as an illegitimate ruler on the throne." *Cuban Literature,* 8. However, in an intriguing and persuasive argument, Pettway claims that it was in Plácido's unpublished, improvised poetry, which he declaimed in cafés, at parties, and in the streets, that he made his most significant contribution to Cuban culture: "Plácido achieved a far greater feat as a spoken-word poet, because improvisation enabled him to evade government censorship and to impart politically sensitive—even revolutionary ideas—within an urban and rural African-descended public." *Cuban Literature,* 15.

52. On the modes of melodrama, see Gillman, "Mulatto, Tragic or Triumphant?"

53. "Correspondencia de ultramar—Isla de Cuba," *El Corresponsal* (Madrid), 15 July 1841, 2. See also "Habana a 25 de Mayo de 1841," *Gazeta de Puerto-Rico* (San Juan), 22 July 1841, 346; and Negrín Fajardo, "Orihuela y la educación popular," 52.

54. Negrín Fajardo, "Orihuela y la educación popular," 52, 56.

55. Orihuela, "Pormenores," 3.

56. Hernández Paz, *Andrés Orihuela Moreno,* 186, 197.

57. *Memorias de la Sociedad Económica de la Habana* 100 (February 1844): 241.

58. Hernández Paz, *Andrés Orihuela Moreno,* 215.

59. "Comisión Provincial de Instrucción Primaria," *Diario de la Marina* (Havana), 18 Nov. 1844, 4.

60. *Diario de la Marina,* 12 Apr. 1845, 1; 25 July 1845, 1; 18 Aug. 1845, 1; 6 Nov. 1845, 1.

61. Hernández Paz, *Andrés Orihuela Moreno,* 200; see also the announcement of an issue of the newspaper in *Diario de la Marina,* 16 May 1845, 4. The point about satire comes from Méndez Gómez, "'Horrores que afligían,'" 5.

62. Jiménez del Campo, *Escritores canarios en Cuba,* 47, 49.

63. Orihuela to Alejandro José Atocha, Barcelona, 16 Nov. 1848.
64. *El Fomento* (Barcelona), 11 Nov. 1848, 4.
65. Orihuela to Atocha, Barcelona, 16 Nov. 1848.
66. Henderson, *Glorious Defeat*, 159.
67. The precise dates of the lifespans of Galo de Cuendias and Victoria Féréal are unknown.
68. *El Popular* (Madrid), 22 Nov. 1849, 4.
69. *El Clamor Público* (Madrid), 27 Apr. 1852, 3; *El Balear* (Palma de Mallorca), 16 June 1852; "Diccionario de procedimientos judiciales por D. Andres Avelino de Orihuela," *Diario de la Marina*, 1 July 1852, 1.
70. Lazo, *Writing to Cuba*, 7, 82.
71. Gaspar Betancourt Cisneros to Domingo del Monte, Camagüey, 11 Dec. 1842.
72. Mirabal, *Suspect Freedoms*, 44–45.
73. Mestre, "SOL," 300.
74. *Diario de Palma* (Palma de Mallorca), 24 Jan. 1853, 3; Pombo, "A D. Andrés Avelino de Orihuela."
75. Andrés Avelino de Orihuela to Juan Eugenio Hartzenbusch, London, Oct. 6, 1854. Hartzenbusch made a name for himself with his *Los amantes de Teruel* (1838).
76. In a letter to the editor of *El Clamor Público*, of Madrid, José Segundo Florez reports that Orihuela was the literary editor of *El Eco de Ambos Mundos*. *El Clamor Público*, 29 Oct. 1853, 1. Orihuela mentions the Spanish government's ban on *El Eco de Ambos Mundos* in a letter to Hartzenbusch of 8 March 1852.
77. This is according to the catalog listing in the Bibliothèque nationale de France.
78. *La Caprichosa*, Aug. 1859, 113.
79. *El Contemporáneo* (Madrid), 30 Oct. 1861, 4; Pabrón Cadavid, "José María Torres Caicedo," 30.
80. *La Caprichosa*, July 1859, 106; M. Vergara, "Pimienta literaria," *La Iberia* (Madrid), 13 Jan. 1860, 3; *Le Temps* (Paris), 18 May 1862, 2; *Annuaire-almanach du commerce* (1864), 74.
81. For his self-description as a citizen of the United States, see Orihuela, "Pormenores," 2. For his anticolonial and nationalist poems, see Orihuela, "El guajiro independiente"; and Orihuela, "El grito de Hatuey!"
82. On the importance of British West Indian emancipation, on 1 August 1834, to Black and white US antislavery advocates, see Rugemer, *Problem of Emancipation*, chaps. 5 and 6.
83. On *El Mulato*, see Lazo, *Writing to Cuba*, 65, 98, and chap. 4; and Mirabal, *Suspect Freedoms*, 33, 54–58. See also Luis-Brown, "1848 for the Americas."
84. Agüeinaba, "Opinión pública," 198–200.
85. Chamerovzow worked as secretary of the British and Foreign Anti-Slavery Society from 1852 to 1869 and served as the editor of its journal, the *British and Foreign Anti-Slavery Reporter*. He edited the slave narrative *Slave Life in*

Georgia, by John Brown (1855), and a few years later published *Correspondence on Coolie Emigration to the West Indies* (1859). Huzzey, "Chamerovzow, Louis Alexis."

86. Agüeinaba, "Opinión pública," 198–99.
87. Born in Cuba, by 1801 Arango had moved to Spain, where he pursued a military career. In 1816 the government named him head of the Sección de Indias of the Ministry of War. In 1830 he became the secretary of the Sección de Ultramar of the Consejo Real de España e Indias. Novales, "Arango y Núñez del Castillo, Andrés."
88. For an account of the founding of the Sociedad Abolicionista, see Schmidt-Nowara, "'Spanish' Cuba," 117.
89. Hernández Paz, *Andrés Orihuela Moreno,* 210.
90. Pérez Nápoles, *Martí,* 87; *La Prensa* (Madrid), 20 May 1934, 5.
91. For biographical information on Orihuela, see Deschamps Chapeaux, "Hechos y personajes reales"; Hernández Paz, *Andrés Orihuela Moreno;* Jiménez del Campo, *Escritores canarios en Cuba;* and Negrín Fajardo, "Orihuela y la educación popular." These sources do not mention Orihuela's abolitionist activities in the 1860s, and my biography here offers additional details about his migrations and work as an editor and writer.
92. Hernández Paz, *Andrés Orihuela Moreno,* 211.
93. For several brief biographies of Mestre, see "José Manuel Mestre Domínguez, 1832–1886."
94. Mestre, "SOL," 298.
95. Mestre, "SOL," 282.
96. Mestre, "SOL," 300.
97. Mestre, "SOL," 282, my emphasis.
98. *Diario de Palma,* 24 Jan. 1853, 3.
99. Pombo, "A D. Andrés Avelino de Orihuela."
100. Manriquer, "O palmas y fuentes."
101. Deschamps Chapeaux, "Hechos y personajes reales," 12.
102. Jiménez del Campo, "*El Sol de Jesús del Monte.*"
103. Jiménez del Campo, "*El Sol de Jesús del Monte,*" 191.
104. Hernández Paz, *Andrés Orihuela Moreno,* 334, 336.
105. Hernández Paz, *Andrés Orihuela Moreno,* 336.
106. John Ernest, qtd. in Levine, Introduction, 6.
107. Trelles, "Bibliografia Placidiana," 19.
108. A. Cornejo Polar, "El indigenismo," 8, 13.
109. In the title, the *o* in *Relacion* is not accented.
110. Balaguer, *Junto al hogar,* 5–32.
111. Orihuela, *Sol,* 112.
112. Anguera, "Españolismo y catalanidad," 916.
113. Cuccu, "Víctor Balaguer I Cirera," 10.

114. Cuccu, "Víctor Balaguer I Cirera," 6.
115. Anguera, "Españolismo y catalanidad," 918.
116. "Biografía. Víctor Balaguer i Cirera."
117. Cuccu, "Víctor Balaguer I Cirera," 27.
118. For biographies of Balaguer in Catalan and Spanish, see "Biografía. Víeer i Cirera"; Comas i Güell, *Víctor Balaguer i el seu temps;* Cuccu, "Víctor Balaguer I Cirera"; Horrillo Ledesma, "Balaguer y Cirera, Víctor"; and "Víctor Balaguer."
119. The Cuban colonial government locked up the father of Tulita's friend Lolita "en la cárcel por suponerle iniciado en esa conspiración que se llamaba los Soles de Bolívar" (in jail, suspecting him of having masterminded the conspiracy called the Suns of Bolívar). Orihuela, *Sol,* 117.
120. Bakhtin, *Dialogic Imagination,* 341.
121. Baulo, "Novela por entregas," 9.
122. For a comparative analysis of *El Sol* and *Blake,* see Luis-Brown, "La Escalera, Sentiment and Revolution in the Nineteenth-Century Novel." For an assessment of Plácido's popularity as a poet, see Lugo-Ortiz, "Notas en torno a Plácido," 137. On La Escalera, see esp. Paquette, *Sugar Is Made with Blood;* Finch, *Rethinking Slave Rebellion in Cuba;* and Reid-Vazquez, *Year of the Lash.* Although historians in Cuba reached a consensus in the 1960s and 1970s that the Ladder Conspiracy was a ruse by colonial authorities who wanted to destroy the population of free people of color, most contemporary historians now argue that the Ladder Rebellion did exist as a series of loosely linked insurrections, even if the colonial government exaggerated its scope and aims. See Barcia Paz, *Seeds of Insurrection;* Cué Fernández, *Plácido;* Curry-Machado, "Catalysts in the Crucible" and "How Cuba Burned"; Finch, *Rethinking Slave Rebellion in Cuba* and "'What Looks Like a Revolution'"; Llanes Miqueli, *Víctimas del año del cuero;* Mena, "'No Common Folk'"; Paquette, *Sugar Is Made with Blood;* and Reid-Vazquez, *Year of the Lash.* I term La Escalera a series of *anticolonial* rebellions advisedly: according to Robert Paquette, British consular dispatches and the papers of the military commission of Matanzas, which processed the detained, "prove beyond a shade of doubt that [white] Creoles and Afro-Cubans were mulling schemes to overthrow the Spanish government" and that "the government had caught a revolution in the making." *Sugar Is Made with Blood,* 168, 245. For an analysis of La Escalera in the context of the long-standing efforts by members of the *pardo* and *moreno* militias in Cuba, see Landers, *Atlantic Creoles,* chap. 6.
123. Orihuela, *Sol,* 55.
124. Paquette, *Sugar Is Made with Blood,* 259.
125. Paquette, *Sugar Is Made with Blood,* 260.
126. Paquette, *Sugar Is Made with Blood,* 249.
127. Finch, *Rethinking Slave Rebellion in Cuba,* 116–19.
128. Finch, *Rethinking Slave Rebellion in Cuba,* 118.

129. Finch, *Rethinking Slave Rebellion in Cuba,* 119.
130. Finch, *Rethinking Slave Rebellion in Cuba,* 128–29.
131. Reid-Vasquez, *Year of the Lash,* 47–48.
132. Reid-Vasquez, *Year of the Lash,* 48.
133. Reid-Vasquez, *Year of the Lash,* 48–49; Finch *Rethinking Slave Rebellion in Cuba,* 88–92.
134. Finch, *Rethinking Slave Rebellion in Cuba,* 9.
135. Finch, *Rethinking Slave Rebellion in Cuba,* 119.
136. Reid-Vasquez, *Year of the Lash,* 49.
137. Deschamps Chapeaux, *El negro en la economía habanera,* 24; Paquette, *Sugar Is Made with Blood,* 4, 229.
138. Helg, "Race and Black Mobilization," 55.
139. Lazo, *Writing to Cuba,* 74, 84.
140. Lazo, *Writing to Cuba,* 11, 94, 95–98, and chap. 4.
141. Rama, *La ciudad letrada,* 23.
142. "Cuba. Aprendizaje africano."
143. "A los habitantes de Cuba."
144. "Impugnacion."
145. Plácido, *Poesías de Plácido,* 3; Plácido, *Poesías de Gabriel de la Concepción Valdés.* The debates on Plácido necessarily took place outside of Cuba: from 1844 to as late as 1867, the Cuban colonial government prohibited a public discussion of Plácido's poetry. Bueno, *Acerca de Plácido,* 11.
146. Del Monte, "Dos poetas negros."
147. *Liberator* (Boston), 15 Nov. 1844; Whittier, "Juan Placido." Alexandre Pétion (1770–1818) was president of Haiti from 1806 to 1818. Toussaint Louverture (1743–1803) was one of the most celebrated military leaders of the Haitian Revolution (1791–1804).
148. The historian Luz María Mena has shown that there were intermittent efforts by Cuban and Spanish clergy and intellectuals to rethink the question of race: in 1814 Don Matías Alqueza, a Spanish resident of Cuba, circulated a leaflet advocating racial equality; Bishop Espada y Landa (1756–1832), who was the bishop of Havana from 1800 until his death, called for widespread interracial marriage in Cuba; and in 1853, Fray Estevan Adoaín, a missionary, remarked that it was "delirious" for anyone to claim pure racial ancestry in Cuba. Mena, "'No Common-Folk,'" 31, 32, 55.
149. Orihuela, *Dos palabras,* 4.
150. Beaumont, *María* (1849), 2:188.
151. Orihuela, *Dos palabras,* 7.
152. Orihuela, *Dos palabras,* 2.
153. Although Villaverde still espoused proslavery views at the time that Orihuela published *El Sol* in 1852, he would later oppose slavery. Brickhouse, *Transamerican Literary Relations,* 155.

154. Although it is true to some extent that Orihuela "applauds" the achievements of *La Verdad* in this pamphlet, as Kahlil Chaar-Pérez has argued, I would amend Chaar-Pérez's perspective by arguing that it is a case of tough love: he also criticizes its lack of commitment to antislavery causes and puts its editorial board on the defensive with his critique, as their lengthy rebuttals in footnotes demonstrate. Chaar-Pérez, "Bonds of Translation," 149.
155. Orihuela, *Dos palabras*, 4.
156. Chaar-Pérez, "Bonds of Translation," 149.
157. Orihuela, *Dos palabras*, 7.
158. Chaar-Pérez, "Bonds of Translation," 150.
159. Chaar-Pérez, "Bonds of Translation," 150.
160. Sibylle Fischer has argued that *Cecilia Valdés* is "the most important novel of nineteenth-century Cuba," repeating verbatim what William Luis argued fifteen years earlier, but I think that *El Sol de Jesús del Monte* gives *Cecilia Valdés* a run for its money without displacing it. Fischer, Introduction, xi; Luis, *Literary Bondage*, 100.
161. For hemispheric framings of these writers, see the following: on Brown, see Brickhouse, "Hemispheric Jamestown," 18–19; on Delany and Melville, see Sundquist, "Melville, Delany and New World Slavery"; on Melville and Stowe, see Marr, "'Out of This World,'" 282–87; on Melville, see Grandin, *Empire of Necessity;* and on Stowe, see Brickhouse, *Transamerican Literary Relations,* chap. 6.
162. Brickhouse, *Transamerican Literary Relations,* 10.
163. Orihuela, *Sol,* 106.
164. Orihuela, *Sol,* 103.
165. Orihuela, *Sol,* chaps. 14, 16, 17, and 18.
166. Orihuela, *Sol,* 103.

Textual Essay

1. Santo Domingo was the capital city of the Dominican Republic, which gained its independence in 1844.
2. Peñas Ruiz, "Semblanza," 2.
3. "Ignacio Boix Blay."
4. Peñas Ruiz, "Semblanza," 3.
5. Peñas Ruiz, "Semblanza," 3.
6. This information comes from a WorldCat search.
7. *La España* (Madrid), 10 Apr. 1853, 4.
8. Keech, "Three-Deckers and Installment Novels," 163, 172, 175.
9. Keech, "Three-Deckers and Installment Novels," 164, 171.
10. Martínez Martín, "La edición artesanal," 67.
11. Botrel, "La novela por entregas," 114, 116.

12. Sánchez García, "Las formas del libro," 126. On the lucrative character of publishing the *novela de entregas,* see Botrel, "La novela por entregas," 111.
13. Sánchez García, "Las formas del libro," 127.
14. O'Neil-Henry, *Mastering the Marketplace,* 23; *La Presse,* 5 May 1842, 4, qtd. in O'Neil-Henry, *Mastering the Marketplace,* 168n1.
15. O'Neil-Henry, *Mastering the Marketplace,* 24.
16. Keech, "Three-Deckers and Installment Novels," 173.
17. Fornet, *El libro en Cuba,* 32.
18. Fornet, *El libro en Cuba,* 104.
19. Botrel, "La novela por entregas," 121.
20. Trelles, "Bibliografía Placidiana," 19. I have been unable to find further bibliographic information on Salinero's text. For the provenance of this text, see the introduction to this volume.
21. Orihuela, "Carta del traductor," 3; Ayguals de Izco, "Advertencia preliminar," 4.

Note on the Translation

1. Piña, "Literatura," 12.
2. Benjamin, "Task of the Translator," 256.
3. De Man, "'Conclusions,'" 25.
4. Benjamin, "Task of the Translator," 258.
5. Benjamin, "Task of the Translator," 257.
6. Benjamin, "Task of the Translator," 253.
7. Rabassa, "No Two Snowflakes are Alike," 12.
8. Ricoeur, *On Translation,* 22.
9. Orihuela, *Sol,* 39.
10. Orihuela, *Sol,* 58.
11. Orihuela, *Sol,* 71.
12. Rabassa, "No Two Snowflakes are Alike," 2.
13. Orihuela, *Sol,* 5.
14. In a footnote, Orihuela describes the *boca-abajo* as follows: "Ninety to one hundred lashings with a leather whip on a naked body; as a result of such punishments slaves tend to fall ill for several days because ordinarily the wounds take a while to scab as a result of the inflammation that sets in, although to cure the wounds they [white overseers] apply a combination of tobacco, urine and sugar cane liquor." Orihuela, *Sol,* 8n1.
15. Orihuela, *Sol,* 59.
16. Orihuela, *Sol,* 90.
17. Zeno Gandía, *La charca,* 9n36.
18. Orihuela, *Sol,* 60.
19. Spivak, "Rethinking Comparativism," 613.

Afterword

1. Del Monte, Letter to the editor, 190.
2. Del Monte, Letter to the editor, 191.
3. Del Monte, Letter to the editor, 195.
4. Del Monte, Letter to the editor, 201, 202.
5. Del Monte, Letter to the editor, 190–91.
6. Orihuela, *Sol,* 98.
7. Orihuela, *Sol,* 61.
8. Orihuela, *Sol,* 98.
9. Martínez Carmenate, *Domingo del Monte,* 170–71.
10. Aguilera Manzano, "Informal Communication Network," 80–82; Aguilera Manzano, "Corrientes," 137; Martínez Carmenate, *Domingo del Monte,* 191, 200, 203, 217.
11. Aguilera Manzano, "Corrientes," 131, 137, 140; Martínez Carmenate, *Domingo del Monte,* 217.
12. Martínez Carmenate, *Domingo del Monte,* 221; Moreno Fraginals, "Definiendo una política," 192.
13. Luis, *Literary Bondage,* 29.
14. Luis, *Literary Bondage,* 29.
15. Luis, *Literary Bondage,* 1.
16. Aguilera Manzano, "Corrientes," 132.
17. Hernández Paz, *Andrés Orihuela Moreno,* 207.
18. Orihuela, "La flor de muerto"; Orihuela, "El mendigo."
19. Aguilera Manzano, "Publicaciones," 312.
20. Aguilera Manzano, "Corrientes," 140–41; Aguilera Manzano, "Publicaciones," 301.
21. Aguilera Manzano, "Corrientes," 141.
22. Aguilera Manzano, "Publicaciones," 302.
23. Aguilera Manzano, "Publicaciones," 304.
24. Aguilera Manzano, "Publicaciones," 305.
25. Orihuela, *Sol,* 10.
26. Aguilera Manzano, "Publicaciones," 317–18.
27. Aguilera Manzano, *La formación,* 91n79, 93n83; Cabrera Saqui, "Vida, pasión y gloria," 7; Luis, *Literary Bondage,* 102; Torres-Cuevas, *José Antonio Saco,* 34.
28. González, "Felipe Poey y Aloy," 7; Martínez Carmenate, *Domingo del Monte,* 127.
29. Opatrny, "Domingo del Monte," 173.
30. Simpson, *La educación superior,* 78. On the Colegio-Seminario de San Carlos, see also Moreno Davis, "La formación de la conciencia cubana."
31. Torres-Cuevas, *Obispo Espada,* 88.
32. Torres-Cuevas, *Félix Varela,* 38.
33. Torres-Cuevas, *Obispo Espada,* 100, 156.

34. Torres-Cuevas, *Félix Varela*, 124.
35. Simpson, *La educación superior*, 112.
36. Torres-Cuevas, *Félix Varela*, 241.
37. Torres-Cuevas, *Félix Varela*, 277.
38. Torres-Cuevas, *Félix Varela*, 317.
39. Benítez Rojo, "¿Como narrar la nación?," 104; Moreno Fraginals, "Definiendo una política," 194; Martínez Carmenate, *Domingo del Monte*, 270. On the Del Monte literary circle, see also Fischer, *Modernity Disavowed*, 107–30.
40. Abreu Arcia, *Por una Cuba negra*, 144; Cabrera Saqui, "Vida, pasión y gloria," 8; Martínez Carmenate, *Domingo del Monte*, 65; Moreno Fraginals, "Definiendo una política," 194; Silverstein, "Cuban Anti-Slavery Genre," 60.
41. Hernández Pérez, Ramírez Pérez, and Ortega Rodrígu, *Cirilo Villaverde*, 19–20.
42. Martínez Carmenate, *Domingo del Monte*, 270.
43. Del Monte, "Dos poetas negros"; Schulman, "Tanco y la literatura antiesclavista," 327. On La Escalera, see the introduction to this volume.
44. Benítez Rojo, "¿Como narrar la nación?," 118; Schulman, "Tanco y la literatura antiesclavista," 325.
45. Abreu Arcia, *Por una Cuba negra*, 87.
46. Moreno Fraginals, "Definiendo una política," 194.
47. Moreno Fraginals, "Anselmo Suárez y Romero," 34.
48. Luis, *Literary Bondage*, 28.
49. Silverstein, "Cuban Anti-Slavery Genre," 67.
50. Orihuela, *Sol*, 70.
51. Rojas, "Esclavitud liberal," 46.
52. Lewis Galanes, "'Hombre misterioso,'" 2n4; Triana y Atorveza, "Dos colombianos en Cuba," 84.
53. Méndez Rodenas, "Abolicionismo transnacional cubano," 69. "Petrona y Rosalía" was first published in *Cuba Contemporánea* in 1925. Bueno, "Narrativa antiesclavista," 176.
54. Tanco y Bosmeniel, "Al que leyere," 255–56.
55. Tanco y Bosmeniel, "Petrona y Rosalía," 114; Tanco y Bosmeniel, "Petrona y Rosalía," trans. Genova, 171.
56. Schulman, "Tanco y la literatura antiesclavista," 325.
57. Tanco y Bosmeniel, qtd. in Schulman, "Tanco y la literatura antiesclavista," 327.
58. Orihuela, *Sol*, 98.
59. Orihuela, *Sol*, 61.
60. Méndez Rodenas, "Abolicionismo transnacional cubano," 69.
61. Tanco y Bosmeniel in Hernández Morelli, "Noticias," 77.
62. Cabrera Saqui, "Vida, pasión y gloria," 20.
63. Silverstein, "Cuban Anti-Slavery Genre," 61.
64. Cabrera Saqui, "Vida, pasión y gloria," 40.

65. Silverstein, "Cuban Anti-Slavery Genre," 62, 65, 67.
66. Suárez y Romero, *Francisco,* 87.
67. Suárez y Romero, *Francisco,* 53.
68. Suárez y Romero, *Francisco,* 85.
69. Suárez y Romero, *Francisco,* 47.
70. See the chapter "Romantic Racialism in the North," in Fredrickson, *Black Image in the White Mind,* 97–129; and see my own analysis of romantic racialism and sentimentalism in Alexander Kinmont in Stowe in Luis-Brown, *Waves of Decolonization,* 39–48.
71. Suárez y Romero, *Francisco,* 53–54.
72. Suárez y Romero, *Francisco,* 53, 54.
73. Suárez y Romero, *Francisco,* 33.
74. Villaverde, "Primitiva Cecilia Valdés," 247.
75. Villaverde, "Primitiva Cecilia Valdés," 244.
76. Villaverde, "Primitiva Cecilia Valdés," 251.
77. Villaverde, "Primitiva Cecilia Valdés," 233.
78. Villaverde, "Primitiva Cecilia Valdés," 248.
79. Villaverde, "Primitiva Cecilia Valdés," 247. Lamarck was one of twelve chairs at the Muséum national d'histoire naturelle in Paris beginning in 1793. For a brief discussion of Lamarck's role at the museum as well as a summary of his thought, see Sloan, "Evolutionary Thought Before Darwin."
80. Villaverde, "Primitiva Cecilia Valdés," 247.
81. Orihuela, *Sol,* 98.
82. Villaverde, "Primitiva Cecilia Valdés," 251.
83. Villaverde, "Primitiva Cecilia Valdés," 251.
84. Orihuela, *Sol,* 39.
85. Villaverde, "Primitiva Cecilia Valdés," 248, 250.
86. Orihuela, *Sol,* 10, 38.
87. Pichardo, *Diccionario provincial,* 216.
88. Paz Sánchez and Hernández, *Esclavitud blanca,* 23.
89. Paz Sánchez and Hernández, *Esclavitud blanca,* 22–23.
90. Naranjo Orovio and García González, *Racismo e inmigración,* 39–41.
91. Hernández García, *Emigración de las Islas Canarias,* 398.
92. Reid-Vasquez, *Year of the Lash,* 58.

Bibliography

Selected Writings of Andrés Avelino de Orihuela

Orihuela, Adrés Avelino de. *Amarguras de la vida: Drama en cinco actos.* Barcelona: Imprenta de la Viuda e Hijos de Mayol, 1848.

———. "Bocetos parisienses. Cuadros fisiológicos. Que comprenden cierta clase de animales raros no clasificados hasta hoy, aunque pertenecen á la historia natural del género humano." *La Ilustración* (Madrid), 1 Oct. 1853, 591–93. Reprinted in *Semanario pintoresco español,* 10 Sept. 1854, 290–92.

———. "Brisas del Mar: Recuerdos poéticos de Don Manuel Nicolás Corpancho." In *Ensayos poéticos de Manuel Nicolas Corpancho, precedidos de varios juicios escritos en Europa y América,* 47–56. Paris: Imprenta y Litografía de Maulde y Renou, 1854.

———, trans. *La cabaña del tío Tom: Novela escrita en inglés por M. Harriett Beecher Stowe.* Paris: Libreria Española y Americana de D. Ignacio Boix, 1852. Schlesinger Library, Harvard University.

———, trans. *La cabaña del tío Tom: Novela escrita en inglés por M. Harriet Beecher Stowe.* Barcelona: D. Juan Oliveres, 1853.

———, trans. *La cabaña del tío Tom.* By Harriet Beecher Stowe. Bogotá, 1853. British Library.

———, trans. *La cabaña del tío Tom.* By Harriet Beecher Stowe. Buenos Aires: Imprenta del Comercio, 1853. Biblioteca Nacional de Chile, Sala Medina.

———. "Un cadáver sobre el trono." In *La Crónica* (San Francisco, CA), 28 Feb. 1855, 1.

———. "Carta del traductor a Ms. Harriet Beecher Stowe, después de haber leido su novela, *Uncle Tom's Cabin.* París, octubre 12 de 1852." In *La cabaña del tío Tom,* by M. Harriet Beecher Stowe, trans. Orihuela, 2–3. Paris: Libreria Española y Americana de D. Ignacio Boix, 1852. Schlesinger Library, Harvard University.

———. *Dieguiyo Pata de Anafe.* Madrid: Imprenta de V. de Lalama, 1849.

———, ed. *La discusión: Diario democrático de la mañana.* Madrid, 1871.

———. *Dos palabras sobre el folleto "La situación política de Cuba y su remedio."* Paris, 1852; New York: La Verdad, 1852. Biblioteca Nacional José Martí, Havana, Cuba.

———. *Ecos del Guadalquivir: Poesías andaluzas.* Havana: Imprenta de Manuel Soler y Gelada, 1846.

———. "La flor de muerto sobre el sepulcro de mi amada." *Noticioso y Lucero,* 10 July 1838, 3. Library of Congress.

———. "El grito de Hatuey! Leyenda cubana (siglo XVI)." *El Eco de Cuba*, 1, 10, 20 July 1855, 1.

———. "El guajiro independiente: Cantos populares cubanos." *El Eco de Cuba* (New York), 22 June 1855, 1.

———. *El jornalero: Comedia en un acto*. Madrid: Imprenta del Centro Industrial y Mercantil, 1865.

———. Letter to Alejandro José Atocha. Barcelona, 16 Nov. 1848. Atocha Manuscripts, Lilly Library, Indiana University.

———. Letter to Juan Eugenio Hartzenbusch. Paris, 8 Mar. 1852. Biblioteca Nacional de España.

———. Letter to Juan Eugenio Hartzenbusch. London, 6 Oct. 1854. Biblioteca Nacional de España.

———. *Lo que puede la ambición*. Havana, 1839.

———. *Memorias de la hija del Yumurí*. Havana, n.d.

———. "El mendigo." *Noticioso y Lucero*, 16 Mar. 1838, 3. Library of Congress.

———, ed. *Panorama Universal: Lecturas amenas é instructivas*. Paris: Ultramar/El Eco Hispano-Americano, 1854.

———. *Perlas y lágrimas*. Matanzas, 1868.

———. "Poesía. A Napoleón III. Con motivo del atentado del 14 de enero de 1858. Presentada por el autor a S. M. la Emperatriz de los Franceses." *La Caprichosa*, July 1859, 106.

———. "Poesía. Costumbres andaluzas. Un baile de Candil." *La Caprichosa*, August 1859, 120–21.

———, ed. *Poetas españoles y americanos del siglo XIX*. Paris: M. S. Albert, 1851.

———. "Pormenores sobre la emancipacion de los esclavos en las colonias inglesas durante los años 1834 y 1835. Tomados de los documentos oficiales presentados al Parlamento ingles e impreso de su orden." *El Eco de Cuba*, 1 Sept. 1855, 3–4; 10 Sept. 1855, 2.

———. *Proscriptos y encarcelados; corona cívica, dedicada a los mártires de la libertad española*. Madrid: Fuertes, 1845.

———. "Recuerdo. Un baile en el hotel de ville, en 1859." *La Caprichosa: Revista Universal del Nuevo Mundo* (Paris), March 1859, 34–36.

———. "Revista biográfica. Personajes célebres de América. Siglo XIX." *La Caprichosa*, May 1859, 69.

———. "Revista científica." *La Caprichosa*, May 1859, 74–75.

———. "Revista literaria. Poesía. A mi amigo Mariano G. Manrique." *La Caprichosa*, June 1859, 90.

———. "Revista satírica: Costumbres andaluzas—Los Dos Marineros." *La Caprichosa*, April 1859, 55–57.

———. "Ritornelo: La vida y la muerte." *El Indicador* (Veracruz Llave, Mexico), 11 Jan. 1846, 3.

———. *El Sol de Jesús del Monte*. Paris: Boix, 1852. Cornell University Library. Reprint, ed. Miguel David Hernández Paz. Santa Cruz de Tenerife, Canary Islands: Ediciones Idea, 2007.

———. "Últimas horas del poeta cubano, Gabriel de la Concepción Valdés, Plácido." Ca. 1844. José Augusto Escoto Cuban History and Literature Collection, Houghton Library, Harvard University, ser. 2, no. 559.

———. "¡Una Coburgada!" *Diario de la Marina* (Havana), 9 Mar. 1845, 3; 5 Apr. 1845, 3. Word Newspaper Archive: Latin American Newspapers. Readex.

———. "Una turca soberana." *Los hijos de Eva: Semanario de literatura, ciencias y artes* (Alicante, Spain) 1.8 (4 Mar. 1849): 125–26.

———. "Variedades. El festin de Baltasar. Estudio bíblico." *La Caprichosa,* August 1859, 124–26.

———, trans. *El voluntario, novela*. By Paul Féval. Paris: Mme. Denné Schmitz, 1854. Bibliotèque nationale de France.

Orihuela, Adrés Avelino de, S. Cancio Bello, and M. F. Viondi, eds. *Jardín romántico*. Havana, 1838. Biblioteca Nacional José Martí, Havana.

Orihuela, Adrés Avelino de, and Teodoro Guerrero, eds. *Quita-Pesares: Biblioteca clásico-romántica de costumbres, literatura, sana moral y burlas*. Havana: Imprenta de Manuel Soler y Gelada, 1845. Biblioteca Nacional José Martí, Havana.

Orihuela, Adrés Avelino de, and Eugène Guillernot, eds. *La satira de ambos mundos: Revista mensual de chismes políticos y literarios, burlas*. Paris, 1859–61.

Newspapers

El Balear (Palma de Mallorca). 16 June 1852. Biblioteca Virtual de la Prensa Histórica. Biblioteca Nacional de España.

La Caprichosa: Revista Universal del Nuevo Mundo (Paris). July, Aug. 1859. Gallica. Bibliothèque nationale de France.

El Clamor Público (Madrid). 27 Apr. 1852, 29 Oct. 1853. Hemeroteca Digital. Biblioteca Nacional de España.

El Contemporáneo (Madrid). 30 Oct. 1861. Hemeroteca Digital. Biblioteca Nacional de España.

El Corresponsal (Madrid). 15 July 1841. Hemeroteca Digital. Biblioteca Nacional de España.

Diario de la Marina (Havana). 28 Sept., 18 Nov. 1844, 12 Apr., 16 May, 25 July, 18 Aug., 6 Nov. 1845, 1 July 1852. Library of Congress.

Diario de Palma (Palma de Mallorca). 24 Jan. 1853. Biblioteca Virtual de la Prensa Histórica. Biblioteca Nacional de España.

El Eco de Cuba (New York). 22 June, 1, 10, 20 July, 1, 10 Sept. 1855. New York Public Library.

La España (Madrid). 10 Apr. 1853. Hemeroteca Digital. Biblioteca Nacional de España.
El Filibustero (New York). 22 Aug. 1853, 1.
El Fomento (Barcelona). 11 Nov. 1848. Hemeroteca Digital. Biblioteca Nacional de España.
Gazeta de Puerto-Rico (San Juan). 22 July1841. Chronicling America: Historic American Newspapers. Library of Congress.
La Iberia (Madrid). 13 Jan. 1860. Hemeroteca Digital. Biblioteca Nacional de España.
The Liberator (Boston). 1 Jan. 1831, 15 Nov.1844. Accessible Archives.
Memorias de la Sociedad Económica de la Habana. Feb. 1844. Google Books.
El Mulato (New York). 1854. Biblioteca Nacional de Cuba.
The North Star (Rochester). 7 Dec. 1849. African American Newspapers Series 1, 1827–1998. Readex.
Noticioso y Lucero (Havana). 1 Jan. 1838–31 Dec. 1839. Library of Congress.
El Popular (Madrid). 22 Nov. 1849. Hemeroteca Digital. Biblioteca Nacional de España.
La Prensa (Madrid). 20 May 1934. Hemeroteca Digital. Biblioteca Nacional de España.
Le Temps (Paris). 18 May 1862. Gallica. Bibliothèque nationale de France.
La Verdad (New York). 14 May 1848, 1; 15 June 1849, 6.

Other Sources

Abreu Arcia, Alberto. *Por una Cuba negra: Literatura, raza y modernidad en el siglo XIX*. Madrid: Hypermedia Ediciones, 2017.
Agamben, Giorgio. "Bartleby, or On Contingency." In *Potentialities,* trans. Daniel Heller-Roazen, 243–74. Stanford, CA: Stanford University Press, 1999.
Agüeinaba. "La opinión pública y las reformas liberales en las Antillas Españolas." In *Revista Hispano-Americana, Política, Científica y Literaria,* ed. Antonio Angulo et al., vol. 1, Nov. 1864–January 1865, 197–202. Madrid: Redacción y Administración Cervantes, 1865.
Aguilera Manzano, José María. "Las corrientes liberales habaneras a través de las publicaciones periódicas de la primera mitad del siglo XIX." *Cuban Studies* 38 (2007): 125–53.
———. *La formación de la identidad cubana (El debate Saco–La Sagra)*. Seville: Consejo Superior de Investigaciones Científicas, 2005.
———. "The Informal Communication Network Built by Domingo Del Monte from Havana between 1824 and 1845." *Caribbean Studies* 37, no. 1 (2009): 67–96.
———. "Publicaciones periódicas e imprentas de la Habana entre 1824 y 1845 en los archivos cubanos y españoles." *Anuario de Estudios Americanos* 64, no. 1 (2007): 293–328.

Agustí, David. *Los almogávares: La expansión mediterránea de la Corona de Aragón*. Madrid: Silex, 2004.
"A los habitantes de Cuba." *La Verdad* (New York), 14 May 1848, 1.
Anderson, Benedict. *Imagined Communities: Reflections on the Origin and Spread of Nationalism*. New York: Verso, 1991.
Anguera, Pere. "Españolismo y catalanidad en la historiografía catalana decimonónica." *Hispania* 61, no. 209 (2001): 907–32.
Annuaire-almanach du commerce, de l'industrie, de la magistrature et de l'administration: ou almanach des 500.000 addresses de Paris. Paris: Firmoin Didot Frères, 1864.
Ayguals de Izco, Wenceslao. "Advertencia preliminar." In *La choza de Tom: Ó sea Vida de los negros en el sur de los Estados Unidos, novela escrita en inglés por Enriqueta Beecher Stowe*, trans. Ayguals de Izco, 3–4. Madrid: Imprenta de Ayguals de Izco Hermanos, 1852.
Bachiller y Morales, Antonio. "Plácido." In *Revista Cubana*, 2:547–61. Havana: Establecimiento Tipográfico de Solor, Álvarez y Comp., 1885.
Bakhtin, Mikhail. *The Dialogic Imagination: Four Essays* [excerpts]. In *Theory of the Novel: A Historical Approach*, ed. Michael McKeon, 321–54. Baltimore: Johns Hopkins University Press, 2000.
Balaguer, Víctor. *Bellezas de la historia de Cataluña*. Barcelona: Impresa Narciso Ramirez, 1853.
———. *Junto al hogar: Misceláneas literarias*. Vol. 1. Barcelona: Imprenta A. Brusi, 1852.
El bandolerismo en Cuba. 2 vols. Havana: Imprenta O'Reilly, 1890.
Barcia Paz, Manuel. *Seeds of Insurrection: Domination and Resistance on Western Cuban Plantations, 1808–1848*. Baton Rouge: Louisiana State University Press, 2008.
Baulo, Sylvie. "La novela por entregas a mediados del siglo XIX: ¿Literatura al márgen o del centro?" *Ínsula* 693, no. 9 (2004): 8–11.
Beaumont, Gustave de. *Maria, ó la esclavitud en los Estados Unidos: Cuadros de costumbres Americanas*. 2 vols. Mexico City: R. Rafael, 1849.
———. *María, o la esclavitud en los Estados Unidos: Pintura de costumbres en la América del Norte*. Cádiz: Libreria de D. D. Jeros, 1840.
———. *Marie, or Slavery in the United States: A Novel of Jacksonian America*. 1835. Trans. Barbara Chapman. Stanford, CA: Stanford University Press, 1958. Reprint, ed. Robert Reid-Pharr. Baltimore: Johns Hopkins University Press, 1999. Originally published as *Marie, ou l'esclavage aux États-Unis, tableau des moeurs Américaines* (Brussels: Hauman, 1825).
Benítez Rojo, Antonio. "¿Como narrar la nación? El círculo de Domingo Delmonte y el surgimiento de la novela cubana." *Cuadernos Americanos* 45 (1994): 103–25.

Benjamin, Walter. "The Task of the Translator." 1923. In *Illuminations,* ed. Hannah Arendt, trans. Harry Zohn, 11–25. New York: Schocken Books, 1969. Reprint. New York: Mariner Books, 2019.

———. "The Task of the Translator." In *Walter Benjamin: Selected Writings. Vol. 1: 1912–1926,* ed. Marcus Bullock and Michael W. Jennings, 253–63. Cambridge, MA: Harvard University Press, 1996.

Betancourt, José Victoriano. "Chucho Malatobo." In *Artículos de costumbres,* ed. Mario Sánchez Roig and Mario Cabrera Saqui, 65–69. Havana: Publicaciones del Ministerio de Educación, 1941.

Betancourt Cisneros, Gaspar. Letter to Domingo del Monte, Camagüey, 11 Dec. 1842. In *Centón Epistolario,* by Domingo del Monte, ed. Sophie Andioc, 2:102. Havana: Imagen Contemporánea, 2002.

"Biografía. Víctor Balaguer i Cirera." http://www.escriptors.cat/autors/balaguerv/pagina.php?id_sec=2290.

Botrel, Jean-François. "La novela por entregas: Unidad de creación y consumo." In *Creación y público en la literatura Española,* by Jean-François Botrel, Serge Salaün, and Andrés Amorós, ed. Botrel and Salaün, 111–55. Madrid: Editorial Castalia, 1974.

Brickhouse, Anna. "Hemispheric Jamestown." In Levander and Levine, *Hemispheric American Studies,* 18–35.

———. *Transamerican Literary Relations and the Nineteenth-Century Public Sphere.* New York: Cambridge University Press, 2004.

Brown, William Wells. *Clotel; or The President's Daughter.* Ed. Robert S. Levine. Boston: Bedford/St. Martin's, 2000.

Bueno, Salvador, ed. *Acerca de Plácido.* Havana: Editorial Letras Cubanas, 1985.

———. "La narrativa antiesclavista en Cuba de 1835 a 1839." *Cuadernos hispanoamericanos* 451–52 (1988): 169–86.

Cabrera Saqui, Mario. "Vida, pasión y gloria de Anselmo Suárez y Romero." In *Francisco, El ingenio, o las delicias del campo,* by Anselmo Súarez y Romero, 7–42. Havana: Publicaciones del Ministerio de Educación, 1947.

Calcagno, Francisco. *Diccionario biográfico cubano.* New York: N. Ponce de León, 1878.

Cárdenas y Rodríguez, José M. de. *Colección de artículos satíricos y costumbres.* Havana: Imprenta del Faro Industrial, 1847.

Carpentier, Alejo. *Music in Cuba.* Ed. Timothy Brennan. Trans. Alan West-Durán. Minneapolis: University of Minnesota Press, 2001.

Castellanos, Jorge, and Isabel Castellanos. "The Geographic, Ethnologic, and Linguistic Roots of Cuban Blacks." *Cuban Studies* 17 (1987): 95–110.

Cavendish, Richard. "Publication of *Uncle Tom's Cabin.*" *History Today* 51, no. 6 (2001). https://www.historytoday.com/archive/publication-uncle-tom's-cabin

"Cerro (La Habana)." EcuRed. https://www.ecured.cu/Cerro_(La_Habana).

Chaar-Pérez, Kahlil. "The Bonds of Translation: A Cuban Encounter with *Uncle Tom's Cabin.*" In *Uncle Tom's Cabins: The Transnational History of America's Most*

Mutable Book, ed. Tracy C. Davis and Stefka Mihaylova, 139–64. Ann Arbor: University of Michigan Press, 2018.

Childs, Matt D. *The 1812 Aponte Rebellion in Cuba and the Struggle against Atlantic Slavery.* Chapel Hill: University of North Carolina Press, 2006.

"City of Potosí." UNESCO World Heritage List. http://whc.unesco.org/en/list/420/.

Comas i Güell, Montserrat, ed. *Víctor Balaguer i el seu temps.* Barcelona: Publicacions de l'Abadia de Montserrat, 2004.

Conway, Christopher. *Nineteenth-Century Spanish America: A Cultural History.* Nashville: Vanderbilt University Press, 2015.

Cornejo Polar, Antonio. "El indigenismo y las literaturas heterogéneas: Su doble estatuto socio-cultural." *Revista de Crítica Literaria Latinoamericana* 4, no. 7/8 (1978): 7–21.

Cornejo Polar, Jorge. *El costumbrismo en el Perú: Estudio y antología de cuadros de costumbres.* Lima: Ediciones COPÉ, 2001.

Cruickshank, D. W. "The Lovers of Teruel: A 'Romantic' Story." *Modern Language Review* 88, no. 4 (1993): 881–93.

"Cuba. Aprendizaje africano." *El Filibustero* (New York), 22 Aug. 1853, 1.

Cuccu, Marina. "Retrat 25: Víctor Balaguer I Cirera (1824–1901)." Collecció retrats, Ajuntament de Vilanova I la Geltrú. https://www.vilanova.cat/doc/doc_19556797.pdf.

Cué Fernández, Daisy. *Plácido, el poeta conspirador.* Santiago de Cuba: Oriente, 2007.

Curry-Machado, Jonathan. "Catalysts in the Crucible: Kidnapped Caribbeans, Free Black British Subjects and Migrant British Machinists in the Failed Cuban Revolution of 1843." In *Blacks, Coloureds and National Identity in Nineteenth-Century Latin America,* ed. Nancy Priscilla Naro, 123–42. London: Institute of Latin American Studies, 2003.

———. "How Cuba Burned with the Ghosts of British Slavery: Race, Abolition and the *Escalera.*" *Slavery and Abolition* 25, no. 1 (2004): 71–93.

Dadabhoy, Ambereen. "'Going Native': Geography, Gender and Identity in Lady Mary Wortley Montagu's *Turkish Embassy Letters.*" In *Gender and Space in British Literature,* ed. Mona Narain and Karen Gevirtz, 49–66. London: Ashgate, 2014. Reprint. New York: Routledge, 2016.

Daut, Marlene L. *Tropics of Haiti: Race and the Literary History of the Haitian Revolution in the Atlantic World, 1789–1865.* Liverpool: Liverpool University Press, 2015.

Delany, Martin R. *Blake, or the Huts of America.* 1859, 1861–62. Boston: Beacon, 1970.

Del Monte, Domingo. *Centón Epistolario.* 3 vols. Ed. Sophie Andioc. Havana: Imagen Contemporánea, 2002.

———. "Dos poetas negros: Plácido y Manzano." 1845. In *Acerca de Plácido,* ed. Salvador Bueno, 54–56. Havana: Editorial Letras Cubanas, 1985.

———. Letter to the editor of *El Globo* (Paris), August 1844. In *Escritos de Domingo Del Monte,* ed. José A. Fernández de Castro, 1:189–202. Havana: Cultural, 1929.

De Man, Paul. "'Conclusions' on Walter Benjamin's 'The Task of the Translator.' Messenger Lecture, Cornell University, March 4, 1983." *Yale French Studies* 97 (2000): 10–35.

Denzel, Markus A. *Handbook of World Exchange Rates, 1590–1914.* Burlington, VT: Ashgate, 2010.

Deschamps Chapeaux, Pedro. "Hechos y personajes reales en *El Sol de Jesús del Monte, novela de costumbres cubanas.*" *La Gaceta de Cuba* 99 (1972): 12–14.

———. *El negro en la economía habanera del siglo XIX.* Havana: UNEAC, 1971.

Domingo Acebrón, María Dolores. "Los Reformistas cubanos en París, 1838–1878." *Caravelle* 74 (2000): 105–17.

Domínguez, Daylet. "Cuadros de costumbres en Cuba y Puerto Rico: De la historia natural y la literaturas a las ciencias sociales." *Revista Hispánica Moderna* 69, no. 2 (2016): 133–49.

Escobar, José. "Costumbrismo: Estado de la cuestión." In *Romanticismo 6: Actas del VI Congreso, Nápoles, 27–30 de marzo de 1996; el costumbrismo romántico,* 117–26. Roma: Bulzoni, 1996.

"Fernández Madrid de Castro, José." mcnbiografías. http://www.mcnbiografias.com/app-bio/do/show?key=fernandez-madrid-de-castro-jose.

Finch, Aisha K. *Rethinking Slave Rebellion in Cuba: La Escalera and the Insurgencies of 1841–1844.* Chapel Hill: University of North Carolina Press, 2015.

———. "'What Looks Like a Revolution': Enslaved Women and the Gendered Terrain of Slave Insurgencies in Cuba, 1843–1844." *Journal of Women's History* 26, no. 1 (2014): 112–34.

Fischer, Sibylle. Introduction to *Cecilia Valdés or El Angel Hill,* by Cirilo Villaverde, trans. Helen Lane, xi–xxx. New York: Oxford University Press, 2005.

———. *Modernity Disavowed: Haiti and the Cultures of Slavery in the Age of Revolution.* Durham, NC: Duke University Press, 2004.

Fornet, Ambrosio. *El libro en Cuba, siglos XVIII y XIX.* Havana: Editorial Letras Cubanas, 1994.

Franco, Jean. *An Introduction to Spanish-American Literature.* 3rd ed. New York: Cambridge University Press, 1994.

Fredrickson, George. *The Black Image in the White Mind: The Debate on Afro-American Character and Destiny, 1817–1914.* New York: Harper & Row, 1971. Reprint. Middletown, CT: Wesleyan University Press, 1987.

Gillman, Susan. "The Mulatto, Tragic or Triumphant? The Nineteenth-Century American Race Melodrama." In *The Culture of Sentiment: Race, Gender and Sentimentality in Nineteenth-Century America,* ed. Shirley Samuels, 221–43. New York: Oxford University Press, 1992.

Gillman, Susan, and Kirsten Silva Gruesz. "Worlding America: The Hemispheric Text-Network." In *A Companion to American Literary Studies,* ed. Caroline F. Levander and Robert S. Levine, 228–47. Malden, MA: Wiley-Blackwell, 2011.

González, Rosa María. "Felipe Poey y Aloy: El naturalista por excelencia." In *Felipe Poey y Aloy: Obras,* 1–28. Havana: Imagen Contemporánea, 1999.

Grandin, Greg. *The Empire of Necessity: Slavery, Freedom, and Deception in the New World.* New York: Picador, 2014.

Griffin, Jon. "Marímbula—The Cuban Thumb Piano." Salsa Bianca: Cuban Music & More. https://salsablanca.com/cuban-instruments/marimbula-the-cuban-thumb-piano/.

Hartzenbusch, Juan Eugenio. *Los amantes de Teruel.* Madrid: Imprenta de José María Repullés, 1838.

Helg, Aline. "Race and Black Mobilization in Colonial and Early Independent Cuba: A Comparative Perspective." *Ethnohistory* 44, no. 1 (1997): 53–74.

Henderson, Timothy J. *A Glorious Defeat: Mexico and its War with the United States.* New York: Hill & Wang, 2007.

Hendler, Glenn. *Public Sentiments: Structures of Feeling in Nineteenth-Century American Literature.* Chapel Hill: University of North Carolina Press, 2001.

Hernández García, Julio. *La emigración de las Islas Canarias en el siglo XIX.* Gran Canaria, Spain: Excmo. Cabildo Insular de Gran Canaria, 1981.

Hernández González, Manuel. "La emigración Canaria a Cuba en la primera mitad del siglo XIX." *Studia Historica: Historia Contemporánea* 15, no. 1 (1997): 71–83.

Hernández Morelli, Rolando. "Noticias, lugar y texto de 'Un niño en La Habana,' espécimen narrativo inédito de 1837." *Círculo* 15 (1986): 73–84.

Hernández Paz, Miguel David. *Andrés Orihuela Moreno y El Sol de Jesús del Monte: La novela histórica antiesclavista de un canario en la Cuba del siglo XIX.* Santa Cruz de Tenerife, Spain: Ediciones Idea, 2007.

Hernández Pérez, Pedro, Jorge Freddy Ramírez Pérez, and Gerardo Ortega Rodríguez. *Cirilo Villaverde: Patriota entero y escritor útil.* Havana: Editorial de Ciencias Sociales, 2012.

Horkheimer, Max, and Theodor W. Adorno. *Dialectic of Enlightenment.* Trans. John Cumming. New York: Continuum, 1999.

Horrillo Ledesma, Victoria. "Balaguer y Cirera, Víctor (1824–1901)." mcnbiografías. http://www.mcnbiografias.com/app-bio/do/show?key=balaguer-y-cirera-victor.

Howard, June. "What Is Sentimentality?" *American Literary History* 11, no. 1 (1999): 63–81.

Howard, Philip A. *Changing History: Afro-Cuban Cabildos and Societies of Color in the Nineteenth Century.* Baton Rouge: Louisiana State University Press, 1998.

Hunt, Robert. "Cashmere." In *Ure's Dictionary of Arts, Manufactures and Mines,* ed. Hunt, 1:631–32. London: Longman, Green, Longman & Roberts, 1860.

Huzzey, Richard. "Chamerovzow, Louis Alexis." *Oxford Dictionary of National Biography*. Accessed 27 May 2010. http://www.oxforddnb.com.ccl.idm.oclc.org/view/10.1093/ref:odnb/9780198614128.001.0001/odnb-9780198614128-e-101107?rskey=Keolgq&result=1.

Iarocci, Michael. "Romantic Prose, Journalism, and Costumbrismo." In *The Cambridge History of Spanish Literature,* ed. David T. Gies, 381–91. New York: Cambridge University Press, 2004.

"Ignacio Boix Blay." Filosofía en español. http://www.filosofia.org/ave/003/c094.htm.

"Ignacio Boix y Blay (Tarragona, 1807–Valencia, 1862) [Semblanza] / Ana Peñas Ruiz." Biblioteca Virtual Miguel de Cervantes. http://www.cervantesvirtual.com/nd/ark:/59851/bmcnw1h8.

Iguacel. "Almogobars/Almogávares, los guerreros olvidados." *Aragonando* (blog). 17 May 2012. http://aragonandonogara.blogspot.com/2012/05/almogabars-almogavares-los-guerreros.html.

"Impugnacion á las 'Ideas sobre la incorporacion de Cuba en los Estados Unidos, por Dn. José Antonio Saco.'" *La Verdad* (New York). 15 June 1849. 6.

Jiménez del Campo, Paloma. *Escritores canarios en Cuba: Literatura de la emigración.* Las Palmas: Ediciones del Cabildo de Gran Canaria, 2003.

———. "*El Sol de Jesús del Monte,* novela de costumbres cubanas, del canario Andrés Avelino de Orihuela." *Anales de Literatura Hispanoamericana* 26, no. 1 (1997): 189–94.

Johnson, Sara E. *The Fear of French Negroes: Transcolonial Collaboration in the Revolutionary Americas.* Berkeley: University of California Press, 2012.

"José Manuel Mestre Domínguez, 1832–1886." Filosofía en español. http://www.filosofia.org/ave/001/a256.htm.

Keech, James M., Jr. "Three-Deckers and Installment Novels: The Effect of Publishing Format upon the Nineteenth-Century Novel." PhD diss., Louisiana State University, 1965.

Kriukelyte, Erica. "The Creation of Modern Prisons in the Russian Empire." International Institute of Social History Research Paper 48. 2012. https://socialhistory.org/sites/default/files/docs/publications/respap48.pdf.

Kuss, Malena. "Puerto Rico." In *Music in Latin America and the Caribbean: An Encyclopedic History,* ed. Kuss, 2:151–88. Austin: University of Texas Press, 2007.

Landers, Jane. *Atlantic Creoles in the Age of Revolutions.* Cambridge, MA: Harvard University Press, 2010.

Lane, Jill. *Blackface Cuba, 1840–1895.* Philadelphia: University of Pennsylvania Press, 2005.

Latour, Bruno. *Reassembling the Social: An Introduction to Actor-Network-Theory.* New York: Oxford University Press, 2005.

Lazo, Rodrigo. *Writing to Cuba: Filibustering and Cuban Exiles in the United States.* Chapel Hill: University of North Carolina Press, 2005.

Ledesma, Victoria Horrillo. "Balaguer y Cirera, Víctor (1824–1901)." mcnbiografias. http://www.mcnbiografias.com/app-bio/do/show?key=balaguer-y-cirera-victor.

Levander, Caroline F., and Robert S. Levine, eds. *Hemispheric American Studies.* New Brunswick, NJ: Rutgers University Press, 2008.

Levine, Robert S. Introduction to *Clotel; or The President's Daughter,* by William Wells Brown, 3–28. Boston: Bedford/St. Martin's, 2011.

Lewis Galanes, Adriana. "'El hombre misterioso'/'el cura': El texto del segundo relato en las *Escenas de la vida privada en la isla de Cuba* por Félix Manuel Tanco Bosmeniel." *Anuario de Estudios Americanos* 51, no. 1 (1994): 185–211.

"Liceo de la Habana." EcuRed. https://www.ecured.cu/Liceo_de_La_Habana.

Llanes Miqueli, Rita. *Víctimas del año del cuero.* Havana: Editorial de Ciencias Sociales, 1984.

Llaverias y Martínez, Joaquín. *Contribución a la historia de la prensa periódica.* Havana: Publicaciones del Archivo Nacional de Cuba, 1957.

Lohnes, Kate, and Donald Sommerville. "Battle of Thermopylae." *Encyclopaedia Britannica Online.* https://www.britannica.com/event/Battle-of-Thermopylae-Greek-history-480-BC.

López Lemus, Virgilio. *La décima constante: Las tradiciones oral y escrita.* Havana: Fundación Fernando Ortiz, 1999.

Lugo-Ortiz, Agnes. "Notas en torno a Plácido." *Encuentro de la Cultura Cubana* 10 (1998): 133–46.

Luis, William. *Literary Bondage: Slavery in Cuban Narrative.* Austin: University of Texas Press, 1990.

Luis-Brown, David. "An 1848 for the Americas: The black Atlantic, 'El negro mártir,' and Cuban Exile Anticolonialism." *American Literary History* 21, no. 3 (2009): 431–63.

———. "La Escalera, Sentiment and Revolution in the Novels of Delany and Orihuela." In *African American Literature in Transition, 1750–2015: Volume 4: 1830–1850,* ed. Benjamin Fagan, 244–67. New York: Cambridge University Press, 2021.

———. *Waves of Decolonization: Discourses of Race and Hemispheric Citizenship in Cuba, Mexico and the United States.* Durham, NC: Duke University Press, 2008.

Lyon, John B. "'The Science of Sciences': Replication and Reproduction in Lavater's Physiognomics." *Eighteenth-Century Studies* 40, no. 2 (2007): 257–77.

Malleson, G. B. *Studies from Genoese History.* London: Longmans, Green, 1875.

Manriquer, Mariano G. "O palmas y fuentes: A mi amigo el señor don Andrés de Orihuela." *El Mosaico* (Bogotá), 15 Dec. 1860.

Marichal, Carlos. "Money, Taxes and Finance." In *The Cambridge Economic History of Latin America,* ed. Victor Bulmer-Thomas, John H. Coatsworth, and Roberto Cortés Conde, vol. 1, *The Colonial Era and the Short Nineteenth Century,* 423–60. New York: Cambridge University Press, 2006.

"Marímbula." National Museum of American History. http://americanhistory.si.edu/collections/search/object/nmah_601901.

Marr, Timothy. "'Out of This World': Islamic Irruptions in the Literary Americas." In Levander and Levine, *Hemispheric American Studies*, 266–93.

Marrero, Juan. *Dos siglos de periodismo en Cuba*. Havana: Pablo de la Torriente, 1999.

Martínez-Alier, Verena. *Marriage, Class and Colour in Nineteenth-Century Cuba*. London: Cambridge University Press, 1994.

Martínez Carmenate, Urbano. *Domingo del Monte y su tiempo*. Maracaibo, Venezuela: Dirección de Cultura de la Universidad del Zulia, 1996. Reprint. Matanzas, Cuba: Ediciones Matanzas, 2009.

Martínez-Fernández, Luis. *Fighting Slavery in the Caribbean: The Life and Times of a British Family in Nineteenth-Century Havana*. Armonk, NY: M. E. Sharpe, 1998.

Martínez Martín, Jesús A. "La edición artesanal y la construcción del mercado." In *Historia de la edición en España, 1836–1936*, 29–71. Madrid: Marcial Pons, 2001.

"The Martyr Poet Placido." *The Liberator*, 15 Nov. 1844. Accessible Archives. http://www.accessible.com/accessible/print?AADocList=1&AADocStyle=STYLED&AAStyleFile=&AABeanName=toc1&AANextPage=/printFullDocFromXML.jsp&AACheck=1.5.1.0.1.

Melville, Herman. *Benito Cereno*. In *Melville's Short Novels*, ed. Dan McCall, 34–102. New York: Norton, 2002.

Mena, Luz María. "'No Common Folk': Free Blacks and Race Relations in the Early Modernization of Havana (1830s–1840s)." PhD diss., University of California, Berkeley, 2001.

Méndez Gómez, Salvador. "'Horrores que afligían a la raza de color': Identidades afrocubanas en el discurso literario de Andrés Orihuela." In *XXII Coloquio de Historia Canario-Americana*, ed. Elena Acosta Guerrero, 1–19. Las Palmas de Gran Canaria: Cabildo Insular de Gran Canaria, 2017.

Méndez Rodenas, Adriana. "El abolicionismo transnacional cubano: Los relatos antiesclavistas de Félix Tanco y 'el tiempo de la nación.'" *América sin nombre* 19 (2014): 61–72.

Mestre, J. M. "EL SOL DE JESÚS DEL MONTE: Novela de costrumbres cubanas, por A. A. de Orihuela.—Paris, 1852." In *Revista de la Habana*, ed. R. M. de Mendive y J. de J. Q García, 3:281–82, 298–301. Havana: Imprenta del Tiempo, 1854. http://books.google.com/books?id=gD0tAAAAYAAJ&printsec=frontcover&dq=Revista+de+la+Habana+1854&source=bl&ots=rxOUQ2lnVG&sig=bcWzXxPvGa7M9A5KHU1rPg2Uxns&hl=en&ei=CAGDTM_AD4H8AbooDdAQ&sa=X&oi=book_result&ct=result&resnum=1&ved=0CBUQ6AEwAA#v=onepage&q=Revista%20de%20la%20Habana%201854&f=false.

Mirabal, Nancy Raquel. *Suspect Freedoms: The Racial and Sexual Politics of Cubanidad in New York, 1823–1957*. New York: New York University Press, 2017.

Morales y Morales, Vidal. *Iniciadores y primeros mártires de la Revolución Cubana.* Havana: Imprenta Avisador Comercial, 1901.
Moreno Davis, J. C. "La formación de la conciencia cubana." *Revista Lotería* 181 (1970): 5–28.
Moreno Fraginals, Manuel. "Anselmo Suárez y Romero (1818–1878)." In *Órbita de Manuel Moreno Fraginals,* ed. Alfredo Prieto and Oscar Zanetti Lecuona, 29–39. Havana: Ediciones Unión, 2009.
———. "Definiendo una política." In *Cuba/España, España/Cuba: Historia común,* 190–205. Barcelona: Grijalbo Mondadori, 1995.
Morton, Julia F. "Mamey." The New Crop Resource Online Program, Purdue University. https://www.hort.purdue.edu/newcrop/morton/mamey.html.
Naranjo Orovio, Consuelo, and Armando García González. *Racismo e inmigración en Cuba en el siglo XIX.* Madrid: Ediciones Doce Calles, 1996.
Negrín Fajardo, Olegario. "Orihuela y la educación popular." In *Profesores canarios en Cuba durante el siglo XIX,* 47–73. Las Palmas: Ediciones del Cabildo de Gran Canaria, 2000.
Noble, Marianne. "The Ecstasies of Sentimental Wounding in *Uncle Tom's Cabin.*" *Yale Journal of Criticism* 10, no. 2 (1997): 295–320.
Novales, Gil. "Arango y Núñez del Castillo, Andrés." mcnbiografías. http://www.mcnbiografias.com/app-bio/do/show?key=arango-y-nunnez-del-castillo-andres.
Nwankwo, Ifeoma. *Black Cosmopolitanism: Racial Consciousness and Transnational Identity in the Nineteenth-Century Americas.* Philadelphia: University of Pennsylvania Press, 2005.
Ocasio, Rafael. *Afro-Cuban Costumbrismo: From Plantations to the Slums.* Gainesville: University Press of Florida, 2012.
O'Neil-Henry, Anne. *Mastering the Marketplace: Popular Literature in Nineteenth-Century France.* Lincoln: University of Nebraska Press, 2017.
Opatrny, Josef. "Domingo del Monte en la discusión sobre la trata y esclavitud." In *Proyectos políticos y culturales en las realidades caribeñas de los siglos XIX y XX,* ed. Opatrny, 167–81. Prague: Universidad Carolina de Praga, 2016.
Ortiz, Fernando. *Un catauro de cubanismos: Apuntes lexicográficos.* Havana: Revista Bimestre Cubana, 1923.
———. "La fiesta afrocubana del Día de Reyes." In *Los cabildos y la fiesta afrocubanos del Día de Reyes,* 25–38. Havana: Editorial de Ciencias Sociales, 1992.
———. *Los instrumentos de la música afrocubana.* Vol. 3. Havana: Publicaciones de la Dirección de Cultura del Ministerio de Educación, 1952.
Pabrón Cadavid, Jhonny Antonio. "José María Torres Caicedo: El nacimiento de la identidad latinoamericana, las construcciones nacionales y el derecho de autor." *Revista la Propiedad Inmaterial* 16 (2012): 21–55.
Palmer, Steven. "From the Plantation to the Academy: Slavery and the Production of Medicine in the Nineteenth Century." In *Health and Medicine in the*

Circum-Caribbean, 1800–1968, ed. Juanita de Barros, Palmer, and David Wright, 53–75. New York: Routledge, 2009.

Paquette, Robert L. *Sugar Is Made with Blood: The Conspiracy of La Escalera and the Conflict between Empires over Slavery in Cuba*. Middletown, CT: Wesleyan University Press, 1988.

"Parfait amor (licor)." EcuRed. Accessed 15 Jan. 2021. https://www.ecured.cu/Parfait _amour_(licor).

Parker-Pope, Tara. "How to Mother a Mother." *Well* (blog), *New York Times*, 11 May 2012. http://well.blogs.nytimes.com/2012/05/11/how-to-mother-a-mother/?_r=0.

Paz Sánchez, Manuel de, and Manuel Hernández. *La esclavitud blanca: Contribución a la historia del inmigrante canario en América. Siglo XIX*. Santa Cruz de Tenerife: Centro de la Cultura Popular Canaria, 1992.

Pendle, Karin. "Eugène Scribe and French Opera of the Nineteenth Century." *Musical Quarterly* 57, no. 4 (1971): 535–61.

Pérez Guzmán, Francisco. "Cuba bolivariana." *Revista de la Biblioteca Nacional José Martí* 27, no. 3 (1983): 5–30.

Pérez Nápoles, Rubén. *Martí: El poeta armado*. Madrid: Algaba Ediciones, 2004.

Pettway, Matthew. *Cuban Literature in the Age of Black Insurrection: Manzano, Plácido and Afro-Latino Religion*. Jackson: University Press of Mississippi, 2020.

Pichardo y Tapia, Estéban. *Diccionario provincial casi-razonado de vozes y frases cubanas*. 1875. Havana: Editorial de Ciencias Sociales, 1976.

———. *El fatalista: Novela cubana*. Havana: Imprenta Militar de M. Soler, 1866.

Piña, Ramón. *Historia de un bribón dichoso: Novela*. Madrid: Manuel Tello, 1860.

———. "Literatura: Las traducciones." *Revista de la Habana*, 1 Oct.–Dec. 1856, 11–17.

Plácido [Gabriel de la Concepción Valdés]. "Goodbye to My Mother—Sonnet." Trans. William Henry Hurlburt. In "The Poetry of Spanish America," by Hurlburt. *North American Review* 68, no. 142 (1849): 148.

———. *Poesías de Gabriel de la Concepción Valdés*. New Orleans: Imprenta de La Patria, 1847. Biblioteca Nacional José Martí, Havana, Cuba.

———. *Poesías de Plácido*. Veracruz: Imprenta del Censor, 1845. Biblioteca Nacional José Martí, Havana, Cuba.

"Plaza de Armas—Havana City Guide." lahabana.com.

Poblete, Juan. "Lectura de la sociabilidad y sociabilidad de la lectura: La novela y las costumbres nacionales en el siglo XIX." *Revista de Crítica Literaria Latinoamericana* 26, no. 52 (2000): 11–34.

Pombo, Rafael. "A D. Andrés Avelino de Orihuela, autor de 'El Sol de Jesús del Monte,' en su viaje proyectado para Méjico." New York, 6 Sept. 1855. Ms. Biblioteca Nacional de Colombia. https://catalogoenlinea.bibliotecanacional.gov.co /client/es_ES/search/asset/68966.

Portuondo, José Antonio. "Landaluze y el costumbrismo en Cuba." In *Letras: Cultura en Cuba*, ed. Ana Cairo Ballester, 4:361–84. Havana: Editorial Pueblo y Educación, 1987.

Quevedo y Villegas, Francisco de. *Historia de la vida del Buscon, ejemplo de vagamundos y espejo de tacaños.* Zaragoza: Pedro Verges, 1626.
———. *The Life and Adventures of Buscon, the witty Spaniard.* London: Herringman, 1657.
Quiroga, José. "Bitter Daiquiris: A Crystal Chronicle." Trans. Elisabeth Enenbach. In *Havana beyond the Ruins: Cultural Mappings after 1989,* ed. Anke Birkenmaier and Esther Whitfield, 270–85. Durham, NC: Duke University Press, 2011.
Rabassa, Gregory. "No Two Snowflakes are Alike." In *The Craft of Translation,* ed. John Biguenet and Rainier Schulte, 1–12. Chicago: University of Chicago Press, 1989.
Rafa. "Bocato di Cardinale." *Fraseomanía: Desnudando dichos y palabras* (blog). 3 Feb. 2018. https://fraseomania.blogspot.com/2018/02/bocato-di-cardinale.html.
Rama, Ángel. *La ciudad letrada.* Hanover, NH: Ediciones del Norte, 1984.
Reid-Vazquez, Michele. *The Year of the Lash: Free People of Color in Cuba and the Nineteenth-Century Atlantic World.* Athens: University of Georgia Press, 2011.
La reina de las Antillas, ó sea, Situación actual de la isla de Cuba. In *Nuevo viajero universal.* ed. Don Nemesio Fernández Cuesta, vol. 3, *América,* 723–821. Madrid: Imprenta y Libería de Gaspar y Roig, Editores, 1861.
Ricoeur, Paul. *On Translation.* Trans. Eileen Brennan. New York: Routledge, 2006.
Riesgo, Pascual. *Conchita la habanera: Novela de costumbres.* Havana: R. Oliva, 1846.
Rivers, Christopher. *Face Value: Physiognomical Thought and the Legible Body in Marivaux, Lavater, Balzac, Gautier, and Zola.* Madison: University of Wisconsin Press, 1994.
Rodríguez O., Jaime E. "'Equality! The Sacred Right of Equality': Representation under the Constitution of 1812." *Revista de Indias* 68, no. 242 (2008): 97–122.
Rojas, Rafael. "La esclavitud liberal: Liberalismo y abolicionismo en el Caribe hispano." *Secuencia* 86 (2013): 29–52.
Román, Manuel Antonio. *Diccionario de chilenismos.* Vol. 3. Santiago de Chile: Imprenta de San José, 1913.
Rugemer, Edward Bartlett. *The Problem of Emancipation: The Caribbean Roots of the American Civil War.* Baton Rouge: Louisiana State University Press, 2008.
"Las ruinas de La Cotorra en Guanabacoa." *Radio Televisión Martí.* 10 Apr. 2018. https://www.radiotelevisionmarti.com/a/171884.html.
Ryer, Paul. *Beyond Cuban Waters: Africa, La Yuma, and the Island's Global Imagination.* Nashville: Vanderbilt University Press, 2018.
Sánchez Andrés, Agustín. "La búsqueda de un nuevo modelo de relaciones con los territorios ultramarinos durante el Trienio Liberal (1820–1823)." *Revista de Indias* 57, no. 210 (1997): 451–74.
Sánchez-Eppler, Karen. *Touching Liberty: Abolition, Feminism, and the Politics of the Body.* Berkeley: University of California Press, 1993.

Sánchez García, Raquel. "Las formas del libro: Textos, imágenes y formatos." In Martínez, *Historia de la edición en España, 1836–1936,* 111–34.
Schmidt-Nowara, Christopher. "'Spanish' Cuba: Race and Class in Spanish and Cuban Antislavery Ideology, 1861–1868." *Cuban Studies* 25 (1995): 101–22.
Schulman, Ivan A. "Tanco y la literatura antiesclavista." In *Homenaje a Lydia Cabrera,* ed. Reinaldo Sánchez and José Antonio Madrigal, 317–32. Miami: Ediciones Universal, 1977.
Schwab, Christiane. "Social Observation in Early Commercial Print Media: Towards a Genealogy of the Social Sketch (ca. 1820–1860)." *History and Anthropology* 29, no. 2 (2018): 204–32.
Scribe, Eugène. *Judith ó el Palco de la opera.* Trans. José Lesen y Moreno. Madrid: Imprenta y Casa de la Unión Comercial, 1843.
———. *Judith, ou la loge d'opéra, nouvelle contemporaine.* In *Tonadillas; ou, Historiettes en action,* 2:1–159. Paris: Dumont, 1838.
"Significado de Boca de siri." Salud Cytan. http://salud.cytan.com/boca-de-siri/.
Silverstein, Stephen. "The Cuban Anti-Slavery Genre: Anselmo Suárez y Romero's *Colección de artículos* and the Policy of *Buen Tratamiento.*" *Revista Hispánica Moderna* 68, no. 1 (2015): 59–75.
———. *The Merchant of Havana: The Jew in the Cuban Abolitionist Archive.* Nashville: Vanderbilt University Press, 2016.
Simpson, Renate. *La educación superior en Cuba bajo el colonialismo español.* Havana: Editorial de Ciencias Sociales, 1984.
Sloan, Phillip. "Evolutionary Thought Before Darwin." Stanford Encyclopedia of Philosophy Archive, Winter 2019 Edition. Ed. Edward N. Zalta. https://plato.stanford.edu/archives/win2019/entries/evolution-before-darwin/.
Sommer, Doris. *Foundational Fictions: The National Romances of Latin America.* Berkeley: University of California Press, 1991.
Spivak, Gayatri. "Rethinking Comparativism." *New Literary History* 40 (2009): 609–26.
Staum, Martin. "Physiognomy and Phrenology at the Paris Athénée." *Journal of the History of Ideas* 56, no. 3 (1995): 443–62.
Stowe, Harriet Beecher. *La cabaña del tío Tomás.* Mexico City: Imprenta de Vicente Segura Argüelles, 1853.
———. *La cabaña del tío Tomás.* Mexico City: Imprenta de Andrés Boix, 1853.
———. *La choza del tio Tom, o vida de los negros en la América del Norte.* Lima, 1853.
———. *La choza de Tom ó sea vida de los negros en el sur de los Estados Unidos.* Trans. Wenceslao Ayguals de Izco. Madrid: Imprenta de Ayguals de Izco Hermanos, 1852.
———. *Uncle Tom's Cabin, or Life Among the Lowly.* 1852. Second edition. New York: Norton, 2010.
Suárez y Romero, Anselmo. *Francisco, El ingenio, o las Delicias del campo.* Havana: Publicaciones del Ministerio de Educación, 1947.

Sublette, Ned. *Cuba and its Music: From the First Drums to the Mambo.* Chicago: Chicago Review Press, 2004.

Sundquist, Eric J. "Melville, Delany and New World Slavery." In *To Wake the Nations: Race in the Making of American Literature,* by Sundquist, 135–224. Cambridge, MA: Harvard University Press, 1993.

Surwillo, Lisa. "Representing the Slave Trader: Haley and the Slave Ship; or Spain's Uncle Tom's Cabin." *PMLA* 120, no. 3 (2005): 768–82.

Sutton, Keith, L. Carl Brown, Abdel Kader Chanderli, and Salah Zaimeche. "Algeria." *Encyclopaedia Britannica Online.* Accessed 16 Mar. 2020. https://www.britannica.com/place/Algeria.

Tanco y Bosmeniel, Félix. "Al que leyere" and *"Escenas de la vida privada en la isla de Cuba."* *Cuba Contemporánea* 39, no. 156 (1925): 255–60.

———. "Amor," "El Himeneo," "América," "La Modestia," "El Juego," "Consuelo," and "Las Postrimerías." In *Rimas americanas,* ed. Ignacio Herrera Dávila [Domingo Del Monte], 1:120–65. Havana: Imprenta de Palmer, 1833.

———. "Petrona y Rosalía." 1838. In *Cuentos cubanos del siglo XIX,* ed. Salvador Bueno, 103–31. Havana: Editorial Arte y Literatura, 1975.

———. "Petrona y Rosalía." Trans. Thomas Genova. *Metamorphoses: A Journal of Literary Translation* 25, no. 1 (2017): 170–93.

"Teatro Tacón." EcuRed. Accessed 18 Mar. 2020. https://www.ecured.cu/index.php?title=Teatro_Tacón&oldid=3542400.

Tepaske, John J., and Herbert S. Klein. *The Royal Treasuries of the Spanish Empire in America,* vol. 2, *Upper Peru (Bolivia).* Durham, NC: Duke University Press, 1982.

Thomas, Hugh. *Cuba: La lucha por la libertad.* New York: Vintage Español, 2013.

Ticknor, George. *History of Spanish Literature.* Vol. 3. New York: Harper & Brothers, 1849.

Tompkins, Jane P. *Sensational Designs: The Cultural Work of American Fiction, 1790–1860.* New York: Oxford University Press, 1985.

———. "Sentimental Power: *Uncle Tom's Cabin* and the Politics of Literary History." 1978. In *Uncle Tom's Cabin,* ed. Elizabeth Ammons, 554–76. 3rd ed. New York: Norton, 2017.

Torres Caicedo, José María. *Unión Latino-Americana.* Paris: Libreria de Rosa y Bouret, 1865. https://books.google.com/books?id=AqTUAAAAMAAJ&printsec=frontcover&source=gbs_ge_summary_r&cad=0#v=onepage&q&f=false.

Torres-Cuevas, Eduardo. *Félix Varela: Los orígenes de la ciencia y con-ciencia cubanas.* Havana: Editorial de Ciencias Sociales, 1995.

———. *José Antonio Saco: La polémica de la esclavitud.* Havana: Editorial de Ciencias Sociales, 1984.

———. *Obispo Espada: Ilustración, reforma y antiesclavismo.* Havana: Editorial de Ciencias Sociales, 1990.

Trelles, Carlos M. "Bibliografía Placidiana." *Cuba y América* 15, no. 1 (1 July 1904): 17–19.

Triana y Antorveza, Humberto. "Dos colombianos en Cuba: José Fernández Madrid (1780–1830) y Félix Manuel Tanco y Bosmeniel (1796–1871)." *Boletín de Historia y Antigüedades* 92, no. 828 (2005): 65–94.

Tuhus-Dubrow, Rebecca. "Why Won't This New Mom Wash Her Hair? The Fascinating Postpartum Customs of Women from Around the World." Slate. 11 Apr. 2011. http://www.slate.com/articles/double_x/doublex/2011/04/why_wont_this_new_mom_wash_her_hair.html.

V., F., and M. B. *Colección de refranes y locuciones familiares de la lengua castellana.* Barcelona: Librería de Juan Oliveres, Editor, 1841.

"Víctor Balaguer." Biografías y Vidas. http://www.biografiasyvidas.com/biografia/b/balaguer_victor.htm.

Villaverde, Cirilo. *Cecilia Valdés.* Havana: Imprenta Literaria, 1839.

———. *Cecilia Valdés.* Ed. Ivan A. Schulman. Caracas: Biblioteca Ayacucho, 1981.

———. *Cecilia Valdés, ó la Loma del Ángel.* New York: Imprenta El Espejo, 1882.

———. *Cecilia Valdés or El Angel Hill.* Ed. Sibylle Fischer. Trans. Helen Lane. New York: Oxford University Press, 2005.

———. "La primitiva Cecilia Valdés." *La Siempreviva* 2 (1839): 75–87, 242–54. Reprinted in *Homenaje a Cirilo Villaverde,* 232–51. Havana: Comisión Nacional Cubana de la Unesco, 1964.

Whittier, John Greenleaf. "Juan Placido." *The North Star,* 7 Dec. 1849. Accessible Archives. http://www.accessible.com/accessible/print?AADocList=3&AADocStyle=STYLED&AAStyleFile=&AABeanName=toc1&AANextPage=/printFullDocFromXML.jsp&AACheck=2.3.3.0.1.

———. "Placido, the Slave Poet." 1845. In *The Complete Writings of John Greenleaf Whittier,* 6:261–69. New York: Houghton, Mifflin, 1892.

Williams, Linda. *Playing the Race Card: Melodramas of Black and White from Uncle Tom to O. J. Simpson.* Princeton, NJ: Princeton University Press, 2001.

"Zapateo cubano." EnCaribe. http://www.encaribe.org/es/article/zapateo-cubano/430.

Zeno Gandía, Manuel. *La charca.* Ed. Asima F. X. Saad Maura. Buenos Aires: Stock Cero, 2005.

Writing the Early Americas

Letters from Filadelfia: Early Latino Literature and the Trans-American Elite
    Rodrigo Lazo

Sifilografía: A History of the Writerly Pox in the Eighteenth-Century Hispanic World
    Juan Carlos González Espitia

Creole Drama: Theatre and Society in Antebellum New Orleans
    Juliane Braun

The Alchemy of Conquest: Science, Religion, and the Secrets of the New World
    Ralph Bauer

www.ingramcontent.com/pod-product-compliance
Lightning Source LLC
Chambersburg PA
CBHW021333140825
31109CB00002B/21